African
Myster.

African American Mystery Writers

A Historical and Thematic Study

FRANKIE Y. BAILEY

McFarland & Company, Inc., Publishers
Jefferson, North Carolina, and London

Library of Congress Cataloguing-in-Publication Data

Bailey, Frankie Y.
    African American mystery writers : a historical and thematic
study / Frankie Y. Bailey.
      p.   cm.
    Includes bibliographical references and index.

    ISBN 978-0-7864-3339-1
    softcover : 50# alkaline paper

    1. American fiction — African American authors — History
and criticism.   2. Detective and mystery stories, American —
History and criticism.   3. American fiction — Themes, motives.
4. African Americans — Intellectual life.   5. Popular literature —
United States — History and criticism.   6. African Americans in
literature.   I. Title.
PS374.N4B27   2008
813'.087209896073 — dc22   2008039048

British Library cataloguing data are available

Cover photographs ©2008 Shutterstock

Manufactured in the United States of America

McFarland & Company, Inc., Publishers
  Box 611, Jefferson, North Carolina 28640
  www.mcfarlandpub.com

Table of Contents

Preface

In "Silver Lining," a short story in Walter Mosley's collection, *Six Easy Pieces* (2003), African American protagonist Easy Rawlins makes an observation about Black men's lives: "Freedom for us has always been dangerous. Freedom for us has been a crime as far back as our oldest memories" (p. 99). Mosley's story is set in the 1960s, and Easy is musing on the "slave heritage" that has meant whenever Black men acted too free, someone was "nearby with a rope and a collar, a shotgun and a curse" (p. 99). This book is about crime and justice as depicted in the works of African American writers. The biological significance of race has diminished in the face of modern science.[1] However, the *idea* of race is still potent. Though we might wish it to be different, we do not live in a color-blind society. In the criminal justice system, race continues to be a factor in the quality of justice received by both victims and offenders (see e.g., Gabbidon and Greene, 2005).

Mystery writers are among those who participate in the construction of images of crime and justice. In this book, the questions posed are about modern African American mystery writers. These writers are the literary descendants of the Black antebellum writers who used their pens to wage a struggle against bondage. Modern African American mystery writers are the genre-writing descendants of generations of Black writers who have dealt in their fiction with the twin perils of "unequal protection" and the "unequal enforcement" (see Kennedy, 1997) that African Americans experience in the criminal justice system. Because as a genre mystery/detective fiction focuses on matters of crime and justice, will we find that African American mystery writers use their work as an opportunity to explore the uneasy relationship between Blacks and the criminal justice system? Or will we find that race/ethnicity and crime is a secondary issue in the works of these writers? What worldviews are offered in the works of African American mystery writers?

Because the questions posed require the reader to understand the literary heritage of modern African American mystery writers, Part I of this book provides the background for this discussion. This section examines the evolution of African American writing about crime and justice from the antebellum era

1

through the late twentieth century. Part II focuses on the works of modern African American mystery writers with analysis of the works listed in Appendix B. In Part III, to expand on my own analysis, I present the results of a readers' survey. These data are the first of which I am aware about how readers respond to the works of African American mystery writers. This section also includes comments from African American mystery writers who responded to an author's questionnaire. In addition, I have comments from scholars who responded to a similar scholar's questionnaire. In Concluding Thoughts, I summarize my findings.

I am not a literary theorist, instead a criminal justice professor who studies literature for what it reveals about American culture. As Manzi (2005) observes: "...literature offers the experience of the imagination. Literature can crystallize issues that may not be transparent in other ways" (p. 115). That is why I wanted to have a close look at the works of African American mystery writers. There are now many more of these writers than in 1991 when I wrote my first book, *Out of the Woodpile: Black Characters in Crime and Detective Fiction*. Walter Mosley and several other African American mystery writers first published in the late 1980s and early 1990s. These writers have been followed by an impressive list of newcomers to the genre.

In collecting the books that were analyzed for Part II, I began with a list of all of the published works by African American authors that I could identify. I had a list of approximately 200 books published from 1988 to 2007. I located and read (or often re-read), 139 of those books (see Appendix B). I did not order books from on-line book sellers (e.g., Amazon) or seek out books currently out of print. All books were found in public libraries, bought at bookstores, or ordered (when a title was not in stock, but was available) through local bookstores. The books from my original list that were not included were those that I could not obtain by these means during the time I was collecting and reading the books in this project. In several cases I did add to the list after meeting an author of whom I was unaware. I decided to include the books in my own mystery series in the sample because my protagonist is one of the few academic sleuths created by African American mystery writers. However, I mention my books only when appropriate to provide an additional example.

Although I had planned to use a qualitative data analysis software package, after coding several books I realized the software was not more efficient than manual coding for my purposes. I found that I was better able to code by reading and marking sections of a book, followed by transcription of those sections to computer. I could then read the transcripts and code by hand using various designations. After themes emerged, I returned to the works in the sample. I went through each book again, looking for what I might have missed in the first reading. I made more notes, and I identified sections of text that illustrated a given theme. Finally, I went through the books a third time looking for good examples of the topics not directly related to the crime and justice issues but relevant in analyzing use of African American and/or American popular culture (e.g., clothing, music, popular films) in social commentary. I found that I had much more material than I could include in the body of this book. I have provided additional examples in Appendix E.

Since I relied on either personal knowledge of the writers or on one of the lists of authors that appear in various places (e.g., library websites), it is possible that I may have wrongly identified an author as African American/Black.[2] It is more likely that I have omitted writers who should have been included. Certain subgenres (e.g., romantic suspense and paranormal mysteries) are underrepresented, as are authors who are self-published or e-published. The reader will notice I use "mystery," "detective," and "crime fiction" interchangeably. I am aware that some writers prefer to be called "crime writers" rather than "mystery writers," and that there is a debate about whether thrillers and mysteries constitute two distinct genres. These debates are beyond the scope of this book. My interchangeable use of these descriptive phrases reflects my perception of the common roots of crime fiction. However, I have not included works marketed as "urban street lit." I am at work on another book that focuses on urban street lit and related hip hop fiction in the context of hip hop culture.

I would like to recognize those scholars who have made important contributions to the study of Black characters and Black mystery writers since my own book, *Out of the Woodpile*, was published in 1991. They include Stephen Soitos, author of the seminal book, *The Blues Detective* (1996). Other scholarly contributions include Kathleen Klein's edited volume, *Diversity and the Mystery Novel* (1999), Maureen Reedy's *Traces, Codes, and Clues* (2003), Helen Lock's *A Case of Mis-Taken Identity* (1994) and Adrienne Gosselin's edited volume, *Multicultural Detective Fiction* (1999). References to other scholars and their works appear in Part III of this book and in citations throughout the text.

Two mystery writers who have edited anthologies should be acknowledged for their efforts to bring the fiction of Black mystery writers to the attention of readers. Paula L. Woods' ground-breaking anthology *Spooks, Spies, and Private Eyes* (1996), provided a valuable historical overview of African American contributions to the genre. More recently Eleanor Taylor Bland edited an anthology, *Shades of Black* (2004), which includes short stories from both well-known and new mystery writers.

I would like to thank the mystery writers who have written a sufficient number of books to make my task as a scholar both a challenge and a literary adventure.

PART I

Early Black Writers as Crime Reporters

Shut up in the prison-house of bondage — denied all rights, and deprived of all privileges, we are blotted from the page of human existence, and placed beyond the limits of human regard. Death, moral death, has palsied our souls on that quarter, and we are a murdered people.

— Frederick Douglass
The North Star, Sept. 29, 1848
(quoted in Fishkin & Peterson, p. 75)

Naming the Crime

Early African American writers participated in their own unique forerunner of the modern "victims' rights" movement. They identified a heinous offense (transatlantic and domestic trafficking in slaves) that they defined as a "crime" — a crime that gave rise to other related offenses (kidnapping, false imprisonment, forced labor, physical abuse, rape, even murder). They described the physical, psychological, financial, and social consequences of these crimes not only for the victims but for the offenders and for society. As anti-slavery activists, they sought relief and prescribed change. As survivors, they demanded justice.

Africans caught up in the international market in humans were stripped of their prior identities and socialized by force into a system that restricted and controlled every aspect of their lives. American slavery transformed Africans and their descendants into a special category of humans. Black slaves in the United States experienced "civil death"[3] (Dayan, 2001). In the 1788 *Federalist No. 54*, founding father James Madison offered his "elaborate defense of the Three-Fifths Clause"[4] in the United States Constitution (Ghachen, 2007, p.3). Madison wrote that slaves possessed:

> [t]he mixt characters of persons and of property. This is in fact their true character. It is the character bestowed on them by the laws under which they live [quoted in Bailyn (1993), cited in Ghachem, p. 4].

Mentioned in the Constitution only in the calculus of determining White representation and the balance of power between the states, African slaves and their descendants existed in a legal purgatory. Both chattel property (who could be bred, sold, and inherited) and persons (who could be held responsible for violations of law), they had no rights.

Madison's struggle to explain the legal fiction by which slaves were both property and persons illustrated the tortured reasoning by which slave owners justified the institution in a nation founded on the principle that "all men are created equal." From the beginning, slavery revealed the intellectual, social, and moral contradictions inherent in American society. Thomas Jefferson, drafter of the Declaration of Independence and slave owner, acknowledged that slavery was an offense against morality, harming not only the slaves but those who owned them (Bailey & Green, 1999, p.6). In *Notes on the State of Virginia* (1785), he wrote "Indeed I tremble for my country when I reflect that God is just: that his justice cannot sleep forever...." (Jefferson, 1955, p. 163). But Jefferson believed it impossible for freed slaves and former masters to live together. He believed that Blacks—"inferior to whites in the endowments of both body and mind"—lacked the intelligence required to function effectively as freedmen and women (Jefferson, 1861, p. 138).

Jefferson was not unique among European Americans. As historian Winthrop Jordan writes in *The White Man's Burden* (1974), from their first encounter with Africans, White Europeans saw them as a race apart:

> For Englishmen, the most arresting characteristic of the newly discovered African was his color. Travelers rarely failed to comment upon it. Indeed when describing Africans they frequently began with complexion and moved on to dress (or, as they saw it, lack of it) and manners... [p.4].

Whites based their perceptions of Black inferiority on such travelers' reports and on later experience with Blacks who had been enslaved. Black slaves were alleged by Whites to "smell, sound, look, feel, even taste different (and often inferior) to whites" (Smith, 2006, p. 5). They were "savages" who needed to be both civilized and controlled.[5]

Rooted in the needs of American capitalism, "race" gained increasing significance as a socially-constructed concept. "whiteness" acquired both social and economic value as "blackness" became the stigma of inferiority. The challenge for Africans and their African American descendants was not only to break the shackles of slavery but to claim the status of fully-evolved moral and intellectual beings. They needed to refute the claims used to justify their status as non-persons. As they made arguments against slavery, African Americans initiated a discourse about race, crime, and justice in America that would continue for the next four centuries.

"Justice Must Take Plase"

The 18th century religious revival movement known as the first "Great Awakening" created converts among both Whites and Blacks. On March 29, 1754, a Black male slave named Greenwich, member of the same Canterbury, Connecticut congregation as his master, rose in church to read an attack on slavery. Greenwich asserted that the African slave trade was a violation of the biblical rules governing slavery. He said that it mattered not whether Africans were indeed the descendants of Ham,[6] "Let that be as it will Justice must Take Plase [sic]" (Seeman, 1999, p. 400).

Other than perhaps his master's discomfort, Greenwich's petition had no immediate impact (Seeman, p. 401).[7] But Greenwich's challenge to the status quo did illustrate one of the reasons that Southern slave owners forbade teaching slaves to read and write. Literate slaves might read the bible for themselves and discover that it contained more than the verses used to justify their enslavement. Literate slaves might use their skills to write travel passes to aid escapes or rallying calls for Black insurrection. Yet, even with these slave codes in place, some slaves managed to learn or were taught by Whites because they held positions as favored household servants or artisans or were the subjects of White missionary work (see e.g., Cornelius, 1991).

Despite efforts to repress them, "[s]peech acts of all forms—praying, swearing, cursing, and so forth—burst unremitting from the page in black Atlantic writing" during the 18th century (Molesworth, 2006, p. 123). In 1789, former slave Olaudah Equiano published *The Interesting Narrative of the Life of Olaudah Equiano*. Equiano's *Narrative* shared similarities with the "captivity narratives" written by White settlers who had by held hostage by Indians (Baum, 1994, p. 537). Brought to the "New World" as the slave of a Royal Navy captain, Equiano later served a Quaker merchant. Eventually, he earned enough to purchase his freedom. He published his autobiographical narrative while living in London and involved with the British abolitionist movement.

In pre–Revolutionary America, the owners of the Black slave girl, Phillis Wheatley, taught her to read and write. Wheatley became a celebrity when she displayed talent as a poet. But when her first volume of poetry was published in London in 1773, it was deemed necessary to assure the skeptical reader that no deception was being perpetrated. The preface of the volume carried a statement from seventeen respected men of Boston attesting that Wheatley was the author of the verses. Her identity as a writer (which contradicted beliefs about the intellectual abilities of Blacks) had been established to the satisfaction of her White male examiners, who then served as witnesses on her behalf.[8]

During this era, Wheatley and the few other Black writers were "in a different position from their white counterparts" (Gray, 2004, p. 86). As the literary marketplace expanded with "the growth in readership and printing presses, the proliferation of magazines, almanacs, manuals, and many other outlets for writing," white writers became less dependent on literary patronage. African American writers such as Wheatley and poet Jupiter Hammon remained "dependent on their white 'friends' and patrons" (Gray, p. 86).

Perhaps this is why neither Wheatley nor Hammon launched direct attacks against slavery in their verses.[9] Forbearing to "hurl condemnations" at their readers, the two nevertheless participated in the African American struggle against oppression (Harrell, 2006, p. 169). By the early 1700s, Black writers were positioning themselves to build on "the ambivalences over color and status around them." Focusing on natural rights, African American writers contributed to one of the "more radical legacies of the Revolution" by helping to "inaugurate the democratization of voice in the political realm" (Bruce, 2001,

p. 55). The evangelist minister Lemuel Haynes was forthright in his evocation of Revolutionary ideology. In "Liberty Further Extended or Free Thoughts on the Illegality of Slavekeeping," an address written early in his career (but not published until 1983), Haynes used the first line of the Declaration of Independence to open his argument (Gray, 2004, p. 83).

As Gates (2000) observes, "What was at stake for the earliest black authors was nothing less than the testimony to their humanity" (p. 60). This image of "black absence" from Western culture (Gates, p. 60) was not limited to the enslaved. For free Blacks as well there was "the same fundamental challenge … that of proving their humanity" (Green, 2005, p. 36). Their oppressed status shaped African American perceptions of the legal system. As Robinson (1997) asserts, Blacks respected "the rule of law … for its power rather than any resemblance to justice or a moral order." This was true both for slaves and for free Blacks, who received little protection of their "tenuous status" (pp. 19–20).

Some Black abolitionists became infamous among slaveholders for assertions that slavery was a crime and that slaves had the right to rebel. Reviewing the history of "the African American jeremiad," Harrell (2006) cites the early activism of Prince Hall. Hall "challenged the white supremacy laws" in Boston and founded the African Masonic Lodge, the first African American social organization. Other Black activists included David Ruggle, the publisher of a 1837 pamphlet,[10] and Henry Highland Garrett, who delivered a controversial speech at the National Negro Convention in Buffalo in 1843. Harrell finds that the jeremiad "embodied the tenets of justice and retribution" and was filtered through "powerful Euro-American socio-religious lens" (pp. 165–166).

In 1829, in his *Appeal to the Coloured Citizens of the World*, David Walker urged the slaves of the United States of America to throw off their shackles. Born in Wilmington, North Carolina, the son of a free mother and a slave father, Walker had never been a slave, but he had witnessed slavery. Walker went North and became an agitator for slave freedom. In his 1829 *Appeal*, he indicated his awareness that his readers might focus on the author rather than the text. He wrote:

> But against all accusations which may or can be preferred against me, I appeal to heaven for my motive for writing — who knows that my object is, if possible, to awaken in the breasts of my afflicted, degraded and slumbering brethren, a spirit of enquiry and investigation respecting our miseries and wretchedness in this *Republican Land of Liberty*!!!!! [Walker, p. 13 in Winston, 1994].

David Walker and fellow Boston-based antebellum authors Prince Hall and Maria Stewart, "appropriated the rhetoric of legal pleading used in Revolutionary-era government petitions and freedom suits … to produce a literature of complaint and rights" (McArdle, 2005. p. 183). The document in which Walker made his assertion of rights was banned in the Southern states. Those who were caught distributing the *Appeal* were charged with the crime of inciting insurrection.[11]

In 1843, at the Negro Convention in Buffalo,[12] Henry Highland Garnet delivered his *Address to the Slaves of the United States of America*.[13] Five years later, in 1848, Garnet republished Walker's *Appeal* with the *Address* that he himself had delivered. Garnet noted in the preface that his own speech had been controversial:

> Gentlemen who opposed the Address, based their objections on these grounds.
> 1. That the document was war-like, and encouraged insurrection; and 2. That if the Convention should adopt it, that those delegates who lived near the borders of the slave states, would not dare to return to their homes [Garnet, p. 89 in Winston, 1994].

As did Walker, Garnet appealed to slaves to seek their freedom by any means necessary. He argued:

> Brethren, it is as wrong for your lordly oppressors to keep you in slavery, as it was for the man thief to steal our ancestors from the coast of Africa. You should therefore now use the same manner of resistance, as would have been just in our ancestors, when the bloody foot prints of the first remorseless soul thief was placed upon the shores of our fatherland [Garnet, p. 93 in Winston].

When he delivered his *Address* to the Negro Convention, Garnet hoped that it would be accepted as part of the Convention platform. Instead, he was attacked by those who favored the use of "moral suasion" to end slavery. Garnet responded in *The Liberator* on December 3, 1843, noting that he had been born in slavery and escaped to freedom. He was "astonished ... to think that you should desire to sink me again to the condition of a slave, by forcing me to think just as you do. My crime is that I have dared to think, and act, contrary to your opinion" (quoted in Forbes, 2003, p. 158).

This matter of independent thought and action was a sore point for Black abolitionists. At the time of Garnet's speech before the Negro convention, fellow fugitive Frederick Douglass was a proponent of moral suasion. By the 1850s, Douglass too had come to believe that the strategy urged by White abolitionist William Lloyd Garrison was ineffective in changing the hearts and minds of slave owners.[14] In August 1857, Douglass, now more militant, complained, "Your humble speaker has been branded as an ingrate, because he has ventured to stand upon his own right, and to plead our common cause as a colored man, rather than as a Garrisonian" (Foner, 1950, p. 437).

On the abolitionist lecture circuit, Douglass had his first encounter with the restrictions he would face as he tried to speak about slavery and freedom. The White abolitionists with whom he traveled, urged Douglass not to deviate from his set speech (Bruce, 2001, p. 255). To Douglass's annoyance, even though his eloquence was acknowledged (Bruce, p. 226), his performance as a speaker — his narrative — was controlled by others.

As speakers on the lecture circuit, former slaves, "participated in a larger abolitionist rhetoric that figured slavery as a crime, slaveholders as perpetrators and defendants, slaves as victims and eyewitnesses, and abolitionists as advocates for the slave" (DeLombard, 2001, p. 249). In this rhetoric, the body of the escaped slave, scarred by physical abuse, was "the space of transcription" (Feldman, 2004, p. 188). For the Northern abolitionist audience, with little experience of personal violence and "ensconced in bourgeois rectitude," the body of the black narrator provided "authentication of his/her spoken biography" (Feldman, p. 188). But at the same time, the Black body was objectified by the White gaze to which it was displayed.

The desire of former slave Douglass to be more than a speaking subject, to become his own advocate, placed him in conflict "with a subtle racial hierarchy within abolitionist rhetoric" (DeLombard, p. 250). The movement from spoken rhetoric to the written word was a natural and necessary progression for African American activists. However, Douglass and other 19th century Black writers faced barriers as they attempted to reach their audiences.

The Black Newspaper and the Slave Narrative

Even as more African Americans acquired literacy in the 19th century, they had limited access to the means of publication. They responded "creatively" by writing for newspapers and magazines, self-publishing pamphlets, and placing their novels with larger publishing houses (Vogel, 2001, p. 4). Antebellum abolitionists such as David Walker placed importance on print "rather than oratory" as a means of linking "the disparate and scattered black communities" (Levine, 2001, p. 18). Walker and other African American activists wanted "to prove themselves mental workers and citizens" (Vogel, 2001, p. 44). Their efforts reflected the awareness that their published works might well reach two audiences—one Black, one White.

As *American* literature, African American writing was "not self-contained." Instead it was responsive to the political, literary, and even legal narratives being produced on both sides of the Atlanta. Black writers referenced both the American Declaration of Independence and the remarks by British observer, Dr. Samuel Johnson, scolding "the slave-driving authors" of that document. Black writers responded both to the observations about race by Thomas Jefferson in his *Notes on the State of Virginia*, and to Justice Roger B. Taney's devastating decision in the *Dred Scott* case[15] (Moses, 2005, pp. 623–624). Therefore, it is not surprising that the first Black newspaper, *Freedom's Journal*,[16] was a direct response to defaming remarks made by White editor Mordecai M. Nash in the pages of the *New York Enquirer*. In the inaugural issue of *Freedom's Journal*, on March 16, 1827, editors John Russwurm and Samuel Cornish addressed a front page, several column prospectus "To Our Patrons." Explaining one of the reasons their newspaper was needed, they wrote:

We wish to plead our own cause, too long have others spoken for us. Too long has the publick been deceived by misrepresentations in things which concern us dearly, though in the estimation of some mere trifles; for though there are many in society who exercise toward us benevolent feelings; still (with sorrow we confess it) there are others who make it their business to enlarge upon the least trifle, which tends to the discredit of any person of color ... and denounce our whole body for conduct of this guilty one... [The Editors, p.1].[17]

The images of Blacks in the antebellum era reflected the need to justify slavery as an institution by presenting Blacks as passive, childlike, savage, oversexed, compliant, lazy, hapless, sullen, ignorant, and/or happy. These images appeared in Southern print culture (e.g., journals and newspapers). The minstrel shows that appeared in the 1830s featuring characters such as "Sambo" and "Zip Coon" helped to proliferate stereotypes that would spread well beyond the South by the 1900s. Free Blacks who strove for respect and respectability needed first to refute such racial imagery (see Bailey and Green, 1999).

Aside from the negative stereotypes of Blacks in the mainstream media, there was also the contradictory and parallel "invisibility" of African American issues and concerns (Jacobs, 2000, p. 35; see also Ernest, 2002, pp. 415–419). Accordingly Cornish, the co-editor of *Freedom's Journal*, declared the newspaper would provide a forum for free Blacks to engage in dialogue and communication and to mobilize "national opinion on behalf of African Americans" (Jacobs, 2000, p. 35)

Before the Civil War, forty-two Afro-American newspapers were founded and published for varying lengths of time (Simmons, p.13). The goal of creating an independent Black press attracted men such as Thomas Hamilton, the editor of New York's *Anglo-American Magazine* and Frederick Douglass, who founded a newspaper in Rochester, New York. Hamilton, who published his paper without White support, proclaimed in his January 1859 first issue that African Americans "must speak for themselves, no outside tongue, however gifted with eloquence, can tell their story" (quoted in Mulvey, 2004, p. 21).[18]

Even though he had some White supporters, Frederick Douglass discovered that his determination to start his own newspaper, the *North Star* (founded in 1847, renamed *Frederick Douglass's Paper* in 1851), put him at odds with his friend and associate, White abolitionist William Lloyd Garrison.[19] Garrison was the publisher of *The Liberator*, a newspaper that was the "avowed 'organ' of free blacks and the enslaved," and he had a "loyal readership" among "politically organized African Americans" (Fanuzzi, 2001, p. 57). The struggle to sustain his own newspaper forced Douglass to "travel to the heart of Garrison's subscriber base, Boston itself, to argue for the legitimacy of his colored newspaper" (Fanuzzi, 2001, p. 65). His inability to woe large numbers of Black subscribers from Garrison's newspaper (which had been in existence since 1831), left Douglass bitter, but reflected "the crossing over of white and black identity in and through the printed medium" (Fanuzzi, p. 65). Even with his difficulties, Douglass continued to publish his newspaper as a weekly until 1860, and as a monthly for three more years. In 1870, he entered newspaper publishing again as the owner and editor of a weekly newspaper in Washington, D.C.

Before he became a newspaper publisher/editor,[20] Frederick Douglass achieved fame on the abolitionist lecture circuit and as the author of *The Narrative of the Life of Frederick Douglass, an American Slave,* published in Boston in 1845. Concerning Douglass's *Narrative,* Clark (1999) observes that he "attempts to situate his tale within a framework of American 'success' narrative ... with the requisite testimonial-like preface by two white male abolitionists" (p. 197). The narratives by Douglass, William Wells Brown, Harriet Ann Jacobs, and other slaves who had escaped from bondage to the North formed a unique genre of American literature.[21] However, Mulvey (2004) notes the connection between these "non-fiction" narratives written by former slaves, the accounts in Black newspapers of the experiences of slaves, and the fictional works produced by Black writers of the era.

As a genre, narratives "enjoyed wide popularity between 1850 and 1863." The works of ex-slave authors such as Frederick Douglass and William W. Brown "far outsold those by Henry David Thoreau and Nathaniel Hawthorne." Even though the primary audience for the slave narratives was White, the narratives reached "a part of the African American communities and enjoyed wide readership there as well" (Rooks, 2004, p. 12). But when White abolitionist writer Harriet Beecher Stowe published her novel, the playing field changed. *Uncle Tom's Cabin: or, Life among the Lowly* appeared first in 1851 as a "magazine novel' in the *National Era.* Published in book form in late 1852, the novel sold over 300,000 copies (Mulvey, p. 19). When Frederick Douglass and William Wells Brown "impelled themselves in to print in 1853, they did so because the most successful of all New England novels had appropriated their narratives and outstripped their sales" (Mulvey, p. 19).

Okker (2003) argues for the importance of the "magazine novel" in the 19th century. She notes that although Stowe's book appeared in the "antislavery paper the *National Era,*" it provides "a paradigm of the nineteenth-century America magazine novel precisely because its composition, content, and reception highlight social relations" (p. 10). The publication of Stowe's novel signified the role that the magazine novel would play in "the political upheavals of the 1850s" (Okker, p. 79). That Stowe drew on slave narratives in crafting her novel is indicative of the extent to which these narratives had become a genre that was familiar to White readers.

The slave narratives reflected what Ostrowski (2006) refers to as the "intertextuality" of antebellum print culture. In the "overlapping print cultures of abolition and labor reform," the slave narrative "shared numerous points of contact" with the city-mysteries novel of the 1840s and 1850s (Ostrowski, p. 493). Although it is not clear how much the urban working class audience at which the city-mystery novels were aimed and the middle-class abolitionist audience for slave narratives overlapped, the two genres were linked by "a network of intertextual relationships within the publishing field of reform literature." They were also linked by

> direct plundering of one genre by authors of the other. The latter appears to be true of the influence of the *Narrative of the Life of Henry Box Brown* on Thompson's *City Crimes* and Lippard's *The Empire City*, a case in which the white authors borrowed from and effaced a black writer's work emerges with unusual even startling clarity [Ostrowski, p. 484].

In the publishing environment of the late 1840s and 1850s, the author of sensational novels "pushed the envelope in the interest of titillating and shocking their readers." In a print culture that was becoming "ever more permissive in the depiction of graphic violence," African American writers may well have "began to regard shocking violence as an aid rather than an impediment to establishing their credibility" (Ostrowski, p. 503).

Generally, authors of slave narratives adopted a formula that appealed to the readers of the 19th century sentimental novel. Sentimental novels focused on the plight of the weak and/or innocent protagonist. Examining the slave narrative in the context of the victim in this literature, Bryant (1997) observes, "Many readers of the slave narrative would surely have recognized the figure of the suffering slave — Innocence, helpless before unjust Cruelty — and would be ready to respond compassionately" (p. 13). For the reader of the sentimental novel, the plight of "the helpless— the orphaned child, the seduced and abandoned young woman, the pathetically insane, the tragically imprisoned" evoked compassion. For these bourgeois readers, the politically correct response to such tales was tears and pity (Bryant, p. 13).

But even when empathetic White readers were inclined toward pity, African American women found it risky to recount the true nature of their experiences as slaves. Because of both gender and racial stereotypes, a former slave such as Harriet Jacobs, "risked having her account misread as a confession" (DeLombard, 2001, p. 251). The sexualized nature of slavery for Black women and the lascivious imaginations of the White audience caused the female narrator to find her "sexual self, rather than the crime of slavery and its perpetrators [had been] placed before the bar of public opinion for judgment" (DeLombard, p. 251).

For Harriet Jacobs, the problem "[was] how to use language as a way of achieving liberation, when language itself [was] a part of her oppression" (Cutter, 1996, p. 209). In constructing her narrative, Jacobs demonstrated her awareness of Northern print culture of the 1840s and 1850s.[22] In literary works, the "fallen woman" appeared in the "two distinct social spaces" created in the North by the exploitation of free labor and in the plantation South by the abuse of slaves (Greeson, 2001, pp. 278–279). In her narrative, Jacobs rejected the "generic outline" (Greeson, p. 287) of the story of trials and triumph favored by male narrators. Instead she adopted "the formula of the antebellum narrative of the fallen woman ... presenting her autobiographical protagonist's loss of chastity as the climatic turning point of her tale" (Greeson, p. 287). This adoption of "urban gothic tropes" allowed Jacobs to "galvanize her Northern audience" (Greeson, p. 288). Because the slave narrative as a genre "was not completely amenable to the issues faced by female slaves," Jacobs engaged in a process of reconfiguring that allowed her to address the intersection of race and gender issues (Patton, 2000, p. 54). In *Incidents in the Life of a Slave Girl*, "motherhood" becomes "the lens to analyze gender and race" (Patton, p.54).[23]

Examining the slave narrative as a genre, Coles (1999) asserts that the slave narrative (or Black autobiography) became the first contribution of Black writers to American literature not only because it "most faithfully rendered the oppressed conditions of black people" in the 18th and 19th century, but because "to write imaginative literature black people first had to be free" (pp. 15–16). He points to the influence of the slave narrative as a genre on the works of future Black (as well as some White) writers. The slave narrative contributed motifs that included "the success story; the first-person account; the documentation of escape, injustice, and religious hypocrisy — all of these devices would re-emerge in various forms in later literary texts" (Coles, p. 28).

Whatever contributions the slave narrative made to future Black writing, the genre limited antebellum Black writers who adopted a formula intended to appeal to sympathetic White readers. In a genre which had an "almost total focus upon the feeling reader," Black writers lacked "the kind of autonomy required for true freedom" (Bryant, 1997, p. 23). Byrant (1997) points to a pivotal event in Frederick Douglass's *Narrative*. Douglass describes his encounter with the slave-tamer Covey. Douglass refuses to be whipped (brutalized) and symbolically claims his manhood. Yet Douglass does not present himself as a violent hero. In his account of his physical struggle with Covey, Douglass uses "low-level self-defensive violence that does permanent harm to no one. ... it is easy for Douglass's White, abolitionist, northern audience to approve of such an act, for it reinforces rather than challenges their racial sentiments" (Bryant, 31). No Nat Turner,[24] Douglass is not a Black man that his White readers need fear would use lethal violence to obtain his freedom. The White readers of his narrative are not required to "contemplate the kind of serious resistance" in which Black rebels would kill Whites "to liberate themselves from slavery, or simply to protect their own" (Bryant, 31).

But even with the restrictions of the form, King (2003) argues that the narratives written by ex-slaves such as Douglass and Harriet Jacobs served to illuminate the "faulty logic" and the "ideological assumptions that supported the institutional apparatus of American chattel slavery and the racialization of deviance" (p.75).[25] For Blacks, both slave and free, conditions worsened with enactment of legislation which included the Fugitive Slave Law of 1850. This law required that Northern law enforcement officers assist slave masters in reclaiming their escaped property. The ability of White Southerners to lay claim

to Blacks who they alleged were their slaves created a situation in which neither fugitives nor free Blacks were safe. Some Blacks fled to Canada; others, such
as activist and novelist Martin R. Delany, discussed with increasing urgency the
possibility of migration to Africa (see Bruce, 2001, pp. 270–271; see also Bailey and Green, 1999). The brewing tensions in the decade before the Civil War,
nurtured an African American literary voice and "a new language of moral
defiance focused on the need to resist the law became a common part of African
American rhetoric from the time of its [the Fugitive Slave Law] passage" (Bruce,
2001, p. 271).

The arguments made by David Walker and Henry Highland Garnet that
slaves should seize their freedom by any means necessary — including violent
rebellion — gained more widespread support among Black abolitionists. The
violent hero who had not found a place in the genre slave narrative appeared
in Black fiction.

Black Fiction in the Antebellum Era

The ex-slaves who published narratives about their lives in bondage often
faced accusations from Southern slaveholders and others that the true authors
of the works were White abolitionists who served as "ghost writers." The pro-
slavery faction charged that the ex-slaves lacked both the intellectual ability and
the literacy to commit to paper the accounts of their lives that they told on the
lecture circuit. Black writers of slave narratives such as Frederick Douglass
needed to prove their authenticity as authors. They also needed to respond to
charges that their narratives were not true stories but rather fiction concocted
to appeal to the sentiments of their Northern audiences.

For modern scholars who accept the authenticity of Black authorship of
the narratives, the boundary between non-fiction and fiction becomes murky
when we turn to the articles and stories that appeared in African American
newspapers.[26] To quote Mulvey (2004), "The border between fact and fiction
is a broad territory, not a dividing line" (p. 17). He offers the example of an
article about a former slave that appeared in the New York *Anglo-American
Magazine* in the September 1859. In what was presented as an interview with
a reporter, the ex-slave confessed that he had killed each of his consecutive
masters. After each owner died a mysterious death, there came a time when no
one else was willing to buy him, and he obtained his freedom. The article was
titled "Patrick Brown's First Love." Mulvey observes, "It is remarkable that a
slave would spend a lifetime concealing the fact that he is a murderer and then
allow his story to be told in a newspaper." Given this unlikely circumstance,
Mulvey suggests that this "may in fact be the first African American short story"
(p. 17).

The fact that authors who wrote non-fiction accounts of incidents in the lives of slaves later used similar events in their fiction also blurs the line between the genres. For example, William Wells Brown, author of a slave narrative, wrote an article in 1852 for a British abolitionist newspaper in which he tells the story of the sale of a beautiful mulatto woman at a Richmond, Virginia slave auction. That same incident appears in his novel, *Clotel* (1853) as a chapter titled "The Negro Sale." Such merging of fact and fiction makes it impossible to identify the definitive first short story by an African American writer (Mulvey, pp. 18–19).

What is clear about the expansion of African American writers into fiction is that fiction provided literary and social space for a more nuanced exploration of the consequences of slavery and the impact of the institution on Black lives. Fiction also provided Black writers with an opportunity to present the heroic slave or free Black who was willing to use lethal violence in resisting slavery. Frederick Douglass presented such a hero when he published his novella, titled "The Heroic Slave" in 1853 (serially in *The North Star* and as his contribution to an anti-slavery anthology). Douglass's story was inspired by the 1841 revolt aboard the slave ship *Creole* led by a slave named Madison Washington. Bruce (2001) notes that Douglass had been interested in Washington's revolt for several years (p. 297). He concludes that the timing of the novella reflected Douglass's own movement away from "Garrisonian nonresistance" and "helped to elaborate more connections among heroism and moral authority, black testimony and anti-slavery ideals" (Bruce, pp. 297–298).

In his second autobiography, *My Bondage and My Freedom*,[27] published in 1855, Douglass drew again on his own observations of the brutalities and acts of violence committed by slaveholders and disregarded by the criminal justice system. He asserted:

> Slaveholders have made it almost impossible for the slave to commit any crime known either to the laws of God or to the laws of man. If he steals, he takes his own; if he kills his master, he imitates only the heroes of the [American] revolution [Douglass, p. 149].

Viewed in the context of his evolving beliefs about Black revolution, "The Heroic Slave" is important because in it Douglass "both continues and extends the themes and strategies of his antebellum journalism; in particular, he turns to the techniques of fiction to accomplish what factual writing would not allow him to do" (Fishkin and Peterson, 2001, pp. 81–82).

Bryant (1997) notes that "the first three African American male novelists ... in the decade before the Civil War" all deal with the issue of violence in the name of liberation or self-defense (p. 31). These novelists are William Wells Brown in *Clotel; or, The President's Daughter* (1853), Martin R. Delany in *Blake*[28]; *or, The Huts of America* (1859–62), and Frank J. Webb in *The Garies and Their Friends* (1857). Bryant asserts that, "In addressing this question, they appreciably broaden the consideration of violence in African American letters." He describes the "prototypes" imagined by these three authors as the "foundation for all future treatments of the topic in the African American novel" (Bryant, p. 31). In *Blake*, Delaney, who is often described as the father of Black nationalism in the United States, offers prototypes of "the heroic rebel, the avenger, and the forgiving Christian" which are picked up at century's end by Sutton Griggs and Charles Chesnutt and explored in new forms (Bryant, p. 43). In *The Garies and Their Friends*, Webb moves the examination of the impact of slavery to the North. In *Clotel*, Brown examines the dilemma of the mulatto as a product of miscegenation. These two themes in African American literature — urban racial conflict and the "tragic mulatto," respectively — would evolve during the 20th century, but never disappear.

Mulvey (2004) describes antebellum African American fiction as "a literature of fusion" which combined elements of "slave narrative, Gothic mystery, satire, pastoral, novel of manners, document, and polemic" (p. 27). He notes that in the 1930s when African American literary critics begin to focus on antebellum Black fiction, the commentary "is negative" (p. 29). However, the 1960s and 1970s brought new attention to this fiction, particularly to Delany's *Blake* as an early Black nationalist text. Mulvey calls *Blake* "the book that Black Power critics were looking for" (p. 30). However, some antebellum Black fiction continued to fare poorly in critical assessment.

One such example is Frances Ellen Watkins Harper's short story, "The Two Offers" published in the New York *Anglo-American Magazine* in 1859. The story has no African American characters. The protagonist, a White woman with two offers of marriage, makes the wrong choice. She marries a man who is charming but dissolute. He breaks her heart, and her friend sits at her bedside as the dying woman waits for the husband who does not return. Learning from this experience, the friend decides to remain single and dedicate her life to working for good causes. As Mulvey points out, this story was published by the editor, Thomas Hamilton, who also published a revised version of *Clotel* and *Blake* (p. 21). Examining the placement of Harper's short story in the magazine, Mulvey discovers some political significance in the fact that it appeared on the same page as "Patrick Brown's First Love." He suggests that Hamilton "radicalized its reading by linking Harper's discussion of white women's lives to Brown's discussion of white men's deaths" (p. 21).

This suggestion of how Black readers might have been encouraged to link the two stories is intriguing, as is recent critical assessment of Harper's post–Civil War novel, *Iola Leroy* (1892).

Black Fiction Writers and Postbellum Violence

In the aftermath of Reconstruction, the year 1892 marked the peak of lynchings of African Americans in the South. Bryant (1997) suggests that it is no coincidence that this was also the year that Frances E.W. Harper, well-known poet and activist, published her novel, *Iola Leroy; or, Shadows Uplifted* (p. 71). The plot of *Iola Leroy* (1892) revolves around family separation and postwar reunion. Ernest (1992) asserts that the novel "about the breakup of African American families and the search for mothers after the war embodies a 'signi-fyin(g)' strategy for returning American cultural discourse to a stable concep-tion of justice" (p. 500). He points out that one of the often overlooked elements of *Iola Leroy* is Harper's use of the concept of "mystery." For example, Harper reveals a cultural mystery that her White readers would have been unable to interpret: "In the first page of the first chapter, Harper draws readers into a 'shadow' culture — that of the slaves— and introduces her readers to the dis-cursive network of that culture, the 'mystery of market speech'" (Ernest, p. 502). White readers would have encountered other such mysteries in the novel, "each of which reveals the cognitive and moral limitations inherent in and enforced by the dominant cultural system" (Ernest, p. 503). These mysteries include the unexpected behavior of Iola Leroy, the apparently White Southern lady, who Dr. Gresham observes tenderly kiss one of the Black patients she is caring for in the field hospital. But, as Ernest notes, the "central demystifying confrontation" occurs when Iola Leroy confronts her own self-identity (p. 504).

In another aspect of the signifying that occurs in the novel, Ernest (1992) and other scholars point to the name of Harper's protagonist, Iola Leroy. *Iola* was the pen name used by Ida B. Wells (later Wells-Barnett), the Black female journalist who was an outspoken crusader against lynching. Harper was acquainted with Wells, and, as a member of the Negro clubwomen's move-ment, Harper was active in the social reform movement, including the cam-paign against lynching (see e.g., Foreman, 1997). With *Iola Leroy*, she wrote the first novel by an African American that interprets the post–Civil War era "from a Black point of view and that refers to the increasing practice of whites lynch-ing blacks" (Bryant, 1997, p. 72).[29]

Between 1882 and 1968, approximately 3,445 African Americans were lynched (Zangrando, 1980). As noted above, the number of African Americans lynched each year reached its bloody zenith in the 1890s. Thereafter, the annual death toll decreased (see Tolnay and Beck, 1995; Bailey and Green, 1999). How-ever, because this form of lethal vigilante violence continued into the 20th cen-tury, it remained an issue that Black writers dealt with in their fiction. Parallel discussions of the causes and effects of lynching and of the appropriate responses to lynching by Blacks, Whites, and the federal government occurred in news-papers,[30] magazines, sociological studies, and public forums.[31]

As they had during the antebellum abolitionist movement, African Amer-ican writers used fiction as another medium through which to communicate their concerns about crime and justice. Between the publication of Harper's novel in 1892 and the publication of Jean Toomer's *Cane* in 1922 (launching the Harlem Renaissance), sixty or more novels by African Americans were published (Bryant, 1997, pp. 72–73). Twenty-four of these novels contained references to lynching. All of the major African American writers except Paul Laurence Dunbar "wrote at least one novel in which lynching was an issue" (Bryant, 1997, p. 73). During the 1920s and 1930s, when attempts were underway to pass a federal anti-lynching bill, African American women such as Angelina Weld Grimké, Georgia Douglas Johnson, and Mary Burrill wrote "lynching plays" that "focused on how the lynching of black men affected the lives of black women" (Hester, 1994, p. 251; see also Allen, 2005).

This continued attention by African American writers to lynching reflected the fact that lynching was not only a crime but a form of terrorism. The impact was felt not only by the individual victim or victims of a given episode but by all those Blacks who heard about the event. As had stories of the violence and oppression of slavery, stories of the "rope and the faggot" became a part of Black oral tradition.[32] Although linked to the rural South, lynching continued to haunt the minds of the Black migrants[33] That a Black man (occasionally woman or child) could be lynched — not only hanged but often mutilated and burned — by White vigilantes, and that the federal government failed to enact anti-lynching legislation, made it clear that freedom for Blacks had not brought the protection of the law. This violence became a subtext of the literary works that African Americans created as they made the transition to the city, moving symbolically into the age of modernity.

In their fiction, Black writers explored the appropriate response to White violence. Were Blacks to be "warriors," "avengers," or "forgiving Christians"? As scholars (see e.g., Bryant, 1997; Kennedy, 1997; Bailey and Green, 1999) have noted the issue of the use of violence created a dilemma for African Americans. This was particularly the case for middle class Blacks. On one hand, they were committed to the crusade against lynching and understood the need for self-assertion and even self-defense. On the other hand, they sought to establish themselves as law-abiding, respectable citizens who did not engage in the violence commonly associated with the lower classes. The meaning of lynching in the context of this intersection of race, class, and gender was an issue Black writers felt compelled to examine in their fiction.

Aside from novels and plays, African American writers produced short stories and poetry that included references to lynching. Trained as a legal stenographer and court reporter, Charles Chesnutt was better known as a writer. One of the short stories in his volume, *The Wife of His Youth* (1899), was titled "The Sheriff's Children." A White sheriff saves a Black (mulatto) man suspected of murder from a lynch mob. During a painful confrontation with his prisoner, the sheriff learns that the young man is the slave son that he sold to pay his debts. The sheriff's (White) daughter shoots and wounds the prisoner that she sees threatening her father. Belatedly the sheriff decides to investigate the murder his son is accused of committing. He returns to the jail to find that his son has committed suicide by ripping the bandage from the wound inflicted by his White half-sister and allowing himself to bleed to death. In *The*

Marrow of Tradition (1901), inspired by the real-life Wilmington, North Carolina riot of 1898, Chesnutt deals with White mob violence. Here too there is an ironic ending involving the Black doctor (whose own child is killed) and the White parents who must come to him to save their child.[34]

Conclusions

Historically, African Americans moved from non-fiction accounts of their lives in slave narratives and newspapers, to the use of fiction to reach a wider audience and speak to that audience in ways not possible in non-fiction. African Americans adapted and modified the genres (e.g., the sentimental novel) and the tropes (e.g., the "tragic mulatto") of mainstream fiction to fit their own needs. As African American writing became a strand of "American literature," White writers (such as Harriet Beecher Stowe) drew on and from the texts produced by Black authors who offered a first-hand account of oppression and injustice.

In a letter to Walter Hines Page, White Southern journalist, diplomat, and crusader for reform, Charles Chesnutt "expressed his dismay at the steady erosion of blacks' civil rights in turn-of-the-century America" (Ianovici, 2002, p. 33). Chesnutt observed that "the Supreme Court of the United States is a dangerous place for a colored man to seek justice" (quoted in Ianovici, p. 33). By the end of the 19th century, African Americans who had spent three centuries struggling for recognition of their humanity, had gained technical freedom from slavery. However, the decision of the Supreme Court in *Plessy v. Ferguson* (1896), affirming segregation of public accommodations as "separate but equal" had been a serious setback in the struggle for equal rights. African American writers were engaged in an effort to counteract the virulent, racist images of authors such as Thomas Dixon, whose popular novel *The Clansman* (1905) would become the basis for D.W. Griffith's blockbuster film *The Birth of a Nation* (1915).

Negative stereotypes of Black men and women were not restricted to popular culture. Such depictions were a part of the social science literature and the historical works of the period as the Southern view of African Americans was disseminated and accepted throughout the country (see Bailey and Green, 1999, pp. 87–89). As late as 1923, the Virginia chapter of the United Daughters of the Confederacy proposed a national monument "in memory of the faithful colored mammies of the South." The proposal was carried forward on their behalf by Mississippi Senator John Williams (Johnson, 2005, p. 62). The movement to erect a statue to the mythic Old South mammy was challenged by African American clubwomen as they were working to preserve the home of Frederick Douglass (Johnson, 2005, pp. 63–64). The struggle to control representation and "memory sites" reflected the understanding on both sides that "the images they promoted, the texts they wrote, and the monuments they erected legitimized collective memories" (Johnson, pp. 63–64).

As African American authors moved into the 20th century, they were better educated and had a growing audience of literate Black readers. However, the ability to reach those readers continued to be limited by Black access to the means of publication. The first appearance of stories and novels that we now identify as having elements of crime and detective genre fiction was in African American newspapers and magazines rather than mainstream publications. In the next chapter, I examine these early works.

Early Genre Writers*

In her anthology, *Spooks, Spies, and Private Eyes* (1995), Paula L. Woods describes Pauline Elizabeth Hopkins as the "foremother of African American mysteries" (p. 16). Hopkins was born in Portland, Maine, in 1859, on the eve of the Civil War. She began her writing career when her first play, "Slaves Escape; or the Underground Railroad," was produced in 1880. During her tenure as a contributor and editor of *Colored American Magazine* Hopkins produced fiction incorporating elements of mystery and detection.[35] Hopkins's "The Mystery Within Us," a play about mysticism, or the paranormal, was published in *Colored American Magazine* in May 1900. Five months later, Hopkins's short story, "Talma Gordon," was published in the same magazine. In March 1901, *Colored American* began serializing Hopkins's novel, *Hagar's Daughter; A Story of Southern Caste Prejudice* under Hopkins's pen name, Sarah A. Allen.

Commenting on Hopkins and her contemporaries, Gunning (1996) observes that Black feminists at the turn-of-the century did not wholeheartedly embrace "the received conventions of true white womanhood" (p. 76). Instead the Black feminists worked "to adapt, supplement, and culturally rewrite these conventions" to be inclusive of women "of all colors, economic stations, and personal histories, who had traditionally been excluded from respectability" (p. 79). One "shift in self-representation" by these feminists of color during the late 19th and early 20th centuries was "toward the triumph of black female strength of character" (Gunning, p. 79). Middle-class Black women pursued their involvement in "racial uplift" and various reform movements (Gunning, p. 79, see also Bailey and Green, 1999).

As literary editor of the *Colored American Magazine*, Pauline Hopkins had a reputation for "a certain aggressiveness that was presumably not attractive in a turn of the century woman" (Gunning, p. 96). Hopkins would later leave the magazine when it came under the control of Booker T. Washington through

---

*In this chapter and the next, the solution to the mystery is revealed in the discussion of several of the works. This is necessary for thorough analysis of the texts. In Section II in which the works of modern mystery writers are discussed, I do my best to avoid "spoilers" (i.e., revelations of key plot points or solutions to the mystery).

his associate, Fred Moore (Gunning, p. 56). But while there, she wrote commentaries on women and politics in a column titled "Women's Department" (Gunning, p. 97). These twin concerns—politics and providing a voice for African Americans, particularly women—characterized Hopkins's work throughout her literary career (Cordell, 2006, p. 52).[36]

Cordell asserts that what distinguished Hopkins's fiction and journalism from her contemporaries, both Black and White, was "her blunt depiction of brutality and violence and the explicit link that she draws between violence and social, political, and racial oppression" (p. 53). In her short story, "Talma Gordon," Hopkins presents a scenario in which a daughter falls under suspicion for her father's murder. Hopkins's story incorporates elements of the real-life Lizzie Borden case, in which the daughter of a wealthy Fall River, Massachusetts, businessman stood trial in 1892 for the alleged slaying of her father and step-mother. Borden was acquitted of the murders by a jury of White males, who historians suggest found it impossible to believe that a respectable upper middle-class White female could commit such brutal acts. The Borden case inspired a nursery rhyme and numerous short stories, plays, operas, ballets, and novels.

In "Talma Gordon," Hopkins examines violence and "true womanhood" in the context of a uniquely African American tale. The murdered man was a bigot who rejected his two daughters when he learned their mother had Negro blood. The setting of "Talma Gordon" is a dinner party hosted by the prominent Boston physician who narrates the story. The topic of discussion for the evening is empire and racial "amalgamation." The story intertwines the doctor's narration with his account of the stories told by other characters, including the reading of letters. Cordell (2006) argues that this "story-within-a-story technique" (p. 52) allows Hopkins to examine the violence against Black women and "the extent to which white, upper middle-class identity depends upon perpetuating and hiding that violence" (p. 53).

As a mystery, Nickerson (1998) observes that "Chinese-box structure of the story" is "a metaphor for the layers of secrecy surrounding the murders." She points out that Hopkins also "borrows from the 'locked room' type of detective story, in which it seems that no one could have gotten into or out of the room in which a body is found" (pp. 190–191). Patricia Turner (1998) notes use of the White doctor to "recount several colliding family histories" allows Hopkins "in part to generate the suspense required in the *mystery* genre" (p. 2, italics in original). The final revelation of the story comes when the doctor reveals to his White male listeners that he is married to Talma Gordon, the beautiful heroine with the "drop of black blood" who was once tried for the murder of her own father. This revelation comes after he has revealed to them the identity of the true killer. Hopkins leaves to the reader's imagination how these men react when the doctor invites them to come with him and meet his wife.

The presence of a doctor-suitor in this story parallels the appearance of similar characters in other books of the era. Birnbaum (1999) notes the presence of physicians who represent the "man of science" in both Harper's *Iola Leroy* and in liberal, White author W.D. Howell's *An Imperative Duty*. In each of these novels, the physician challenges the idea of the taint of Black ancestry and dominant views about miscegenation by urging the female protagonist to choose to live as his "White" wife. In Harper's novel, *Iola Leroy*, the heroine is courted by two physician-suitors. She chooses marriage with the Black physician rather than the White and commitment to the uplift of the African American race with which she now chooses to identify. In "Talma Gordon," with the mystery center-stage, Hopkins does not explore this choice by the female protagonist to marry the White doctor.

As in the Borden case, Hopkins gives Talma Gordon a sister. Talma's sister, Jeanette, wanted to kill their father when she learned he intended to change his will, disinheriting his daughters in favor of his son with his second wife. However, Jeanette's ill will toward their father was a secret rage because the truth about their mother's lineage was not revealed. It is Talma, whose suitor was rejected by their father, and who would have shared his fortune with her sister, who seemed to have the motive. As the doctor tells his listeners, "The case was very black against Talma" (Hopkins, p. 10).

The doctor and Hopkins make a sly pun in describing the case against Talma, but as she sat in the courtroom she enjoyed the privilege of "whiteness." The secret of her racial identity was not revealed during the trial. The judge and the jury saw her as a wealthy young White woman of good family. As in the real life Borden trial, the evidence against Talma Gordon is "entirely circumstantial." The judge in his summary of the evidence gives "the prisoner the benefit of the doubt" (Hopkins, p. 11). The jury finds Talma not guilty. But she is — as was Lizzie Borden — convicted in the court of public opinion. Even though she has been acquitted, Talma is ostracized. She and her sister, Jeanette, take refuge in Rome.

When Talma arrives at the clinic of the doctor/narrator, he sends for her fiancée. Talma tells her lover about the letter that Jeanette wrote on her deathbed. In the letter Jeanette recounts how after overhearing their father's plans to disinherit them, she demanded to know why he had always practiced such "monstrous injustice" toward his daughters (p. 14). Their father told Jeanette about the birth of their brother, his third child with their mother, a boy that was "dark as a mulatto, with the characteristic features of the Negro!" (p. 15). He accused his wife of infidelity which sent her into convulsions. He sent for her Northern-born parents who admitted that their daughter had been adopted. The child's birth mother had been an octoroon woman who was abandoned by her lover.

With the death of both his wife and their baby, Captain Gordon took control of his wife's estate. He intended passing it on to the son of his second marriage. Learning this, Jeanette reacted with outrage, declaring her desire for "revenge upon this man, my father" (p. 15). But, as the doctor reveals to his listeners, Jeanette was pre-empted in her murderous intent by someone else who wanted revenge. The son of the partner that Captain Gordon betrayed, an East Indian posing as White, killed the family. By coincidence, he too was at the clinic, suffering from tuberculosis. On his death bed, he confessed to the murders. He accused his victim, Captain Gordon, of greed for gold and piracy: "His blackest crime was the murder of my father, who was his friend, and had sailed with him for many a year as his mate" (p. 17).

All of this information comes to Talma and the doctor in the form of death-bed confessions. In her effort to clear her name, Talma had hired investigators: "By her direction the shrewdest of detectives were employed and money flowed like water, but to no purpose; the Gordon tragedy remained a mystery" (Hopkins, p. 11). Nickerson (1999) observes that Hopkins's use of plot elements from the Borden case are "very much in the tradition of" Anna Katherine Green and Metta Victoria Fuller Victor (pseudonym of Seely Regester) (p. 192). Green and Victor were White female mystery writers, contemporaries of Hopkins. Nickerson (1998) also finds that Hopkins displays similarities to Mary Roberts Rinehart in her punishment of the murderer while suggesting "that under the conditions of injustice woven into the fabric of American culture, murderous ideas in a woman's head are understandable, if not justified" (p. 190). But Hopkins's use of the Borden story is unique because she places miscegenation and racism at the heart of the plot.

Hopkins's novel, *Hagar's Daughter*, appeared in monthly installments in *Colored American Magazine* from March 1901 to March 1902 (Brooks, 1996 in Gruesser, p. 120). Brooks observes that in this story of "maternal inheritance" and the "mysteries of identity," Hopkins follows the pattern of other African American women novelists of the period whose "focus on strong female characters and their relations to each other relegates the male characters to the margins of the narrative" (Brooks, pp. 120–121).

DeLamotte (2004) describes *Hagar's Daughter* as "an early twentieth-century romance that is both a revolutionary revisioning of traditional Gothic mystery and an oppositional deployment of the relatively new figure of the detective" (p. 70). In Hopkins's novel, slavery is revealed as "the originary crime underlying all the others" (DeLamotte, p. 71).

The novel begins in Maryland in 1860–62, when St. Clair Enson, a wastrel aristocrat, learns that his brother Ellis has married and is now the father of a baby daughter. With the help of Walker, a slave trader, St. Clair destroys his brother's idyllic family life by revealing that his brother's wife has Negro blood. Ellis recovers from his initial despair and plans to take his wife and child abroad. But he fails to return from his trip to make the arrangements. A body, face destroyed by a pistol blast, is found with Ellis's papers and watch. Ellis has apparently committed suicide. His wife, Hagar, is unwilling to believe this. She suspects St. Clair and confronts him:

Ellis was killed, murdered — shot down like a dog. What did the pistol prove? Nothing. His pockets had not been rifled. That proves nothing. Neither his great trouble brought to him by his marriage with me — a Negro — would have driven him to self-destruction. He was murdered [Hopkins, p. 60].

St. Clair dismisses Hagar's shrewd analysis of the planted evidence of suicide as the ravings of a "madwoman." He declares: "This is too much for any man to stand from a nigger wench" (p. 61). He tells Hagar that she and her child are going to be sent to the slave market. Hagar falls "into a state of melancholy from which nothing aroused her but the needs of the child" (p. 64). As O'Brien (2003) observes, Hagar "must reconcile her 'black blood' and the racist assumptions about Black women instilled in her as a White woman with what she knows as her own personal strength and dignity" (p. 121). Hagar finally rouses herself enough to attempt an escape. She manages to slip past her captors and attempts to make it into the woods. When she is trapped on the bridge, she plunges into the Potomac River with her baby in her arms. She and the child apparently drown.

When Chapter 9 opens, it is 1882, twenty years later. The focus of the novel is now on Senator Zenas Bowen. The senator is a self-made millionaire from California. His wife, a beautiful, well-bred lady, is the step-mother of his daughter, Jewel. Jewel has taken D.C. society by storm and won the heart of Cuthbert Sumner, the aide to General Benson, head of the Treasury Department. However, as the reader learns, Benson is a member of a trio of con artists. The other members of the team are Major Madison and his boldly beautiful daughter, Aurelia (contrasted with the innocent, demure Jewel). Aurelia was once involved with Cuthbert Sumner, and she plots to reclaim him from Jewel, who she has befriended. When Jewel comes upon Aurelia in Sumner's arms, she breaks her engagement to him. According to the con artists' plan this should leave General Benson free to claim Jewel — and her inheritance — as his own.

The plan goes awry when Sumner rejects Aurelia. He is then framed for the murder of Benson's secretary (who has been the victim of Benson's sexual harassment and is the mother of his illegitimate child). When Benson learns that Jewel and Sumner have reconciled and have secretly married even though Sumner is in jail, he arranges for Jewel to be kidnapped. Imprisoned at the abandoned Enson mansion, she encounters another prisoner, Aunt Henny, the old Black woman who works at the Treasury Department. Aunt Henny knows that Sumner did not commit the murder.

Indeed, it is Aunt Henny who holds the key to the mystery of General Benson's identity. But Aunt Henny must be rescued, and her granddaughter, Venus, assumes the role of detective to find her missing grandmother. Venus's father, Issac, has been working for General Benson. Issac turns up unexpectedly with the money that Venus's hardworking mother needs to pay the mortgage. Given Issac's history as a ne'er-do-well and conman, Venus is not inclined to believe he came by the money honestly. She suspects it is somehow linked to the murder at the Treasury Department and the fact that her grandmother has gone missing. After questioning her brother Oliver, the college student, about their father, Venus concludes she must take action because "[t]he police are slower 'n death" and her father is "up to his capers." Even if her mother is fooled by her father, she is not.

> It's a burning shame for Dad to go on this way after all Miss Jewel's kindness to us. But I'll balk him. I'm see him out on this case or my name ain't Venus Johnson [Hopkins, p. 195].

As Venus adds, she intends to "see if this one little black girl can't get the best of as mean a set of villains as ever was born" (Hopkins, p. 195). With this goal in mind, Venus offers her assistance to Mr. Henson, the Secret Service chief, who is investigating the murder. Henson, who seems to function as a PI, was hired by Jewel prior to her kidnapping. Even though he is convinced General Benson is behind it all, he has no way to prove it. Then Venus walks into his office with her suspicions about her father, Issac. She tells him about witnessing an encounter between the general and Jewel's step-mother, Mrs. Bowen, that sent Mrs. Bowen into a swoon. That was when Venus realized that General Benson was a serious threat, and "that I'd got to cook his goose or he'd cook mine" (Hopkins, p. 201). Venus explains that the general is a "sly old villain" (p. 201). She has been offended by his flirtatious behavior toward her — his "loving servant girls on the sly" (p. 202). Concerning this scene between Venus and Henson, Knadler (2002) observes that what would have stood out for Black female readers was "not Venus's sassy and risible pretensions" but the fact that Mr. Henson, the detective, "is impervious to racial and gender violence perpetrated by the white character" (p. 76).

Eventually convinced of Venus's cleverness and the relevance of her information to his case, Henson decides to send her undercover as his operative. She is to masquerade as "Billy," the grandson of Henson's Black operative, who is posing as "Uncle Henry," a crippled old Negro who is fond of liquor (Hopkins, p. 202). Arriving in the vicinity of Enson Hall, Uncle Henry establishes himself as a favorite among the locals who congregate at the general store. Meanwhile, Venus gains entry to the grounds of the Hall. She locates Jewel and Aunt Henny, her grandmother, and brings about their rescue.

Aunt Henny testifies during Cuthbert Sumner's trial even though the prosecutor objects that "the evidence of a Negress" should be used to impugn the good name, "the honour" of a soldier and "brave gentleman" (Hopkins, p 229). Knadler (2002) observes that in this scene, Aunt Henny with "the voice and traumatic memory of the slave woman" challenges "the power of the white patriarchal government." She is able to detect the brute beneath the general's masquerade of civility" when the police and those in authority cannot penetrate his disguise as a gentleman (p. 59). During her testimony, Aunt Henny identifies Benson as St. Clair Enson, who as a young slave master, age seven, hit her with a block of wood and left her scarred (p. 228). Aunt Henny has taken the stand to identify the man who murdered a White woman, but she also testifies about the crime of slavery (written on her Black body as it was on the bodies of the escaped slaves who displayed their scars for abolitionist audiences).

When Henson of the Secret Service takes the stand, he has other revelations about General Benson. In the climatic scene of the novel, he reveals that General Benson is St. Clair, and Benson's friend, Major Madison, is the slave trader, Walker. When Henson declares that he himself is Ellis Enson, Jewel's step-mother, Mrs. Bowen, the wife of the dead Senator, stands up in the courtroom and declares, "Ellis, Ellis! I am Hagar" (Hopkins, p. 233).

The long-separated couple is reunited, but Hagar is immediately rendered an outcast from White society. Cuthbert Sumner is relieved that Jewel is Hagar's White step-daughter, and that they can go on with their marriage. Crediting the power of socialization for his bigotry, Hopkins relates that Sumner "was born with a noble nature" but has been shaped by "environment and tradition" (p. 237). Inspired by noblesse oblige, he made donations to Negro colleges "on the same principal" that motivated him when he "gave liberally to the Society for the Prevention of Cruelty to Animals and endowed a refuge for homeless cats" (p. 237). Sumner admits to Ellis Enson that he could not love Aurelia Madison after he discovered that she had Negro blood (Hopkins, p. 241).

This admission foreshadows his reaction to the next revelation. Hagar remembers that before he died Senator Bowen told her to look in his old trunk. She discovers the clothing in which she wrapped her own baby and a letter from Bowen left in the trunk to certify that he rescued a child from the Potomac when he was a river boatman. He found the child floating on a log and took her home to his now deceased first wife. They adopted the child, Jewel. Unbeknown to her, Hagar married the man who saved her child and has been step-mother to her own daughter. Jewel is Hagar's daughter.

When she learns this secret of her identity, Jewel sends Sumner a note. She knows and even understands his feelings about race-mixing. Before his "good angel" can triumph (p. 250), Jewel is taken off to Europe by her parents (who have remarried). Sumner waits a year for their return, then goes to Enson Hall, only to discover Jewel's grave. She has died of a fever while abroad. Hopkins writes: "Cuthbert Sumner questioned wherein he had sinned and why he was so severely punished" (p. 252). Hopkins concludes that Sumner has paid for the sins of the nation which "must be washed out." In the final scene, Sumner observes the child of St. Clair Enson (General Benson) and his murdered secretary (Elise Bradford) playing on the lawn of the Hall. Sumner thinks of the impact of slavery not only on Black families but "the sacred family relation" (p. 252). On this somber note, the novel ends.

In *Hagar's Daughter*, Hopkins brings together a team of detectives that challenge both racial and gender assumptions. The Black male and the Black female operatives are clever enough to go undercover. As an operative, Venus Johnson crosses gender lines to "pass" as an adolescent boy. It is indicative of Hopkins's own feminist leanings that it is Venus, not her college student brother, who takes on the role of sleuth. Also worthy of notice is Hopkins's subtext of gender tensions in the Johnson family created by the union of a hard-working wife/mother and a shiftless husband/father. Tellingly, it is Venus, rather than her mother who is most critical of her father's behavior. Having learned that some men cannot be depended on, Venus depends on herself. Arguably, Hopkins' *Hagar's Daughter* is not only a milestone in the evolution of mystery fiction by African Americans but also of feminist mystery/detective fiction.

In another early venture into genre fiction, John Edward Bruce's *The Black Sleuth* was serialized from 1907 to 1909 in *McGirt's Magazine* (see Seraile, 2002). In the University Press edition of the novel, Gruesser (2002) observes that *The Black Sleuth*

> is, in fact, only partially a mystery. The West African hero, Sadipe Okukenu, does not become a detective until the second half of the novel, and the crime he is investigating, the theft of a large, flawless diamond, never really takes place [p. ix].

As a cultural outsider, Sadipe has a perspective on race relations different from that of native-born African Americans. Sadipe comes to the United States in the company of Captain Barnard. Barnard is "a down-easter, and like most of the men from that part of America, he had a great deal of genuine sympathy for the Negro" (Bruce, p. 22). Sensitive to racial injustice, Barnard acknowledges the truth of the observations made by Sadipe's "wily old" father about the "manstealers[s]" in the United States who engaged in the slave trade and the "men-killers" who still were lynching Black men (p. 24). Barnard responds:

> ... their crimes have disgraced the American name and made it a byword and hissing among the nations, and our children, and our children's children will bear the stigma and suffer the consequences of these crimes against God and man for generations yet unborn [p. 24].

This frank acknowledgment of American guilt by the captain convinces the father that he can trust Barnard to place his son in an American school. After a pleasant sojourn in a school in New England, Sadipe Okukena goes South to a Black industrial college. En route he encounters racial prejudice both during a stopover in Washington, D.C., and on board the train. The ticket-taker, "a coarse, gruff, red-haired Irishman" (p. 30), punches Sadipe's ticket, then slaps him on the back, saying, "There's yure train, old man; step lively now." Outraged, Sadipe responds, "You're an insolent, impudent brute; how dare you strike me?" (p. 30). He informs the Irishman that he has "a great notion to slap your face." The "spunky boy" is saved from the consequences of his threat by "a gentleman" who steps forward. The gentleman, a stockholder in the railroad, accompanies Sadipe to make a complaint. The ticket-taker is called to the office by the superintendent and required to apologize for "his bad manner" (p. 30).

This is not the end of Sadipe's troubles. When the train crosses the Virginia line, he is ordered to move to the colored car (p. 31). Possessing a first-class ticket, Sadipe resists. The two Black porters ordered to remove him refuse to obey, one of them as a matter of conscience, the other because he doesn't like the look in Sadipe's eye and fears he may be armed (p. 33). Again, a White man, "evidently a man of influence and culture," (p. 34) observes the episode and comes to the aid of the African youth. This gentleman sits down beside Sadipe and gives him a six-shooter to use if he needs to protect himself. The gentleman, General R. M. DeMortie, is from the West and the commander of "one of the crack Negro regiments." He regards Negro soldiers "as the bravest and the best in the service" (p. 34).

Sadipe receives a third shock when he arrives in Gordonsville. The sleepy Southern town is the home of Eckington College for Colored Youth, to which he has received a scholarship. Sadipe is dismayed by the indolent, "hungry-looking poor whites" who laze about why Negro men and women sell food to the train passengers (p. 35). He is further disheartened when he sees the school. In a letter to General DeMorti, he writes that although the promoters of the school "have a most extraordinary ambition to make it a college," the curriculum is inadequate, not even of the quality of "our little village school in Maine" (p. 43). Sadipe reminds the General of his offer to help him in securing employment with the General's friend who is establishing "an international Detective Bureau" (p. 42). In his response, the General agrees, "The South is a veritable hell for a man of your culture and taste" (p. 44). He promises to help Sadipe secure a position.

Meanwhile, Sadipe, still oblivious to the racial etiquette governing interactions in the South, has angered the local Whites. The professor (principal of the school) explains that they attracted attention because they "were better dressed than any white man or boy that we met in our walk ... and our prosperous appearance angered them" (p. 45). Even worse for Sadipe, he is a stranger and his manners are different "from the everyday, ordinary Negro they meet" (p. 45). To the professor's relief, Sadipe has left town by the time the White men come looking for him. When the mob comes at midnight, the professor greets them in his robe and tells them that he expelled Sadipe from the school (p. 56). They search the principal's house and not finding Sadipe, depart.

Three years later, Sadipe is employed by the International Secret Service Bureau. He has been successful as a detective, spurred on by an overheard comment from a client. The client, Captain De Forrest, came to the Bureau for help finding a stolen diamond. In the opening line of the novel, he declares, "Do you mean to tell me that that nigger is a detective, and that you are going to put him on this case, Mr. Hunter?" (p. 3). The narrator describes De Forrest as person "who would easily be mistaken for a gentleman — only gentleman do not use the word 'nigger' when speaking of Negroes, nor spell it with two gs when writing about them" (p. 3).

After establishing the outstanding reputation of the detective agency, the narrator describes the Black sleuth as a native of "Ekiti Country in Yorubaland on the West Coast." His value to the agency is enhanced by his superior education (graduate of Eton College "with high honors"), his abilities ("a fine linguist, an expert at chess"), and his physical condition ("as perfectly developed physically as an Apollo Belvidere"). For all his attributes, Sadipe is also "the personification of modesty" (Bruce, p. 4).

Sadipe goes undercover as a waiter named "Randolph" at a fashionable English hotel, where the suspects are accustomed to dine. In this regard, "he was admirably fitted in view of the fact that his black face disarmed all suspicion as to his true character" (p. 67). Among Sadipe's other advantages in the investigation is that Mandeville, one of the men he has under surveillance, would never suspect that Sadipe knows French, the language in which Mandeville converses in the presence of strangers (p. 76). Sadipe also makes the acquaintance of the two female servants who work in the house of the suspects by presenting himself as an African native who sells curios and tells fortunes. Throughout the investigation, Mr. Hunter, Sadipe's chief, praises his progress and expresses his "implicit confidence" in Sadipe's skills as a sleuth. Justifying his faith, Sadipe locates the rendezvous of the "shrew swindlers" who have "eluded the vigilance of the best detectives of Scotland Yard" (p. 92).

Sadipe's background and his competence as well as his employment as a PI by a detective agency make him unique among the early Black sleuths.[37] As Gruesser (2002) points out, Bruce's fiction reflected his political views. Bruce was involved in Black organizations such as the American Negro Academy and, with Arthur Schomburg, founded the Negro Society for Historical Research. Acquainted with a number of Black leaders and involved in forging connections with Africans and West Indians, Bruce served as host to Marcus Garvey, when Garvey arrived in the United States. He was a liaison between Garvey's Universal Negro Improvement Association (and his Back-to-Africa movement) and African organizations. When Bruce died in Harlem in 1924, his funeral drew more than five thousand people (Gruesser, p. xiii).

W. Adolphe Roberts, a journalist, became the first Black mystery writer to publish a novel in non-serialized form. *The Haunting Hand* (1926) features:

> ... a spunky young white woman who works for a Long Island film company and relies on her intuition to solve the crime that occurs in her boarding house. The only black character in the novel is the Negro maid of one of the film company's female stars. She makes two brief, barely visible appearances [Bailey, 1999, p. 53].

Jamaican by birth, Roberts arrived in the United States at an early age. He worked as a newspaper reporter in New York and San Francisco before serving as a front-line correspondent during World War I. Although Roberts wrote two other crime novels, *The Mind Reader* (1929) and *The Top Floor Killer* (1935), Blacks played minor roles in his books. *The Mind Reader* features two sibling heroes battling a psychic who wants to control the world. *The Top-Floor Killer* features a detective, who grew up in the slums, on the trail of a serial killer. Perhaps more indicative of Roberts' political views is his non-genre novel, *The Strange Career of Bishop Sterling* (1932). Written under the "Irish" pseudonym, Stephen Endicott, the novel focuses on violence by the Ku Klux Klan. However, both the protagonist (a morally ambivalent male) and the victim (a female school teacher involved with a politician) are White (Bailey, p. 53).

Roberts was publishing during the Harlem Renaissance. The fact that Roberts did not focus on Black characters and Black issues brings him into the debate that was at the heart of the Renaissance about the obligations of Black writers.

Of "Respectability" and "Primitivism"

Wintz (1988) argues that although associated with the physical location of Harlem in New York City, the Renaissance "was basically a psychology — a state of mind or an attitude — shared by a number of Black writers and intellectuals who centered their activities around Harlem in the late 1920s and early 1930s" (p. 2). The participants in this literary and cultural movement were not always physically present in Harlem. Bremer (1990) finds that "the best publicized 'New Negro' leaders of the Harlem Renaissance were more often away then in residence during the 1920s" (p. 49). Literary activity by African American writers was going on elsewhere, abroad and in other American cities, such as Chicago. But Harlem was "the symbolic center of African American" life (Bremer, p. 49).[38] It attracted not only writers and artists, but the migrants who arrived to work in the service-oriented industries of the city (Bremer, 49).

One of the issues during this literary movement was the role that the Black writer should play in improving the status of the race. What Peplow (1980) describes as "the critical debate of the Harlem Renaissance" was "whether a black author should write *black* or as an American who *happens* to be black ... [should] the black writer ... project racial themes or universal ones?" (p. 31). With an eye not only to this question but to the larger one of the depiction of Black characters, W.E.B. Du Bois, editor of *The Crisis*, the journal of the National Association for the Advancement of Colored People (NAACP),[39] solicited the opinions of writers. In a 1926 symposium that appeared over several issues of the journal, Du Bois invited well-known writers (both Black and White) to respond to the question "The Negro Image in Art: How Shall He Be Portrayed?"[40] (see Bailey, 1991, p. 121).

The symposium served to highlight the varied opinions among the writers about a special responsibility with regard to the depiction of the Negro race. This was an aspect of the larger question of whether "art" should also be "propaganda." In 1928, in an article for H. L. Mencken's *American Mercury*, poet, novelist, and race leader, James Weldon Johnson described the problem of the double audience:

> ... the Aframerican author faces a special problem which the plain American author knows nothing about — the problem of the double audience. It is more than a double audience; it is a divided audience, an audience made up of two elements with differing and often opposite and antagonistic points of view. His audience is often both white America and black America ... [quoted in Scruggs, 1977, p. 543].

For Black writers, this vexing issue of the duty/obligation to portray Blacks in a certain way was complicated by the debate regarding "lower class" culture and whether it should be excluded from depiction. In Harlem, as in other urban Black communities, class tensions became more complex in the first decades of the 20th century as the pace of Black migration from the South increased.[41] Urban communities were increasingly segregated by mechanisms such as restrictive covenants,[42] but this residential segregation did not keep Whites out of Harlem. The Prohibition era — organized crime, speakeasies, and a generation recovering from the psychological impact of World War I — created a situation in which Whites were present in Black communities not only as business owners and merchants, but as "slummers," "interlopers," and "patrons" of the arts (Lewis, 1997; Bernard, 2005). In her book about Manhattan in the 1920s, historian Ann Douglas (1995) observes that if jazz was the rage then

> ... white urban Americans wanted to go straight to the source to get more of it. By the mid–1920s, Harlem was being advertised as the "Nightclub Capital of the World." About 125 nightclubs led by the Cotton Club and Connie's Inn, served up African American music and dancing to white patrons eager to enjoy a little regression back to jungle life and to participate, only as voyeurs, in what was palpably the most exciting entertainment scene America had ever boasted [p. 74].

The juxtaposition of high-flying night life and the daylight realities of the ghetto during the "Jazz Age" created a phenomenon that some African American writers wanted to portray in their works. The "high life" and the "low life" of Harlem pitted Black political activists such as W.E. B. Du Bois, who believed that respectability and assimilation into the dominant society was the key to gaining Black rights, against more bohemian young writers and artists who were attracted to "primitivism." A sore point in this debate for Du Bois and others was the influence wielded on Black arts and letters by wealthy Whites who had acquired their ideas about primitivism from Europe where there was a fascination with African art and culture. These Whites sought primitivism in Harlem, and a number of them became patrons of the Harlem Renaissance. Thus both Langston Hughes and Zora Neale Hurston at various times received financial support from, Charlotte Mason, a wealthy White matron who was interested in anthropology and demanded that the several young writers and artists she sponsored emphasized "what she identified as folk culture or primitivism" in their works (Kellner, 1997, p. 124).

Carl Van Vechten, the most prominent of the patrons, spent significant amounts of time in Harlem and invited the Black writers and artists that he befriended to gatherings in his home. Socially-connected, he introduced them to the mainstream editors and publishers, who were among his other guests. However, Van Vechten stirred a firestorm of controversy and created ill-will among some of the Black leaders who had offered him hospitality when he published a sensational novel titled *Nigger Heaven* (1926). The title referred to the segregated balcony seating of Negroes in theaters. The novel was about the descent of an educated young Black man into the seductive underworld of Harlem. Black race leaders such as Du Bois, who advocated the use of literature for racial progress, were outraged. Several of the young Black writers, who had served as Van Vechten's consultants during the writing of the novel, continued to support him. One of them was Rudolph Fisher.

Rudolph Fisher

The existence of the Black ghetto contributed to the evolution of African American mystery fiction. Harlem Renaissance physician and writer Rudolph Fisher brought Black mystery writers into the genre mainstream with the publication of a mystery set in the Black community. Fisher died at the age of 37 in 1934 after "a third operation for an intestinal aliment" (Perry, 1987). In the decade from 1925 to 1935, two novels, fifteen short stories, as well as "journalistic pieces and scientific articles" by Fisher were published (Balshaw, 2000, pp. 30–31). Although Fisher was neglected in later decades, he was popular in the 1920s and received "extensive notice in the African American press as well as being one of the very few Black writers who consistently published in many mainstream white magazines, particularly *Atlantic Monthly* ... but also *McClure's Magazine* and *Story*" (Balshaw, p. 31).

Fisher's only mystery novel, *The Conjure-Man Dies* (1932) is classic detective fiction. In this book, his other novel, *The Walls of Jericho* (1928), and his short stories, Fisher assumes the self-assigned role of "Harlem's interpreter" (quoted in Perry, 1987, p. 3). He addresses the dilemmas faced by his characters as they encounter the opportunities and the obstacles of urban life. Adept at depicting the culture shock experienced by the Blacks who left the South during "the Great Migration," Fisher focuses on "Harlem's complex and ambiguous meaning for black people as mecca and hell." At the same time, Fisher examines "the intraracial and interracial problems and the identity crisis fomented by differences in pigmentation" (Deutsch, 1979, p. 159).

In one of his better-known short stories, "City of Refuge" (1925), Fisher's protagonist, King Solomon Gillis, has fled North Carolina to avoid being lynched for shooting a White man. Gillis made his getaway in an automobile that he later sold to a Washington, D.C., bootlegger. The bootlegger gave him "a hundred dollars and directions to Harlem" (Fisher, p. 28). Harlem is indeed a refuge from White vigilante violence, but Gillis remains at risk. He falls prey to Mouse Uggam, a Black con man and drug dealer. Uggam arranges for Gillis to work in a grocery store owned by an Italian named Tony Gabrielli. Then he sends his own customers in to make special purchases.

Mouse Uggam calls to mind the observations by W.E. B. Du Bois in his ground-breaking sociological study, *The Philadelphia Negro* (1899). Regarding the group that he referred to as the "submerged tenth," Du Bois observed:

> Their nucleus consists of a class of professional criminals, who do not work ... and migrate here and there ... these are a set of gamblers and sharpers who seldom are caught in serious crime, but who nevertheless live from its proceeds and aid and abet it ... they stand ready to entrap the unwary and tempt the weak ... [p. 586].[43]

As Whalen (2005) points out Uggam was among those Black men who was sent abroad during World War I and returned to the United States with a greater sense of the world. In Uggam's case, his war experience aids his duplicity. He peppers his conversation with Anglicized French phrases such as "toot sweet" (for "*tout de suite*"). His sophisticated air helps him to persuade Gillis to accept what seems to be a legitimate job offer. He is also able to convince Gillis that the pills he wants him to sell are "some valuable French medicine as yet unavailable in the United States" (Whalen, p. 785).

Fisher offers a perverted twist on the supposed bond among Southern migrants. Gillis has heard neighbors back home in North Carolina boast about one of their sons who fought in France and then settled in Harlem. When Uggam picks Gillis out as his mark, Gillis is delighted when he looks at Uggam's card and discovers that he has met his neighbors' son. Uggam has been instructed to befriend Gillis by his boss (a former Pullman porter turned cabaret owner). When he comes to call, Gillis is more than willing to listen to his suggestions about how to get on in Harlem.

Mouse Uggam represents modernity. Gillis is the product of a rural prewar past (Whalen, p. 785). Fresh from the rural South, Gillis reacts with amazement to the subway, the sounds of the city, and its people. At the end of the story, as he and Uggam sat in a Harlem cabaret, Gillis confides, "Ain but two things in dis world, Mouse, I really wants. One is to be a policeman. Been wantin' dat ev'y since I seen dat cullud traffic-cop dat day. Other is to git myse'f a gal lak dat one over yonder!" (Fisher, p. 38). When two White detectives who have been observing Gillis's activities in the grocery store, arrive to arrest him, Uggam claims that he happened to be sitting at the same table and that Gillis offered to sell him pills to help him sleep.

When one of the detectives pulls the envelope containing the pills from

Gillis's coat pocket, he begins to realize that he has been set up. Even at that moment, he is distracted by an argument between the "girl with the green stockings" (Fisher, p. 38), that he has been admiring, and her escort. He jumps up to go to her aid. The detective mistakes his movement as an attempt to escape and whistles for reinforcements. Gillis entertains the cabaret regulars by resisting arrest — until he sees a uniformed Black policeman: "He stopped as if stunned. For a moment, he simply stared. Into his mind swept his own words like a forgotten song, suddenly recalled: —'Culled policemans!'" Still amazed by this phenomenon of the city, Gillis relaxes with a grin on his face that "had something exultant about it" (Fisher, p. 40). As Deutsch notes, in this story, the instruments of oppression are "subtle and frustrating" and justice is "achingly elusive" (p. 160; see also McCluskey, 1981, p. 56).

Deutsch (1979) observes that in describing the "physical topography" of Harlem, "Fisher reconstructs the black community, block by block. Practically every story is set on a specific street or cluster of streets" (p.160). Moreover, the streets "are revealed to the reader in both graphically realistic and metaphorically imaginative terms" (p. 160). Fisher contrasts the bustle and excitement of the city street with the place Gillis finds lodging. He has been sent to the address by the bootlegger to whom he sold his car. The room is "half the size of his hencoop back home, with a single window opening into an airshaft." In this tenement room, the odors of cabbage, chitterlings, and liver and onions do battle with each other. The sounds of a couple fighting, a baby crying, music —"a sewer of sounds and smells"— bombard his senses (Fisher, p. 31). During this era in Harlem's history, the tawdry and the wretched exist along side the signs of Negro progress.

As one of the new generation of Black writers, Fisher felt no obligation to present only positive images of Blacks. Although he was a minister's son and inclined to take a moralistic tone in his fiction (Perry, 1987, p. 12), Fisher was open to literary experimentation. In an inscription to Carl Van Vechten, the wealthy White patron of the Harlem Renaissance,[44] Fisher described *The Conjure-Man Dies* as an "experiment in technique" (quoted in Tignor, 1982, cited in Gosselin, 1999, p. 611). Regarding this aspect of his work, Gosselin (1999) writes:

> Like Dashiell Hammett, Rudolph Fisher ... experimented with the clue puzzle format dominating the so-called Golden Age of detective fiction in the 1920s and early 1930s. Also like Hammett, Fisher's experiment involves combining classical detective fiction with elements of the newly developing hard-boiled formula [p. 1].

In *The Conjure-Man Dies* (1932), Fisher introduces Perry Dart, an African American police detective leading a homicide investigation. Dart is the first of ten Negro members of Harlem's police force to be promoted to detective. Born in Manhattan, Dart attended public school. He possesses a clear sense of the community, "having himself grown up with the black colony, [he] knew Harlem from lowest dive to loftiest temple" (Fisher, p. 14). The novelty of a Black detective in Harlem is highlighted during Dart's interview with Mrs. Ararmintha Snead, an older woman who was in the conjure-man's waiting room when the murder occurred. She objects when he tells her that he is a member of the NYPD, "Police detective? T'ain't so. They don't have no black detectives." To this Dart responds, "Your informant was either ignorant or color-blind, madame" (Fisher, 1932, p. 79).

Dart's team applies modern methods of crime scene investigation, but Dart lacks the esoteric scientific knowledge required to unravel the deeper mysteries of the apparent murder of Frimbo, the African prince and Harlem "conjure-man." Dart solicits the aid of Dr. John Archer, the physician who lives across the street from the house in which the murder occurred. Dr. Archer has a "lean, light-skinned countenance" (Fisher, p. 11). By his own account, Dr. Archer is underpaid and underappreciated by his patients, and he is pleased when Dart requests his assistance (p. 22). Later in the book, Archer describes how his training/habits as a physician are similar to those of a detective: "The criminal I chase is as prime as rascal as you'll ever find — assailant, thief, murderer — disease. In each case I get, it's my job to track disease down, identify it, and arrest it. What else is diagnosis and treatment" (209).

Archer's analogy between the work of the physician and that of the detective is intriguing because in his mystery Fisher comments on the variety of social ills, including organized crime and violence, plaguing the Black community. Not all of these comments come from the two protagonists. The perspectives of working-class Harlem residents are also offered in exchanges between the third sleuth, Bubber Brown, and his best friend, Jinx Jenkins. Bubber and Jinx appear as moving men in Fisher's other novel, *The Wall of Jericho* (1928). In *The Conjure-Man Dies*, Bubber has given up his job in the sanitation department to become an unlicensed private investigator, a "family detective," specializing in domestic matters. As Gosselin (1999) notes, Bubber Brown has often been "overlooked by critics," but he plays a crucial role in the novel (1999, p. 1).

When Jinx is arrested for Frimbo's murder based on the circumstantial evidence that Bubber unintentionally provides, Bubber sets out to prove Jinx's innocence. This involves assisting the police in locating an elusive suspect, an experience that Bubber finds exhilarating. But his visit to Jinx in jail reminds him of the gravity of the situation. Jinx tells Bubber that even if Frimbo (whose body has disappeared) does turn out to be alive, Jinx could still get twenty years in prison for assault. Bubber objects, "...But shuh, man, they can't do that to you." To which Jinx replies, "I know they can't. You know they can't. But do they know they can't?" (p. 194). Here Jinx raises the possibility of a criminal justice system that functions to produce miscarriages of justice. His perspective was undoubtedly shared by many working-class Black men in Harlem in the 1930s.

As it turns out, the mystery of the murder of Frimbo is complex enough to require the efforts of all three detectives. A clue to the solution appears on the first page in the form of a popular song being sung by pedestrians strolling along the street. The narrative voice of this song, a cuckolded husband, wishes his rival ("you rascal you") dead. Fisher presents this clue in the context of the free-and-easy gaiety of the nightlife on Harlem's Seventh Avenue (Fisher, p. 3). What seems to be local color (no pun intended) turns out to be germane to the plot.

After slipping in this clue, Fisher immediately distracts the reader by drawing a contrast between this brightly-lit avenue and a dark and silent side street. There is a Gothic element, reminiscent of Edgar Allan Poe, to his description of one of the houses on this street: "[It] reared a little taller and gaunter than its fellows. So that the others appeared to shrink from it and huddle together in the shadow on either side" (p. 4). There are two signs over the door of the house, one for "Samuel Crouch, Undertaker," and the other for "N. Frimbo, Psychist" (p. 4). The sense of foreboding is explained when Bubber Brown runs out of the house and across the street to fetch Dr. Archer to the murder scene.

A Harvard-educated African prince, Frimbo has set up practice on the upper floor of the building owned by Crouch, the undertaker. During his session with Jinx, the conjure-man is apparently murdered by a blow to his head and Jinx's handkerchief is stuffed down his throat. After Archer examines the body, the corpse disappears from its temporary resting place in the funeral home downstairs. Later Frimbo reappears, alive and claiming to have been in a state of suspended animation that only resembled death. Archer, the man of science, doubts Frimbo's story and is certain the matter is somehow linked to Frimbo's missing manservant.

Faced with this complex situation, Detective Dart relies on Archer, the physician, to help him detect the sleight of hand related to the corpse. But Archer is less useful as an consultant about the intimate relationships of the various suspects. Bubber, the source of comic relief, offers Dart the most relevant insight into gender relation when he explains why he became a "family detective." As he puts it, "monkey-business" always flourishes, even during hard times:

> Monkey-business. Cheatin'—backbitin,' and all like that. Don't matter how bad business gets, lovin' still goes on; and long as lovin' is goin' on, cheatin' is goin' on too ... [Fisher, 49].

Bubber anticipates making a good living as a gatherer of information for concerned spouses. Dr. Archer, the bachelor physician, dismisses his own fleeting thought of an illicit affair between Frimbo and Martha Crouch, the undertaker's wife:

> "If it was anybody else besides Martha, I might be suspicious of—"
> "Of what?"
> "What she might have laid for Frimbo" [p. 93].

Dart, the police detective, is even more certain that the "outraged husband the-ory" doesn't apply in this case because Frimbo "was not interested in women" (p. 93). Dr. Archer suggests Dart remember to "check up" anyway because of his distaste for Crouch, a man who was glad that he had collected that month's rent before his tenant was murdered (p. 93).

Martha Crouch's involvement with her husband's tenant is the key to the mystery of who would kill—or try to kill—a conjure-man. In the lethal tri-angle popular in the hard-boiled fiction of the era, she is an unhappy wife who turns to a virile lover. Gosselin (1998) notes that Stanley Crouch, the under-taker, "epitomizes the direction of the black middle class by the 1920s" (p. 614). But his business activities and socializing at his private club leave his wife with time on her hands. Martha Crouch, "pampered and suitably bored" takes on the task of collecting the rent from her husband's tenants and becomes involved with Frimbo (Gosselin, p. 615).

Unlike the husbands in James M. Cain's novels,[45] Martha Crouch's spouse does not become the victim. Instead he kills his rival. Because of his alibi and a clever disguise, Crouch is not one of the prime suspects. That he is the killer, demonstrates Fisher's awareness of the conventions of the genre. A witty exchange occurs between Dr. Archer and the medical examiner (the only White character in the book) about mystery fiction. Archer claims that the Mrs. Aramintha Snead, "devout church-member and long-suffering housewife" is the "least likely person" to have committed the crime and therefore certain to be the guilty party. The medical examiner counters that Archer has "very adroitly neglected to mention the really most unlikely person on the case," Dr Archer himself. Archer replies that this is "quite possible" and his motive for killing Frimbo would be "professional jealousy" (p. 154). Fisher ends this exchange between the two by having Archer threaten to someday write a mys-tery in which the murderer is "the most likely suspect." The medical examiner assures him, "You'd never write another" (p. 155).[46] This conversation would have indicated to fans of the genre that Fisher was acquainted with the con-ventions of "Golden Age" detective fiction. The reader also might have sus-pected Fisher of making a tongue in cheek reference to Agatha Christie's *The Murder of Roger Ackyrod* (1926).[47]

More in keeping with the Jazz Age's interest in Freudian psychology (see Douglas, 1995, pp. 127–129) than with classic detective fiction, sex is at the heart of Fisher's mystery. Frimbo, the conjure man, keeps male sex glands among the bottles in his laboratory. Gosselin (1998) asserts that the mention of the "rite of the gonad" is "a parody of Freud" (p. 616). Frimbo dismisses sex as a bodily function, "necessary to comfort, like blowing one's nose" (Fisher, p. 268). He considers the study of biochemistry as more "vital" to his existence. Citing this passage, Gosselin (1998) argues that what Frimbo "shares a num-ber of characteristics with other detectives derived from the Dupin-Holmes tradition" (p. 609). This tradition is of the erudite, eccentric detective who values intellect over heart. Sex remains at the heart of the book because although Frimbo views Martha Crouch as only a passing fancy, she — or, at least, her jealous husband — proves his undoing. Having survived the first attempt on his life, Frimbo is assisting the police in re-enacting the crime when the cuckolded husband strikes again.[48]

Frimbo is not the only character in the novel involved in a sexual relationship that erupts in violence. The victim of domestic violence, Mrs. Aramintha Snead, the church woman, was waiting to see the conjure man about her problem. She tells Perry Dart that she has prayed that her husband will stop beating her when he is drunk.[49] Prayer having failed, she has come to Frimbo seeking another remedy. If prayer won't work, she will "now take it to the devil" (p. 81). She has heard about Frimbo from people in the neighborhood, "Everybody knows 'bout this man Frimbo — say he can conjure on down" (p. 81). She reminds Dart of the coverage in the *Amsterdam News* of the young man who survived having a knife broken off in his head. People say it was because Frimbo had put a charm on the victim to protect him from a boy who was out to get him (p. 82). Given Frimbo's reputation, Mrs. Snead believes he will be of more use than the police to her.

Regarding the violent characters in Fisher's Harlem, Bryant (2003) comments on Fisher's use of the "badman type" to which he brings a "diverting quick wit and a polished literary style." One such character is Tiger Shade, who Bryant notes is "very much in the tradition of Stagolee and John Hardy. Tiger 'was by a fair margin the tallest, widest, and thickest man in Harlem,' and he 'was bad as he was big'" (Bryant, p. 45). However, as a middle-class Black professional Fisher was writing for an audience that would "appreciate and be amused by his symmetrical locutions" (Bryant, 46) rather than for those working-class African Americans who actually might describe a man such as Tiger in the language of legend and folklore.

The potential for on-stage violence by Harlem residents is most evident in the encounters the hapless Bubber has in poolrooms and elsewhere. In one scene, Bubber turns into "a quiet side street" and finds that people are gathering as an argument escalates between two men over a woman. The girl has accused one of the men of insulting her. Her "protector" knocks the other man off the stoop and a fight erupts. The accused man draws a knife. The girl yells out a warning to her defender, and the crowd disperses as the man goes for his gun. Two shots are fired, and "the victim lay huddled with wide staring eyes at the foot of the stoop." The girl and the man with the gun retreat back into the building and take the elevator upstairs (p. 189). Bubber, too, retreats from the scene. He remarks, "Damn! What a place! What is this — an epidemic?" (p. 189). He has been present at two murders on two consecutive nights, and wonders, superstitiously, if there will be a third (p. 189).

Yet, even as Fisher presents Black male violence, he spends significant space depicting the strong bonds of friendship between Bubber and his friend

Jinx. They are a study in contrast, the short, bouncy Bubber, and the tall, taciturn, Jinx. But Fisher demonstrates the strength of their friendship by the exchanges between them that do not lead to violence. The normal rules of engagement regarding personal insults and "signifying" do not apply between the two men. For example, in the jail visit scene, Jinx taunts Bubber about his skin color:

> "African boogies ain't dumb," explained Jinx. They 'jes dark. You aint' been away from there long, is you?"
> "My folks," returned Bubber crushingly, "Left Africa ten generations ago."
> "Yo' folks? Shuh. Ten generations ago, you-all wasn't folks. You-all hadn't qualified as apes" [Fisher, p. 33].

The reader is told that it was only because "the hostility" between Bubber and Jinx "concealed the most genuine affection for each other" could the two men "come so close to blows that were never offered" (Fisher, p.33).

Frimbo, the African prince, also demonstrates loyalty and a sense of obligation to another man. Frimbo's missing manservant was the victim of the first attack. Frimbo creates confusion by stealing the servant's body from the funeral home and pretending to have himself been the victim in order to carry out the ritual required by one member of his clan toward another. He must burn his servant's body before sunset on the third day after his death (p. 304). As his king, he is obliged to find his servant's killer and ensure he or she receives punishment. Frimbo agrees to abide by Western law (p. 305), a moot issue when Frimbo himself is killed.

In her introduction to an edited collection of Fisher's short stories, Perry (1987) notes that Fisher tended to cast a cynical eye on Harlem. *The Conjure-Man Dies* addresses the tendency of Harlem residents to turn to practitioners such as Frimbo for solutions. During a conversation between Archer and Dart, the police detective asks the physician about Frimbo's occupation:

> "How'd he get into a racket like fortune-telling?"
> "Ask me another. Probably a better racket than medicine in this community. A real clever guy could do wonders" [Fisher, p. 27].

One of the suspects in the case confesses that he is there because he believes Frimbo is killing his brother with voodoo (p. 111).

In "Dr. Archer Nose," Fisher's only other work featuring Dart and Archer, the physician again encounters alternatives to his professional methods. The plot involves a murder in the home of a woman who practices folk medicine. Her folk practice is revealed late in the story, but when he arrives at the scene of the crime Dr. Archer sniffs out the vital clue. In a Holmesian turn, he comments on the uniqueness of odors, "M-m. Peculiar — very. Curious thing, odors. Discernible in higher dilution than any other material stimulus. Ridiculous that we don't make greater use of them" (p. 185). The odor turns out to be from a concoction that the folk healer makes for her clients. Archer views the woman and her practice with disdain. As a trained physician, he is angry and frustrated by the woman's gullible customers, including the father-turned-killer who went to her for a charm to cure his ailing son. When the boy died, the father sought revenge.

In *The Blues Detective* (1996), Soitos offers a detailed and ground-breaking analysis of the use by Fisher of a variety of African American cultural material, including folklore, religion, and superstition. Soitos describes four tropes as characterizing African American detective fiction: "alteration of detective persona, double-consciousness,[50] Black vernaculars, and hoodoo" (p. 27). He identifies all four tropes in Fisher's *The Conjure-Man Dies*.

Applying this criteria to "Dr. Archer's Nose," published three years later, Soitos finds the story "lacks the wit, the descriptive talent, and the use of the extended metaphor that makes the novel so fascinating." Soitos suggests that the short story form might have been "inadequate for Fisher's talents." Or, perhaps, Fisher "may have been arguing for a position he intellectually understood but emotionally questioned" (p. 121). This intellectual argument is John Archer's criticism of Afrocentric religions and the practice of folk medicine, which as Soitos observes seems "out of character when compared to his enthusiasm for Frimbo in the novel" (p.121). The female practitioner in the short story is "unsophisticated" in her methods and without the voice given to Frimbo (p. 121).

As Soitos implies, the level of sophistication of the practitioner seems to be the key to understanding the difference in depiction. Fisher, the author, was also Fisher, the physician and man of science. It makes sense that Archer, Fisher's fictional alter ego, should display fascination with and even grudging respect for Frimbo. Possessed of the arcane knowledge of his African culture and a Harvard education, Frimbo represents the synthesis of African primitivism and European modernism. The female "root woman" in "Dr. Archer's Nose" is uneducated, superstitious, and willing to risk the health of those like herself in order to bring a few more dollars into her household. From its inception in 1847, the American Medical Association (AMA) lobbied for professionalism and pushed for the criminalization of unlicensed practice by non-physicians. Given his professional training, Archer might logically be expected to have little respect for a woman who represents the ignorance that he considers an affront to modern medicine. Unlike Frimbo, the root woman in "Dr. Archer's Nose" offer no challenge to Archer's worldview or his assumption of superiority.

Whatever its literary quality, "Dr. Archer's Nose" should interest social scientists because of the impact of poverty on the lives of Harlem residents. The root woman's son shared his bed with a border. This "hot bed" system of using a bed in shifts allowed poor Harlem residents to cope with high rents and limited housing during the mass migration of the early twentieth century. Boyd (2000) finds that, "[t]he number of Black families that needed to take in boarders was considerable." Boyd cites estimates (offered originally by Henri (1976) in her book on Black migration from 1900 to 1920) that "'at least one-third' of Black families took in boarders (Boyd, p. 651). Although this practice was indicative of the economic straits of poor ghetto families, Boyd notes that one positive aspect was that it provided an opportunity for an "informal family economy" that facilitated "community-based networks" and allowed women to combine their housekeeping activities with "income-producing activity" (pp. 651–652).

Another aspect of Harlem life that Dart and Archer discuss as they try to identify the killer are the social conditions that sometimes led young people to alcohol or drug use and created situations in which mothers felt helpless to save their children. The victim's mother becomes a suspect in his murder because she was distressed by the "bad habits" that her son had fallen into under the influence of undesirable companions. The son had tuberculosis, the disease that killed his father. In real life, substance abuse/addiction and infectious diseases had plagued the poor of New York City since Irish immigrants lived in 19th century tenements (see e.g., Sante, 1992; Courtwright, 1996). These problems continued in the poverty and overcrowding of early 20th-century Harlem.

Discussing the mother in the story as a suspect, Dart and Archer have an exchange about the limits of "mother-love" and situations in which mothers "can go crazy," Dart mentions unwed mothers who "try to smother their kids—and sometimes succeed." Archer responds that this is quite different from the crime they are investigating because mothers who commit infanticide "aren't yet mothers, emotionally. They're just parents, biologically. With a wholly unwanted and recently very painful obstruction between themselves and happiness" (p. 196). This is a statement worthy of modern theorizing about neonaticide (see e.g., Riley, 2005).

George Schuyler

A contemporary of Fisher, George S. Schuyler, also contributed to the development of the genre. Between 1936 and 1938, Schuyler, a journalist and satirist, published two serialized novellas in the *Pittsburgh Courier*.[51] A combination of science fiction, adventure, romance, and political intrigue (the Ethiopian struggle against Italian invasion), the novellas, "The Ethiopian Murder Mystery" and "Revolt in Ethiopia," have been reissued as *Ethiopian Stories* (1994). The editor of the Schuyler volume, Robert A. Hill (1994), notes that in a review of Fisher's *The Conjure-Man Dies*, Schuyler praises the novel, saying that it "contains all the elements of a good mystery story" (p. 7). Schuyler seems to have been influenced by Fisher's novel:

> The story appears to have supplied Schuyler with the idea for "The Beast of Bradhurst Avenue," a mystery story about a series of gruesome beheadings in Harlem, which he published in the *Courier* in weekly installments from March through May 1934 ... [Hill, p. 8].

Schuyler's story features a Black police officer, Detective Sergeant Walter Crummel. It also features a star-crossed love affair between an African princess and a young White man. The princess and another young Black woman are murdered and their headless bodies placed in sacks. The culprit turns out to be a German scientist who is experimenting with transplanting a human brain into a dog's skull and needed the brains of the young women (Hill, p. 9). Aside from Fisher's influence, the story also reflects the influence of Schuyler's grandmother, who, he recalled, used to "regale me with strange and hair-raising tales about ghosts and witches" (quoted in Hill, p. 10). The choice of villain suggests Schuyler's concern about Nazi Germany (p. 9).

Schuyler's novella, "The Ethiopian Murder Mystery," was originally published in the *Pittsburgh Courier* from October 1935 to February 1936. This work features black detectives. The Black press provides sensational coverage of the murder and an arrest. The "screaming headlines" proclaim that "Harlem Society Woman, "Pretty Octoroon" has been charged with "African Prince's Murder":

> "Police Say Harlem Girl Killed African Prince."
> These and other screaming headlines blazoned from ten thousand newsstands. The news flashed across the continent and the oceans. Reporters besieged the Van Dyke residence [Schuyler, p. 69].

In African American newspapers, real-life crime coverage also could be sensational. Commenting on coverage of domestic violence during the Harlem Renaissance, Knadler (2004) finds:

> In the near weekly stories of domestic violence particularly those focusing on "women with knives," as opposed to those potboilers dealing with husbands who beat or murdered their wives, both the New York Age and the Amsterdam News disseminated that idea that emotional excesses and possessiveness were "natural" for black women ... [p. 101].

Knadler hypothesized that these stories were actually reassuring for male readers because they "reaffirmed a woman's dependence on her man" during a time when gender norms were in flux (p. 101). This sensational coverage of violence between men and women was not confined to African American newspapers. In the 1920s and 1930s, in the age of "jazz journalism," mainstream newspapers also covered male-female violence with blaring headlines (e.g., Bailey & Hale, 2004).

In Schuyler's novella, a reporter is the suitor of Crissina, the young woman who is suspected of the murder. He sets out to prove her innocence. Crissina's attorney, a former attorney general and the "highest-priced lawyer in Harlem" (p. 69), observes the first meeting of his client and the reporter after she is released on bail:

> ... They made a nice-looking couple, he thought, he quite black and she almost white, and both handsome. But what would old man Van Dyke say to such a

match? There had never been any black folks in his family as far back as could be remembered. But how circumstances change attitudes! (p. 71).

Here Schuyler, who achieved notoriety among his contemporaries with his satirical novel, *Black No More* (1931) is commenting on intra-racial color prejudice. In upper-class African American society and among the lower class, light-skin color was a visible marker of race-mixing. During slavery, slaves who were related to White slave owners were often house slaves and more likely than field hands to receive some education. They were also more likely to be freed. By the twentieth century, light-skin had become associated with higher social and economic standing. Assimilating White attitudes and beliefs about skin color, some light-skinned Blacks practiced (still practice) discrimination against those of darker skin color. This explains the lawyer's thoughts about how Crissina's father might react to a relationship between his "almost white" daughter and the "black" reporter.

The murder occurs in the famed Sugar Hill section of Harlem where the Ethiopian prince has an apartment. When the prince is found murdered, one of the other suspects is Mme. Helene Curtis, "a socially prominent Harlem matron and hairdresser" (Hill, 1994, p. 3).[52] Even though he is not the social equal of Crissina, who is the daughter of a wealthy Harlem undertaker, Rod, the reporter, is clever and determined. He is well-placed to aid Crissina because he has the casual, friendly relationship with the police common to reporters who cover crime beats. He discusses the case with Lieutenant Willston, one of the detectives, in witty exchanges reminiscent of Fisher's *The Conjure-Man Dies*.

Commenting on Schuyler's body of work, Putnam (2006) points out that Schuyler often makes uses of "a detective-like character as protagonist":

> The hero of his first novel, *Black No More*, was a man named Max Disher, who was likely patterned on Rudolph Fisher.... While not an actual detective, Disher exemplified the character type: he was resourceful and able to transverse multiple social spaces.... Moreover, he spoke the languages of multiple classes ... [p. 247].

Further Developments

With regard to genre detective fiction, it was Schuyler's contemporary, Rudolph Fisher, who laid the groundwork for future development by African American mystery writers (see Bailey, 1991; Soitos, 1996; McCluskey, 1987). Balshaw (2000) writes: "Comparison of Himes's detectives Gravedigger [sic] Jones and Coffin Ed with Fisher's Dart and Archer moves one from the gentleman sleuth to the hard-boiled 'tec, in African American terms, such is the difference between them" (p. 31). But Gosselin (1998) asserts that in *The Conjure-Man Dies*, Fisher's "narrative strategy of giving the last words to Bubber, the street-smart detective, sets the stage for Chester Himes and the hard-boiled detective tradition" (p. 617).

It would be more than three decades before the 1957 publication of Himes's first detective novel. Another writer, Hughes Allison, created a detective that can be viewed as an intermediary between Fisher's Dart and Archer and Himes's tough guy detectives. In July 1948, Allison became the first African American to have a short story published in *Ellery Queen Mystery Magazine* (*EQMM*). Titled "Corollary," the story features Joe Hill, the only Black detective in the Oldhaven Police Department. In a letter to the *EQMM* editors, Allison said that his detective differed from White detectives such as Sam Spade and Ellery Queen because Hill "is equipped to think with his skin" (Bailey, 1991, p. 70).

Hill's ear for details helps him to solve a case that is the "corollary" to a major bust of a gang of robberies who have committed several murders. Even though he and the other detectives work around the clock for two days to get statements about the twenty robberies from the suspects, Hill later recalls something he was told by the Black chauffeur, who was the get-away driver for the four White men. The chauffeur said that he had done a favor for a neighborhood psychic on the morning of the last hold-up. This turns out to be the key to solving another case when a little Black girl and her prim White teacher come to the police station with a finger in a box. The little girl refuses to talk to the White police detectives because she is afraid of them, a view that the teacher starts to explain is shared by others in the community. She is cut off by Hill's supervisor who has called him back to work to hear the girl's story. Hill's knowledge of con games in the Black community allows him to quickly connect what the chauffeur told him earlier to the finger in the box.

As do Fisher's Dart and Archer before and Himes's detectives after, Hill brings a perspective to his work that his White colleagues lack. As the only Black detective on the force, Hill has the added pressure of being there whenever a Black offender or victim needs a cop with whom he or she feels comfortable. But Hill himself brings passion to his work, displaying righteous anger when he realizes the psychic/cult leader has been preying on elderly Blacks in the community. Hill's supervisor, Inspector Duffy, does not reprimand Hill when he displays his disgust for the con man by punching him in the mouth.

The evolution of police procedural novels and other genre fiction occurred as African American writers of non-genre fiction were making significant contributions to the literary discourse about crime and punishment. To fully appreciate the context in which Chester Himes created the most famous of the pre–Civil Rights era African American detectives and the influences that continue to shape modern mystery writers, the works of these non-genre writers should be examined.

The Non-Genre Crime Writers

Rodgers (1997) comments on the "notably harsh views of migration" exhibited in George Washington Lee's *River George* (1937), Richard Wright's

Native Son (1940), William Attaway's *Blood on the Forge* (1941), Curtis Lucas's *The Flour is Dusty* (1943), and Carl Offord's *The White Face* (1943). Rodgers finds in these works a "'fugitive migrant' impulse" (p. 98). Arguably, the best known of these novels is Richard Wright's *Native Son*. Wright was born in 1908 in Natchez, Mississippi, the year before Chester Himes was born in Jefferson City, Missouri. As adults, the already successful Wright would praise and befriend Himes, the first-time novelist. Wright believed "that Himes was not just a new black talent but a new genre of writer" (Fabre, 1973, p. 290). As for Wright, himself, his recognition and fame as a writer came with the publication of *Native Son* (see Fabre, 1973, pp. 178–180 on critical response). Rodgers (1997) writes of the novel:

> From the moment in March 1940 when Wright jarred the American reading public awake with *Native Son*, his unapologetic portrait of Bigger Thomas, this angry, terrified and terrifying young man has come to represent the archetypal urban racial misfit [p. 100].

In *Native Son*, Wright drew on his own experience as a migrant. For a decade (1927–1937), Wright shared a "cramped and dirty" South Side of Chicago flat with his aunt, mother, and brother. Later, when he became an insurance agent, Wright "visited hundreds of similar dwellings" Kinnamon (1969, p. 67). In "How Bigger Was Born," the now-famous introduction to *Native Son* (first delivered as a speech at the Schomburg Library in Harlem), Wright mentioned the real-life models for his protagonists. In the "Black Belt" of the South, he had known defiant young men who were killed or confined in an asylum or prison.[53] In the North, such young men were physically contained by the boundaries of the ghetto and provided with distractions such as the programs at the South Side Boys' Club where Wright had worked (Wright, 1940, Introduction). In *Native Son*, Bigger becomes first a migrant to the outside world of the rich slumlord who employs him as a chauffeur and then a fugitive fleeing across the winter landscape of Chicago after he accidentally kills his employer's daughter, Mary, and then murders his own girlfriend, Bessie (Rodgers, 1997; see also Guttman, 2001, on violence against women in *Native Son*).

In one telling scene, Bigger, a young Black male who has already violated the most sacred of racial norms by killing a White woman, contemplates the sacredness of White space:

> He walked to Dalton's through the snow. His ring hand was in his coat pocket, his fingers about the kidnap note. When he reached the driveway, he looked about the street carefully.... He walked up the steps and stood in front of the door. He waited a moment to see what would happen. So deeply conscious was he of violating dangerous taboo, that he felt the very air or sky would suddenly speak, commanding him to stop [Wright, 173].

Walls (1985) comments on Richard Wright's early interest in mystery fiction. In *Black Boy*, Wright wrote that *Flynn's Detective* was among his youthful reading material. In a 1940 article in *Atlantic Monthly*, Wright observed ironically:

> If there had been one person in the Dalton household who viewed Bigger
> Thomas as a human being, the crime would have been solved in half an hour....
> The one piece of incriminating evidence which would have solved the "murder
> mystery" was Bigger's humanity ... [quoted in Walls, p. 126].

Rodgers (1997) writes, "*Native Son* is the most pronounced example of what one contemporary reviewer, summing up the Black novelists of the age, called the 'spirit of defeat' that permeated their fiction" (p. 99). Influenced by the Chicago School of urban sociology, Wright drew on this "sophisticated academic model" to explain "the disturbing psychological and social dislocations brought on by the exodus." In this respect, *Native Son* emerges as "Wright's case study of Chicago theories" (Rodgers, p. 104).[54]

Wright's knowledge of these theories came via his connections with the School's faculty. The caseworker for Wright's own family, Mary Wirth, was the wife of Louis Wirth, who was one of the principal investigators involved in a "massive urban study" of Chicago's South Side (Rodgers, 105). Wright also became friends with Horace Cayton, Wirth's research associate (Rodger, 105). When Cayton and anthropologist St. Clair Drake, both African Americans, co-authored *Black Metropolis* (1945), Wright wrote an introduction to the study.

Another important influence on Wright's work was his political affiliation with the Communist Party (see Reilly, 1972; Zirin, 2000; Fabre, 1973). As a correspondent for the Communist newspaper, the *Daily Worker*, Wright had covered the trials of the Scottsboro Boys (nine Black youths accused in 1931 of gang raping two young White women on a slow-moving Alabama train). International Labor Defense (ILD), the Communist Party's legal arm, had vied with the NAACP over who would provide defense for the Boys. When the ILD won the favor of the parents of several of the boys, it hired famed New York City attorney Samuel Liebowitz to lead the defense team. During the several trials that followed, through the series of appeals that went twice to the United States Supreme Court, the Communist Party propelled the case into an international *cause celebre*. When Ruby Bates, one of the alleged victims, recanted her testimony, the case became symbolic both of "racial hoax"[55] and recalcitrant Southern justice in the face of Northern criticism (see Acker, 2007). Wright himself was well aware of the dangers White women presented to Black men. This was a theme that recurred in his work, including short stories such as "The Man Who Killed a Shadow" (1946),[56] inspired by a true incident.[57]

As Wright was writing *Native Son* (1940), he asked his friend Margaret Walker, an African American poet, to collect and send him the newspaper articles about a real-life case going on in Chicago at the time. An eighteen year old Black man, Robert Nixon, was on trial, accusing of murdering a White mother of two with a brick when she surprised him as he was burglarizing her apartment (Fabre, 1973, p. 172). Nixon had been persuaded to give the Chicago police a confession to this crime and two other attacks on White women "as well as five attempted murders of which it was not at all certain he was guilty" (Fabre, p. 172). In its coverage of the case, the *Chicago Tribune*

> immediately transformed the murder into a sexual crime and made a great deal out of a charge of rape, although the prosecution never explicitly brought this charge against Nixon. If the article that Bigger read about himself in prison seems unduly exaggerated, it is well to remember that Wright was quoting word for word from the *Tribune* reports of the Nixon case ... [Fabre, p. 172].

Another Chicago case was perhaps even more important to Wright in understanding his protagonist's mental state. While he was writing *Native Son*, Wright did research on the Leopold and Loeb murder case. In one of the "crimes of the century," Nathan Leopold and Richard Loeb, two wealthy University of Chicago students stood trial in 1924 for the "thrill-killing" of 14-year-old Bobby Franks. Intellectually-gifted and inspired by the philosophy of Friedrich Nietzsche, Leopold and Loeb had conspired to commit the "perfect crime." Their attorney, Clarence Darrow, admitted the guilt of his clients but offered an eloquent challenge to the death penalty. Wright absorbed both the psychiatric explanations of Leopold and Loeb's mental state when they killed and the argument made by Darrow as he struggled to save their lives (Butler, 2005).

Wright's interest in psychiatry was reflected in his support of the efforts by Dr. Frederic Wertham to establish a psychiatric clinic in Harlem. Known today for both his research on juvenile delinquency and his controversial campaign against crime comic books, Wertham opened the Lafargue Psychiatric Clinic in Harlem in 1946. That year, Wright wrote an article titled "Psychiatry Comes to Harlem," supporting the clinic (Fabre, 1973, p. 293). Wright himself had been the subject of Wertham's experiments on the association of ideas and writing. Wertham based an article, "An Unconscious Determinant in Native Son" (1944) on Wright's description of his dreams and daydreams, Wertham offered "a sexual interpretation of the famous scene where Bigger burns Mary's body" (Fabre, p. 292).

For Wright himself, a more overt influence on his works was his admiration for H. L. Mencken, the American journalist, editor, and satirist. Wright read and re-read Mencken's books. Through H. L. Mencken, he discovered the works of the Russian novelist, Fyodor Dostoevsky, author of *Notes from the Underground* (1864) and *Crime and Punishment* (1866). Wright's interest in Dostoevsky was shared by his fellow authors Ralph Ellison and James Baldwin. Bloshteyn (2001) concludes that Wright "learned a great deal from reading Dostoevsky and he did manage to incorporate much of it into his novels."

At the same time, Wright's African American vernacular helped to shape the aesthetics of his works. Gussow (2003) notes the influence of blues music on Wright's writing. Novelist and critic, Ralph Ellison discusses this influence in a 1945 review essay titled "Richard Wright's Blues."[58] In an oft-quoted passage from the essay, later reprinted in *Shadow and Act* (1964), Ellison wrote:

The blues is an impulse to keep the painful details and episodes of a brutal experience alive in one's aching consciousness, to finger its jagged grain, and to tran-
scend it, not by the consolation of philosophy but by squeezing from it a
near-tragic, near-comic lyricism. As a form, the blues is an autobiographical
chronicle of personal catastrophe expressed lyrically [1964, p. 90].

This formulation of "The Blues School of Literature" was extended by Earl
Conrad, a writer for the *Chicago Defender* in an article in which he referred not
only to Wright, but to Ellison himself[59] and to Chester Himes. Conrad wrote
that Himes, "in his first novel, *If He Hollers Let Him Go*, also portrays one of
those frustrated characters, Robert Jones, a man who has been hard hit and is
pretty devoid of hope" (quoted in Gussow, 2003, p. 138).

Yarborough (1981) examines this novel by Himes, along with Ann Petry's
The Street (1946) and Ralph Ellison's *The Invisible Man* (1952) in an article
titled "The Quest for the American Dream in Three Afro-American Novels."
Yarborough's article was published at the beginning of a decade that would be
identified with Reaganomics and conspicuous consumption by the upwardly
mobile (the late 20th century version of the American dream). Coined by historian James Truslow Adams in his book, *The Epic of America* (1931), the phrase
"the American dream" gave a name to an ideal—a myth—shared by immigrants to America. African Americans, even though their ancestors had arrived
as slaves, shared this myth. As Yarborough (1981), observes, "Despite severe
disappointments, however, Afro-Americans have generally been among the
most fervent believers in the American Dream" (p. 33).

By the 1940s, the tension generated by a reality that fell so short of the
dream became intense. Among African American writers, the novels of Himes,
Petry, and Ellison — all influenced by Richard Wright — exemplified "this acute
sensitivity to the frustrations of the Black individual striving for the American
ideal of success" (Yarborough, p. 35). If the 19th century writers were attempt-
ing to write African Americans into humanity, Wright and those who followed
him were depicting the consequences of Black exclusion from the social and
economic mainstream.

In Petry's novel, *The Street*, Lutie Johnson, hardworking and ambitious,
suffers a series of setbacks in her attempt to achieve the American dream. Her
marriage ends, her attempt to launch a singing career fails, and her son is
arrested. Lutie's dream is finally shattered when she kills Boots Smith, the Black
bandleader who has been sexually harassing her and must flee from New York
to Chicago. As Davis (2005) observes:

There is little safety in *The Street*, as moments of potential freedom are quickly
interrupted by the social and political realities of the racial climate in the 1940s.
Readers are continually presented with images of violence that circumscribe not
only one's attempt to establish a home and vital homeplace, but one's physical
and emotional wholeness as well ... [p. 36].[60]

In a 1971 interview, Petry recalled that *The Street* was inspired by a newspaper article she read. Although the item had occupied "perhaps an inch of space," she had been struck by the story of an eight year old boy who had been taught to steal letters from mailboxes by the superintendent of an apartment building in Harlem (Morgan, 2004, p. 245). With this inspiration, she wrote the story of a mother whose child is lost to the social forces that she struggles against. After her son's arrest, Lutie goes to the Children's Shelter to see him. She is told that his case will come up on Friday, but she may see him for a few minutes if she cares to wait:

> Lutie sat down near the back of the room. It was filled with colored women, sitting in huddled over positions. They sat quietly, not moving. Their patient silence filled the room, made her uneasy. Why were all of them colored? Was it because the mothers of white children had safe places for them to play in, because the mothers of white children didn't have to work? [Petry, 1946, pp. 408–409].

When she sees three "foreign-looking" White women, Lutie thinks maybe it isn't race. She thinks that perhaps they are all there because they are poor (p. 409). Later, as she flees New York on a train, Lutie thinks that her son is expecting her to visit him tomorrow: "He would never know why she had deserted him and he would be bewildered and lost without her" (p. 435). She tells herself that he will be better off if he goes to reform school, better off without her because the "best [she] could give him wasn't good enough" (p. 435). As Lutie traces a design on the train window, she remembers a teacher from her childhood who wondered why "they have us bother to teach you people to write" (p. 435). Lutie has been defeated by the forces aligned against her. She tries to figure out how she ended up on the train, leaving her son: "Her mind balked at the task. All she could think was, it was that street. It was that god-damned street" (p. 436).

The American dream also tantalizes and eludes the protagonist of Ellison's and Himes's novels (Yarborough, 1981; see also Jackson, 1999). The narrator of Ellison's *Invisible Man* travels from a Tuskegee-like Black Southern college to New York City. A would-be "Horatio Alger," he is seeking success in the city.[61]Instead, the narrator finally retreats underground to a basement hideaway. In *If He Hollers Let Him Go*, Himes's protagonist, Bob Jones, a worker in the war industry in Los Angeles, finds that instead of achieving upward mobility, he is defined by White America "as incompetent, unworthy of associating with whites, and finally a rapist" (Yarborough, p. 54).

Yet these writers vary in their assessment of the meaning of the American dream for Africans Americans. Yarborough asserts that Himes and Petry "repudiate the relevance" of the concept in the face of overwhelming White racism "against which the individual's weapons of idealism, determination, diligence, and even violence are inevitably blunted." Ellison on the other hand, despite his protagonist's retreat from the world, finds some hope in Black self-determination (Yarborough, p. 57).

Conclusions

Looking backward, Joseph (2002) asserts, "taken as a body of work evolving over time ... [f]ew authors have pondered the theme of justice more explicitly and incessantly" than Zora Neale Hurston. Joseph points to Hurston's works, the short stories, "Spunk" (1926) and "The Bone of Contention" (unpublished) and her two novels, *Jonah's Gourdvine* (1934) and *Their Eyes Were Watching God* (1937). All of these works "hinge on court cases and they invite us to consider not merely a legal decision but the court's methods of deciding" (p. 457). Hurston is certainly not a genre crime fiction writer. However, she shared the awareness of the Harlem Renaissance writers that something was at stake.

Hurston became involved in a legendary war of words with Richard Wright after he asserted that her novel, *Their Eyes Are Watching God* (1937), "perpetuated the 'minstrel show tradition and the clichés about black life so dear to the white reading public'" (Fabre, 1973, p. 143). A few years later, in the *Saturday Review of Literature*, Hurston took Wright to task for the violence in *Native Son* (1940) that he "attributed to interracial relations in the South," for "his Communist message," and his use of violence, particularly violence toward women (Fabre, pp. 161–162). Whatever their positions on how African Americans and their lives should be depicted, African American writers from Hopkins and Bruce to Hurston and Wright shared the perception that their audience included both Blacks and Whites, and that words could be important in shaping the relationship between the races and changing American culture.

In the last days of the Great Depression, Wright, the literary father of the modern protest writers, was more cynical then his turn of the century and Harlem Renaissance era predecessors about social justice in America. However, even he believed art might offer the possibility for redemption. After *Native Son* was published, Wright received numerous letters from Black prisoners asking Wright for help. In 1940, a letter from an elderly woman led Wright to spearhead a campaign to gain the release of Clinton Brewer. Eighteen years old when he was convicted in 1923, Brewer was serving a life sentence for the murder of a mother of two who had refused to marry him. Brewer had been studying musical composition in prison, and Wright was successful in getting one of his pieces recorded by Count Basie. The possibility that Brewer could successfully re-enter society seen high. Three months after he was released, Brewer killed another woman who refused his proposal.[62]

Wright had read Frederic Wertham's book *Dark Legend* (1941), and turned to him for understand what "motives or psychological abnormality had made this second murder possible" (Fabre, 1973, p. 237). Wertham found a lawyer for Brewer and helped to save him from execution. This was the beginning of the friendship between Wright and Wertham. Later Wright would turn to Brewer's story as inspiration for his novel, *Savage Holiday* (1954). As Fabre (1973) states after the Brewer case, Wright continued to explore "the areas of conflict between society and the inner world of the individual" (p. 237). The question of how African Americans coped with oppression was as relevant in the 1940s as it had been at the turn of the century.

During the first half of the twentieth century, both genre and non-genre fiction laid the groundwork for the emergence of post–World War II African American mystery writers. In the final chapter in this section, we focus on mystery writer Chester Himes and the Civil Rights era preceding the modern "renaissance" of Black writers.

3

From Himes to Hip Hop

In 1968, James A. Emanuel and Theodore L. Gross, editors of *Dark Symphony, Negro Literature in America*, observed:

> The diversity in recent novels by Negroes—even in novels by a single author—is evidenced by Negro participation in an internationally popular genre: the detective novel. First tried by Rudolph Fisher in *The Conjure Man Dies* (1932) the genre has been congenial to the talents of Chester Himes ... [p. 360].

During World War II, Himes was "the most popular and frequent contributor" to *Negro Story* magazine. Over the two years of the magazine's existence, Himes contributed stories with soldier and civilian protagonists who were engaged in simultaneously combating "racism and class oppression on a day-to-day basis in wartime America" (Mullen, 1996, p. 9).[63] When the "Zoot Suit riots" occurred in Los Angeles in 1943 (between off-duty military servicemen and young Mexican American males), Himes wrote an essay for *The Crisis* titled "Zoot Riots are Race Riots." Written that same year of 1943, his novel, *If He Hollers Let Him Go*, features a protagonist, Bob Jones, who recognizes his own jeopardy as a man of color while reflecting on the forced removal of Japanese Americans from the West Coast (Itagaki, 2003). By the 1940s, Himes himself had a life-time of experience with racism in America. Chester Himes became a European expatriate.

It was at the request of his French editor, Marcel Duhamel, then director of Gallimard's detective story series, La Serié Noire that Himes created a detective series (Reed, 1988, p. 124). Although the novels between *If He Hollers Let Him Go* (1945) and *For Love of Imabelle* (1957, republished in U.S. as *A Rage in Harlem*) were not genre crime fiction, arguably Himes always had been concerned with issues of crime and justice in both his fiction and his life. Himes's first encounter with the criminal justice system came after a series of personal setbacks that took him from college student to prison inmate (1929–1936). In his 1971 autobiography, *The Quality of Hurt*, Himes wrote, "I grew to manhood in the Ohio State Penitentiary. I was nineteen years old when I went in and twenty-six years old when I came out..." (p. 60). Himes recalled that he was safe from assault in prison because "I had such violent seizures of rage that I made men twice my size quake with fright" (p. 62). His prison experiences served as a crucible for Himes's evolution as a writer of crime fiction.

During his seven years in prison for armed robbery, Himes contributed short stories to African American periodicals and to *Esquire* magazine (Breen, 2001; see also Skinner, 1989). Himes (1971) observed that writing:

> protected me, against both the convicts and the screws. The black convicts had both an instinctive respect for and fear of a person who could sit down at a typewriter and write, and whose name appeared in newspapers and magazines outside...
>
> My first short stories were published in weekly newspapers and in magazines published by blacks ... [p. 64].

These early short stories "were not racially oriented." During his incarceration, Himes "wrote about crimes and criminals, mostly about the life in prison" (Himes, 1971, p. 65). Breen (2001) notes that the two police detective protagonists that would eventually appear in Himes's series "had precursors in the early story 'He Knew,' which Himes published in *Abbott's Weekly* and *Illustrated News* in 1933" (p. 35). With his early short stories and the later novels, Himes established himself as a writer of hard-boiled fiction. In *Hard-Boiled Masculinities*, Breu (2005) describes Himes's novels as occupying

> a contradictory yet overlapping series of border zones between high and popular culture, noir and hard-boiled fiction, the political and the psychological, modernism and post modernism, social protest literature and expatriate modernism, African-American and Anglo-American literary traditions ... [Breu, p. 143].

In his detective fiction, Himes's Harlem, the setting of his police procedural novels,[64] is as much psychological and metaphorical space as physical setting. In the eight novels published between 1957 and 1969, Himes offers an increasingly despairing view of race relations in America. In his ninth and final novel, *Plan B*, an unfinished work published in 1993 (nine years after Himes's death), the threatened racial war finally erupts. From first book to last, Himes created a fictional Harlem that served as a commentary on life in a Black ghetto and on the value of Black life in America. Skinner (1998) writes:

> Himes doesn't act as an apologist for his race in these novels, but he does show a cause-and-effect relationship between racial oppression outside the ghetto and prostitution, armed robbery, and murder inside Harlem [p. 3].

Skinner asserts that Himes depicts two kinds of victims: one, scraping by "in his ghetto prison"; the other "turned bestial by white oppression" (p. 3). In such a world being too innocent or too trusting (i.e., "a square") makes one vulnerable. In *A Rage in Harlem* ([*For Love of Imabelle*,1957]), Jackson, an undertaker's assistant, falls for Imabelle, a femme fatale (but see below). He is set up as the fall guy in a con game. Imabelle introduces him to some men, one of whom is supposed to be able to raise the denomination of currency. When all of Jackson's hard-earned cash is apparently destroyed in an exploding stove and Imabelle and the men disappear, Jackson, a good Christian, turns to theft from his employer. He steals $500 to pay off a fake U.S. marshal and to get more money converted. On the lam, he seeks the help of his twin brother, Goldy, who has his own con game going as a female "Sister of Mercy" who sells tickets to heaven.

By the time the police detectives, Grave Digger Jones and Coffin Ed Johnson, enter the novel in Chapter 8, the game is already afoot. Goldy has already taken on the task of finding the missing Imabelle. Like Bubber Brown in Rudolph Fisher's *The Conjure-Man Dies* (1932), Goldy functions as a third sleuth. It is he who finds an early lead by calling everyone from Jackson's irate landlady to Imabelle's prim and proper sister, pretending that he is a "U.S. Federal Attorney." In his guise as Sister of Mercy, Goldy goes down to the post office to have a look at the wanted posters of the three men who are wanted for robbery and murder down South. It is Goldy who briefs the two police detectives on the con and the wanted men, and on Imabelle, who after the robbery down South fled North leaving behind a husband and bringing along a trunk that Jackson claims contains gold ore. Goldy becomes one of those victims that Skinner describes, with his throat slit by a more dangerous predator.

In this first book in the series, the two police detectives experience an episode of personal victimization that will haunt them throughout the rest of the series. Coffin Ed has acid thrown in his face by one of the men they are pursuing. Gun in hand, "a blind man with a pistol" (a recurring image in the series), he staggers about calling for his injured partner. Thereafter, Coffin Ed, his face scarred by the acid, has little control over his surges of rage. Post-traumatic stress disorder (PTSD) is not uncommon among police officers who are wounded on the job or who are themselves forced to kill. Symptoms of this disorder include flashbacks, nightmares, and panic attacks (see e.g., Sheehan & Van Hasselt, 2003). In the case of his traumatized partner, Grave Digger tries to keep Coffin Ed from killing someone during one of his blind rages.

But Grave Digger himself is also physically battered on (and by) the job. In *Cotton Comes to Harlem* (1965), he returns from sick leave:

> It was Grave Digger's first night back on duty since he had been shot up by one of Benny Mason's hired guns in the caper resulting from the loss of a shipment of heroin. He had been in the hospital for three months fighting a running battle with death and he had spent three months at home convalescing ... [Himes, p. 16].

Other than the "finger-size scar obliterating the hairline at the base of his skull," (p. 16) Grave Digger's scars are concealed by his clothing. He will be injured and hospitalized again by the end of *The Heat's On* (1966).

In spite of their battle scars earned in urban crime fighting, when their supervisor, Lieutenant Anderson, looks at his two "ace detectives" he has a recurring impression. To him, "with their identical big hard-shooting, head-whipping pistols, [they] had always looked like two hog farmers on a weekend in the Big Town" (Himes, *Cotton Comes to Harlem*, p. 17). In fact, the two detectives go home each night to family life with their supportive spouses in Astoria, Long Island. As do many real life police officers, Grave Digger and Coffin Ed live outside the community they police. They straddle two worlds.

In policing Harlem, a violent ghetto, their attitudes lean more toward "crime control" than "due process."[65] The two detectives believe that in order to do their job they must be tough enough to merit the respect of the "hoodlums" they police. Watters (1994) observes:

> As cops, Coffin Ed and Grave Digger have official sanction from the white police department to be excessively brutal ... their license for brutality is based on the police department's utter reliance on them as skilled readers of Harlem's behavioral and linguistic codes [p. 618].

Yet in *Cotton Comes To Harlem* (1965), Lieutenant Anderson warns them that the commissioner feels that they have "killed too many people in this area" and that the newspapers "have been yapping about brutality in Harlem" (Himes, p. 18). To this Coffin Ed responds that it is the White cops "who commit the pointless brutality" (p. 18). As for himself and his partner:

> "Digger and me ain't trying to play tough."
> "We are tough," Grave Digger said [p. 18].

Their toughness is directed not at petty criminals but at those predators whose crimes have the greatest impact on the community. Such big-time criminals include the fake minister, Deke O'Malley, who in *Cotton Comes to Harlem* (1965) swindles hard-working Black people out of $87,000 with his Back-to-Africa scheme. But the deepest hostility on the part of the two cops is reserved for drug dealers. In *The Heat's On* (1966), Grave Digger responses with rage to the suggestion from an assistant district attorney that the suspect who was killed while peddling dope was committing "a minor crime":

> "All the crimes committed by addicts—robberies, murders, rape.... All the fucked-up lives.... All the nice kids sent down the drain on a habit.... Twenty-one days on heroin and you're hooked for life.... Jesus Christ, mister, that one lousy drug has murdered more people than Hitler. And you call it *minor!*" His voice sounded like it was filtered through absorbent cotton [Himes, p. 55, ellipses in the original].

In this case, Grave Digger and Coffin Ed have used excessive force. Applying their own methods, they punched the suspect in the stomach to make him vomit up the evidence he had swallowed. Their actions were witnessed by three firemen and two patrol officers. The suspect was a White man, and although the commissioner asks for more time to investigate, he suspends the two detectives. Anderson assures them that, "It's just the newspaper pressure," that will "blow over" (Himes, p. 57). But Grave Digger responds, "It's all right to kill a few colored people for trying to get their children an education, but don't hurt a mother raping white punk for selling dope" (Himes, p. 57).

Van Deburg (1997) comments on the interrogation methods used by Grave Digger and Coffin Ed: "To encourage compliance with the law, the black detectives [make] extensive use of "pigeon's nest"—a windowless, soundproof basement interrogation room reputed to have hatched more than all the rooftop rookeries in Harlem (p. 177). Yet, the two detectives operate by their own ethical code. They strive to retain their own "personal integrity amid corruption" by refusing to take bribes "sexual, monetary, or culinary" and it is painful to them that the people they police believe "that every cop [has] a price" (Van Deburg, p. 177).

Himes wrote that he himself rejected the idea that one should make excuses for Black men who committed crimes by considering them "victims of racism":

> Black victims of crime and criminals might be foolish and hare-brained, but the soul brother criminals were as vicious, cruel, and dangerous as any other criminals—I knew because I'd been one—the only difference being they were absurd [quoted in Reed, 1988, pp. 126–127].

The viciousness that Himes attributed to criminals is portrayed in the pages of the books in the series. French intellectuals such as Jean-Paul Sartre and Boris Vian classified Himes's novels with those of Dashiell Hammett and James M. Cain and "relatively continuous with social realist novels of black protest and black criminality such as *Native Son*...." (Breu, 2005, p. 35)

The significance of race is the thread that runs through the series. When Jackson, the undertaker's assistant in *A Rage in Harlem* (1957), is fleeing after the shootout in which Coffin Ed has acid flung in his face, he recalls "an old folk song that he'd learned in his youth." The words of the song are "Run, nigger, run; De patter-rollers catch you" (p. 73). The patter-rollers (or paddy rollers) were the able-bodied White males who patrolled the countryside monitoring the movement of slaves. Echoing this theme, a non-series crime novel that Himes published two years later has the title *Run Man Run* (1959). In a Hitchcockian game of cat and mouse, a young Black law school student is pursued by a homicidal White detective. The student, Jimmy Johnson (no relation to Coffin Ed), has a job as a night porter. He is there when Matt Walker, the White detective, walks into the luncheonette and kills two of his co-workers. But Jimmy has difficulty convincing even his blue-singer girl friend, Linda, that the cop is a killer. Walker is a psychopath, subject to alcoholic blackouts, who has beaten a prostitute badly enough to put her into the hospital. Bailey (1991) observes that in the novel, Himes examines "police corruption and race hatred" and the moral choices made by the characters:

> As violent as the Grave Digger and Coffin Ed novels, it is Himes's attempt to point out that it is not only the Blacks in Harlem who are crazy, blind, and full of rage. Matt Walker, white Anglo-Saxon, all American boy with a college education and a nice sister also makes his contribution to this madness [p. 58].

In his first autobiography, *The Quality of Hurt* (1971), Himes recalls a time when he himself should have run. Thirty-two years earlier when he was confronted by a clerk while cashing bogus checks: "I could have run. I should have run. But, unfortunately, I never did run" (p. 46).[66] In his second autobiography, *My Life of Absurdity* (1976), Himes relates that he got the "experience and the background" for his novel *Run Man Run* while working as a porter at a luncheonette (p. 28).

For Jimmy Johnson, Harlem offers only an illusion of safety as he is pursued by the White cop. But Himes's Harlem is not without places of comfort and respite. Coffin Ed and Grave Digger hang out in Mammy Louise's restaurant. While eating barbecued ribs, black-eyed peas, rice, okra, collard greens, and apple pie, they observe with humor the "slick young black man" (Himes, *Cotton Comes to Harlem*, p. 140) with whom the widow has replaced her "short fat" husband (pp. 140–141). They listen to the music the young people are playing on the junk box (pp. 141–142). When they are introduced in *A Rage in Harlem* (1957), the two detectives are providing security at the Savoy where a ball is taking place. Such social events symbolize the more respectable aspects of Harlem life.

As in other communities, respectability in Harlem can be a façade. Braham (1997) notes the interweaving of the problems of race and gender in the novels. Himes's books are "unusually dense with sexually indeterminate characters" (p. 3). Goldy, Jackson's cross-dressing brother in *A Rage in Harlem*, lives with two other men who are involved in questionable business enterprises, Big Kathy, the "madame" of a whorehouse, and Lady Gypsy, a fortuneteller. On the quiet street where they reside, their neighbors are unaware of how they earn their livelihoods. Known as "the Three Black Widows," they have a reputation for unblemished respectability (Himes, p. 34). Goldy spends Thursdays and every other Sunday afternoon at the flat his wife, a domestic servant, maintains for use on her days off (Himes, pp. 34–35).

This relationship between Goldy and his wife reflects the complexity of gender (as a construct) and sexual relationships in Himes's Harlem. Bailey (1991) notes the graphic language of Himes's men and women, whose favorite epithet is "Mother-raper":

> Sex is in the air — often crude and lustful, sometimes preceded by violence. High yellow temptresses with swaying hips seduce and betray squares. Young black girls become the prey of the perverts who come up to Harlem seeking sex. Madames run whorehouses; prostitutes in dime-store perfume sit on barstools ... [Bailey, p. 65].

In *Cotton Comes to Harlem* (1965), a cheerful young assistant medical examiner at a homicide scene sings, "I'll be glad when you're dead, you rascal you" (p. 148). The medical examiner is White, but perhaps not coincidentally this song that was popular when Rudolph Fisher wrote *The Conjure-Man Dies* (1932) still captures the conjunction of sex and violence in Himes's Harlem. In a recent article, Crawford (2006a) asserts the complexity of Himes's female characters who are "raucous, outspoken and often violent ... yet, Himes portrays these Harlem female characters as physically beautiful and, on many levels, as the most respected members of their fictional community group" (pp. 193–194). Crawford goes on to assert that Himes's *femmes* are not in the tradition of hard-boiled detective fiction. They "go against the grain" not only of these images but also "the long and enduring history of literary and popular culture images of black female characters as emasculating, bestial, unnaturally masculinized, and consequently, ugly women" (p. 194). As Crawford argues, the characters in Himes's Harlem both reference and challenge the genre archetypes.

Commenting on his detective fiction, Himes is said to have told an interviewer, "I just made the faces black" (quoted in Kelly, 2000). Although his work has been described as "absurdist literature" (McCann, 2002), Himes claimed, "I thought I was writing realism.... Realism and absurdity are so similar in the lives of American blacks one cannot tell the difference" (quoted in Kelly, 2000). One of the absurdities of Himes's Harlem is that his two African American detectives are violent to protect the residents from the greater violence that might be employed by White law enforcement. The detectives employ street justice at their own risk, suffering reprimands, suspension, and negative media coverage.

Within what Walters (1994) describes as Himes's "discourse of *protection* articulated in the detective novels" (p. 628), there is the evolving sense that safety will only be obtainable through Black revolution. This is the premise of *Plan B* (1993). Walters (1994) compares Himes's final work to the Black nationalism fiction of the late 1960s, such as Sam Greenlee's *The Spook Who Sat By the Door* (1969). She also notes antecedents in Sutton Griggs's 19th century novel *Imperium in Imperio* (1899) (Walters, p. 629).

Another important book in this context is John A. Williams's 1967 novel, *The Man Who Cried I Am*. Williams's work is about a Black writer, dying of cancer, who is in Amsterdam because of the mysterious death of a colleague. The book has been praised for its literary merit as an autobiographical examination of Black history and culture, However, Gilyard (2001) and Boyd (2002) note that although fictional, Williams's description of "an international conspiracy to exterminate all people of African descent" that he calls "the King Alfred Plan" (Boyd, 2002) became one of the conspiracy theories abroad in the Black community. According to Boyd (2002), in a brilliant marketing ploy, Williams Xeroxed excerpts from the novel and left them on subway seats to create a buzz about the forthcoming book.

These works by Greenlee and Williams came at a time when the hopeful era of the early Civil Rights movement had given way to pessimism. Media images of the urban inner city increasingly portrayed a dangerous place inhabited by violent Black men. Stabile (2006) observes:

> By the end of the 1960s, the historical threat that black men were said to pose to white womanhood had been mostly subsumed beneath narratives featuring vio-

lent, angry, and armed black men. Nevertheless, the link between black men and crime had expanded from an openly racist one based on fears of miscegenation (and a specific threat to white women) to a now generalized threat to society as a whole [p. 154].[67]

In the mid–1960s, rioting occurred in inner cities across the country. Police officers and National Guardsmen crashed with Black citizens in the streets. As the Kerner Commission reported in 1968, until the riots began the mainstream media (and much of dominant society) ignored what was going on in urban ghettos (see e.g., Jacobs, 2000, p. 50). In *The Quality of Hurt* (1971), Himes wrote, "The only thing that surprised me about the race riots in Watts in 1965 was that they waited so long to happen. We are a patient people" (p. 74). In Himes's final novel, *Plan B*, Grave Digger and Coffin Ed have not been able to quell the violence. Their investigation exposes a conspiracy that puts the two partners on opposite sides. Grave Digger shoots Coffin Ed. In turn, he is shot by Tomsson Black, the most respected African American man in the country, who is financing the purchase and distribution of guns to Black citizens. As Bunyan (2003) observes:

> In *Plan B*, Digger and Ed will be denied even the option to stand aside. In this, the final work in the series, the forces that drive the action are untouchable historical forces, under which racial tensions have been building for four hundred years ... [p. 12].

The racial politics of the 1960s were being played out not only in the streets and the courtrooms but in popular culture. A more liberal Supreme Court recognized the rights not only of racial minorities and women, but of suspects and defendants in the criminal justice system. In the mystery genre, changing attitudes about race provided an opportunity for White writers such as John Ball and Ernest Tidyman to create Black sleuths (Virgil Tibbs and John Shaft, respectively) with cross-over appeal for White readers. These sleuths reached an even wider audience in the films, *In the Heat of the Night* (1967) featuring Detective Virgil Tibbs and *Shaft* (1971), featuring Harlem PI John Shaft. Both sleuths later made the transition to television.

The success of these films and the discovery by Hollywood of a Black audience hungry for African American protagonists led to the era of so-called "black exploitation" (or "blaxploitation") films. These controversial, action films featured strong Black heroes (some of them female) who took on corrupt cops, organized crime, and homicidal racists. To the dismay of critics, some of the more popular films in this genre featured protagonists who were criminals. "Priest," the drug dealer in *Super Fly* (1977), who wanted to make one more big score before getting out of the business, was an often cited example of why these films provided negative role models for Black youth.

However, a criminal protagonist as hero was not unusual in American popular films. Americans of all racial/ethnic groups have historically enjoyed stories about "good bad men" who challenge and defeat "bad bad men," the true villains. The arrival of good bad *Black* men in films coincided with the increased focus on the urban inner city — particularly poor Black neighbor-hoods — as the social location of violent crime. Critics of the blaxploitation films initiated a discourse about crime, popular culture, and role models for Black youth that would continue through the 1970s and into the 1980s with "urban hood" or "new jack" films inspired by hip hop culture (see e.g., Smith-Shomade, 2003; Henry, 2004).

The urban environment changed as "White flight" to the suburbs esca-lated. This flight had begun in the aftermath of World War II as affordable housing in the cities became more difficult to find and family cars and trains made commuting more practical. As the G.I. Bill subsidized the purchase of homes by White families in suburban subdivisions, Black families succeeded White in the neighborhoods that they were deserting. With the deindustrial-ization of the cities, as industries in the Northern and Midwest "rustbelts" moved to the "sunbelts" of the South and Southwest, those who remained in the urban inner cities were increasingly the poor who sociologist William Julius Wilson (1993) describes as "the truly disadvantaged." In the post–Vietnam era as the focus turned from the war abroad to the "war on crime," an increasingly punitive criminal justice system focused on crime in the inner city.

As Barlow (1998) concludes in her analysis of newsmagazine coverage of crime before, during, and after the riots of the 1960s, the face of the criminal identified in the media and by law enforcement, and finally by social scientists, was increasingly young, poor, and black or brown. The "war" being waged against crime was accompanied by expanded popular discourse about "Cadil-lac welfare moms," "crack babies," and "young Black super-predators" that joined traditional descriptions of "violent Black males" and "street criminals" (see e.g., Goetz, 1996) The "underclass," a concept that had been originally employed by social scientists to describe a minority of citizens that were out-side the economic mainstream, became to be a code word for the Black inner city poor (see e.g., Jargowsky & Yang, 2006). These residents were said to live in "killing fields"[68] in which drive-by shootings by gang members were fre-quent occurrences. Increasingly, in states such as New York and California, progression from juvenile facility to adult prison became a rite of passage for young African American and Hispanic males.

The changes occurring in the inner city were depicted in the hard-hitting street fiction popularized by Donald Goines and Robert "Iceberg Slim" Beck. Goines and Beck appealed to readers because they wrote with the credibility of men who had been "in the life." Goines, who wrote about drug dealers, pimps, and prostitutes, and survival in the streets, had served time in prison. Goines published sixteen books, including the Kenyatta series, written under the pseu-donym, Al C. Clark (Osborne, 2001). His titles included *Dopefiend: The Story of a Black Junkie* (1971), *Whoreson: The Story of a Ghetto Pimp* (1972), *White Man's Justice, Black Man's Grief* (1973), and books featuring Jomo Kenyatta, the leader of a Black revolutionary organization. As Phillips (1998) observes, the books were "published by the white owned, but black audience directed (included the 'girlie' magazine *Players*) Holloway House, located in Los Angeles" (Phillips, p.30). Home of much of the street lit of the era, Holloway House also published Robert Beck, author of the autobiographical *Pimp: The Story of My Life* (1967), and titles including *Trick Baby* (1967), *Mama Black Widow* (1969), and *Death Wish* (1976). Other Black crime writers of this era included Roosevelt Mallory, who wrote about "Radcliff," a hit man.

Stirred by the fervor of the Civil Rights movement, "literary writers" such as Leroi Jones ventured into new territory. Jones became "Amiri Baraka," one of the leading spokespersons for the use of art as political propaganda. Davis (2005) observes:

> For African American writers in the 1960s and 1970s, interpreting black experience largely meant doing so in the context of the black nationalist movement ... black nationalism was proposed as the route to liberation — liberation that was to garner support in the works of black artists and the development of a black aesthetic that stressed racial stability and solidarity ... [p. 24].

The Black Arts Movement rejected Eurocentric standards of literature and criticism. Two writers, Ishmael Reed and Clarence Major brought Afrocentric perspectives to genre detective fiction. In *Mumbo Jumbo* (1972) and *The Last Days of Louisiana Red* (1974), Reed featured the Hoodoo Detective, Papa LaBas. In *Mumbo Jumbo*, LaBas is in search of 'Jes Grew, the embodiment of African American culture. In this book and in *Louisiana Red*, Reed challenges the traditional mystery novel formula. Clarence Major goes even further in *Reflex & Bone Structure* (1975), an anti-detective novel that recounts the murder of Cora, who was involved in a romantic triangle with the narrator and another man. The solution to the crime is complicated by the fact that the victim dies repeatedly in different ways, characters are manipulated at the whim of the narrator (who is in the process of creating the story), and the narrator himself proves unreliable. *Reflex and Bone Structure* emerges a "parody" that "undermines the conventions of the detective story" (Hogue, 2002, p. 172). There are "a series of continuous disruptions" that complicate the narration, and the mystery of the double murder of Cora and her lover, Dale, is never solved (Hogue, p. 172)

In their books, Major and Reed subvert the expectations of Eurocentric genre fiction that the mystery can be solved and that once the solution has been reached, order will be restored in the fictional world. In *The Signifying Monkey* (1988), his book about Black literature, Henry Louis Gates describes Reed's *Mumbo Jumbo* "as a textbook complete with illustrations, footnotes, and a bibliography" (quoted in McCoy, 2005, pp. 612–613). Soitos (1996) agrees that Reed is not confined by genre (p. 182), but instead draws on the improvisational techniques of jazz and the blues, performing "a riff on the detective story" (p. 184). Weixlmann (1991–1992) described PaPa LaBas as "above all else intuitive" (p.61), rejecting the rational approach of the Holmesian detective and dramatizing "the direct confrontation between Euro- and Afro-centric thought and culture (p. 61). In this respect, Balshaw (2000) notes that both Ishmael Reed and Rudolph Fisher have "a shared interest ... in the multiplicity of voices that make up an alternative Africanist tradition of vernacular history, what Reed calls 'Jes Grew'" (p. 32).

In Major's *Reflex and Bone Structure* (1975), the narrator tells the reader: "I want this book to be anything it wants to be. A penal camp. A bad check. A criminal organization. A swindle. A prison. Devil's Island. I want the mystery of this book to be an absolute mystery ... (p. 59). Yet, Major incorporates references to the realities of Black oppression in his narrative. One flashback deals with Cora's mythic encounter with police violence in small Georgia town. She is being gang-raped by "fifty white cop" in the backseat of a police car, when she miraculously gives birth:

> While the last cop is opening his pants, a boy child slides out of Cora's vagina, grows up instantly. A big, strong, young man. Suddenly he starts beating the shit out of the fifty cops. With his bare fists he beats them into a pile of pulp. He releases his mother than vanishes [p. 118].

Later in the book, Cora as a child witnesses her father's humiliation by a White man. Her mother denies the event could have happened, forcing Cora to repeat, "My father is a brave and strong man and nobody pushes him around" (p. 125). Still later, Cora is married to a policeman and living in Queens. Her husband "wears his gun all the time" and one night comes home and "shoots up the joint" (p. 133). In *Reflex and Bone Structure*, time is elastic. Both Reed and Clarence Major incorporate elements of what Lock (1994) describes as the Afrocentric tradition in mystery writing, linked to the Osiris myth of destruction and rebirth rather than to the Oedipus myth of discovery and punishment found in the Eurocentric tradition.

Lock applies her theory of the Afrocentric tradition to works that are not considered genre fiction. In her book, *A Case of Mis-taken Identity: Detective Undercurrents in Recent African American Fiction* (1994), in addition to discussing Fisher's *The Conjure-Man Dies*, Lock examines several other works including Toni Morrison's *Beloved*. *Beloved* (1987) tells the story of a slave mother who kills her own child. She is haunted by that child in the form of a strange young woman who arrives at her door years later (see Bryant, 2005, on the role of the Gothic in this novel).

In *Beloved*, which has parallels to the real-life case of slave mother Margaret Garner,[69] Morrison explores the concept of remembering the slave past as a necessity for racial wholeness. In her book of literary theory, *Playing in the Dark* (1992), Morrison examines the role of blackness in works by four White authors, i.e., the Black presence in White American literature. In her own works, Morrison argues that the violence and brutality of that past must be remembered and understood. In *Beloved*, after Sethe, the slave mother kills her child, she is approaches by her mother-in-law, Baby Suggs:

"It's time to nurse your youngest," she said.
  Sethe reached up for the baby without letting the dead one go.
  Baby Suggs shook her head, "One at a time," she said and traded the living
one for the dead, which she carried into the keeping room. When she came back,
Sethe was aiming a bloody nipple into the baby's mouth. Baby Suggs slammed
her fist on the table and shouted, "Clean up! Clean yourself up!" [Morrison, p.
152].

The two struggle, and Baby Suggs slips in the dead child's blood. Sethe goes on
nursing her baby, Denver. "So Denver took her mother's milk right along with
the blood of her sister." Sethe is still nursing her living child when the sheriff
returns with a neighbor's cart to take her away (Morrison, p. 152).

This scene imagines the complexity of the emotions of the slave mother
who kills her child rather than see the child returned to bondage. The mother,
in shock at her own act, feeds the blood of one child to the other with her breast
milk — the nurturing mother and the murdering mother are embodied in one
woman. The literary exploration of violence in the context of race, class, and
gender oppression emerged in its modern form with Morrison and other women
writers in the 1970s. However, as Spilka (1997) observes, one of Ann Petry's
early stories, "Like a Winding Sheet" (1945), "deals with the unexpected impetus toward domestic violence in a Black working class household, and so anticipates recent treatments of that theme by Black women writers" (Spilka, p. 262).
Even earlier, during the years of the Harlem Renaissance, and through the Great
Depression, other female writers such as Marita Bonner, offered disturbing
narratives of women's lives. In Bonner's stories, Balshaw (2000) finds

repeated again and again across stories whereby women and children find themselves victim of the racialized socio-economic structures they are mired within.
Children, die, or kill themselves, get put in reform school or prison, aspire to
become numbers runners as their mothers turn to drugs, or find themselves
unable to find a way out of the ghetto except through violence [p. 94].

In the modern era, Black women writers moved to the literary forefront,
sometimes offering feminist and womanist critiques of the male-dominated
ideology of Black nationalism. Michelle Wallace in *Black Macho and the Myth
of the Superwoman* (1979) and the autobiographies of activists such as Angela
Davis and Elaine Brown described "sexism and the restricted roles for women
in the movement" (Davis, 2005, p. 25). Davis (2005) asserts that in the midst
of the Black nationalist movement, women writers such as

Alice Walker, Gayl Jones, Toni Cade Bambara, Toni Morrison, Ntozake Shange,
and Louise Meriwether complicated notions of black unity and revolution by
collectively showing that nation-building could not occur without discussing the
relationship between black men and women and addressing the specific realities
of black women's lives ... [p. 24–25].

Yet even though African American female authors made contributions to
American literature that helped to open doors for other writers, they stirred

controversy. More controversial than Morrison, Alice Walker (*The Color Purple*, 1992) and Gayl Jones (*Eva's Man*, 1976) were accused of bashing Black males with their depictions of Black men. Walker in *The Color Purple* (and in the Steven Spielberg film adaptation) tells the first-person story of a woman who is sexually and physically abused and psychologically oppressed by the men in her life. Jones's *Eva's Men* includes a scene of male castration by her protagonist.

Commenting on her own book, Jones observed, "In many ways, *Eva's Man* is a horror story" (quoted in Clabaugh, 2006, p. 651). *Eva's Man* is about an abusive relationship that ends in murder as told by the incarcerated female protagonist. Young (2005) describes the book as a "prison narrative" (p. 377) in which the police enact "a disciplinary gaze" suggesting "Jeremy Bentham's Panopticon, a highly centralized system of observation and surveillance" (p. 386). Young argues that in Jones's novel, there are no safe or "free" spaces for women in prison or outside. Even as a child, Eva has witnessed "punitive" violence in her parent's marriage as her father raped and abused her mother (p. 390).

Neither Jones's novel nor the works by Morrison or Walker are genre detective fiction. But these works are significant in that they focus on images of crime and examine the nature of oppression and injustice in women's lives. Sharpe et al. (1990) assert that Harlem Renaissance era–writer Zora Neale Hurston and contemporary writers Morrison and Walker "subtly show how rape, molestation, incest, and murder of black women by Black men may be exaggerated responses to Black men's own treatment at the hands of white male society..." (p. 147).

Significantly, literary scholar Trudier Harris (1995) has identified a problem in the construction of female characters in African American literature that she refers to as "this disease called strength" (p. 105):

> This [literary] landscape ... is peopled with black women who are almost too strong for their own good, whether that strength is moral or physical, or both. Historically, black writers have assumed that strength was the one unassailable characteristic they could apply to black women. If black women could be attacked for being promiscuous, they certainly could not be attacked for being strong ... [Harris, p. 110].

As Harris observes, this strength "frequently perpetuates dysfunction in literary families" because the strong female characters become "malignant growths upon the lives of their relatives" (Harris, p. 110). The task for African American writers becomes to create female characters who can cope with the challenges in their lives without becoming closed off from emotion. At the same time, these female characters must find a way to deal with the violence in their lives without being emotionally vulnerable to the point of mental breakdown.

As Mullen (2001) notes, at least since the late 1970s, when William Julius Wilson's sociological text, *The Declining Significance of Race* (1978), was published, "analysis of black social class formation has been stepped up in the liberal and academic press." This has "given dramatic impetus to best-selling new black fiction" and non-fiction (p. 158). Works dealing with the Black middle class have, Mullen argues, "been predictably accompanied by intensified demonizing of the black urban poor, black youth, crime, and gangsterism" (p. 158). In this environment, some male African American writers also have explored the intersections of race, class, and gender, focusing particularly on Black masculinity.

A number of these male writers, such as John Edgar Wideman and Ernest Gaines, have incorporated crime elements into their works. For example, Gaines's *A Gathering of Old Men* (1984) is set on a Louisiana plantation where a White Cajun man "with a protracted history of killing blacks is murdered" (Clark, 1999, p. 200):

> On the surface Gaines appropriates standard literary genres, not only the protest novel, but also the detective novel. These modes center both violence and plot in rather traditional ways; not surprisingly, the white characters' primarily concern in the novel is "whodunit" [Clark, p. 205].

Commenting on Gaines's use of the mystery structure, Wesley (2003) asserts: "By significantly changing the style and content of the narration, rescinding the control usually reserved for the detective, and by revising the conventional conclusion, Gaines reconstructs racial power relations" (p. 114). Wesley describes the display of "heroic black manhood" by the old men in Gaines's novel as bearing similarities to Frederick Douglass's description in his *Narrative* of his confrontation with the slave breaker Mr. Covey (p. 115). In Gaines's novel, the old Black men who give the novel its title all confess to the crime of which one of them is accused. Gaines explores "the importance of violence in black men's construction of masculinity" and their "ability to invent creative means to reform themselves" (Clark, p. 205).

Wesley (2003) in a chapter in her book *Violent Adventure* titled "Detecting Power" compares Gaines's *A Gathering of Old Men* (1983) to Walter Mosley's mystery novel, *Devil in a Blue Dress* (1990). Citing sociologist Michel Foucault, Wesley observes that "stories of detection" can function as "pertinent inquiries into the practical operation of power" and for the "negotiation of racial inequalities." Gaines and Mosley examine the "new possibilities of black empowerment in the aftermath of the civil rights struggle and the second World War, respectively." (Wesley, p. 113)

Even as Black writers reconfigure the genre to explore Black empowerment, the tensions within African American culture continue to complicate depictions of Black life. The rise of "hip hop culture" and Black neo-conservatism, two parallel phenomena in a "postmodern era," provoke debate about how African Americans should present themselves and how they should be presented. This debate is played out both in mainstream American culture and in African American popular culture. In the late 1990s, "urban street lit," a controversial literary descendant of the hard-boiled street lit of the 1960s and '70s, became the best-selling fiction among young African American readers (see e.g., Young, 2006; Wright, 2006).

Conclusions

In an article about comic strips in Black newspapers in postwar Toledo, Nelson (2005) writes of the two series she has analyzed:

> Swing Papa and Barry Jordan have a few common characteristics. Both featured African American male musicians (although Barry Jordan was also an amateur detective) and both are adventure continuity comic strips set in the city ... [p. 5].

Nelson (2005) notes that the two comic strips "were created and published" after World War II, during a time "when America was reconstituting itself on several levels domestically and internationally" (p. 2). Thus, the creators of these two comic strips were influenced by African American cultural vernacular, specifically music. They also were influenced by mainstream White comic strip characters such as Dick Tracy and Steve Canyon. Nelson (2005) finds that although "Barry Jordan was an 'everyman' hero from an African American male's perspective," he also "embodied many of the same characteristics of the white male hero found in literature, stage, radio, film, and (increasingly) television" (p. 4).

Increasingly, in the postwar era, African Americans were challenging the barriers that were keeping them from moving into the American mainstream. This was reflected in the protest novels of the 1940s and '50s and in the Black Nationalist literary movement during and after the 1960s Civil Rights movement. But, at the same time, African American writers were participating in the creation of late 20th century American literature. Thus, in 1974, Percy Spurlark Parker, following in the genre footsteps of Fisher, Himes, and Allison published *Good Girls Don't Get Murdered*. This mystery novel features Big Bull Benson, gambler and hotel/bar owner. During his conversation with a mysterious woman who comes into the bar, Bull acknowledges that he was mentioned in the paper eight months ago when, "I helped a friend out of a murder rap" (p. 8). He promised to tell her about it "some day." He never has the chance, as he is walking her home, someone shoots at them. She is killed.

This has been Parker's only full-length novel to date, but he has continued to writer about Bull Benson and other characters. His stories have appeared regularly in *Alfred Hitchcock Mystery Magazine* (AHMM), *Ellery Queen Mystery Magazine,* and other short story magazines. Similarly, Marc Olden, who wrote a men's adventure series (*Black Samurai*) for Signet Books in the 1970s, continued to publish crime fiction until his death in 2003. Olden was nominated for an Edgar for Best Paperback Original Novel in 1978 for *They've Killed Anna*, from his *Harker File* series about an investigative reporter. During the course of his career, Olden wrote a mystery featuring Edgar Allan Poe (*Poe Must Die*, 1978), and more recently novels with police protagonists, *The Ghost* (1999). *Fear's Justice* (1996), and *Kisaeng* (1991) among them.

Although he wrote only two mysteries in the 1980s, playwright Clifford Mason also helped to lay the groundwork for the significant movement of African American writers into the genre. Mason's novel's *The Case of Ashanti Gold* (1985) and *Jamaica Run* (1987) feature P.I. Joe Cinquez, a Harlem reporter turned private eye. The two books have an international flavor, involving Joe with a Zulu warrior and South African gold smuggling in the his first case, and a trip to Jamaica to sold his landlady's murder in the second.

In the late 1980s to the 1990s, African American mystery writers began an unprecedented era of contributions to genre crime fiction. Roth (2004) in his book, *Inspecting Jews*, writes, "American Jewish detective stories thrive in the busy and contested intersection of modern Jewish literature and American popular culture ... a crossroads where literary conventions, mass media, and ideologies merge and collide" (p. 2). Much the same may be said of African American crime fiction. Section II focuses on the works of contemporary African American mystery writers.

PART II

Modern African American Mystery Writers

A basic premise of this book is that African American mystery writers are participants in the creation of popular culture. As cultural workers, they are involved in the social construction of the concepts of "crime" and "justice." Social constructionists argue that we each create our own "reality" based on the varied sources of information available to us (Berger and Luckman, 1966). With regard to the criminal justice system, most citizens have only limited personal experience as either victims or perpetrators of crime. Most citizens derive their information about the system and how it functions from other sources, particularly from the mass media (Surette, 2007).

As do popular films and television crime shows, mystery fiction as a genre offers consumers information in the form of narratives. As do legal narratives, news reports, and true crime books, mystery novels contribute to the totality of images from which citizens draw in developing beliefs about crime and the criminal justice system.

In his research on attitudes about crime, Theodore Sasson (1995) identifies five "frames" that are commonly used by citizens when they talk about crime. These frames are: (1) faulty system; (2) social breakdown; (3) blocked opportunities; (4) media violence; and (5) racist system. Each frame is used by citizens who adopt it to explain what is often referred to as the "crime problem." The two versions of the faulty system frame see the system as faulty either because it is too lenient or because it is ineffective. The social breakdown frame sees the crime problem as a symptom of societal woes (with liberal and conservative versions of the sources of those woes). The blocked opportunities frame attributes crime to a social structure that denies the poor and minorities legitimate opportunities for success. The media violence frame points to the proliferation of images of violence and asserts the negative impact of these images on society, particularly children. Lastly, the racist system frame asserts the existence of institutionalized racism in the criminal justice system.

We might expect that mystery writers will create characters that hold beliefs and attitudes that reflect these frames. Attitudes toward the criminal justice system, crime, and offenders found in mystery novels reflect the popular discourse of the era. For example, when Edgar Allan Poe wrote the stories that established him as "the father of the mystery short story," his works reflected the attitudes toward race prevalent among White Southern males of the antebellum era. In the post–Civil Rights era and in the wake of the modern feminist movement, societal attitudes changed, and these changes were reflected in mystery fiction. More female protagonists joined the ranks of fictional detectives. More racial/ethnic minority characters began to appear and eventually were depicted as protagonists. Writers of the genre, both male and female, expanded their focus on social issues.

African American writers have been influenced by the "conventions" of the genre. At the same time, they have contributed "inventions."[70] The question is whether their unique social history has shaped the perspectives of Black mystery writers in ways that are identifiable in their works. Writers create fictional "universes," imaginary "worlds," that they populate with an assortment of characters—fictional people—that move through time and space. The world created by the author provides a fictional space in which problems are worked through by the protagonist and other characters. Do modern African American mystery writers create characters, plots, and settings that reflect racial issues? When depicting the criminal justice system, are African American mystery writers prone to use "blocked opportunities" or "racist system" frames—frames favored by many African Americans in real life?[71]

With these questions in mind, the chapters in Section II will examine the sleuths and their worlds; the social location of crime; victims and offenders, and the functioning of the criminal justice system in the works of modern African American mystery writers.

The Sleuths and Their Worlds

In the social sciences, ethnographers go into the field to observe, record, and later describe the activities of groups. Arguably, the sleuth in a mystery novel performs similar functions. As the sleuth investigates the crime and places it in context, he or she serves as the eyes, ears, and legs of the reader. The fictional world of the novel is processed through the mind of the sleuth who interprets it for the reader. Malmgren (2001) observes that, "Every detective story necessarily contains an interpretant, someone engaged in decoding signs, and therefore a foregrounded figure of the reader" (p. 28). Describing the ethnic detective in the works of Chester Himes, Harry Kellerman (Jewish rabbi), and Tony Hillerman (Native American tribal police), Peter Freeze, "identifies a 'cultural mediator' or a narrator who introduces the reader to an unfamiliar ethnic culture" (cited in Jablon, 1997, p. 146).

Illustrating this function of the cultural mediator, Jablon (1997) describes Easy Rawlins's role as narrator in Walter Mosley's *Black Betty* (1994)*: "His [Easy's] voice chaperons the reader on a guided tour through the 'bad' part of town…. A clue to the fact that he is talking to outsiders is his repeated efforts to explain life on the street" (p. 149). Jablon notes that Easy also explains the working life of a "poor man" (p. 149). In his description, Easy "serves as an interlocutor, a narrator who uses standard English to bracket dialogue in the vernacular. He even interrupts conversations among characters to instruct his readers in what is going on" (p. 149).

However, as is true of real-life ethnographers, even the most skilled and knowledgeable fictional sleuth is likely to have certain personal biases. If the sleuth is fully developed as a character, he or she has a "back story," a biography that has shaped his or her personality. The sleuth has grown up in a world in which race/ethnicity and various other characteristics that he/she possesses affect how others respond to him or her. Like real people, fictional sleuths are conscious of their own personal and cultural histories. In this regard, Kelly (1998) observes: "In creating a fictional investigator, every writer necessarily

Hereafter, I will cite the edition of the books that I used in my research. To check the copyright year of a book go to Appendix B.

defines a "stance," a way of being in a fictional world, the features of which are also of the author's choosing and creating" (p. 138).

In this chapter, we look at who the sleuths are and how their biographies shape their worldviews.

Who the Sleuths Are

The majority of the sleuths created by African American mystery writers are African American. The social and work worlds that they inhabit often bring the sleuths into contact with others from diverse cultural and racial/ethnic backgrounds. The sleuths range in age from college student to senior citizen (not including in this discussion the several juvenile sleuths). Some have lived or are living abroad. They do not share one common philosophy that could be described as *the* worldview of the sleuths created by African American writers. Their political positions range from far left to somewhat conservative. Most are middle class in education and aspirations, if not always in financial resources. They are not all Protestant, but most are heterosexual. They are not all anti-police. Their lifestyles vary as much as their physical attributes and tastes in clothing. They have a variety of occupations (see Table 1 for a representative look at series sleuths).

Table 1: Sleuth's Professions

Author	*Sleuth*	*Profession of Sleuth*
Bailey, Frankie Y.	Lizabeth ("Lizzie") Stuart	Criminal justice professor/ crime historian
Baker, Nikki	Virginia ("Ginny") Kelly	Stockbroker
Bates, Karen Grigsby	Alex Powell	Newspaper columnist
Bland, Eleanor Taylor	Marti MacAlister	Police detective
Camacho, Austin S.	Hannibal Jones	Former cop, now troubleshooter
Carter, Charlotte	Nanette Hayes	Street saxophone player
Carter, Charlotte	Cassandra Lisle	College student
Chambers, Christopher	Angela Bivens	FBI special agent
Darden, Christopher and Lochte, Dick[72]	Nikki Hill	Lawyer (prosecutor)
Davis, Kyra	Sophie Katz	Mystery writer
DeLoach, Nora	Grace "Candi" Covington ("Mama") and daughter Simone	Social worker (mother); Paralegal (daughter)
Edwards, Grace	Mali Anderson	Former cop, now social worker
Greer, Robert O.	C.J. Floyd	Bail bondsman

Author	Sleuth	Profession of Sleuth
Grimes, Terris McMahan	Theresa Galloway (and her mother)	Personnel officer in state agency
Hayes, Teddy	Marcus "Devil" Barnett	Former CIA assassin, now tavern owner
Haywood, Gar Anthony	Aaron Gunner	Private investigator
Haywood, Gar Anthony	Joe and Dottie Loudermilk	Retired cop and wife
Henry, Angela	Kendra Clayton	Part-time GED instructor
Holton, Hugh	Larry Cole	Police detective/unit commander
Joe, Yolanda (writing as Ardella Garland)	Georgia Barnett	TV reporter
Kelley, Norman	Nina Halligan	Professor/former prosecutor/PI
Meadows, Lee	Lincoln Keller	Private investigator
Mickelbury, Penny	Carole Ann (C.A.) Gibson	Lawyer (defense attorney/security firm)
Mickelbury, Penny	Mimi Patterson and Gianna Maglione	Investigative reporter; Police detective
Mosley, Walter	Ezekiel "Easy" Rawlins	Confidential agent, later licensed PI
Mosley, Walter	Paris Minton and Fearless Jones	Bookstore owner; World War II vet
Neely, Barbara	Blanche White	Domestic worker
Phillips, Gary	Ivan Monk	Private investigator
Phillips, Gary	Martha Chainey	Casino courier
Samuels-Young, Pamela	Vernetta Henderson	Lawyer
Singer, Gammy	Amos Brown	Landlord
Smith-Levin, Judith	Starletta Duvall	Police detective
Thomas-Graham, Pamela	Nikki Chase	Economics professor
Tramble, Nichelle D.	Maceo Redfield	Former baseball star
Walker, Blair S.	Darryl Billups	Journalist
West, Chassie	Leigh Ann Warren	Police officer
Wesley, Valerie Wilson	Tamara Hayle	Private investigator
Woods, Paula L.	Charlotte Justice	Police detective

Before exploring their occupational socialization, we should have a look at some of the events that shaped these protagonists and their varied world-views.

Where They Come From

The backgrounds of the sleuths are as diverse as the authors who created them. Some are from small Southern towns (e.g., Barbara Neely's[73] Blanche White and Frankie Y. Bailey's Lizzie Stuart). Others are transplants from the

Midwest (e.g., Pamela Thomas-Graham's Nikki Chase). Most are urbanites by birth and/or choice (e.g., Grace Edwards' Mali Anderson; Paula L. Woods' Charlotte Justice; Valerie Wilson Wesley's Tamara Hayle; Robert Greer's CJ Floyd). In Gammy Singer's *A Landlord's Tale* (2005), protagonist Amos Brown says:

> My Harlem. Born and bred here and proud of it. The facades of the buildings were weathered, but there was a grandeur that lingered, waiting to be revived, spruced up, ready to go again. Like me, I guess [p. 3].

Many of the protagonists in mysteries by African American writers are — as are many real-life African Americans—first-generation middle class. For example, Eleanor Taylor Bland's police detective Marti MacAlister is a Chicago's native whose parents worked for the railroad; her mother cleaned the trains and her father was a porter. A few of the protagonists grew up in middle or even upper middle-class homes. For example, Charlotte Justice's father is a chemist who created make-up for Black Hollywood stars; her mother is from an old Los Angeles family. Nikki Chase, now an economics professor at Harvard, grew up in an upper middle-class family in Detroit. The economic status of Charlotte Carter's character, Cassandra Lisle, improved significantly when her grandmother died and she went to live with her great aunt and uncle, Hyde Park residents who have both money and style.

Some protagonists faced early obstacles that threatened not only their upward mobility but might have ended their lives. These obstacles included desertion by one or both parents, abuse by parents or caregiver, death of caregiver, and drug addiction or criminal lifestyle of family members. Many of the protagonists have experienced neighborhoods with drugs, gangs, and disorder. Some are from what urban ethnographer, Elijah Anderson describes as "street families" who, he asserts, have different orientations/ values than respectable or "decent families" (Anderson, 2000). African American mystery writers echo these distinctions with protagonists who describe growing up either in stable families and avoiding the streets, or losing family members and friends to the streets. In *Hidden in Plain View* (1999), Blair Walker's journalist Darryl Billups, tells the reader that in spite of his living arrangements (i.e., unmarried cohabitation with his girlfriend), he is a "traditionalist in other ways":

> The Billups family — me, my father and mother, Camille, and my brother, James Jr.— before he died in Vietnam — always lived in a house.... From the time I turned thirteen, my family lived in a neat, detached two-story.... My father always saw to it that his family was surrounded by four well-maintained walls that belonged to us. And my mother made sure the occupants were always well taken care of and never went wanting for anything including spiritual sustenance [p. 38].

In contrast to this rock solid family structure, Jessie King, Gary Hardwick's protagonist in *Double Dead* (1997), now a Detroit assistant district attorney, comes from a family that was outside the American mainstream:

> When they got older, Jesse, his sister Bernice, and their brother, Tyrus, all acquired their mother's welfare mentality....
>
> He grew up knowing what it was like to want. There were times when they didn't have enough food and had to scrounge for what they could get around the neighborhood. They wore old clothes and had to suffer the humiliation of hand-outs...
>
> After they moved from Herman Gardens, Jesse fell in with a group of neighborhood boys from the east side ... [p. 25].

Jesse King began to retreat from street life when one of his friends was picked up for burglarizing a house. The friend, who couldn't read, signed a confession to the rape of a young girl. He was sent to prison where he was gang raped. When another close friend was killed, Jesse decided to go back to school. He came to the attention of a teacher who became his mentor and went on to college, then law school. He became a political conservative, who believes "that blacks were wretched only because they chose to be" (p. 26). He applies this philosophy to his own sister, Bernice: "She was a drug addict, a crackhead mostly, although she'd use anything if she had the money" (Hardwick, p. 56).

On occasion, characters from impoverished backgrounds who have achieved middle or even upper class status found their careers and lives in jeopardy. In these circumstances, a return to their roots is presented as both therapeutic and life-saving. Jesse King explains to his upper class fiancée Connie that he is leaving her for Ramona, the woman with whom he was on the run from both the police and the bad guys. He has much more in common with Ramona, who grew up in the ghetto as he did: "We both walked out of a bad world into a better one; only she never forgot where she started like I did. She gave me something back, Connie. She gave me back myself" (Hardwick, p. 356).

The protagonist who returns to his or her roots—both physically and psychologically—has an opportunity to regroup. He may find the help needed to resolve the crisis he is facing. In Eric James Fullilove's *Blowback* (2001), Richard Whelan, Harvard-educated national security advisor to the president, finds himself framed for the murder of the White woman, daughter of a corporate mogul, with whom he has been romantically involved. He turns to his half-brother Marcus Blaze, his mother's son from her failed first marriage. Marcus is a street-smart, criminal defense attorney, with whom Whelan has never wanted a familial relationship—until he finds himself in trouble. Marcus points this out to Whelan when he comes to the jail:

> "...You called me because you need me for once. Let's forget about all the times I needed you and you were like, Marcus-motherfucking-who, okay?"
>
> "Fine, Marcus. Let's just call a truce for now."
>
> Marcus sat on the edge of a chair. "Because, and I wanna hear you say, it, bro, because you need me."
>
> Richard Whelan sighed. "Okay. Because I need you" [p. 41].

Whelan and his half-brother met for the first time when Marcus turned up at Whelan's Harvard dorm with "a six-pack of beer and a couple of reefer"

(p. 48). In the eyes of Whelan and his White quad mates, Marcus was a "street thug." He came from a background that Whelan rejected. But Marcus is among those characters who survive troubled and/or impoverished backgrounds and achieve success. As a group, these characters tend to provide similar explanations of how they avoided the fates that befell many of the people with whom they grew up:

    a. their own determination
    b. academic and/or athletic abilities
    c. supportive parents or other relatives
    d. a mentor who served as role model and provided resources
    e. observing what happened to their less fortune or cautious peers
    f. seizing and making full use of opportunities

In the lives of many of these protagonists, family members or pseudo-kin were important in their early socialization and are continuing sources of support.

Family Matters

In his defining essay, *The Simple Art of Murder* (1944), Raymond Chandler described the private investigator (PI) as a "lonely knight." The modern fictional detective — whether PI, cop, or amateur — is less likely to be lonely. If he or she has no blood relatives, often a circle of friends provide support. Focusing only on female writers, Décuré (1999) asserts that "two features emerge as important and original in black women's crime fiction." One is the tendency to "break the pall of silence" concerning interracial relations. The other feature is the "greater role" of "the heroine's personal relations with family, friends and lovers/husbands" (p. 162). Décuré argues that the attention to these intimate relationships in the works of Black women writers "differ[s] quite markedly from White women's fiction" (p. 162).

In her Introduction to *Shades of Black* (2004), the anthology that she edited, mystery writer Eleanor Taylor Bland, asserts that in the works of African American mystery writers, loved ones are especially valued:

> In my opinion, the most significant contribution we have made, collectively, to mystery fiction, is the development of the extended family; the permanence of spouses and significant others ... children who are complex, wanted, and loved; and even pets ... [p. 1].

Bland demonstrates this in her own series. Her widowed sleuth, Marti MacAlister remarries, creating a blended family of her two children and her new husband's son. They share their home with Marti's mother. Both Marti and her husband, Ben, a paramedic/firefighter, have work partners who have spouses and families. Other friends and relatives enter their lives and become a part of the family group, sharing holidays and special occasions. The pets

Bland mentions in her comments include not only the two dogs belonging to their own household, but the four-legged guests who accompany their owners to gatherings. *A Cold and Silent Dying* (2004) ends with a Thanksgiving celebration at Marti and Ben's home. The guests include the formerly nomadic veteran, who was a suspect in the murder investigation, but has now found a welcome in this extended family.

The extended family in the fiction of Black mystery writers has its parallel in the research of social scientists and historians who write about the presence and the importance of the extended family in the lives of real-life African Americans. Historians discuss the "fictive kin" who constituted a part of the slave community and who provided some insulation against a system in which spouses, parents, and children might be sold away from each other at any time. Scholars (see e.g., Sarkisian, 2007; Stewart, 2007) also point to the continued importance in the post-slavery era and even today of the extended family which includes elders (grandparents) and an array of uncles, aunts, and cousins. Such families also include relatives by marriage or informal adoption ("taking in to raise").

This willingness to define family as more inclusive than a nuclear family of parents and children or even blood relatives is one of the mechanism that allowed African Americans to survive. Novelist Toni Morrison describes the concept of "other mothering" or "other mothers," the women who are not mothers by birth or sometimes even related by bloodline, but who carry out the functions of mother by providing nurturing and caring (O'Reilly, 2004). Banks-Wallace and Parks (2001) state: "In contrast [to dominant society definitions] African American definitions conceptualize motherhood as a group activity that is public and concerned with the welfare of all children" (p. 93). The members of extended families, fictive kin, and other mothers (and fathers) are readily apparent in the works of African American mystery writers (Décuré, 1999; Reddy, 2003).

An example of the creation of an extended "family" composed of people who were strangers occurs in Gammy Singer's *A Landlord's Tale* (2005) and its sequel, *Down and Dirty* (2006). Protagonist Amos Brown was raised by his Aunt Reba. His only remembered contact with his father "was one time when I was twelve and Aunt Reba called him to come discipline me" (p. 33). In *A Landlord's Tale* (2005), he tells Catherine, a young woman to whom he is attracted:

> My aunt was more than overjoyed when the police picked me up and deposited me in a state prison. She probably dusted her hands together and said, "Good riddance." Hell, I don't blame the woman. I was sullen, angry, and nobody's child. I wouldn't have wanted to raise me either [p. 33].

When Amos inherits his father's apartment buildings, he moves into one of them. He discovers to his dismay that one his tenants, Wilbur, is homosexual.

He calls him "The Fag" (p. 16). His other tenants include Miss Ellie, a former Cotton Club dancer, and Winnie, a young mother with a small daughter, Josie. During the course of this book and in *Down and Dirty* (2006), Amos forms bonds with these tenants, particularly with Wilbur, who is wasting away from an illness for which the doctors in the 1970s don't yet have a name.

However, even with the attention given to familial relationships in this and other series, the sleuths of African American writers are not immune to the loss of family members or significant others. Traumatic losses by death will be discussed in greater detail below. But relationships also end by other means. Hugh Holton's Chicago police detective, Larry Cole, has a wife and a son. He and his wife eventually divorce because of his job. Walter Mosley's Easy Rawlins loses his wife because of his inability to confide in her. Another relationship with a woman he loves also fails. Blair Walker's Darryl Billup meets an attractive nurse's aide named Yolanda when he is hospitalized after being mugged in *Up Jumped the Devil* (1997). He reluctantly provides her with shelter when she and her son must flee her abusive boyfriend. In *Hidden in Plain View* (1999), he and Yolanda and her son have rented a house and become a family. But in *Don't Believe Your Lying Eyes* (2002) the relationship unravels after Darryl and his snobbish sister go to meet his fiancée's parents. A roach running across the dinner table and insults exchanged between Darryl's sister and his future mother-in-law make clear the class differences that Darryl has been pondering.

But as Bland asserts, among African American protagonists, there is a strong tendency toward bonds that are sustained. The protagonists first bonds are with their birth families, who are sources of both comfort and stress. Paula L. Woods' Charlotte Justice and her siblings refer to their parents' home as "the Nut House" not only because of the variety of nut-colored skin tones in the family, but because of family craziness. Charlotte joins the family for scheduled gatherings such as "movie night." When she acquires a lover, Aubrey, he becomes an accepted part of the family. Charlottes finds this irritating at those moments when he seems more in tune with her family than with her. In *Strange Bedfellows* (2006), Charlotte wants to talk about a conflict she is having with her brother, Perris, the lawyer. Her family with " not so-subtle maneuvering" diverts the conversation to the upcoming Academy Awards. Charlotte tells her Uncle Syl that she has been too busy to see any of the nominated movies.

> Aubrey kissed my ear and whispered: "I've been trying to get you to go."
> I could feel another argument tickling the back of my throat which I doused with a swallow of Scotch. Aubrey knew I'd been preoccupied the past few months, between the jobs and the months I'd spent working with Perris and my Police Protective League rep to fight that last suspension, so why was he rubbing it in? [Woods, p. 79].

As might be expected, the protagonist often comments on the dynamics of family life and intimate relationships. Sometimes a recollection from childhood involving family members is used to describe a moment when the protagonist became aware of adult concerns and adult pain. In Gary Phillips' *Perdition, U.S.A.* (1996), Ivan Monk recalls a happy family outing that was marred by racism. At an amusement park with his parents and sister, he won a teddy bear for his mother in a ring toss game. His moment of pride is short-lived:

> ... several drunk, laughing sailors, reeling from a rollercoaster ride, sloshed by. When one of them mumbled something about "niggers," his dad was going to take off after the crew but his mother restrained him. She reminded him that if the police were called, it would be himself— not the sailors— arrested [p. 45].

Later, Ivan finds his father drinking late at night. He shows Ivan his honorable discharge from the Korean War and recalls that he was told to fight to keep the world free. Holding Ivan close, "with alcohol emanating from him like a backed-up sewer," he asks, "But what about ours, boy? What about ours?" (p. 46).

In Nikki Baker's *The Lavender House Murder* (1992), Virginia ("Ginny") Kelley remembers her father's love of the beach and the family's summer condo in Delaware. Her father also loved long hair. Her sister had hair "that black people will sometimes call 'good' ... fine and nearly straight" (p. 9), but Ginny had her father's hair, thick and coarse. She was unable to wear the styles that he saw on White women in magazines. She felt she "let him down" (p. 9). Because of her hair, Ginny could never enjoy summer at he beach — where her mother avoided the problem of wet hair by staying out of the water, reading paperback novels on the beach.

During those summers, Ginny realized the condo that was a part of her father's "middle-class dream achieved" (p. 8) only made her conscious of being "different from the hundreds of white faces on that dirty stretch of sand" (p. 8). When her parents sold the condo to finance their retirement, her father had tears in his eyes at the closing. Ginny's memories of those summer days was that they were "lukewarm and lonely, as I was an African American princess with the fatal flaw of kinky hair" (p. 8).

The other aspect of her memories of being twelve also had to do with gender and race: "People said that I favored my father when I was a girl and the remark engendered my dislike. I imagined that with my kinky hair and broad features, I was being told that I looked like a man" (p. 9). Ginny Kelly is one of the few African American protagonists in genre fiction who is gay.[74] In this respect, her memories of childhood describe not only her socialization into race and gender but are linked to her discovery of her sexuality (see Soitos, 1999 on Ginny as lesbian sleuth).

For Terris McMahan Grimes's protagonist Theresa Galloway, her family issues revolve around the competing demands of her mother and her husband and children. In *Somebody Else's Child* (1996), Theresa recalls the death of her sister from leukemia and her brother's decision to join the Army (that led to his being stationed in Germany and marrying a White woman):

Carolyn's death and then Daddy's, and Jimmy's defection, created a huge vacuum in Mother's life that I felt compelled to fill. I ended up being caught smack
dab in the middle of the "sandwich generation," trying to juggle a career, raise a
family, and be there for Mother, too [p. 58].

Although single, Nora DeLoach's Simone Covington is often called home
by her mother, Grace ("Mama"), a social worker and small town amateur sleuth.
Because she lives in Atlanta, Simone has some ability to negotiate with her
mother about when she will visit. In *Mama Rocks the Empty Cradle* (1998),
Mama is having bunion surgery and wants Simone to come home while the
lawyer Simone works for is out of the country for six weeks. When Simone
starts to use her boyfriend, Cliff, as an excuse not to visit, Mama counters:

"You and Cliff will have at least two weeks left to do something together. But,
tell you what I'll do," Mama said, and I knew I was about to be bribed. "You
come home on Friday, you and I will shop and cook on Saturday, then Cliff can
drive here and have Sunday dinner with you, me, and your father" [p. 7].

Simone weakens as "[t]he thought of how much Cliff and I both loved Mama's
cooking whirled through my mind..." (p. 7). She goes home to visit her mother.
      In *Sex, Murder, and a Double Latte* (2005), Kyra Davis' Sophie Katz must
make time for her sister while trying to deal with a stalker.

"I've got to get out of the house."
      "Leah, this really isn't a good time." I collapsed onto the love seat. Ever since
my sister had given birth to my nephew a year and a half ago, our contact had
been reduced to frequent quasi-therapy sessions in which I listened patiently
and pretended to empathize with her trials and tribulations as a stay-at-home
mom. Normally I could rise to the occasion, but at the moment I was a bit too
caught up in the trials and tribulations of being a potential homicide victim
[p. 107].

Sophie Katz is bi-racial, the child of a White Jewish mother and an African
American father. Also bi-racial, Austin S. Camacho's Hannibal Jones grew up
in Europe. In *Blood and Bone* (2006), when a young woman tells him that he
doesn't know what it's like to be "raised a half-breed," he takes off his sunglasses
and pushes his face toward hers. He tells her, "Take a good look."

"My father was a black soldier, a military policeman," Hannibal said, his voice
still low but hard now. "My mother was a German girl he met while stationed in
Berlin. He left me there when they sent him to Vietnam. But he never came
back. My mother raised me in Berlin, among the American military community,
at a time when mixed marriages weren't really accepted. Children of those marriages even less so. I think that qualifies me to say I know exactly what you're
about ... [p. 179–180].

For the protagonist, whatever his or her background, crime-solving activities complicate creating a family of his or her own. Conversely, these activities also may bring people into the life of the sleuth. For example, Walter
Mosley's protagonist Easy Rawlins informally adopts the two children that he

rescues. Jesus, the boy, who becomes his son, was the victim of a wealthy pedophile. His daughter, Feather, was the daughter of a woman who was murdered.

Sometimes the sleuth is called upon to protect the family he has created from the threats posed by criminals. During one investigation, Hugh Holton's police detective Larry Cole must rescue his young son from a woman who has targeted Cole and his team. Robert Greer's CJ Floyd learns how vengeful his enemies can be when his long-time lover Mavis is kidnapped by the female psychopath who has been stalking Floyd to avenge her own brother's death. The difficulty of creating a safe space in a dangerous world is a matter with which Eleanor Taylor Bland's sleuth Marti MacAlister and her husband, Ben, also deal. In the aftermath of events such as those involving the psychopathic ex-husband of Marti's friend and former housemate, Sharon, Marti and Ben have a security system. In addition, one of the canine members of the family is a trained guard dog, appropriately named "Trouble."

But even though familial bonds make the sleuth vulnerable to enemies, the presence of loved ones generally strengthens the sleuth. Even when the kin are no longer physically present, they may contribute to the sleuth's well-being. Relatives who are dead and buried often remain a part of the sleuth's cosmos. The names of these relatives are evoked as sources of wisdom or insight. In *Do or Die* (2001), when Grace Edwards's protagonist, Mali Anderson, faces the difficult situation of providing care for her father and his friend (whose daughter has been murdered):

> ... What I needed at the moment was what Mom used to call "wake and worry" food. Eat all you can at the wake and worry about your weight later.
> Wake food, she had said, was down-home heavy, with enough fat and calories to drown the deepest sorrow and heavy enough to get you back on your feet in no time. Not necessarily smiling, but back on your feet where you belonged [pp. 35–36].

Sometimes the dead kin provide an apt phrase that captures the essence of a situation in which the protagonist finds himself. In *The Devil's Hatband* (1996), CJ Floyd, Robert Greer's bail bondsman protagonist, considers the possibility he may have been set up by the two men who offered him a job looking for a federal judge's daughter and some missing documents:

> He also wondered if he hadn't just stepped into the kind of manure pile his uncle used to like to call "home-grown cornbread Negro shit." Like most black people, CJ had spent a good part of his life looking in the rearview mirror, making certain that his ass wasn't hanging out unprotected in a white man's world. Now he was standing two steps from a dead black woman, flanked by two raw-boned white country cops, on a failed rescue mission that had blown up in his face ... [p. 62].

The presence of departed kinfolk who are evoked as sources of guidance and acerbic commentary is in keeping with an Afrocentric view of the cosmos that recognizes the existence of spirits who maintain a connection with those who they loved. This connection remains as long as they are remembered and called upon. Expressing her beliefs about this connection, Barbara Neely's protagonist Blanche White has her own spiritual practice and rituals,

> including reverence for her Ancestors and the planet, and seeking energy from trees and healing from the sea. Some things she'd learned from African, Afro-Caribbean, Native American, and Asian ways ... but she always added her personal twist [*Blanche Passes Go*, 2001, p. 12].

Blanche has rejected organized religion, "the Christian or the Muslim or any other religion that played a part in African slavery" (Neely, 2001, p. 12). The protagonists of other African American mystery writers hold a variety of views about religion. However, the church appears in many of the novels as a reference point in the lives of the protagonists and an institutional presence.

The Church

African American mystery writers acknowledge both organized religion in the form of the church and spirituality, in the form of "an individual's personal relationship with a God or acknowledgment of a higher power" (Sanchez & Carter, 2005, p. 280). In his book, *The Blues Detective* (1996), Soitos emphasizes the distinctive difference in worldview between Black detective fiction and "mainstream white detective fiction ... exemplified in the religions and socio-philosophical beliefs of the characters" (p. 43). Soitos describes "the use of hoodoo" in the text as "[o]ne of the two primary ways in which worldview is communicated" (p. 43). Here, hoodoo refers to "indigenous, syncretic religions of African Americans in the New World" (p. 42). As a worldview, hoodoo challenges the European perception of time and space. Smitherman (1985) writes:

> In the traditional black church, and in Black American culture generally this aspect of the traditional African world view strongly continues in the emphasis on spirituality ("soul") rather than materiality. Black Americans believe that soul, feeling, emotion, and spirit serve as guides to understanding life and their fellows. All people are moved by spirit-forces, and there is no attempt to deny or intellectualize away that fact [p. 92].

Some protagonists, such as Eleanor Taylor Bland's Marti MacAlister or Terris McMahan Grimes's Theresa Galloway, attend church with their families. Marti MacAlister is involved in the church community and draws on its resources to help people she encounters who are in need. She stands in contrast to those protagonists who have rejected or are ambivalent about organized religion. In *Chosen People* (2006), Kathy Grisby Bates's newspaper columnist, Alex Powell, is taken by surprise when her cosmopolitan lover, Paul, takes her to church. She is even more surprised by his revelation afterwards:

"...Here's the deal. I grew up going to church, as we all did, and a few years ago, I decided to go back when I could get there."

"Do you go every Sunday?"

"Many Sundays. I'm not a fanatic."

I pondered this in silence [p. 184].

However, Alex, herself, is not a stranger to the minister, who welcomes them and praises her work to the congregation, describing Alex as:

"...a voice for the voiceless, especially the African-descended voiceless in this city. To do what many journalists have forgotten to do over the decades[!] to, in the words of Saint Paul, comfort the afflicted and afflict the comfortable."

"Yes, *indeed!*" one old lady breathed [pp. 176–177].

This warm, if personally discomforting, reception by the congregation that Alex, a Los Angeles newspaper columnist, receives, is in contrast to the reception that greets Christopher Darden and Dick Lochte's protagonist, assistant district attorney Nikki Hill. In *The Trials of Nikki Hill* (1999), her attendance at the church she belongs to is greeted with antipathy by at least some members of the congregation. The Los Angeles DA's office has charged a beloved African American diva with murder. After the service, Nikki finds that people she has known much of her life are avoiding her, and people that she doesn't know are sending her hostile glances. An elderly churchwoman, Sister Mumphrey, confronts Nikki:

"Law people," Sister was saying. "Police people."

"I'm not exactly a po—"

"Supposed to be defending us from the evil of the world. Instead you spend your time making life difficult for good folks like Djuana Cooper. A minister's daughter" [p. 227].

Nikki's father and step-mother, from whom she is estranged, do not rush to her defense. Instead, Nikki's friends, Loreen and Victoria, take on Sister Mumphrey. The three friends walk out of the church with arms linked, "giddy as schoolgirls" (p. 228).

This scene with Sister Mumphrey, in which she tells Nikki that as someone in a position of power, Nikki should be "doing good in this world, 'stead of trying to bring down the righteous" (Darden and Lochte, 1999, p. 227) illustrates what criminologist Kathryn Russell (1998) has described as "black protectionism," the tendency of members of the African American community to rally around a Black person, particularly a celebrity, who has been accused of a crime. We will look at African American perceptions of justice in Chapter 7.

The next section focuses on work, an aspect of their lives which brings protagonists both satisfaction and stress.

Work and Work Places

The degree of psychological ownership of the job that an individual feels is one measure of workplace satisfaction. Pierce, O'Driscoll, & Coghlan (2004) write:

Creating and maintaining work settings that empower individuals and enable them to exercise control over important aspects of their work arrangements should — we would argue — enhance their sense of ownership, which may promote the manifestation of work-related attitudes (e.g., job satisfaction, organization-based self-esteem) and behaviors (e.g., nurturing, protecting) [p. 529].

However, most jobs involve a certain amount of stress. Barak & Levin (2002) describe stress as "the psychological state that is or represents an imbalance between people's perceptions of the demands placed on them and their ability to cope with those demands" (p. 138). On their list of "job stressors," Ortega, Brenner & Leather (2006) include:

Bureaucracy and politics
Nature of work and tasks
Interpersonal conflicts
Training (need for/lack of availability)
Poor communications
Role issues [p. 40].

An example of bureaucracy and politics occurs in Hugh Holton's *Red Lightning* (1998), when police commander Larry Cole's investigation is interrupted by political gamesmanship:

Cole had never been called before the Chicago City Council before, but he was aware of a number of their past hearings that were usually covered by the media. Some of them were fairly serious affairs aimed at probing issues of importance to the citizens of Chicago. A number were no more than political debates.... A few of them, like the one Kingsley and Alderman Edwards were cooking up tomorrow morning had an agenda [p. 240].

For those who work within any bureaucratic structure, oversight and threatened disciplinary action prove stress-inducing. Real-life police officers identify bureaucracy and politics as a major source of work life stress (see e.g., Toch, 2001).

Of course, a formal organization is not required for a stressful workplace. As a domestic worker, Barbara Neely's Blanche White is the descendant of the many African American women who have dealt with the trails and tribulations of being both "invisible" and oppressed by employers, who sometimes berate, cheat, and/or abuse them. The tasks expected of a domestic worker by employers and the ways in which they expect these tasks to be done contribute to an oppressive work place (Bailey, 1999). Moreover, as Blanche points out in *Blanche on the Lam* (1993), many of her White employers are still yearning for "Aunt Jemima," a Black servant who will listen to their troubles and offer comfort and advise (p. 39).[75]

In general, work that involves high-levels of interaction with other people in unpleasant situations is stress-inducing. In their work lives, many of the protagonists who are professionals occupy the position of "outsider within." This term was coined by African American feminist scholar Patricia Hill Collins in her book *Fighting Words* (1998). As Willett (2001) describes:

Collins replaces romantic themes of the alienated man torn by a double consciousness or the exoticized Other who does not speak with her more politically? concept of the "outsider within...." The concept of the "outsider within" draws attention to the fact that modern alienated subjects do not inhabit—in fact do not aspire to—some space beyond the reach of modern social and economic structures, including capitalism. In the modern world, individuals are situated at the intersections of diverse source of power ... [p. 158].

Berlant (1993) describes the "outsider within" as "the minority subject who circulates in a majoritarian public sphere." This subject may be seen as "exemplary" because she "has distinguished herself from the collective stereotype." However, Berlant argues that at times this subject may be expected to provide "personal testimony" about "her alien 'people'" (p. 551). Social scientists have applied the concept of "outsider within" to research on Black female police officers (Martin, 1994) and Black female firefighters (Yoder & Berendsen, 2001).

In Jake Lamar's *If 6 Were 9* (2001), his protagonist, Clay Robinette, relates with tongue in cheek how when he was a journalist the expectation that he be exemplary—better than his White colleagues—led to his downfall.

A credit to the race was the compliment back in the olden times. Well, Janet Cooke[76] was considered a debit to the race. Though my case was never exposed to as much publicity as hers was ... I, too, was regarded by some as a disgrace to black people. I never felt that way about myself. Hey, I was a mediocre journalist. I never aspired to anything but mediocrity. You know how black folks always say a black person has to be twice as good as a white person to get as far? Well, that may or may not be true. All I want to do is uphold my right to mediocrity ... [p. 7].

At a university in Ohio, Robinette has achieved some measure of happiness with a wife and twin daughters—until he makes another misstep and has a brief affair with a White female student who ends up dead. Then both his marriage and his position are in jeopardy.

Ellis Cose (1993) observes that for African Americans in careers that provide middle-class status:

In the workplace, the continuing relevance of race takes on a special force, partly because so much of life, at least for middle-class Americans, is defined by work, and partly because even people who accept that they will never be treated fairly in the world often hold out hope that their work will be treated fairly ... [that society] will properly reward hard labor and competence [p. 55].

In the mystery fiction by African American writers, Black protagonists tend to find satisfaction in their work. However, some also experience stress related to the responses of co-workers and others to the protagonist's race/ethnicity and/or gender. In one of the longest running series by an African American mystery writer, Eleanor Taylor Bland's homicide detective, Marti MacAlister, has achieved a relationship of mutual respect with her partner, Vik Jessenovik, and with Slim and Cowboy, the two vice cops with whom they share

office space. The working relationship that Marti enjoys with her male colleagues, and that Judith Smith-Levin's Lieutenant Starletta Duvall enjoys with
the men in her unit, stands in contrast to the work environments experienced
by several other female protagonists. In John Ridley's *Those Who Walk in Darkness* (2003), Soledad "Bullet" O'Roark, who is indifferent or oblivious to much
of the day-to-day social interaction that occurs around her, becomes aware of
the hostility toward women on display in her unit:

> But there was that picture and there were other pictures [of well-endowed
> women] torn and ripped and tacked and scotch-taped all over Parker Center —
> this desk, that locker.... And there was that detective by the window, the one
> with the coffee mug. The one with the coffee mug that read: SAVE A MOUSE.
> EAT THE PUSSY. How long had he had that thing? Was she just noticing it, saw
> as she was just now noticing ... [p. 91].

Soledad O'Brien is an officer in a special unit in the Los Angeles of a parallel
science fiction universe. In Paula L. Woods' series set in Los Angeles in the
early 1990s, Charlotte Justice is scheduled to testify in the harassment hearing
of a supervisor who forced her colleague, an inexperienced female detective,
into a sexual liaison. In Grace Edwards' series, Mali Anderson has bitter memories of the treatment she received while on the NYPD. Mali perceived the gender bias she encountered as inseparable from the racial bias displayed by her
fellow officers. In *Sympathy for the Devil* (2001), Christopher Chambers' protagonist, FBI agent Angela Bivens, has won a class action racial and sexual discrimination suit against the Bureau.

In real life, one of the issues for police officers is the perception that only
another police officer can understand the stresses related to the "job." Many
officers prefer not to "bring the job home" (see e.g., Toch, 2001). In this respect,
the relationship that Bland's Marti MacAlister has with her second husband,
Ben, is different than her relationship with her first husband, Johnny. Johnny
was a police officer, but he was psychologically fragile, sometimes silent, because
of his experiences in Vietnam. Marti felt she always had to be strong. With
Ben, even when she does not go into the details of her cases, he is able to offer
comfort and moral support. But in *Too Beautiful to Die* (2003), Glenville Lovell's
Blade Overstreet finds that his former assignment to an NYPD street unit and
his related inability to respond to his wife's needs have damaged his marriage.

Another aspect of work-related stress has to do with the competing
demands (roles) of job and home life. In Pamela Samuel-Young's *Every Reasonable Doubt* (2006), Vernetta Henderson, an attorney who has been assigned
as co-counselor in a high-profile murder case, must explain to her husband,
Jefferson, that having a baby might need to be postponed. In the second book
in the series, *In Firm Pursuit* (2007), Jefferson, an electrician, remains supportive. But he wonders aloud why Vernetta wants to be a partner in a law firm
where she is now the only Black female associate and under continuous pressure to perform. In Keith Lee Johnson's *Sugar & Spice* (2003), FBI agent Phoenix

Perry's husband objects to the fact that she is thinking about a murder case while they are on vacation:

> ... One of the things that bothered him were all the hours I spent working my cases. You would think he'd understand, having been an agent himself. But it's like that when you're a woman. Men expect everything from you, regardless of your chosen vocation [p. 22].

In Hugh Holton's *Violent Crimes* (1997), the reader sees the demands of the police officer's job from the perspective of protagonist Larry Cole's wife. Through the intervention of Cole's colleague, Blackie, and his wife Marie, Lisa Cole has returned to her husband following an estrangement. His pager goes off after they have made love:

> ... Larry's pager was on her nightstand. It was turned low and didn't wake him, although he shifted on his side. She reached down and shut it off. There was only one number for him to call when the little black box went off. Lisa had watched him make that call many times before. He would say little as he listened, his body tensing and the muscles of his face going rigid. Then he would go out into the night, leaving her. On many such occasions it had been for hours—once, for two days. Not tonight, she vowed shutting it off [p. 250].

After debating with herself, she wakes him. As he reaches for the phone, she thinks, "*Damn, being a cop's wife can be hard....* But she knew now that she was in it for the duration" (p. 251). Later in the series, the Coles divorce, and she moves to another city with their son.

On the job, the nature of the protagonist's relationship with his or her supervisor affects every aspect of work life and may spill over into personal life. The ethical dilemmas some protagonists face because of requests or orders from their supervisors will be discussed in greater detail in Chapter 7. A more common problem for protagonists are personality and work style conflicts with supervisors. Eleanor Taylor Bland's Marti MacAlister, has a new supervisor, Lieutenant Nicholson. Nicholson has limited street experience and demonstrates her authority in ways that her subordinates consider petty. After summoning Marti and Vik to her office, she always makes them wait outside the door before calling them in. Marti, who dislikes change and liked and respected her former boss, has developed a physical symptom of stress. She has acid reflux.

In *A Cold and Silent Dying* (2004), Marti, called to her supervisor's office, compares her own appearance to that of the slender, stylish lieutenant. Nicholson, who has delicate features and curly hair, wears a dark suit and blouse as her "uniform":

> Looking at her, Marti thought of the extra ten pounds she had put on since September and the annual physical that was coming up, and for the first time in years felt uncomfortable with her size and unhappy about the weight gain. One hundred plus sixty-five pounds [Bland, p. 37].

However, Marti feels competent in her own abilities as a detective. Because Bland writes from multiple points of view, the reader has an opportunity to view the situation from Lieutenant Nicholson's perspective. In *A Cold and Silent Dying* (2004), Nicholson thinks with scorn about how Marti depends on "haphazard, I've-got-a-hunch methodology" to solve her cases (p. 22). At the same time, she is intrigued by Marti's family life. She has seen the popsicle-stick pencil holder and photos of her children in Marti's office:

> Occasionally she wondered what a life like MacAlister's might be like, she thought of her own childhood, growing up hungry and poor with eight siblings all lighter and brighter than she was, and no daddy. She had no regrets because she chose not to marry, no guilt because she preferred contraceptives to childbirth [p. 22].

Even though Nicholson expresses her contentment with her personal life and her career trajectory, she is disliked by the police officers that she supervises. In spite of her own irritation with Nicholson, Marti disapproves of jokes about her. In *A Dark and Deadly Deception* (2005), Marti thinks about the double standard applied to women in command and how she herself achieved credibility in the department:

> ... She didn't have any sympathy for Nicholson, but if she [Nicholson] were a male, there would be no sexual innuendos or comments about her ability to manage stress, no "lemon" nicknames, not to mention the humor associated with undermining or circumventing her authority [p. 134].

At the same time, Marti is concerned that Nicholson is making it more difficult for other female cops to get rank and hold command. Marti has worked hard to earn respect and her nickname, "Big Mac." She has made it "easier for a woman to be accepted as a cop, and without saying much of anything. Now along comes Nicholson, tearing that down" (p. 134). However, Marti has no desire to be a supervisor because she prefers being out in the field. She enjoys the "thrill of the chase." She acknowledges to herself that she cannot "imagine anything else giving her the high she got from actively investigating someone's death, as morbid as that might sound" (p. 134). Normally, she likes her job, even when working conditions are unpleasant. She attributes much of her present stress to her supervisor, a Black female who sees Marti as a threat and would like to be rid of her.

Marti MacAlister is not the only protagonist to make such an observation about another African American in his or her workplace. In Blair Walker's *Hidden in Plain View* (1999), Darryl Billups says that he expected the only other Black assistant editor at his newspaper — who he has nicknamed "King Handkerchief Head" — to react badly to Darryl's promotion to that position: "Because black folks like him usually battle ferociously to remain the lone speck of pepper in a sea of salt, rather than help lift up other black faces" (p.11). In *Orange Crushed* (2004), Pamela Thomas-Graham's Nikki Chase describes similar hostility from Janice Borden, a Black female professor in another department. Nikki tells the reader that Borden has "viewed me as a rival since the day we met" and has even spread stories about how Nikki was "her protégé in college." So she finds it hard to trust Borden:

> ... What was true was that we had both grown up as certifiable members of the black upper middle class—she in Los Angeles and me in Detroit—and now we were both successful black women at Harvard. We should have been close friends and allies—but apparently Janice felt that the place was too small for the two of us. And she would be thrilled to see me gone. It was sad, but true: the old-school HNIC phenomenon (that would be Head Nigger in Charge) was very much alive and well in our generation [p. 168].

Janice Borden is on the fast track for tenure in the Afro-American Studies Department. She is rumored to be having an affair with the chairperson, whose wife has gained a great deal of weight since her third pregnancy (p. 168). In contrast, Borden, although heavy-set, is stylish with henna highlights in her hair and a Hermes scarf "flung casually over her rust-colored cashmere twin set" (p. 167).

The issue of appearance in the workplace provides an opportunity for African American characters to display unity in the face of criticism. In Walker's *Hidden in Plain View* (1999), Darryl Billups reports with both amusement and annoyance the attempt by his White superiors to have him persuade his friend, "Mad Dawg," a sportswriter on the newspaper, to cut his dreadlocks. Although there is "no official dress code for reporters, the powers that be would love to see Mad Dawg shorn. His dreads have been deemed unprofessional, if not a touch threatening" (p. 10). However, the White editors are afraid to approach Mad Dawg because they don't want "to appear racist" (p. 10). Darryl declines the request. Although Mad Dawg's lifestyle sometimes dismays Darryl, he considers him a reliable friend and ally.

In fact, a number of the protagonists do have another Black person in the work place who they consider an ally. In *Orange Crushed* (2004), the murder victim was Nikki Chase's friend. A senior professor at Princeton, he was her sounding board and mentor. In Paula Woods' series, Charlotte Justice relies on the "sisterhood" of other Black female officers in the Georgia Robinson Society, the benevolent association to which she belongs. In *Strange Bedfellows* (2006), one of those officers, Billie Truesdale, has transferred into her unit, and Charlotte is grateful for her presence:

> ... In a department where watching your back was as necessary to the job as carrying a weapon, Billie was one of the people I never had to worry about. In addition to being a sure-nough sister from the 'hood, what made me like Billie was the fact that she was a warrior, cunning enough to have survived both the violence-prone streets of her neighborhood and the testosterone-laden halls of South Bureau Homicide, where she'd worked for several years before getting called up to RHD ... [p. 27].

In less dire straits, Karen Grigsby Bates' Alex Powell still seeks the office of her friend, Georgie Marks, the fashion editor, to ventilate about the ways of the "white folks" with and for whom they work. In *Chosen People* (2006), Alex is outraged when her editor tells her that she will have to choose, "Between being a member in good standing of your community and being a good reporter" (p. 63). After challenging his suggestion that being Black and being a good reporter "are mutually exclusive" and pointing out he never questions the objectivity of other reporters who socialize with the people they report on, she goes off to talk to Georgie about it. Georgie, an expert in office politics, suggests Alex "blind-carbon" her follow-up to the discussion her editor said they would finish later to the editor in chief.

> We beamed at each other. The current editor in chief was a true gentleman, a silver-haired Southern-raised, second-generation civil rights activist from a borderline Southern state and he would be appalled to, uh, *accidentally* learn of Fine's latest observation ... [Bates, p. 67].

This scene illustrates that allies and sources of support that Black protagonists have in the work place are not limited to other African Americans. Particularly for those Black protagonists who are working in professional settings such as police departments, universities, and newsrooms, work place friends and allies may be as diverse as the setting. In Charlotte Carter's Cassandra Perry series, hippie college student Cassandra shares a bond with Owen, one of her professors, a laid-back, pot-smoking White Southerner who had a Negro nanny when he was a child but is estranged from his wealthy family and his birthplace. In Judith Smith-Levin's series, African American homicide lieutenant Starletta Duvall, has an Italian American partner, Dominic Paresi, who is romantically involved with Vee, African American, mother of three, and Star's best friend. Star's lover is the medical examiner, Mitchell Grant, who is both White, Harvard-educated, and old money. In Robert Greer's CJ Floyd series, his assistant and now partner, Flora Jean Benson, was a sergeant in the Army during the Gulf War. Her lover is her former commanding officer, General Alden Grace, who maintains his intelligence connections and has been a source of information in several cases. Flora Jean resisted Grace's efforts to turn their liaisons into a serious relationship. In *The Fourth Perspective* (2006), the two walk hand-in-hand:

> Flora Jean and Alden Grace recognized that they stood out, and neither of them liked it much. But they'd long ago learned to deal with the idiosyncrasies of a black-white love affair, coming to grips with the fact that a tall, buxom black woman walking hand in hand with a six-foot-four inch, square-jawed, blue-eyed white man with a crew cut would certainly — during their lifetime and perhaps forever — draw stares in America [p. 221].

African American protagonists — who draw stares to themselves by their actions or mere presence — tend also to be aware of the "invisibility" of African Americans and other people of color who hold low status jobs in the work place. In *Orange Crushed* (2004), Pamela Thomas-Graham's Nikki Chase, an economics professor at Harvard, has a friendship with the building superintendent.

> Percy Walker embraced me. He always reminded me of my grandfather; over the years we've become good friends. And as my brother Eric has also learned at Princeton, it is always good policy to have friends in the Building Department [p. 174].

It is Eric's friend in the Building Department who provides Nikki with the key she needs to get into the office of her murdered mentor at Princeton.

Later Nikki observes Butch Hubbard, the chair of Harvard's Afro-American Studies Department, as he joins a workers' rally for higher wages. After her initial suspicion that Hubbard is there for the media spotlight, she acknowledges that he is

> giving voice to people who had none. No one else would listen to what Percy had to say—but they'd listen to a tenured Harvard professor who happened to make for great television [p. 176].

But empathy for the voiceless notwithstanding, the question remains why the protagonists of African American mystery/detective fiction become crime solvers. Why have the professionals—the cops and the PIs—make this their life's work? Why do the amateurs become involved in investigations?

Self-Identity as a Crime Solver/Fighter

Paula Woods opens *Inner City Blues* (1999), the first book in her series featuring Charlotte Justice with these lines:

> Twelve years, eleven months, and fifteen days into living out my *Top Cop* fantasies—Christie Love[77] with a better hairdo—my Nubian brothers down on Florence and Normandie had to go and pitch a serious bitch and mess up my cha-cha [p. 11].

A page later, Charlotte says:

> As I watched the city I loved go to hell in a handbasket, I kept reminding myself that the Los Angeles I wanted to protect and to serve was basically composed of law-abiding citizens, not mad looters dragging microwaves down Pico Boulevard—near *my* house, no less [p. 12].

Charlotte has a degree in criminology. Over a decade earlier, her husband, a professor conducting gang research, and her baby daughter were gunned down in their driveway. Her desire to protect and serve her community is linked to this personal trauma from which she has never fully recovered. Charlotte Justice is one of several protagonists who has experienced a life-changing event. Eleanor Taylor Bland's police detective, Marti McAllister, was widowed when her husband, Johnny, also a Chicago police officer, was killed. Former prosecutor, Nina Halligan, Norman Kelley's protagonist, knows who killed her husband and two children but she must wait to obtain justice because the killer is out of reach.

Being involved in a shooting is a traumatic event for a police officer. In *Sunrise* (1994), Chassie West's D.C. police officer, Leigh Ann Warren, has come back to her hometown in North Carolina to recuperate and to decide if she can go on being a police officer. In the prologue, she recalls the incident during which she and her partner, "Duck" (Dillon Upshur Kennedy), were wounded:

> The kid was going to shoot me; that was a given. He had nothing to lose; he'd already shot one cop. Duck, fellow crimefighter, car pool partner, friend, sat slumped at the kid's feet, his back against the wall, a pool of blood widening around him [p. 1].

Leigh Ann ("tired, evil, and I wanted to go home") barreled into the apartment building to find out what was keeping Duck, who went to see his sister (p.1). She found herself looking "down the barrel of a ridiculously small nickel-plated revolver aimed right at my head" (p. 2). Both she and Duck survived, but she already had lost someone close to her to violence. Her fiancée, an undercover cop, was killed the night after they became engaged, and now she and her partner have been shot. She explains to her foster mother, Nunna, why she became a police officer:

> ... Aside from you and Mrs. Totten [school principal], the people I've admired the most were policemen. A beat cop saved my life. He ran into our apartment building to warn people that it was on fire. He found me in the stairwell full of smoke and carried me out. There was nothing he could do for Mom and Dad [p. 35].

When Nunna says she heard the story of her family's death from Leigh Ann's cousins, Leigh Ann says she could never talk about it before because of "survivor guilt" (p. 35). She went to law school because everyone had such high expectations of her. But after her fiancé was killed, she "realized that life's too short to waste trying to fulfill other people's expectations." She joined the police force right after law school (p. 35).

A minority of African American protagonists, female police officers born into a police family are even rarer. In Judith Smith-Levin's series, Lt. Starletta Duvall's father was a much-admired and respected police officer who was killed on duty. In R. Barrie Flowers' *Justice Served* (2005), Nina Parker, the daughter of a cop, has been a homicide detective for seven years:

> Nina Parker had known she wanted to be a policewoman since she was five years old, which was her earliest memory of her father as a cop with the Detroit Police Department. When the family moved to the Pacific Northwest after her father retired, she kept her own dream alive, entering the police academy in Portland at twenty-one. By the time she was twenty-five she had been on patrol, done vice, and gotten married and divorced [p. 29].

This description of a police officer's career path is in contrast to protagonists who join the force and find the working environment intolerable. This may be a temporary state of affairs, as in the case of West's protagonist, Leigh Ann Warren. In *Sunrise* (1994), she tells her foster mother, Nunna, about what drew her to the work, but then notes the negative aspects, "the stress, the emotional tugs-of-war, the daily encounters with malice" (p. 162). But what has brought her to this crisis is what she felt when she shot the kid who shot her partner. What she felt scared her.

> ... that kid became every thief I'd ever had to deal with, every pusher, wife beater, child abuser, rapist, mugger, every piece of garbage I'd soiled my hands with over the last six years. I was an avenger, a female Charles Bronson— [p. 103].

The kid was a pizza delivery man who had been beaten up and robbed three times and mistook her off-duty partner, who was running toward him, for an attacker. The man she shot didn't die, but Leigh Ann experiences the psychological turmoil common to officers involved in shooting incidents. She must deal with emotions she finds unacceptable, but she comes to the realization that she is committed to being a police officer. The work is something she is good at and wants to go on doing.

In contrast, Edwards's Mali Anderson views her time on the NYPD as an error in judgment. Leaving the department — and filing a law suit — she returns to graduate school and becomes a social worker. In *Fear of the Dark* (1988), the reader learns that Gar Anthony Haywood's protagonist Aaron Gunner became a private investigator after he was expelled from the LAPD for "rearranging the face of an overzealous self-defense instructor" (p. 16). Valerie Wilson Wesley's Newark PI, Tamara Hayle, was the only woman and the only African American in the Bevington Heights, New Jersey police department. She resigned after an incident involving the harassment and assault of her son and his friends by officers in the department (*Easier to Kill*, pp. 42–43). She still respects her former boss, the police chief who was her "reluctant" mentor and supporter.

Glenville Lovell's Blade Overstreet decided to go into law enforcement because of his brother's addiction to drugs. In *Love and Death in Brooklyn* (2004), he recalls:

> My thinking was that if I could get rid of all the drug dealers than my brother would be safe. Of course, experience quickly snuffed out those romantic notions.... It became about the chase, outwitting and outthinking the dealers.... It became more about inflicting pain and punishment on barbaric men and women who didn't care who they hurt in their thirst for money ... [p. 293].

Overstreet left the NYPD after settling a $2.5 million civil-rights violation suit. He is now owns a music store (with a partner from Trinidad) and is an investor in a nightclub (p. 10). However, his wife, an actress, who has returned to him is still unsure about their relationship. She wonders if he has gotten the violence of the NYPD out of his system or if it is his nature (p. 131).

Another protagonist who joined the police department to pursue a particular group of offenders, John Ridley's Soledad "Bullet" O'Roark is a member of the LAPD's elite M-Tac squad. In *Those Who Walk in Darkness* (2003), mutants with superpowers have appeared on earth. The superheroes were welcomed initially as protectors. As a young Black girl growing up in Wisconsin, Soledad was thrilled when, "the Nubian Princess," a Black female superhero, appeared:

> Tough, proud, and as costumes go she actually had fashion sense. To me she was a symbol and an inspiration, and I wanted nothing more in the world than to be like her [p. 35].

When a battle between superheroes and supervillians destroyed the city of San Francisco, the disillusioned and angry non-mutant humans turned against the mutants. An adult Soledad joined the LAPD, qualified for the high-risk, special tactical unit, and has now turned her efforts to create a special weapon that will destroy even the intangibles, mutants with the power to disappear.

Another protagonist with a mission, Luther Green in Gary Hardwick's *The Executioner's Game* (2005), is a government assassin. Among "the best and the brightest," he was recruited by the government when he graduated from West Point. He is pragmatic about what he does, the fact that he is a "killing machine":

> Luther believed in America, but he was practical about it. If his country wasn't the leader of the world, another country would have assumed that position, and it would be no less protective of its interests. A true patriot knew that everything in life was the lesser of two evils.
> This was how he and the other E-1 agents justified their occupation. The men and women they eliminated were plagues on humanity [p. 70].

When Luther becomes aware of unapproved activities being carried out by operatives within the government, he is designated a rogue agent. He goes in search of another agent who can provide him with crucial information. That agent has been hiding out in East Baltimore. As Luther tells the colleague who is helping him, "The ghetto is a no-man's land to the government. Alex taught me that at E-1" (p. 80).

Among the non-law enforcement professionals and the amateur sleuths, the fate of the world is usually not at stake. In the case of sleuths who are not criminal justice professionals or in professions that involve them in criminal investigations, there are often several reasons for getting involved. Such strong motivation is expected by readers of the genre, who are willing to suspend their disbelief, but who also prefer sleuths to have good reasons for taking on often dangerous investigations rather than leaving them to the professionals. The amateur sleuth may be seeking answers to questions from his/her own past or present, or aiding a friend or loved one who is in jeopardy. Ideally, if genre readers are to be satisfied, the modern amateur sleuth is motivated by more than curiosity.

Distrust of the police motivates some African American protagonists to get involved in criminal investigations. Such sleuths include Grace Edwards' Mali Anderson, in present-day Harlem, and Cassandra Lisle, the 1960s college student protagonist of Charlotte Carter's Cook County series. Whatever their opinion of law enforcement, the sleuths are also motivated by personal situations. In Grace F. Edwards' *The Viaduct* (2004), Marin Taylor, a Vietnam vet in 1970s Harlem, searches for his kidnapped infant. In Stephen L. Carter's *The Emperor of Ocean Park* (2002), Talcott Garland, an Ivy League law professor needs to solve the puzzling message left him by his father, a judge who might have been murdered. In Yolanda Joe's *Video Cowboys* (2006), television newswoman Georgia Barnett has to find the daughter of the man who has taken hostages in a bank because her camera man is among those being held. In Norman Kelley's *The Big Mango* (2000), series protagonist, Nina Halligan, has a chance to avenge the murders of her husband and children. In *A Landlord's Tale* (2005), Gammy Singer's protagonist Amos Brown, is drawn into a criminal investigation when a skeleton is found in the wall of one of the apartment buildings that he inherited from the father from whom he was estranged. In Gary Phillips's *Shooter's Point* (2001), casino courier Martha Chainey is not pleased when she finally acknowledges what is driving her to find out who was behind two shootings:

> Until she'd said it, the courier hadn't been forced to articulate what it was about the murder that had gotten to her. But she knew, and was bothered by the answer. "When I saw her body in that economy room, Victoria, alone and far from home, two nasty holes in her, it was me" [p. 219].

Although his career as a sleuth begins as a matter of financial necessity, Walter Mosley's Easy Rawlins, acquires a reputation as an investigator and trouble-shooter for people in his community. In *A Red Death* (1991), the second book in the series, Easy says:

> People would come to me if they had serious trouble but couldn't go to the police. Maybe somebody stole their money or their illegally registered car.... I settled disputes that would have otherwise come to bloodshed. I had a reputation for fairness and the strength of my convictions among the poor. Ninety-nine out of a hundred black folk were poor back then, so my reputation went quite a way [p. 5].

By the third book, *White Butterfly* (1992), Easy has settled into his identity as a detective:

> In my time I had done work for the numbers runners, church-goers, businessmen, and even the police. Somewhere along the line I had slipped into the role of a confidential agent who represented people when the law broke down. And the law broke down often enough to keep me busy. It even broke down for the cops sometimes [Mosley, pp. 9–10].

Panek (2000) observes that Easy Rawlins, an originally reluctant detective, "develops tradecraft from his sociability, his wide acquaintance in his community, his intelligence and knowledge, and from his capacity for subterfuge" (p. 198). His reward for doing what he does is "a wage and some approbation from his community as well a measure of recognition from the police who come to him to help solve crimes in Watts" (p. 198). But, as Panek observes, being a detective is not without cost, it "becomes increasing painful and stressing to Easy" to play "a dual role" (p. 198).

Sleuthing may be stressful. However, as M.C. Wesley (2003) observes, because of the historical restriction of acquisition of knowledge by African Americans, "The violation of this restriction is certainly one of the major appeals of the Black detective novel" (p. 123). A motivation common to African American protagonists is the desire to acquire knowledge and use it to resolve the disruption caused by the crime in a fashion that seems just. More than other detectives perhaps, they are concerned with the possibility that those with power are not only corrupt but malevolent.

The protagonists as a group display an aptitude for dealing with the situations caused by criminal events. This is true of characters as diverse as Mosley's ex-prisoner protagonist Socrates Fortlow in *Always Outnumbered, Always Outgunned* (1998) and Nora DeLoach's small town social worker in her "Mama" series. Fortlow is a man trying to find his place in the world after spending much of his adult life in prison for murder. Nora DeLoach's protagonist, Grace "Mama" Covington, has been compared by reviewers to fictional sleuths, Miss Marple and Jessie Fletcher. As her daughter Simone explains, her mother's interest in crime began as a game that they would play to amuse themselves when they were traveling the world as a military family. Now, as a social worker and good neighbor, Mama puts her skills to use. In *Mama Stalks the Past* (1997), Simone relates:

> Although Mama loves helping people, I know that her real passion is digging up bits and pieces until she's solved a mystery, and there is nobody better at doing that. Long ago, I don't remember when, Mama decided that if we could get at the truth of a problem, we would have made a contribution to humankind ... [pp. 32–33].

In more elite settings, Pamela Thomas-Graham's protagonist Nikki Chase, becomes involved in murder investigations in the Ivy League universities where she teaches and visits. She acknowledges that she has begun to take seriously her reputation as a "Nancy Drew"—even though her sleuthing activities could jeopardize her chances of receiving tenure in the economics department at Harvard.

For Nikki Chase and the other protagonists becoming involved in an investigation may involve not only career risks, but physical and psychological dangers as well. Protagonists who are police officers have partners and are able to call on the services of other criminal justice professionals and civilian experts. Protagonists who are PIs and amateur sleuths need people who will provide backup.

Sidekicks and Social Networks

Kelly (1998) observes that one of the issues for the fictional detective is "whom and on what basis" he or she can trust the "various persons encounter[ed]" (p. 111). In an uncertain world, a detective finds it useful to have a reliable ally in carrying out required tasks. One of the most problematic relationships in the mystery genre exists between Walter Mosley's protagonist, Easy Rawlins, and his childhood friend Raymond "Mouse" Alexander. Schwartz (2002) calls Mouse "Easy's violent, homicidal guardian agent" (p. 63). In contrast, in Mosley's other series, Paris Minton, a mild-mannered bookseller has as his sidekick Fearless Jones, a World War II veteran and hero.

Among the sidekicks are two daughters, who are their mother's "Watsons." As noted above in Nora DeLoach's "Mama" series, Simone Covington narrates her mother's exploits. Similarly—but more reluctantly—Theresa Holloway in Terris McMahan Grimes plays this role for her mother. In the first paragraph of *Somebody Else's Child*, (1996), Theresa tells the reader that her mother "has always been rather excitable."

> What can I say, she's my mother and I love her. But the truth of the matter is, she gets into other people's business and she gets carried away in the process. Now, I'm fully aware of Mother's excesses, and I try to stay clear when I sense she's getting ready to go off the deep end, but somehow I always manage to get sucked right in ... [p. 9].

In Robert Greer's series set in Denver, bail bondsman and occasional bounty hunter, CJ Floyd has a strong social network of people who he can call on. They include Julie Madrid, his former assistant, now lawyer, and his former assistant, now partner, Flora Jean Benson. When he is in need of additional backup, CJ relies on two broken-down ex-rodeo stars and a legendary ranch foreman, Billy DeLong (who perhaps comes closest to the traditional frontier image of a "sidekick"). During the course of the series, CJ also has established relationships with a young motorcycle-riding doctor, who escaped from Vietnam with her aunt, and the white-water expedition leader who is now the doctor's husband. Floyd's network also includes a retired Italian organized crime boss who is a fellow collector of Western memorabilia.

Preferring the tried and true sisterhood of women, Norman Kelley's Nina Halligan relies on the "Bad Girls," who include Anna, her Asian American lawyer. In *A Phat Death* (2003), the degree to which these women and their associates are organized astonishes Nina's new husband, Glen. As they are fleeing their apartment where a young female rap singer has been killed in an explosion, Nina gets on the telephone. She calls a "Code Z," the signal for the people on the Z list to stand by, and then describes her equipment to Glen:

> "Cellular phone. Listening monitor. Handcuffs. Protocols. Two 9mm pistols," I rattled off. "In the other case are a laptop and an electronic surveillance monitor."

"Pistols?"

"Yes, dear. His-and-her matching set."

"It's that serious, huh?"

"Glen, didn't you see that girl's severed head?"

[She loads her clip in her gun as he drives the car].

"You folks are really organized, huh?" he finally said, perspiration forming on his forehead.

"Yep. Some of us aren't sitting around and waiting for affirmation action programs to continue," I replied. "We've *read* and *know* our history" [pp. 89–90].

Although less well-equipped for violent action and less concerned about geo-politics, the circle of sidekicks that surround Karen Grigsby Bates' sleuth, Alex Powell, are effective in her world. These women include two close friends who are journalists, her aunt, and the wealthy White matron who owns the guest house in which Alex lives. These women know the ins-and-outs of Los Angeles society and have contacts across the country.

Lovers and spouses who work in criminal justice constitute another class of allies (or restraints). Gary Philips's PI, Ivan Monk, lives with Japanese-American judge, Jill Kodama. He depends on her for sensible legal advice. Frankie Y. Bailey's protagonist, Lizzie Stuart, is involved with John Quinn, homicide cop turned university police chief. Grace Edward's protagonist Mali Anderson considers meeting her police detective boyfriend, Tad Honeywell, the one good thing that came out of her time on the NYPD.

In general, the sidekicks and other dependable allies in their lives help the African American protagonist to negotiate treacherous ground. Still, for African American protagonists, sleuthing-related stress is complicated by social status. These protagonists require havens.

Safe Spaces

In the novels of African American mystery writers, the protagonists generally have "safe spaces." This phrase is used by Patricia Hill Collins in *Black Feminist Thought* (1990, p. 97). Collins defines these spaces as "places where black women 'speak freely' and where domination does not exist as a 'hegemonic ideology'" (Griffin, 1995, pp. 8–9). In Collins's conception, safe spaces include "extended families, churches, and African American community organizations, as well as cultural traditions like the black women's blues and literary traditions" (Griffin, p. 9). As Griffin notes, some apparently safe institutions may not be safe for all (e.g., homosexuals or women who seek abortions) because safe spaces "can be very conservative spaces as well" (p. 9). In the novels examined here, safe spaces are both physical and psychological. They are sought by men as well as women. We will return to this topic in the next chapter in the context of setting. However, we should look here at physical spaces in relation to the protagonists.

Modern African American sleuths move through spaces and across boundaries much more freely than in the past. They may feel at home in spaces that are popular locales enjoyed by others of similar age, class, and/or gender. Kyra Davis's sleuth, Sophie Katz, a thirty-something, single woman, who is a native of San Francisco, finds sanctuary in her favorite Starbucks with a newspaper and a Grande Caramel Brownie Frappuccino. Other African American protagonists patronize businesses that are Black-owned but that attract a diverse mix of clientele. In Angela Henry's Kendra Clayton series, Kendra's uncle owns Estelle's, a restaurant located near a college campus in Willow, Ohio, that attracts students, staff, and faculty. In Frankie Y. Bailey's Lizzie Stuart series, set in a Virginia university town, the Orleans Café, owned by Miss Alice, a Black matriarch, brings together a cross-section of the town's population.

For those protagonists with roots in the African American community (living and/or working there), the safe spaces that they seek are often located in that community. Robert Greer's CJ Floyd often can be found at Mae's Louisiana Kitchen, the restaurant owned by his lady friend, Mavis Sundee, and her father. This restaurant is an institution in Black Denver. Occasionally, the Black protagonist has his own business over which he exercises control. Gary Phillips's Los Angeles PI, Ivan Monk, owns a doughnut shop where he has an office and interacts with his with his employees and regular customers. In Teddy Hayes's series, after his father is killed at his bar, former CIA agent, Devil Barnett comes home to run the Be-Bop Tavern.

Of course, the places that serve as sanctuaries for the sleuth can be intruded upon. At one point in Robert Greer's series, Mavis Sundee's restaurant is blown up by a woman on a vendetta. In *The Devil's Backbone* (1998), Mavis is twelve months into the rebuilding process. In less spectacular fashion, in Kyra Davis's *Sex, Murder, and a Double Latte* (2005), Sophie Katz has her recuperative ritual disrupted when a man she finds both irritating and intriguing comes into her favorite Starbucks. He takes the last copy of the *New York Times* that she intended to read while she drank her coffee. When she informs him of this, he refuses to surrender the newspaper. His physical and psychological intrusion into her space marks this man as someone who requires watching. He might be a potential lover or he could be the unknown person who has been re-enacting scenes from one of her own murder mysteries.

Often the protagonist's hangout doubles as a setting where the protagonist can learn what he or she needs to know about what is going on in the community in the present or what happened in the past. In *I Heard It Through the Grapevine* (1994), Turner finds that in real life, rumors—information received on the communal "grapevine" in the Black community—can be both incorrect and unfounded. In detective fiction, the sleuth learns over time about the reliability of a source. Grace Edward's Mali Anderson places great reliance on the information she receives from the owner of her favorite beauty shop/hangout. In *Do or Die* (2001), Mali describes her friend Bertha, who she have known for two decades, as "a reliable source of street news, gossip, and any scandal worth repeating" (p. 23). Bertha owns a beauty salon and the news on the grapevine comes to her:

> It flows automatically as early as 7 A.M., when the regulars from Miss Laura's luncheonette arrive with breakfast and news hotter than grits. This is the early edition followed by periodic updates. Then the after work crowd wraps it up in the evening [p. 23].

As will be discussed in the next chapter, beauty shops and other businesses (institutions) provide a place where the protagonist and others in the community can connect. However, as Griffin (1995) points out, African American enclaves are not always safe spaces. Conflicts related to class, gender, and sexuality may intrude. Paradoxically, a temporary "safe space" may be created even in a setting that the protagonist finds discomforting. In Barbara Neely's *Blanche among the Talented Tenth* (1995), Blanche White, who is out of place at an elite Black summer resort, finds solace when she engages in "heart talk" with another woman. Such female conversations contain personal revelations that signal good intentions (p. 95).

The question the protagonist must ask of any place is whether the safety is real or an illusion.

Conclusions

Whether amateur or paid, African American sleuths respond when a crime occurs. They believe, or come to believe, that they are the ones who should or must take action. The genre requires that the sleuth be motivated in order to have a convincing reason for acting. In the cases of African American sleuths who are not law enforcement officers or private investigators, the motivation often comes from a lack of faith in the ability of the criminal justice system to achieve an appropriate result. African American amateur sleuths may well have this in common with other sleuths. However, for the African American sleuth this lack of faith is often based on his or her assessment of historical and contemporary evidence of institutionalized racism and/or neglect on the part of the police and the courts in dealing with cases involving Black citizens as victims and/or alleged offenders.

Those protagonists who are not sworn law enforcement officers face obstacles as they go about their sleuthing. Terris McMahan Grimes' protagonist, Theresa Holloway has a demanding day job and a family as well as a mother who expects her assistance. For those sleuths who are private investigators, there is the problem common to the self-employed business person—finding paying clients. Valerie Wilson Wesley's Newark PI, Tamara Hayle, is a working woman with a teenage son and a battered car. She is always in search of the client that will, as she says in *Easier to Kill* (1999), provide her with the "professional boost" that she needs (p. 20):

Although I am thankful for anybody I can get, I know I am the last stop for many of my clients. They usually end up coming to me because the legal system has done them wrong, and they don't have enough money to go anywhere else [pp. 20–21].

When she is hired by a radio personality, Tamara hopes that this new client will refer her to others like the client who "pay their bills quickly and discretely" (p. 21). Tamara is tired of "chasing down dollars from deadbeats." However, she feels some sympathy for her non-paying clients. She is chasing them down, "knowing even as I chased just how tough meeting those bills can be" (p. 21).

Whoever the protagonists are, whatever their background, social, and economic status, what sees to unite them as a group is their commitment — sometimes grudging and reluctant in the beginning — to follow the case through to the end. Arguably, this is one of the characteristics that they have in common with other genre protagonists. The question is whether their own backgrounds and experiences affect how these protagonists go about seeing the case through to the end. This matter of "doing justice" will be discussed in greater detail in Chapter 7. The next chapter focuses on the social location of crime in works by African American authors.

Place, Crime, and Community

Our City is wide open tonight, at the mercy of people who [don't know][78] right from wrong.
— L.A. TV anchor, 4/29/92

This is the quote that appears on the fly leaf of Gary Phillips's *Violent Spring* (1994), featuring PI Ivan Monk. It is an example of the mainstream media's coverage of the rioting in Los Angeles that followed the acquittal of the White police officers involved in the videotaped beating of Black motorist, Rodney King. The "people" referred to by the TV anchor are the African Americans and Latinos who took to the streets when the verdict was announced. After analyzing the media coverage of the riots in Los Angeles, Bridges (1992) concludes:

> The media fanned the flames of racial and ethnic unrest between blacks and whites, blacks and Latinos, and other groups by reducing complex events to short phrases which were then repeated again and again in news stories. These phrases or key descriptors were often misleading [quoted in Ramaprasad, 1996, p. 79; see also Jacobs, 1996].

The 1992 riot was not the first time civil unrest had occurred in the streets of Los Angeles. In 1943, there had been the "Zoot Suit Riots," involving attacks by off-duty military men on young Chicanos wearing the suits that were than a fad among young Black and Chicano men (Cosgrove, 2005; Alford, 2004). Those riots went on for several days, uncontrolled by the police. In 1965, the Watts riot — triggered by a police stop of a motorist — "thirty-four deaths, 1,032 injuries, over 4,000 arrests, and an estimated $40 million in property damage" (Jacobs, 2000; see also Joiner, 2005, p. 9). Many African American observers viewed the 1965 Watts riot as a warning about the potential for uprisings in inner city communities. They linked the riots to the dominant society neglect of these communities (including poor schools, inadequate health care, and high rates of unemployment) that would be described in the Kerner Commission Report (1968).[79]

In Phillips's *Violent Spring* (1994) the plan to build a shopping complex at the intersection of Florence and Normandie (site of the real-life beating of White truck driver Reginald Denny)[80] is sidelined by the discovery of the body of a Korean American merchant during the ground-breaking ceremony. In a savvy political move—given the tensions between Blacks and Korean Americans[81]—the Korean American Merchants Group hires PI Ivan Monk to investigate the matter.

Paula L. Woods sets her *Inner City Blues* (1998) in Los Angeles during this same political moment. Woods' protagonist, Charlotte Justice, is the only African American woman, one of the two women, in the LAPD Robbery-Homicide unit. Justice lives in racially-torn L.A. and works in a police department that is notorious for its brutality and arrogance toward racial minorities.[82] By her mere presence, Charlotte Justice is engaged in a subversive challenge to the status quo. In this first book in the series, Justice is faced with solving a murder that occurs in the midst of the urban chaos.

Commenting on what urban life symbolized for Black migrants from the South and the subsequent deterioration of Black communities, Massood writes:

> While once promising freedom from the Jim Crow laws and rural poverty of the South, the city began to show the wear and tear of economic depression, segregation, and racial prejudice, and the mecca soon became a ghetto. This was reflected in the literary output of writers of the post–Renaissance period such as Richard Wright, Ralph Ellison, and James Baldwin and has continued to be examined throughout the following decades by more contemporary writers (for example, Donald Goines, Paule Marshall, Louis Meriwether, and Walter Mosley) ... [1996, p. 86].

The last named author, Walter Mosley, is an heir to another tradition in American writing—that of hardboiled detective fiction. In *Imagining Los Angeles* (2000), David Fine observes, "In the 1990s fiction of Gar Anthony Haywood, Gary Phillips, and Walter Mosley the African-American detective operating in Watts and South Central Los Angeles has come to represent a significant component of the local tough guy novel" (p. 144). In *Farewell, My Lovely* (1940), when Raymond Chandler's PI Philip Marlowe and gigantic ex-con Moose Malloy enter Florian's, a once–White, now Black-owned club, Marlowe describes the patrons from a White man's perspective:

> Eyes looked at us, chestnut colored eyes, set in faces that ranged from gray to deep black. Heads turned slowly and the eyes in them glistened and stared in the dead alien silence of another race [Chandler, p. 145].

In *Devil in a Blue Dress* (1990), Mosley describes a similar scene—but this time from the perspective of a Black protagonist. Easy Rawlins relates:

> I was surprised to see a white man walk into Joppy's bar. It's not just that he was white but he wore an off-white linen suit and shirt with a Panama straw hat and bone shoes flashing white silk socks.... He stopped in the doorway, filling it with his large frame, and surveyed the room with pale eyes; not a color I'd ever seen in a man's eyes ... [p. 9].

The geography of "moral space" (see e.g., Whitehead, 2003) that African American mystery writers employ tends to be rooted in Afrocentric interpretations of race, class, and gender interactions that occur in the settings described. That is, the African American protagonist looks at the world with a "Black gaze" as opposed to the "White gaze" of protagonists such as Philip Marlowe.[83] The Black protagonist tends to perceive crime, criminals, and the criminal justice system in the larger context of American social history. Commenting on the connections of memory, self, and place, Lewis (1995) writes:

> for the period 1910–1945, many black residents lived in an almost all-black world, one shaped but not totally defined by limited interaction with whites. In such a world, notions about power changed. In churches, on windowsills, street corners, or other places of congregation, African Americans sermonized, joked, sang, and for moments at a time altered power relations. More important, in these settings concepts like minority, difference, and other meant something other than what we have come to accept. When read from inside the black community outward, place helped resituate the colored "other" [p. 359].

In Mosley's *Devil in a Blue Dress* (1990), the place is Los Angeles in 1948. Easy Rawlins lives in a segregated city, but his own perspective has been affected by his wartime and post-war experiences. He is surprised when a White man walks into Joppy's bar, but not cowered by his presence: "When he looked at me I felt a thrill of fear, but that went away quickly because I was used to white people by 1948" (Mosley, 1990, p. 9). This is just as well because Easy is about to find himself working for this White man, Mr. Albright. Albright needs a Black man who can go where he cannot, to look for the missing fiancée of a wealthy politician, a White woman who frequents Black jazz joints. Easy takes the job because he has a mortgage and has lost his job at Champion Aircraft.

In this first book in the series, Mosley introduces Easy Rawlins as a Black migrant who has come to Los Angeles from Houston. Like some other — and earlier — migrants to urban areas, he is fleeing trouble at home. In Easy's case, the trouble is in the form of his dangerous friend Mouse. But, like other migrants, Easy also has come seeking the opportunities to be found in this city. He has been able to buy a house, and he wants to keep it. As he explains, "Maybe it was that I was raised on a sharecropper's farm or that I had never owned anything until I bought that house, but I loved my little house" (p. 19).

But Easy has found that although it is possible to achieve a part of his American dream in Los Angeles, there are some familiar restrictions. His aircraft factory job was "an awful lot like working on a plantation in the South" (p. 69):

> The white worker would just say, "Sure, Benny, you called it right...." And Benny would have understood that.... But the Negro workers didn't drink with Benny. We didn't go to the same bars. We didn't wink at the same girls [p. 69].

M. C. Wesley (2003) asserts, "Easy's situation rewrites Chester Himes's *If He Hollers* (1945) in which self-respect is not an alternative for protagonist Bob

Jones, who loses his job at Atlas, a Los Angeles shipyard" (p. 126). As he struggles to maintain his pride, Jones is caught up in "an escapable cycle of personal anxiety and possible violence" (p. 126). In Mosley's characterization of Easy Rawlins, World War II has opened up "new options of limited inclusion, the possibility of black male 'respect' and 'freedom'" (Wesley, p. 127).

In *Devil in a Blue Dress* (1990) and subsequent books in the series, Easy takes readers into a world that was alien to the protagonists of White writers such as Chandler and, later, Mickey Spillane. In *One Lonely Night* (1951), Spillane writes:

> Here was the edge of Harlem, that strange no-man's-land where the white mixed with the black and the languages overflowed into each other like that of the horde and the Tower of Babel. There were strange, foreign smells of cooking and too many people in too few rooms. There were the hostile eyes of children who became suddenly silent as you passed [p. 134, quoted in Crooks, 1995, p. 4].

This urban frontier that Spillane describes is one in which the White detective is subject to the hostile gaze of the poor, the foreign, Blacks and Whites, who mix in this border land. According to the myth of American success, what they all have in common is the "American dream" of assimilation and mobility. The life that Easy Rawlins creates for himself in Los Angeles is light years away from the world that he fled after his violent sidekick Mouse involved him in murder (see *Gone Fishin,'* 1998). But Easy is not fully assimilated into the American mainstream. As a detective, he is still required to function along the liminal boundaries that exist between Black and White in Los Angeles. Regarding these boundaries, Bunyan (2003) also compares Easy Rawlins to Raymond Chandler's PI, Philip Marlowe. Easy lacks the "invisibility" that makes Marlowe "self-sufficient":

> ... Marlowe can move freely through the territories of the criminals and the police because he is in possession of knowledge.... Mosley shows Easy slowly becoming aware of the many ways in which he is vulnerable, the ways in which he is never absolutely outside people's territories, never in extra-legal space ... [p. 5].

Bunyan refers here to Easy's first essay into sleuthing in *Devil in a Blue Dress* (1990). In this initial adventure, Easy begins to acquire the skills that he needs in order to operate outside the system and in hostile territory. As Wesley (2003) puts it, Easy has "a series of mentors" who teach him "about the levels and types of violent power" (p. 123). He learns more about violence and power with each book in the series.

In *Little Scarlet* (2005), Easy Rawlins describes the aftermath of the 1965 Watts riot —"a five-day eruption of rage that had been simmering for centuries" (p. 3). After several days, stunned-looking people are beginning to venture back into the street:

> There was the smell of smoking in the building too, but not much. Steinman's Shoe Repair was the only store that had been torched. That was the first night,

> when the fire trucks still braved the hails of sniper bullets. The flames were put
> out before they could spread [p. 5].

Valerie Wesley Wilson's PI, Tamara Hayle was a child in the 1960s, growing up with her older brother, Johnny. In *When Death Comes Stealing* (1994), she recalls Newark, New Jersey before the riots:

> ... Johnny used to talk about how Broad Street stretched out — grand movie theaters, department stores, big-time musicians playing Newark *first*, and you couldn't make it down the streets on a Saturday night. But everything changed after the '67 riots.
>   I grew up in the Central Ward, the Hayes Homes. I was ten when the cops beat up some cabbie right around the corner from where I lived, and word had it that they killed him ... [p. 23].

This was the trigger for the rioting that followed. When the riots were over, "nothing was the same. All the money left, the big bucks, and the little." Tamara's parents moved their family to East Orange. But an adult Tamara came back because she is "a Newark girl at heart, always will be" (Wilson, 1994, p. 23).

Memory and Cultural Vernacular

In *Habits of the Heart* (1986), Bellah et al. assert that there is an American "culture of memory" made up of shared events (such as the urban riots of the 1960s), rituals, and holidays. Within this national culture, racial/ethnic groups possess their own unique cultures of memory. This explains the title — "What To The Slave Is The Fourth Of July?" — abolitionist Frederick Douglass gave to a speech he was asked to deliver in 1852. He answers his own question, "a day that reveals to him, more than all other days of the year, the gross injustice and cruelty to which he is the constant victim" (Douglass, 2005). Douglass was commenting on the fact that when White Americans celebrated their "Independence Day" in 1776, slaves like himself remained in bondage. In the aftermath of the Civil War, African Americans created their own holiday, "Juneteenth," to celebrate the day in 1865 when slaves in the Southwest learned that they had been emancipated.

In the *Blues Detective* (1996), Soitos discusses the use of African American cultural vernacular by Black mystery writers. Fouché (2006) writes, "The black vernacular tradition is primarily associated with the production or performance of music, dance, literature, visual art, and sport" (p. 641). However, as scholars have observed the rituals of food/cooking, dress/style, and even grief are also moments in which production and performance of Black vernacular traditions occurs.[84] In *The Signifying Monkey* (1988), his often-cited volume on African American literary criticism, Henry Louis Gates, Jr., observes, "Whereas black writers most certainly revise texts in the Western tradition, they often seek to do so 'authentically,' with a black difference, a compelling sense of difference based on the black vernacular" (p. 342, quoted in Napier, 2000, pp. 339–347).

In the mystery/detective genre, this practice of difference occurs within the context of place. As Kadonaga (1998) observes, the sleuth in the act of solving a mystery must frequently reconstruct "the complex movement of individuals through space and time ... geography is often a central element in mysteries, even if the author did not intend it to be" (p. 2). Writing about the role of setting in mystery novels, Porter (1981) observes:

> A crime always occurs and is solved in a place that, depending on the tradition in which an author is working, will be evoked with more or less precision, and writers of detective novels are in the realist tradition insofar as they have always tended to anchor crime in a specific location and in certain milieus and social strata [p. 73, quoted in Howell, 1998, p. 3].

One aspect of place in African American literature is the presence of the South even in works set in other regions of the country. The South is the region from which Black migrants departed and the locale that lives on in memory. Page (1999) observes that in contemporary African American novels, whether Southern locales are "literal or metaphorical":

> evocation of the scenes, language, and customs of the rural South is a nostalgic attempt by the novelist and often by their characters, to retain in the contemporary northern city crucial elements of the African-American culture, framed in the rural southern past ... [p. 9].

Especially valued is the sense of communal life found "down home" in the South. In the face of enduring White ambivalence and distrust, wherever they have gone African Americans have created safe spaces/places for themselves shaped by Black vernacular.

Gathering Places

Writing of social spaces in general, Oldenburg (1989) describes what he calls "third places" or "great good places." Such places are neither home nor the workplace, but other places where people find sociability and fellowship. Historically, "great good places" in African American communities have served to strengthen communal ties among individuals by providing gathering places in which a range of activities could occur. Barbershops, beauty parlors, pool halls, neighborhood taverns and restaurants are recognized as such places. Ethnographers have identified the rituals of conduct and etiquette that guide the behavior of the regulars and the process by which a stranger becomes a member of the group. Ethnographers also have studied the forms of discourse that occur in beauty shops (Majors, 2003; Phillips, 2001), barbershops (Marberry, 2005; Abbott, 1992), and taverns (May, 2000).

The beauty shops and barber shops where African Americans are groomed and pampered to face the world are often Black-owned spaces where Whites seldom venture and customers feel free from White surveillance. Conversations in these shops are significant not only for their content but for their language and structure. In her research on "shop talk" in beauty parlors, Majors (2003) found that the speaker "engage[s] in a sharing of personal experience, often in narrative form" (p. 297). Women in Black beauty salons assume roles that include "*stylist, medical expert, teacher*, and *analyst*, as well as a variety of client types" (p. 297). In this setting both problem-solving and the exchange of knowledge occurs (p. 298). Friendships develop and are nurtured. Examining female relationships, Hughes & Heuman (2006) found that the Black women they studied maintained friendships with other Black women by communicating in ways that conferred a "sense of solidarity." They used "black vernacular" and they engaged in "authentic" communication.

In the works of African American mystery writers, time spent in beauty shops (or barbershops) also involves learning about or staying connected with what is occurring in the community. In *Blue Blood* (1999), an entry in Pamela Thomas-Graham's series, protagonist Nikki Chase heads to a beauty shop near an African American church when she needs information about the minister:

> The House of Beauty on Dixwell Avenue reminded me of the hair salon my mother used to take me to when I was growing up: a small glass storefront with a bright pink awning and a sign in the window reading BRAIDS, RELAXERS, PRESS-AND-CURL.... At a half block away, I was counting on at least one of Reverend Leroy's parishioners being a regular customer ... [p. 154].

Nikki finds a customer who has a story to tell that she won't share with the police. She shares it with Nikki there in the beauty shop. Valerie Wilson Wesley's PI Tamara Hayle routinely goes to "Jan's Beauty Biscuit" when she needs to consult her friend Wyvetta Green's grapevine. In *Easier to Kill* (1998), Tamara has a mission. She needs information about three people in her current case:

> I was sure Wyvetta Green could help me answer the questions I had about all three, so I'd stopped by Dunkin' Donuts earlier for two dozen doughnuts and a couple of cups of coffee as an offering. I don't like to call the fact-finding conversations I have at the Biscuit interviews, but that's what they are, and Wyvetta is too sharp to allow herself or her customers to be pumped even discreetly, for information without getting something in return ... [p. 66].

In addition to bringing doughnuts and coffee, Tamara demonstrates her understanding that exchanges of value occur by having her nails done and tipping the manicurist generously, having her hair trimmed, occasionally taking Wyvetta out to lunch, or springing for after-work drinks for whoever wants to come along. Now and then, she even does investigative work for the salon owner based on what Wyvetta can afford to pay (Wesley, 1998. pp. 66–67). Wyvetta and the other beauty shop owners depicted by African American writers are businesswomen in the tradition of the Black female entrepreneurs described by scholars (see e.g., Boyd, 2000; Light & Rosenstein, 1995).

Gar Anthony Haywood's PI Aaron Gunner has his office in the back room of a barbershop. In *All the Lucky Ones are Dead* (2000), the reader learns why this arrangement can be a liability for a private investigator. Potential clients are reluctant to discuss personal matters in a setting where gossip is the order of the day:

> ... where anything said in confidence could be spread to the far corners of the earth by the next rising of the sun. Which was exactly what Mickey's Trueblood Barbershop was, of course. The oddball group of characters who let Mickey clip their hair on a semiregular basis could be counted on for nothing if not the broad and instantaneous dissemination of every word they heard spoken in his establishment ... [p. 26].

Another location for gossip is the neighborhood bar. In Gammy L. Singer's *Down and Dirty* (2006), Amos Brown goes out seeking dinner and information. The regulars get into a discussion about Steadwell, Amos's friend who is suspected of murder. One of the men offers "three cheers for Steadwell" if he did kill Dap, the victim:

> "...Dap wasn't worth the paper it takes to wipe my ass."
> From the other end of the bar someone responded. "Why you say that? That's cold, man. Dap never done nothing to you, did he?"
> "I'm the only one he hasn't done something to."
> Another voice, "Don't believe that nigger — reason Henry's jaw-juicing is because Dap did him in — stole one of his whores right out from under him — ask Sweets, he'll tell you" [pp. 99–100].

Analyzing communication in a real-life tavern, May (2000) found that the regular patrons at Trena's Lounge engaged in "race talk" that had "therapeutic value." The patrons also engaged in "'talking shit'— a stylized, but joking expression of verbal jousting" (May, 2003). In Grace Edwards' *No Time to Die* (1999), protagonist Mali Anderson goes to the Lido Bar on 125th Street in Harlem: "When I stepped in, the barstools on the left were occupied by regulars who didn't swivel an inch when the door opened" (p. 41). Volume down on the television, the regulars are watching "a soundless ball game" (p. 41). Four men in their sixties, "holding court" at a table, tip their hats to Mali as she passes. Taking a seat at the bar, she orders a drink and settles in to "catch the talk of the day" that is "floating above a vintage Joe Williams riff on a jukebox." The regulars are discussing Michael Jackson and O. J. Simpson, both of whom have become isolated from the Black community. They joke about the "industrial-strength suntan lotion" Michael Jackson would need if he decided "to rejoin the tribe" and how O.J. might

> redeem himself in the eyes of black folks now that he was no longer living high on the hog in white heaven, but mostly they ragged Michael.
> "I'm askin' you," a fat man in the group of four said, "did the Man in the Mir-

ror ever look in the mirror? I don't think so. Ghost scare the livin' shit out you, high noon on Times Square" [p. 42].

But one of his table mates objects to the remark, pointing out that Jackson has "more talent in his little toe" than the fat man has in his "whole watermelon head." To which the first speaker responds, "Well, least my watermelon head is black." And it's "nappy," someone at the bar tells him (p. 42).

Such verbal jousting also occurs in barber shops. Gary Phillips illustrates this in a scene from *Only the Wicked* (2000) that takes place in the Abyssinia Barber Shop and Shine Parlor. PI Ivan Monk is one of the customers. The topic is women and sex. When Monk, who has been reading a magazine is asked if he has anything to offer, he responds, "I don't like to be crude, Johnny." But speculation returns to Monk's Merchant Marine experiences in France and Turkey. One of the men observes that Monk is "a circumspect dude":

> "'Cept we talkin' bout the past, man," Patterson exclaimed. He held his smoke in one hand and drank from a bottle of orange juice with the other. "Now, what you hiding, Virgil Tibbs?"
> "I don't want to embarrass you fellas with my—how shall I say it?—my achievements. 'Cause I know how fragile your egos are."
> "Shee-it," Brant exhaled. "That must mean your sorry ass never got off them tubs you were grease monkey on."

The scene achieves two things. First, it shows Monk among other Black men in a situation of camaraderie. The reader has an opportunity to see how Monk is similar to and different from these men. The scene also launches a plot involving one of the men in the barbershop.

Barber shop talk also occurs in Walter Mosley's *Fear Itself* (2003). Bookstore proprietor Paris Minton predicts how the conversation will go in a few days when he drops by the barber shop to play cards. The year is 1955, and a young woman has tried to "pass" for White:

> ... we'd discuss the fate of Lana Tandy, the light-haired, fair-skinned Negro who tried to be the beauty queen of L.A. We'd laugh at the pageant and we'd laugh at her for thinking she could make it that far. Mr. Underwood, the retired porter, would get angry then and tell us that we shouldn't be laughing but protesting like they were doing down south. We'd say, "You're right, George. You're right." And he'd curse and call us fools [pp. 16–17].

Unless Mr. Underwood's given name happened to be "George," the men's response carried a barb. "George" was the name that White railroad passengers often called the Black men who worked as sleeping car porters in the luxury coaches owned by George Pullman (see e.g., Santino, 1991). The fact that the Brotherhood of Sleeping Car Porters, the labor union founded by A. Philip Randolph, was known for its political activism would explain Mr. Underwood's stance and his reference to the younger men as "fools."

Because of his intellectual interests, Paris Minton also finds sanctuary in another communal setting, The Emerald Lounge, "an oasis of sorts in the Negro community." (p. 79). The customers there are different than many he might encounter in the barbershop. Because only classical music is played on the record player by the Jamaican owner, Orrin Nye, the lounge attracts "[m]embers of the church, especially the choir, older ladies who were scandalized by boogie woogie and rhythm and blues, pretentious white-collar professionals and world-weary lovers, mugger, and thieves...." Paris Minton's friend Fearless Jones goes there too, when he is in love (p. 79).

As Brown and Kimball (1995) note there are three areas to which we might profitably attempt to map the terrain of the "black city": civic space and public ritual, conceptualizations of the city, and the moral dimensions of urban space" (p. 297). Describing this terrain in Walter Mosley's *Devil in a Blue Dress* (1990), Coale (2000) writes, "Black men often congregate in bars and barbershops, in pool rooms and on the streets. However marginal their way of life in contrast to the white culture, it has its own rules, clues, customs, and conceits..." (p. 180). Kennedy (1999) writes, "Mosley embeds Easy in local networks of social and cultural relations which play an important part in determining his values and actions" (p. 233). At the same time, Easy is experiencing "a larger and more oppressive system of relations organized by the dominant white world" (Kennedy, p. 233). This might also be said of some of the African American protagonists in modern settings, who also need the rituals and customs of the Black community in order to maintain their equilibrium.

The Faces of Crime and Danger

As discussed above, African American mystery writers often replicate the "talk" that occurs in safe places, the verbal exchanges that scholars have observed in similar real-life settings. Soitos (1996) has observed that the use of language in the mysteries by Black authors is one of their distinctive hallmarks. However, how language is used by a character may be complex. Scholars have identified the phenomenon of "code switching" (see e.g., Greene & Walker, 2004). A speaker may slip into the informal language (or dialect) of family or peers when in their presence; in more formal settings that same speaker may use the language of the classroom or office. Easy Rawlins does this with an awareness that he shares with the reader. In *Devil in a Blue Dress* (1990), he relates:

> I always tried to speak proper English in my life, the kind of English they taught in school, but I found over the years that I could only truly express myself in the natural "uneducated" dialect of my upbringing [p. 10].

Young (1998) describes Easy's code switching as "masking behavior," geared to the situation in which he finds himself (p. 145).

This matter of "proper English" also comes up in Evelyn Coleman's *What a Woman's Gotta Do* (1998). Modern-day protagonist, Atlanta journalist Patricia Conley, a woman given to sharp-eyed and acerbic observations, registers her objections to the way her waitress speaks.

> A different waitress came over and asked me if I'd like a coffee refill. I didn't understand her words at first and it took several repetitions before I got it. I couldn't understand her English and she wasn't a foreigner either. She was speaking what Californians were now calling Ebonics. Well, they hadn't heard Ebonics until they came to Georgia ... [p. 92].

Patricia is thankful that her own grandmother taught her to speak standard English. Her grandmother emphasized "that if you learn how to speak good English and have a solid education, you've won half the battle' (p. 92). Later, en route to a monastery, she is pleased to discover that her taxi driver, "an older black man," is someone "who'd been in Atlanta longer than I had " and speaks without "an accent or the poorest diction you've ever heard." Patricia notes, "You could tell this black man was from the old school. The school where black people knew that it was important to communicate to whites in their language..." (p. 152).

As Patricia Conley implies, the use of language is one of the standards by which African Americans are evaluated by Whites and sometimes by each other. For the African American protagonist — as in real life — the ability to move back and forth across boundaries depends on presentation of self. In their book about the Black image in White America, Entman and Rojecki (2000) write:

> Blacks in American culture are now *liminal* beings, liminal people are by their nature *potentially* polluting, disruptive but not necessarily destructive of the natural order since they are "no longer classified and not yet classified," as Malkki describes the Hutu refugees in Rwanda. Media culture reflects this in its mélange of images, as does the largest segment of the white audience in its mixture of emotions, beliefs, hopes, and fears about Blacks [p. 51].

In Terris McMahan Grimes' *Somebody Else's Child* (1996), protagonist Theresa Galloway, a middle-class, middle manager in a state agency, comments candidly on her fear of crime. Compelled to go out late at night by her mother's urgent call, Theresa tells the reader:

> I may appear to be the intrepid soul sister, but the truth of the matter is, I don't like being out after dark. I've become increasingly paranoid in my old age. Strange children in primary colors make me uneasy, particularly when they start doing peculiar hand signs. I am always on guard for potential muggers and rapists, who as a class, just happen to be partial to the dark. And, I must know the scene of every violent crime committed in Sacramento over the past two decades ... [p. 10].

Although she mentions "[s]trange children in primary colors," Theresa's concern about becoming the victim of a violent crime is free-wheeling, embracing all potential predators. In real-life, African American civil rights activist, the Rev. Jesse Jackson created controversy in 1993 with his statement: "There is nothing more painful to me at this stage in my life than to walk down the street and hear footsteps and start thinking about robbery. Then look around and see somebody White and feel relieved" (quoted in Vedantam, 2005).

The debate about who commits crime and why began in earnest in the late 19th century with the birth of "positivist criminology." Early criminal anthropologists began to collect crude statistical measurements and to theorize based on assumptions about human evolution and a racial hierarchy. In the United States in the late 20th century, media depictions of young Black male "super predators," who were gang members, helped to sustain and perpetuate the image of the Black criminal. "Street crimes" that target strangers are likely to be committed by young males. Young Black males are overrepresented as street crime offenders based on their proportion of the population. They are underrepresented as white-collar and corporate offenders, an area in which wealthy, older White males are the primary offenders (Gabbidon & Greene, 2005). But citizens tend to be more fearful of being mugged than of having their retirement funds embezzled or their water supply polluted. Scholars assert that this is in part due to how the media cover crime (see e.g., Surrette, 2007).

Images of the Black criminal date back to the 19th century South, found not only in newspapers but in "Old South" novels and early films (e.g., *The Birth of a Nation*, 1915). These images have been updated in the context of "law and order" campaigns and the "war on drugs."[85] Fear of crime in urban settings is one of the reasons for both White and Black middle-class flight to the suburbs.[86]

Change and Consequences

Discussing the competing images of the city as "utopia" or "dystopia," Scruggs (1993) observes:

> The city as a symbol of community, of civilization, of home—this image lies beneath the city of brute fact in which blacks in the twentieth century have had to live.... It is one of the aspirations expressed in ongoing dialogue that the Afro-American community has with itself, a dialogue that sets a city of the imagination, the city that one wants against the empirical reality of the city that one has ... [pp. 4–5].

The massive shift in population from rural to urban that occurred in the 20th century brought African Americans into cities that were evolving from modern to post-modern with the accompanying growing pains. In the 19th century, as the pace of immigration from abroad increased, observers described the ethnic succession as one group followed another as residents of urban neighborhoods. In the 20th century, factors such as restrictive covenants, "block-busting," highway construction, urban renewal, White flight, deindustrialization, and gentrification, contributed to the pace and form of neighborhood change. In genre fiction by African American mystery writers, the protagonists and other characters often comment on these changes.

In Gar Anthony Haywood's *Fear of the Dark* (1998), Aaron Gunner sees poverty reflected in the decaying infrastructure of Watts:

> To his way of thinking, pavement was a clear an indicator of a community's well-being as anything that rested above it, and the mutilated tarmac maze of south-central Los Angeles was its most flaring badge of insolvency, a readily available reminder of poverty Gunner didn't need, but could never quite ignore. It said something about the ghetto's place in the heart of City Hall, about the great regard elected officials had for the safety and comfort of the poor ... [pp. 70–71].

In *Love and Death in Brooklyn* (2005), Glenville Lovell's former police detective, Blade Overstreet, also describes the physical signs of community decline in areas of Brooklyn that now "look like wasteland."

> ... a store, a restaurant, an apartment complex; there is something about the scarred face of these buildings, the dingy, dust-covered bricks, the cracked, oiled caked sidewalks that shriek of neglect. Many of these areas are in East Flatbush and East New York, home to many immigrants who become victims of crime [p. 53].

Studying the reactions to violence of real-life inner-city residents in Washington Heights in New York City, Fullilove et al. (1998) found:

> Respondents were depressed by the deteriorating neighborhood, public spaces occupied by drug dealers, stores cluttered by day but shuttered with metal gates at night, and graffiti covering walls and street signs. Drugs were universally held to blame for the deterioration of the neighborhood [p. 5].

The responses of the residents to violence fell along a continuum, from "retreatism," attempts to isolate themselves, to "activism," efforts to stop the violence (p. 6).

In *A Landlord's Tale* (2005), Gammy Singer's protagonist, Amos Walker, tells the reader:

> People I used to deal with every day in my numbers business just weren't civilized anymore, because of drugs. That's why I quit. The criminals and even the cops didn't act like they used to back in the day. Both sides had gone crazy. Street rules were murky ... [p. 6].

In Singer's *Down and Dirty* (2006), Amos has been using up "a lot of energy" in his struggle to hold his ground against drug dealers. Harlem in the 1970s "was a war zone, and good people were leaving":

> Crack houses, like goody-palaces, had surfaced all over Harlem. I'd closed the deal on my third piece of property, another brownstone located just one block over — and the ink hadn't dried before I found out two crack houses, independ-

ent of each other, had set up shop on the same block and were doing thriving business [p. 18].

Across the country and a couple of decades later, In *Bad Night is Falling* (1998), Gary Phillips's Los Angeles PI Ivan Monk is drawn into an apparent gang war when he is hired to investigate the firebombing of a multi-racial housing project. In Austin S. Camacho's *The Troubleshooter* (2004), Hannibal Jones is hired by a White lawyer who wants to create low-income housing. Hannibal must reclaim the apartment building from squatters and hold it against the son of a Italian crime boss who has gone out on his own. Hannibal and the rag-tag team he puts together (with a visit to the soup kitchen where he volunteers) are befriended by the motherly woman who lives next door and her young grandson.

In *The Conjure-Man Dies* (1932), Fisher's characters make references to a community that has experienced demographic changes. Dr. Archer's treatment room was "a butler's pantry in the days before Harlem changed color" (p. 197). In a wry comment, murder suspect Jinx tells his friend Bubber that if he goes to prison for two decades, "Twenty years from now Harlem'll be full o' China-men." (p. 194). In Robert Greer's *Resurrecting Langston Blue* (2005), demo-graphic changes are underway that will help to sustain the community, but will also change the neighborhood's complexion:

> The Points, the core of Denver's black community since early in the twentieth century, was a neighborhood in transition. Urban gentrification and increasing ethnic diversity were becoming more obvious every day. Longtime shades of black were making way for every color in the rainbow [p. 47].

Although in both social science and urban crime fiction, the focus is often on poverty-stricken communities, one aspect of mystery novels by African American writers is that they present the middle and upper middle class African American communities that are also a part of the cityscape and more elite set-ting. In Karen Grigby Bates' *Plain Brown Wrapper* (2001), Alex Powell inves-tigates the murder of a legendary publisher during a Black journalist conference in L.A. She follows the suspects among the Black well-to-do from Los Angeles to Washington, with a stop along the way in Cape Cod. In Paula L. Woods' *Stormy Weather* (2003), Charlotte Justice goes to visit her Uncle Syl, who lives in a large house in an prosperous neighborhood. Even so, Syl and his neigh-bors in this Los Angeles neighborhood are concerned about crime. Charlotte says of her uncle's neighborhood:

> The residents of Lafayette Square, an upper-middle-class, mostly black neighbor-hood southwest of Hancock Park in the Mid-City district, had received permis-sion three years before to erect barriers to stop wholesale cruising down their stately tree-lined streets— and, according to their detractors, to separate them-selves from the hoi polloi just outside the square's half-dozen or so blocks. The riots had made Sylvester Curry and his neighbors look incredibly farsighted ... [p. 169].

But as Charlotte notes, the community has to "bear the brunt of public opinion and the cost of installing and maintaining the barricades" (p. 169). In real-life, in communities across the country, neighborhoods, including those that are ethnically and racially-diverse, have moved to create barriers between themselves and would-be criminals.

In Penny Mickelbury's *Where to Choose* (1999), Carole Ann Gibson is astonished by what is occurring in Jacaranda Estates, the planned community in California where her mother lives:

> She stared in dismay at the destruction before her. The stench of urine was overpowering, even from a distance. The broken beer and wine bottles not withstanding, no child cover ever again play in this sand that held an odor worse than a thousand baby diapers and probably concealed drug needles like land mines [p. 39].

Jacaranda Estates is unique because the founders of the community in the 1950s were a Black man and a Mexican man. Carole Ann remembers the community as a good place to grow up, but now it is under siege.[87]

Small Towns

Although this chapter has focused on urban settings, African American mystery writers also locate their novels in small-town settings. In Chassie West's *Sunrise* (1994), protagonist Leigh Ann Warren describes the small town to which she has returned. The residents have made their yards "immaculate" for a high school reunion, but Leigh Ann observes:

> The black population lived on the west side of Main, the white on the east. East or west, there were only two classes of residents: poor and poorer. There were no mansions in Sunrise ... [p. 22].

Sunrise has only one police officer, Mr. Nehemiah Sheriff, who when he isn't enforcing the law is a farmer (p. 42). Examining coverage of violent events in small towns by big-city newspapers, Frank (2003) finds that in the standard media narrative:

> Small towns are 'sleepy' places where terrible things are not supposed to happen. That is why the residents of small town, all of whom know each other, leave their front doors unlocked and their keys in the ignitions of their cars [p. 207].[88]

Popular images of small town police officers vary by region (e.g., the sheriff in a Deep South town), but small town cops are assumed to be unprepared to deal with violent crime. In reality, Payne, Berg, and Sun (2005) find that rural police officers must deal with "a number of problems that their urban counterparts" do not encounter. Rural officers are required to be "generalists and able to respond to an assortment of departmental and social/community needs" (p. 32). This would describe Nehemiah Sheriff, a secondary but important character, with whom Leigh Ann Warren joins forces in Chassie West's *Sunrise* (1994). Mr. Sheriff appears again to lend a hand in *Killer Riches* (2001) when Leigh Ann's foster mother, Nunna, and Nunna's new husband are kidnapped.

In Eleanor Taylor Bland's series, police detective Marti MacAlister has moved to Lincoln Prairie from Chicago. She is community-oriented, demonstrating awareness of needed services as she goes about her investigations. But, in her small town, doors must be locked and children protected. An article in *USA Today* (12/20/2005) reported that in the first six months of 2004, the homicide rates in some cities with populations of 10,000 or fewer were up 13 percent. Offered explanations from scholars and police officers for "the sudden spike in small-town homicide" included gang activity, illegal drug sales, and "a faltering economy" (p. 03a). In mystery fiction, murders in small towns and country villages are not occasions for surprise.

In small towns, as in big cities, when the norms of the community are violated, murder may follow. In Elaine Meryl Brown's *Lemon City* (2004), the setting is a town in the Blue Ridge Mountains of Virginia that was settled by former slaves. Even though the year is 1973, the town residents still prefer to keep to themselves. Faye, a member of the Dunlap family, has broken the "outsider rule." Harry, the outsider she married, has been murdered. His demise has cast a pall over Thanksgiving dinner:

> Normally when death sneaks up without warning and steals away a family member, the living feel robbed. That wasn't the case with Harry. He was a mean man and had deserved to die, but trouble hadn't died with him, not completely. His demise had raised suspicion about the family, making everyone at the table a suspect ... [p. 17].

As a resident of a small town, the protagonist may be comfortably settled, in as in Nora DeLoach's "Mama" series; may be welcomed back home, as is Chassie West's Leigh Ann Warren; or may realize that even if you can go home again, you may not be able to stay there, as does Barbara Neely's Blanche White. However, in *Blanche Cleans Up* (1999), Blanche notes her preference for her hometown of Farleigh, North Carolina, or for Harlem rather than Boston:

> In either place she could plop herself down and be herself. But she was in Boston now, and the way she was ignored by salesclerks and followed by store security people downtown was just one more sign that this city wasn't putting out the welcome mat for her. Boston didn't seem to allow much room for differences either ... [pp. 91–92].

Conclusions

The people in a community come together in setting where they interact and in the process define the quality of life in that community. One of the features of works by African American mystery writers is that they routinely recreate in their books the community institutions—barber shops, beauty parlors, taverns, and restaurants—where Black people in real life connect with each other. The degree to which the writers replicate the "talk" and the rituals that occur in these settings provide readers who might have little exposure to this side of Black communal life with some sense of the social interactions that occur in these settings.

Because mysteries are about crime, the other aspect of community life that the writers focus on are the situations that give rise to violence. The correlation between community disorganization and rates of crime is well documented in social science research. In poor, inner city communities, some violence grows out of criminal enterprises, such as drug dealing. Other acts of interpersonal violence occur in intimate or social settings. Aggravated assaults and homicides typically involve male-male encounters, often in situations involving alcohol or drugs (e.g., Shihadeh & Flynn, 1996; Oliver, 1994).

In works by African American mystery writers, such violence is often depicted as an aspect of community life. Recall the scene in Rudolph Fisher's *The Conjure-Man Dies* (1932), in which Bubber Brown happens upon a fight between two men prompted by a woman's claim that she was insulted. Such encountered are rooted in age old male beliefs about masculinity, honor, and chivalry played out in an urban setting among men who have suffered racial oppression.[89] Modern mystery writers continue to portray the routine activities of those who engage in crime in poor and racial/ethnic minority communities.

At the same time, reflecting the geographical and social boundary crossing that occurs in modern life, the characters in these works often travel from poor neighborhoods to the gated homes of the wealthy or to small towns. This is not unique in genre fiction. It has been one of the hallmarks of PI fiction since the days of Hammett and Chandler. What is different about this movement in works by African American mystery writers is that it reflects the reality of contemporary African American movement through space.

African American mystery writers recognize that their protagonists, many of whom are middle class, may have much in common with the Black victims and even the offenders that they encounter. The next chapter focuses on the portrayal of victims and offenders in works by African American mystery writers.

6

Victims and Offenders*

In her book about fear of crime in women's lives, *Nothing Bad Happens to Good Girls* (1997), Esther Madriz writes:

> Images of criminals imply that it is strangers who are most likely to do us harm. None of them reflect the reality of violent crime, in which most victims know the perpetrator. With very few exceptions, they do not depict husbands, boyfriends, lovers, or acquaintances as possible predators. Only some few women who reported having been victims of domestic violence said that the typical criminal was someone who abused his partner [p. 111].

Because Madriz was writing a decade ago, one might ask if, in the intervening years, these images have changed. Summing up the present-day media depiction of criminals and crime, Ray Surette (2007) writes:

> Overall, crime is cast in the media within constructions where large differences exist between what the public is likely to experience in reality and what they are likely to gather from the media. Has the portrait changed over time? The portrait of criminals and crimes in the media does display a number of evolutionary trends. Criminals have become more evil, heroes have become more violent, victims have become more innocent, violence has become more graphic, and crimes have become more irrational ... [p. 64].

After media coverage of a number of sensational cases in the 1990s involving alleged "malice domestic," it is possible that the "evil strangers" of popular culture are now rivaled in popular imagination by "evil intimates"—the parents, spouses, and lovers who engage in unspeakable acts. At any rate, whether focused on strangers or intimates as the offenders who prey on innocent victims, this sensationalism is not new (see e.g., Haltttunen, 1998; Bailey

*In the final section of this chapter, it may be necessary to reveal several plot twists or endings in order to illustrate a point. When this occurs, author and title will be provided in an endnote rather than in the text. If the reader wishes to avoid this information, the reader should not go to the endnote when a book is being discussed and no author/title is mentioned in the text. This information is provided in endnotes for the benefit of scholars and other readers who would like to have it. Please note that no attempt will be made to conceal plot details that the author intentionally reveals to the reader (e.g., the identity of the criminal who is being tracked in a thriller or police procedural).

and Hale, 2004). With regard to mass media, since the birth of the "penny press" in the 19th century, sex and violence have been used to sell newspapers[90] The mantra of local television news is often said to be, "If it bleeds, it leads." Non-violent property offenses and public order crimes receive limited attention in some news markets. Citizens who obtain much of their information about crime and criminals from newspapers, television news, and related Internet sites are apt to overestimate the rate of violent crime in their neighborhoods. Citizens often develop "cognitive maps" which identify certain areas of the city as places to avoid. Suburbanites and small town residents may hesitate to travel to metropolitan areas because they fear urban predators (see e.g., Surette, 2007; Lipschultz and Hilt, 2002).

Describing the "altruistic fear of crime" that parents feel for their children, Tulloch (2004) concludes, the "levels of worry reported by parents were generally high and a function of parental age, personal worry about victimization and perception of rising crime rates" (from abstract). Eleanor Taylor Bland illustrates this concept in *A Cold and Silent Dying* (2004). Police detective Marti MacAlister, and her husband, Ben, a paramedic/firefighter, have a discussion with their teenager daughter, Joanna, and her friend, Lisa. Marti wants the two girls to stay home because of the threat posed by DeVonte, the man to whom Lisa's mother, Sharon, was briefly married. Joanna tells her parents that they have "been working on self-defense techniques." When Marti tells her that is not enough, Lisa assures her that she won't be fooled again by DeVonte, who in *Whispers in the Dark* (2001) lured Sharon and Lisa to the Bahamas to kill them.

> Besides, Lisa tells Marti and Ben, "the school is on Code Yellow":
> "Which means...?" Ben asked.
> "Tighter security, random searches, a few more cops walking around," Lisa explained.
> "Why?"
> "Rumor is that there might be a gang fight," Joanna said [p. 215].

Hearing this, Marti and Ben exchange looks. They have already taken their two sons out of public school, but Joanna is a junior and wants to graduate with her class. When Ben asks if they feel safe at school, Lisa explains that their college prep program is located in a separate section of the building. The kids they mingle with are "all preppies"—except for the athletes ("peons") with whom Joanna, a jock, associates (p. 215).

Later, Marti and Ben have this exchange:

> "A guard dog," Marti said. "An alarm system."
> "A Beretta and a service revolver."
> "A cop and a fireman."
> "Security," Ben said. "An illusion..." [p. 216].

In mysteries, security is indeed an illusion. When a crime does occur one of the questions has to do with the actions of the victim.

The Character of the Victim

Wittingly or unwittingly, we place victims on a continuum, evaluating their claims on our emotions. On this continuum, victims range from the "innocent," who did nothing to merit or contribute to his or her mistreatment, to the "blameworthy" or "deserving" victim, who "asked for" what he or she got by his or her own bad or inappropriate behavior. Moreover, there is a process by which a person who has been harmed *becomes* a victim. That process involves, first, realizing that one has been victimized and then having one's victimization recognized by others. These others include police officers, prosecutors, and other participants in the criminal justice process, and also may include politicians who make the laws (see e.g., Elias, 1986).

Commenting on criminal justice from the perspective of the real-life victim — particularly victims of sexual and domestic violence — Herman (2005) asserts, "At every step of criminal proceedings, victims are powerfully reminded of their marginal and dishonored status" (p. 574). In a similar vein, Shklar (1990) observes that "the normal model of justice continues to have severe difficulties in coming to terms with victims" (p. 37). This raises the question, "what justice might look like if the victims were the protagonists, rather than peripheral actors" (Herman, p. 579).

In criminal justice proceedings, the interaction occurs between the State and the alleged offender. Victims play the roles of "accusers" and "witnesses" who offer statements and/or testimony. Participants in the modern victims' rights movement have demanded a larger voice and attempted to change the system. The victims' rights movement is in many ways as controversial as the 19th century abolitionist movement in its assertion of rights and demands for justice. Stabile (2006) observes that victims in American society provide an opportunity

> for mobilizing sympathy, for producing outrage about social injustice, and for political action by both institutions and social movements. To deny victim status to certain groups or to ignore the victimization that occurs to them, is at once to further marginalize the needs of particular communities, as well as their specific hopes and fears, and to construct threats to the social order based on socially constructed assessments ... of worthy and unworthy victims ... [p. 2].

Stabile continues with a historical reference, noting that from "slavery until the contemporary era, with precision and regularity the ranks of worthy victims have long excluded African Americans..." (p. 2).

Whoever the victim, typically the plots of mystery/detective fiction focus on murder and other violent crimes rather than garden-variety, much more common public order offenses and non-violent property crimes. The crime of murder is important enough to justify the time and effort of both the sleuth and the reader.

The Sleuth as Survivor

One aspect of what modern crime fiction does is to describe the impact on those who are left behind when someone is killed. Contemporary protagonists who become "survivors" — in the language of the victims' rights movement — often spend time "working through" the aftermath of the violence. Particularly in the works of several African American female mystery writers, the stages of recovery are depicted.

During the course of the series, Paula L. Woods's Charlotte Justice describes her feelings about the murders of her husband and child. In *Inner City Blues* (1999), the reader learns that Charlotte was motivated to become a police officer by her desire to spare others similar pain. She says she gains satisfaction knowing that she "helped put another criminal behind bars and gave the victims' families a sense of closure I never got from the criminal justice system" (p. 37). In *Strange Bedfellows* (2006), the reader sits in as Charlotte reluctantly seeks help from a therapist and begins to deal with her feelings about her dead husband and her interfering family.

In *Where to Choose* (1999), Penny Mickelbury's protagonist, attorney Carole Ann Gibson resented the attitude of friends and acquaintances in the aftermath of her husband's murder. They treated her "like a pariah." Long-time friends avoided her phone calls as if they thought she was a carrier of "something deadly and contagious." The pleasure she took in "stalking" them and getting in their faces, left her depleted of energy (p. 24).

Norman Kelley's former prosecutor, Nina Halligan, is grief-stricken by the loss of her husband and two children. But in *The Big Mango* (2000), she is plagued by guilt and grotesque nightmares because she is tempted to try to move on with her life. She is sure that her husband and children hate her for reaching out to a former lover and for appearing to waver in her promise to avenge their deaths.

For the sleuths who have suffered a loss through violence, recovery is often linked to their ability to determine what happened and why. All fictional sleuths, whether bereaved or not, ask some basic questions about crimes. In crime fiction, as in some theories of criminal victimization and offending, the focus is on the individual actors. The sleuth is involved in the reconstruction of the process by which the victim and the offender came to the crucial moments of the criminal event.

The Victim-Offender Encounter

In *Crime and Everyday Life*, Felson (2002) identifies what is required for a crime to occur. Crimes occur within "behavior settings," which are generally defined in term of space and time. Within these settings, criminal acts have three "almost-always elements": a likely offender, a suitable target, and the absence of a capable guardian against the offense (pp. 20–21). It is when these elements come together that embezzlement or a mugging or a murder can occur. Readers of crime fiction are aware of the concepts of motive, means, and opportunity. Fictional sleuths—like their real life counterparts—focus their investigations on finding the suspects who had all three.

One of the features of crime fiction by African American writers is the tendency to place both victims and offenders in context. African American mystery writers rarely present either victims or offenders as throwaway characters. This chapter examines some of the situations in which victims and offenders interact in the novels by Black writers.

Domestic Violence

In 1958, criminologist Marvin Wolfgang analyzed the data for homicides in Philadelphia. He concluded that some homicides—whether occurring in a barroom during a brawl or in a kitchen during a marital dispute—could be described as "victim-precipitated." That is the victim was the first to pick up a weapon or the victim dared the other person to act in response to a threat or insult. Wolfgang also reported that the most dangerous rooms in the house were the kitchen and the bedroom. He theorized that it was in these rooms that quarrels were most likely to begin—and end (Wolfgang, 1958). Wolfgang's finding about the quarrels that lead to violence have been replicated in other studies, such as research by Riedel and Best (1998) on intimate partner homicides in California between 1987 and 1996. Wolfgang's conclusions about "victim precipitation" remain controversial.

Perceptions of the victim are often colored by assessments of the victim's behavior. Nowhere, perhaps, is this more common than in domestic violence. This is especially the case when a victim of prior abuse becomes an offender. In Judith Smith-Levin's *Reckless Eyeballin'* (2001), a police officer is shot by his wife as he is eating breakfast:

> Ernestine Henderson shot her husband Willis as he was enjoying his second cup of coffee for the morning. Well, enjoying maybe wasn't the word. He was complaining. Complaining *to* Ernestine *about* Ernestine.
> She'd listened to this routine for twenty-two years. Usually the complaints were punctuated with a fist to the face, or a kick to the belly, or any other place he could reach.
> This morning, he'd started in about the way she fried his eggs ... [p. 8].

Ernestine is exhausted from working the graveyard shift at a factory where she spent eight hours sewing zippers on denim pants. On her way home she stopped at the supermarket to buy oranges and Willis's morning paper. She came home, laid out his uniform and made his breakfast, including freshly squeezed orange juice. Now, as she listens to her husband rant, she knows that when he is done eating the breakfast he is complaining about, he will get up and hit her. She looks at his head and the cast iron skillet. She pours him another cup of coffee, thinking about how he complains about how noisy she is when she drinks coffee in his presence. She thinks about his stinginess, and how he humiliated her in front of a store clerk by complaining when they were shopping for a new coffeemaker. She thinks about how he takes her paycheck, and only allows her to keep twenty-five dollars for emergencies. He belches. She looks again at the "big, black iron skillet." Then she turns and leaves the kitchen. She goes to the bedroom and gets his gun from the bedside table. He looks up when she walks back into the kitchen with the .357 Magnum in her hand. She holds it like she has seen Clint Eastwood do it in movies (pp. 8–15).

> Then he made a big mistake.
> He laughed.
> A bullet hit him right between the eyes, and a gamut of emotions crossed his face in seconds. Anger, shock, surprise, and finally fear ... that was the one that stuck [p. 15].

This scene in which a battered wife shoots her husband is noteworthy because of the attention given by Smith-Levin to depicting the relationship. Ernestine Henderson is caught up in what Walker (1980) described as a "cycle of violence." In a real-life, if Ernestine Henderson's case went to trial rather than being plea-bargained, her defense attorney would probably call an expert witness to testify about the "battered woman syndrome."[91] The expert would explain how Ernestine Henderson saw no escape from the relationship and might well have thought that if her husband continued to beat her, he would some day kill her.[92] In Smith-Levin's novel, when Ernestine Henderson is arrested, Lt. Star Duvall recalls going to the Henderson house in response to a disturbance call when she was a rookie cop. Star regrets the fact that she was not able to do more at the time. She tells the jail matron:

> "Her husband was a wife beater, and in my eyes, that's lower than snail shit. Still, he's going to get the same honors that my father [a hero cop] got." She shook her head. "It pisses me off, Carol; I'm not sure I can even go to the funeral" [76].

The protagonists of African American mystery writers respond to domestic violence offenders with a range of negative emotions, from disdain to righteous outrage. Domestic violence — including child and elder abuse — is one of the more common crimes in works by Black mystery writers. Often it is not the primary focus of the book, but an aspect of a character's biography. In their works, the writers examine not only the immediate impact of abuse but the long-term consequences for victims, especially children who are abused or witness a parent's abuse.

In Barbara Neely's *Blanche Passes Go* (2000), Blanche tells her mother, Miz Cora, about Blanche's neighbor who has three little girls "cute and bright" and who won't leave her abusive husband. "After all," Blanche said, "she's a grown woman. All she's got to do is leave!" This remark makes Miz Cora furious, "You don't know nothin' 'bout it! Not a blessed thing!" Her mother tells Blanche about the violence in their own household by Blanche's father:

> "I never wanted you to know," Miz Cora said when her tears subsided. "But when you started talking all stupid 'bout that poor woman across the street...." You were too young to remember him much. He never struck me in front of you. Especially you. He loved you both, but you were his favorite..." [p. 251].

Although he told Miz Cora that he loved her too, when he was angry or drunk, he called her an "ugly black thing" (p. 252). The physical abuse to which Miz Cora was subjected was accomplished by the psychological abuse common in violent intimate relationships.

Although Blanche did not witness her father's violence, this is not true for children in many homes in which violence is occurring. R. Barri Flowers' *Justice Served* (2005) opens with a scene in which a little girl hides under the bed, listening as her mother is being beaten, raped, and murdered (pp. 1–4). This is the prologue to a story about two Portland, Oregon, detectives' search for a serial killer who targets male abusers released on technicalities or after plea bargains. The reader understands that the vigilante killer is probably the child who witnessed her mother's murder. Several women, including a criminal court judge and the director of a battered women's shelter, are suspects. The domestic violence offenders reflect the diversity of men who batter. They include an African American man and a Hispanic man, both working class, and a White upper class man who has a wife, a Mercedes, and a town house that he uses for meetings with his mistress. The anonymous serial killer believes "that no matter what happened to her there would always be someone to take her place in the battle to regain control over their lives from those who tried to dominate them with their fists." She has determined that, "The bastards had to pay for their sins, one way or the other. And she was going to collect in full force!" (p. 208).

Children who grow up in abusive homes are not limited to females in real-life or in the works of African American mystery writers. In Walter Mosley's *A Little Yellow Dog* (1996), a confrontation occurs between the vice principal and a parent in the school where Easy Rawlins is working as a custodian. Easy observes the argument in the empty auditorium. A big man, the father demands that his son be released to him. The vice principal tries to reason with the father:

> "He's in good hands, Mr. Brown," Bill Preston was saying. "Your son has been badly injured repeatedly over a long period of time. He has broken bones that have never been set right and maybe some internal damage..." [p. 75].

The father claims that his son is "just accident-prone." When Preston doubts that the boy's injuries could be accidental, the father shoves him. Preston tells the father that when he saw Eric's injuries he had to call the nurse.

"She had to call the police. That's the law. They took him to the hospital." (p. 75). The father tells Preston that Eric is his son and he determines where he goes. The much shorter vice principal, a former gym teacher, responds by going into a rage that leaves Brown on the floor with a broken jaw. Easy intervenes before Preston can club the fallen man with the platform extender rod he has found backstage. Easy tells him they need to get their stories straight. They will say Preston acted in self-defense, and that Easy "saw it all." Preston explains that he would not have hit the man "if he hadn't talked about the boy like that.... They shouldn't let people like that have children. They shouldn't even let them live" (p. 77).

Easy becomes angry when Preston decides they should tie Brown up before calling the police. He responds, "Ain't no niggahs gonna be tied up anywhere around here today" (p. 77). Easy takes exception to Preston's superior attitude. He points out that they both know "what really happened" (p. 77) during the fight. Brown is arrested as he (lacking a car) is trying to leave the school on foot. Later, Eric — who was in the nurse's office during the altercation — is taken away from the parents after one of his father's beatings sends him to the hospital. Easy tells the reader that the police beat Brown, "so bad the judge took Eric away to keep his own police from someday being charged with murder" (p. 77). Here the abusive father becomes a victim when the vice principal and police officers engage in "disciplinary" (extra-legal) violence.[93]

In Eleanor Taylor Bland's *A Cold and Silent Dying* (2004), DeVonte Lutrell, the serial killer who romances and disposes of wealthy, older women, was an abused child. His criminal file reveals that his mother killed his father in self-defense when DeVonte was nine years old. "Eight years later, the mother was killed by an unknown assailant" (p. 79). In a flashback, DeVonte remembers his mother's mockery:

> "My son, smart you are, huh? Smarter than this?" And she would hit him. "Or this." And he would be hit again. "How many times have I told you about these young girls you sneak out to meet? You think I don't know?" His mother's hands went around his neck, squeezing until he almost passed out ... [p. 113].

Because of his own unhappy childhood, DeVonte feels protective toward Lynn Ella, the little girl that he intends to use in his plot to get revenge on Marti MacAlister and her friend Sharon, DeVonte's fourth wife. The process by which Lynn Ella falls into DeVonte's hands is an indictment of the foster case system. Lynn Ellen was in an abusive foster home. She was sold to DeVonte, who luckily for her is a killer but not a pedophile.

In a number of the works by African American mystery writers, abuse of children in the foster care system is mentioned or is an element of the plot. In Evelyn Coleman's *What a Woman's Gotta Do* (1998), protagonist Patricia Conley was abandoned as an infant. Her first memory is of a foster home in Baltimore, where "a tall black man with a limp" that she calls "old Cooney" and his wife took in foster children of "all nationalities as a way to make ends meet"

(p. 31). But Cooney hates both the foster children and his own. Patricia recalls: "I was thirteen years old before I knew what hate was, and I applied it to Cooney—after he raped me" (p. 31). Cooney is arrested, but Patricia also is seized. She is dropped off at a shelter. She feels abandoned once again because Mrs. Cooney did nothing to prevent her from being "carted off like a criminal" (p. 32).

In Lee Meadows' *Silent Suspicion* (2000), PI Lincoln Keller investigates the unsolved murder of a journalist. When he goes through her files, he gains "a great sense of the importance of her work."

> Deborah's first professional article was a 1984 in-depth article in the *Michigan Chronicle* that highlighted the growing number of African-American children in the foster care system. She went on to talk about the problem adoption agencies were having finding African-American parents to serve as adoptive parents. The article was poignant, moving, and a call to action ... [p. 87].

The plight of children who become runaways is a recurring theme in Eleanor Taylor Bland's Marti MacAlister series. In *Dead Time* (1992), Marti and her partner, Vik, have a case involving a group of homeless children who are in danger. Vik is unsettled by the search for the children:

> Beside her Vik swore, something he almost never did in her presence.
> "This is really getting to you."
> "We're looking for kids," he said angrily. "We're got a crew digging garbage out of a cellar and looking for dead kids. We're here in this rat-infested, God forsaken part of town looking for children." He spat out another profanity ... [p. 134].

In *Windy City* (2002), Marti and Vik encounter three of the children again. Four years have passed (in series time), and one of the children is 17 with a child of her own. Another is living with an alcoholic mother, and the third, José, is a 15-year-old foster child living in the home of a Hispanic city councilman. When the other foster child in the household, a teenage girl, is murdered, José is a prime suspect.

In Bland's *Scream in Silence* (2001), an elderly woman lives with a psychologically abusive son. When he goes out, she leaves her bed and sneaks to the kitchen to look for strawberry jam. He returns unexpectedly:

> "Mother!"
> She screamed. She didn't mean to. She knew he might be there, watching. She clutched the spoon as he came toward her, holding out his hand [p. 114].

She begs him for the jam. He tells her, "Sweets aren't good for you, Mother. Don't you remember Father telling us that?" (114–115). She knows that he blames her for not protecting him from his father (p. 115).

In Terris McMahan's Grimes' *Somebody Else's Child* (1996), the murder of the woman who lives across the street from Theresa's mother reveals the mistreatment of the elderly woman by her daughter. The daughter's child, who lived in the house with the grandmother, was also endangered by what was happening there. As in real-life, violence in this household is generational in its impact.

African American mystery writers also examine other types of crimes involving power and control.

Sexual Harassment and Assault

In her book about victims of stalking, Dunn (2005) writes about the paradox that in its earlier stages, the victim-to-be may mistake her pursuer's behavior as romantic wooing. She may be flattered, may fall in love, and may even marry him. This makes it difficult for the woman to later convince others that she is being victimized by a relentless and obsessed man. Dunn states:

> Importantly, images of victims created by the claims-makers who seek to advocate for them necessarily construct their *innocence*, typical victims cannot play any part in their own victimization if we are to define them as "true" victims and care about what befalls them [pp. 3–4].

In an article for *Ms. Magazine* about the case of Joan Little, an African American woman standing trial for the murder of the White jailor that she claimed sexually assaulted her, activist and scholar Angela Davis (1975) observed that the stereotype of the Black woman is of "a creature motivated by base — animal-like sexual instincts" (p. 4). The image of the Black woman is used to negate any harm done by raping her and to justify "the overexploitation of her labor." Davis goes on to ask, "How many black women working in the homes of White people have not had to confront the 'man of the house' as an actual or potential rapist?" (p. 4). Historically, the risk of sexual abuse by members of the household in which they were employed as domestic servants was one of the reasons that African American parents wanted to keep their daughters out of domestic service (see Bailey, 1999, pp. 191–194).

In *Blanche on the Lam* (1993), Barbara Neely's sleuth Blanche White recalls being sexually assaulted while on her job. She was making use of her employer's bathtub at the time. Her employer's brother David Lee Palmer caught her there:

> ... He'd made her pay in a much more painful and private way [than being fired]. She hadn't bothered to report it to the police. Even if they'd believed her and cared about the rape of a black woman by a white man, once it came out she'd been attacked while naked in her employer's bathtub, she'd never have been employed in anybody's house in town again. But she still had hopes of fixing that motherless piece of shit one day [p. 63].

When Blanche encounters David Lee Palmer again in *Blanche Passes Go* (2001), he is involved in the murder of a young woman.

This female vulnerability extends to women who might expect to be protected by class-based physical security. In R. Barri Flowers' *State's Evidence* (2006), a judge is murdered and his wife raped in their own home. In Ray Shannon's *Man Eater* (2003), Ronnie Deal, a film studio executive, is having a drink in a bar when a man starts beating up a woman:

> "Stop it!" Ronnie said, speaking out loud, but none of the eight other paying customers at the Tiki Shack seemed to hear. In fact, no one moved except to breathe.

Ronnie — who has had a bad day and is fed up — knocks the man out with a beer bottle. Then in the worst nightmare of anyone who has engaged in "bystander intervention"[94] during a crime, the man tracks her down. He is angry and humiliated, and he breaks into her house and rapes her. During the attack, she tries to be still, not to fight, not give him that pleasure:

> Finally, he was done. He rolled off her, laughing, and began to dress himself, as unhurried and casual as a one-night stand she had brought here of her own volition ... [p. 67].

After he has gone, Ronnie goes into the bathroom and throws up.

> She stayed there on her knees, crying for a long while, then crawled into the shower stall.... Trying to make her mind a blank slate ... the memory was there, and it would not go away ... [p. 68].

Ronnie displays the initial symptoms of physical and psychological trauma. Many rape victims experience — as does Barbara Neely's Blanche White — years of post-traumatic stress related to the event. If the crime is reported to the police and/or goes to trial, the victim often experiences what victim advocates describe as a "second victimization" when she finds her own behavior being dissected and must relate the intimate details of the assault. In spite of the efforts of advocates who argue that rape is a crime of violence and should be treated like any other crime, many rape victims still feel stigmatized and humiliated by the reactions of others to the crime (see e.g., Finch & Munro, 2007).

In Ronnie's case, she has to make up her mind what to do about this man who has not only raped her but threatened her life unless she gives him $50,000 in five days. She is known as a tough, hard-driving woman. Not only her personal safety, but her professional reputation is at stake. Discussing decision making by victims, Baumer (2002) suggest that "victims have two main goals after they define an event as a crime: to reduce the immediate distress they feel as a result of perceived inequitable treatment and to reduce their vulnerability to future victimization" (p. 581). In the plan that she comes up with to deal with her attacker, Ronnie attempts to achieve both goals.

There is another group of women that face particular sexual jeopardy because of their work — prostitutes. They fall into that category of criminal offenders who often become victims in the course of their routine activities. Male offenders who are involved in criminal activities such as pimping and drug dealing also are more likely to become victims than are non-offenders.

Numbers Runners, Prostitutes, Pimps, and Drug Dealers

The "life course" of many offenders follows a trajectory from juvenile delinquency to adult criminality, and then eventually "aging out" of crime. Unlike white-collar and corporate crime, "street crime" is a young man's (or woman's) game. Moreover, most offenders are petty criminals. Most do not engage in serious acts of violence. But those offenders who are involved in "vice crimes" have lifestyles that are more likely than other offenders to involve routine activities that place them in potentially dangerous situations. In such settings, it is not uncommon for an offender to become a victim.

Historically, "red light districts" and "drug marts"— areas in which prostitution, drug sales, gambling, and other related activities occur — often have been located in poor, disorganized, and/or ethnic/racial minority neighborhoods. This was the case in the 19th century, and it is still the case in the 21st century. Since the debut of hard-boiled fiction in the 1920s, mystery/detective fiction with urban settings has portrayed the activities occurring in gambling dens, bars, and hot-bed hotels. In these urban settings, characters involved in illegal hustles are commonplace. Often they are a part of the cityscape, observed in passing. Sometimes they are minor characters and/or recurring characters sought out by the protagonist for information.

In African American popular culture, the status of these characters has reflected the complex reality of their real-life counterparts. As books such as Louise Meriwether's coming-of-age novel, *Daddy Was a Number Runner* (1976), portray, playing the numbers was widespread in Black communities. Many otherwise law-abiding residents placed a bet with a numbers runner on a daily basis. Although playing the numbers has been eclipsed by legal state lotteries, references to this form of gambling— an institution in both urban and small town Southern communities— appears in the works of African American mystery writers. In Gammy Singer's series set in the 1970s, protagonist Amos Brown is a former numbers runner. In Grace Edwards' Mali Anderson series, there is passing reference to the fact that Mali's friend Bertha is the daughter of a numbers runner. Bertha got her start in business with the money that her father gave her after a win. He told her to use it to buy a car, instead she bought a run-down building and renovated it to open a beauty shop.

Equally prominent in African American culture, the pimp has had the status of both folk hero and predatory criminal. Quinn (2001) observes:

> The pimp figure has long been a street cultural anti-hero in black America.... The subcultural pimp type became an emblem of sartorial, gestural, and verbal exuberance in black male sphere ... [p. 211].

In the 1970s, pimp culture was prominent in works by authors of hard-boiled urban fiction such as Robert "Iceberg Slim" Beck and Donald Goines, and in the "blaxploitation" films[95] aimed at a Black audiences. The pimp as entrepreneur was an independent businessman who provided a service. He did so by recruiting and controlling women (his "stable") who engaged in sex work and turned their earnings over to him. He engaged in conspicuous consumption. The pimp "styled" in flamboyant hat, coat, and "pimp-mobile." The rise of the pimp who controlled "street prostitutes" hastened the demise of brothel prostitution controlled by a female "madame."

Regarding the women who are recruited by modern pimps, Norton-Hawk (2004) finds: "Pimp-controlled prostitutes are more likely to be single, to have failed to complete high school, to be non–White, to have never held a legitimate job, and to come from exceptionally dysfunctional families" (p. 189). As might be predicted, pimp-controlled prostitutes were also younger than other prostitutes when "they had their first sexual experience, first used illegal drugs, and first engaged in prostitution" (p. 189).

A picture emerges from the scholarly literature of the life course of such young women as moving from bad (often flight from a dysfunctional home) to worse (a pimp and life on the streets). In Grace Edwards' *Do or Die* (2001), Mali Anderson becomes involved when the daughter of her father's friend is murdered. Although both men are successful jazz musicians, the friend's daughter, Starr, had been involved with a smooth-talking pimp. She was murdered as she was getting her life back together and about to debut as a singer with her father's band. When " Short Change," the pimp, is murdered too, Mali's investigation leads her to the women who worked for him. Identified by the night of the week that he spent with each, they turn out not to be as downtrodden as Mali expects. What she finds out about the prostitutes challenges her assumptions.

Jeanette Beavers ("Tuesday") tells Mali that she does not intend to be recruited by another pimp. "As far as I'm concerned, the script has flipped. I'm on my own. When I fuck, I keep the buck. That's my financial philosophy" (p. 97). Mali watches Tuesday head downtown in a taxi, dressed in a simple skirt and blouse, carrying a small purse and an attaché case. Mali observes, "She looked nothing like the girls who strolled the Point near the Bronx Terminal Market." Obviously, Tuesday is directing her attention to a higher class of client (p. 97). One of the other women, Myrtle Thomas ("Thursday") tells Mali how Starr defied Short Change. Starr was able to do so and escape a beating, but Short Change became obsessed with controlling her. When she tried to break away, rather than let her go, he got her hooked on drugs. Her father rescued her, and helped her to get clean. Myrtle tells Mali that Short Change was "the kind of man that could tip into your dreams" (p. 112). That was how he held his women. Now that she is free, Thursday is on her way to Las Vegas.

When Mali attends the gathering that the women hold in Starr's honor, she meets Martha Golden, the Friday woman. Martha tells her how she met Short Change after she left home. Her step-father had been molesting her, while her mother pretended not to see. Finally, she slashed her step-father with a knife. When her mother slapped her, they argued and Martha left home (pp. 125). But she went back, as she promised herself she would do, "in style." She has married the preacher who was always interested in her and built the two of them a big house. He treats her right, and she intends to learn how to love him (p. 125).

Mali concludes about four of the women that in spite of "the stuff that had happened in their lives—abuse, neglect, rape, the desperate need for love, for money; getting messed up by the wrong promise from the wrong man ... in one way of another, they managed to survive" (p. 155). As for their pimp, Mali discovers from a neighbor that knew him that Short Change (whose given name was Henry Stovall) suffered a physical trauma as a child due to the poor medical care he received. The surgery that he received left him impotent. Ironically, this happened when his mother tried to get him better care by taking him to a hospital outside of Harlem. The neighbor tells Mali that he was a bright boy who might have been a preacher as easily as a pimp. But as he emerges in the stories told about him Henry, alias Short Change, was a smooth-talking manipulator, capable of and given to brutality.

In Eleanor Taylor Bland's *Slow Burn* (1993), vice cops Slim and Cowboy bring in a drug addict to talk to Marti MacAlister about the "baby dolls" that have been passing through Lincoln Prairie. Golden, the addict, is coming down from heroin. Her dealer is in the hospital, and she has been cut off from her supply. She is agitated, pacing, nose running. She tells Marti that she is from Kansas, a place she never wants to go back to because there is nothing in Kansas "but hard times" (p. 178).

> "Hell, ain't nothin' nowhere but hard times." She stood up, sat down, rubbed her jeans. "I got to get out of this. Out of all this. He bring them little girls into this like he brought me, but hustling for a man don't seem so bad five, six years ago. Different now. Better off working for yourself" [p. 178].

She tells Marti, "Them babies was sold like they was nothing. Sold" (178). When she expressed her concerns about this to R.D., her pimp, "He had Brick whip up on me" (p. 178).

The "baby dolls" were sexually abused by "perverts" who made movies. The movies, Golden tells Mali with disgust, were shown to other children to show them what to do (pp. 178–179). She tells Mali about how the doctor the police know about was involved. The doctor made sure that the girls were disease-free and gave them abortions if they became pregnant (p. 179). Golden tells Marti that she doesn't know what eventually happened to the girls. "Marti looked at the girls in the pictures. She wasn't sure she wanted to know what had happened to any of them" (p. 179).

Here prostitution is linked to a financially-lucrative "kiddie porn" operation. The people involved are not flashy pimps like Short Change. Earlier when Marti and Vik find R.D. waiting for them in the interrogation room at the precinct, Marti thinks that she might have "mistaken him for a legitimate businessman":

> There was a boyishness to his dark, round face, the roundness exaggerated by his close-cut kinky-black hair. Conservative in a dark pinstriped suit with a mauve shirt and gray tie, R.D. didn't have the clothes or the mannerisms stereotypical of a pimp [p. 98].

When R.D. is shot in the pool hall where he hangs out, Marti encounters his mother at the hospital. Marti recognizes her as a local real-estate agent. His mother tells Marti that this is the first time that she has seen her son in a month because she has been on a cruise. But he "stops by during the week to see what's cooking and cut the grass, or check the fluid levels in my car" (p. 136). R.D.'s mother confesses that she knows about his "activities." She tells Marti that his father was a gambler and went to prison for armed robbery. She says that although she could get rid of "a shiftless husband. A lot harder when it's your own flesh and blood" (p. 136). R.D. is her only child and a diabetic (p. 137).

In Gary Hardwick's *The Executioner's Song* (2005), protagonist Luther Green, a government assassin hiding out in the ghetto, encounters a young woman named Sticky B. She has made the lucrative transition, moving from prostitute to "manager" of her own drug territory. She and Luther negotiate for information. When she misunderstands his suggestion that she be his girl that night, she is affronted:

> "...Do I look like a ho to you? My flat backin' days are over. I am a playa, a mack, a big, bad-ass daddy with tits." Her face flashed the angry look.

Luther assures her that he didn't "mean any disrespect. What I meant to say was the information on the White man [that he is looking for] is valuable, and I don't need to get it from a third party" (p. 98). Sticky B. refers him to Red, "[t]he only bitch in this city's that's badder than me" (p. 98).

In Gary Hardwick's *Double Dead* (1998), Ramona, the young woman who became a "professional girlfriend" (p. 45) for well-to-do men grew up in a Detroit ghetto. She and her female friends hung out with drug dealers. When the men were killed or sent to prison, the women moved into this lucrative business. Ramona was reluctant to get involved because although "[t]he money was good ... it was too dangerous" (p. 45). This depiction of Ramona's friends moving into drug dealing to fill the vacuum created by the death and imprisonment of the men illustrates in fiction the scholarly discussion of the twin impacts of the "war on drugs" and "crack" cocaine.

The "war on drugs" waged by law enforcement in the urban ghetto has resulted in massive arrests of young males (Walker, 1998).[96] At the same time, the market for crack has provided opportunities for entrepreneurs, including women, to gain a foothold in the drug business. Most women remain at the bottom of the distribution chain. In Hardwick's *Double Dead* (1998), LoLo, the leader of the Nasty Girls, finds herself in a escalating turf war with Gregory Cane, a drug lord.

Cane was born to a heroin-addicted mother. He lost his left eye as his body fought off the drug. His mother became a prostitute, and he began his own criminal career at ten, stealing cars. He grew up in juvenile facilities, fighting off predators. He killed for the first time at age 12, cutting another boy's throat (p. 34). When he was 16, he was almost beaten to death by two corrupt prison guards who were running contraband. Now, he is a man who believes he has survived God's curse and, therefore, controls his own fate. He fears nothing because he is "already dead. Dead in his heart and in the eyes of society" (p. 35).

Gregory Cane sees no other path for himself. The ability of the offender to change his or her life, to become a law-abiding citizen, is a subject of interest to criminologists. In Charlotte Carter's *Jackson Park* (2003), Cassandra Lisle has an unsettling glimpse of her granduncle Woody's past. In the spring of 1968, Cassandra, Woody, and her grandaunt, Ivy, are helping a friend who is searching for his missing granddaughter, Lavelle. Cassandra and her uncle go to a bar called "Puffo and Geneva's" looking for information. It is not the kind of place that Cassandra, a Black "hippie" college student, would normally enter. The people inside are talking and laughing loudly, but they notice when Cassandra and Woody walk in:

> Like something out of a bad Western, a couple of older men who recognized Woody mumbled deferentially to him and then made themselves scarce. Strangers in Dodge City, we were getting appraising eyes from both men and women as we strode steadily toward the rear. Woody cut his usual impressive figure: a tall black man with steely features in his custom-made finery ... [p. 158].

Nuffy, the pimp Woody has come to question about the missing girl, at first mistakes Woody for "a goddamn nigger cop" (p. 87). But to Cassandra's amazement, Woody first pays for the pimp's drink and then uses more violent means to persuade him to talk. Woody and Nuffy, are sitting together in the booth, and Nuffy yelps in pain. Cassandra tells the reader:

> I didn't want to admit what was clearly the truth. My handsome, patient, loving Woody had cut this guy's wrists open and now he was speaking calmly to him ... [p. 89].

Woody points out to Nuffy that time can be an enemy: "The more time that passes, the worse it looks for Lavelle. And now you're in the same boat. Longer we sit here, the more blood you lose" (p. 89). When Nuffy answers his questions, Woody escorts him out to his car and takes him to the White hospital rather than Cook County Hospital, where Black people would normally go.

Woody has connections in city government. He also has a hated ex-rival for his wife's hand named Waddell, who is still a criminal, now a drug lord. In Carter's *Trip Wire* (2005), while conducting her own investigation into the murders of two housemates, Cassandra tracks Waddell down to learn about the drug business. The dealer who told Cassandra where to find Waddell runs his own operation from the back of a barber shop. Waddell has "[a] big place with two well-groomed, deadly German shepherds in the gated front yard" (p. 120). A young man with a gun, a body guard, sits in the kitchen playing solitaire (p. 120). Yet when he learns that Cassandra was living in the house with the two hippies who were killed, Waddell is disturbed. He wanted to know what she was "doing in a place like that" and why her uncle would let her stay there (p. 112). He will discuss the drug business only in hypothetical terms.

In *Jackson Park* (2003), the first book in Carter's series, Cassandra tells the reader how close she herself came to becoming a criminal. Not just a criminal, a mass murderer:

> If things had gone just a little differently — another little turn of the wheel — I might have gone out in a blaze of gunfire. They'd have *taken* me out, like they did that white guy in the Texas tower.[97] Or I might be sending imaginary telegrams from a padded cell. For sure, I wouldn't have fulfilled my dream of going to college.
> For the longest while see, nobody liked me [p. 1].

She presents the reader with a list of four reasons why she was unloved and unlovable, including her mother's desertion and the fact that she was being raised by her grandmother, who'd had a hard life and was "a pitiless old bat whose fortitude and patience was all gone" (p. 150). Adding to Cassandra's woes, she herself had a "gimpy left foot" and her cousin and best friend died of polio. Luckily, as she relates, her grandmother died before Cassandra could act out of her dreams of retaliation against school bullies and the rest of the world (pp. 2–3). She is rescued by her wealthy and elegant grandaunt and uncle, who take her to live with them in Hyde Park (p. 3).

Unlike Cassandra, who is rescued, Gammy Singer's protagonist Amos Brown was raised by his mother's bitter sister, Reba. He became a numbers runner and a compulsive gambler. He served time in prison. Their relationship is contentious, until he makes a discovery about his mother that he shares with Reba. He discovers she is capable of feeling: "A terrible sadness cloaked Reba's form and bent her body farther, head facing the floor as she shuffled around the kitchen" (p. 169).

For both Black victims and offenders in these mysteries, the external circumstances of their lives often test their wills to survive. Before concluding this chapter, we should look at another group of victims and offenders who arguably fall into a special category in real life and in fiction.

White Victims and White Offenders

Historically, in the American criminal justice system and in mainstream culture, White victims have been more highly valued than victims of color.

Even today, an offender, whatever his or her race/ethnicity, who is convicted of murdering a White victim is more likely to receive the death penalty than are killers of victims of color[98] Historically, in crime fiction, the victim was White. The aftermath of World War II brought gradual recognition and more inclusion of non–White victims in mystery fiction. For example, in Ellery Queen's *Cat of Many Tales* (1949), a serial strangler known as "the Cat," who is terrorizing New York City, has among his victim a young Black woman from Harlem. By the late 20th century, White crime writers were significantly more likely to include characters of color in their books. Occasionally these characters appeared as victims, less frequently as the primary victim of the plot.

In real-life, acts of violence tend to be intraracial. That is, victims and offenders tend to be members of the same racial/ethnic group. This is because acts of violence are often unpremeditated, occurring in situations in which the victim and the offender encounter each other during routine activities, often as acquaintances if not intimates, and frequently when either or both are engaged in behaviors such as consuming alcohol or drugs. Many people in this country live in segregated neighborhoods and spend limited time associating — except in work situations and sometimes not even then — with people of other racial/ethnic groups. For these reasons, violence tends to be intraracial. There-fore, when mystery writers create works in which characters are racially diverse, it is of interest to observe why and how these characters engage in violence toward each other. Who kills whom and why?

The White homicide victims in books by African American writers repre-sent a cross-section of humanity. These victims include (but certainly are not limited to) an elderly and beloved male doctor in a Southern town; a young woman trying out for the Olympic swim team; a shoe salesman who was dabbl-ing in blackmail; a middle-class woman who was estranged from her family; the legendary head of a music company who cheated his Black recording artists; an upper-class married woman who was having an interracial affair; a lesbian writer staying at a bed and breakfast on Martha's Vineyard; the young female housekeeper at a private hotel in a British resort town.[99] As is common in mys-tery/detective fiction, some of the White victims engage in acts that the offend-ers considered sufficient provocation for murder. Others simply possess information or stand in the way of some goal the offender wants to achieve. White victims, like victims of color, are sexually assaulted, beaten, robbed, and harmed in other ways.

Although the "nature v. nurture" debate continues among social scientists pure biological theories of criminality have been discredited. The mystery of the precise interaction of individual characteristics with environment remains. Yet, there is minimal effort in the mainstream media to explain why an African American adolescent or adult engages in violent crime. The assumption seems to be that criminality is an innate aspect of the lives of racial/ethnic minori-ties. In contrast, as Miller, Like, & Levin (2006) point out, the mainstream media devote significant space to explaining the violent crimes of White offenders. The assumption seems to be that Whites who commit violent crimes are demonstrating "individual pathology" rather than the expected behavior of members of their racial/ethnic group. "Whiteness" offers most White offenders the possibility of being perceived as "mad" rather than "bad."[100]

In American society, White men are granted the right to engage in a certain amount of acceptable violence. Since the colonial era, American culture has celebrated the exploits of violent (White) men with guns (Slotkin, 1973; Courtwright, 1996; Gibson, 1993). Even White male serial killers and mass murderers often obtain "cult status" (Miller, Like, & Levin, 2006). Given the attention to violent White offenders in popular culture/mass media, it is worth looking at several examples of such offenders in the works of African American mystery writers.

In Blair Walker's *Up Jumped the Devil* (1997), a frustrated neo–Nazi persuades several of his fellow White maintenance workers that they should strike back against Jews and Blacks and others who are making their lives miserable. They began by killing a wealthy Jewish philanthropist. They move on to a series of bomb attempts, one of which goes awry. Reluctantly recruited to the team, one of the men commits suicide when a White friend of his is accidentally killed by one of the bombs left in a garbage can. But the team, including the youthful disciple of the leader, have plans to blow up a building. Reporter Darryl Billups receives tips about the group's activities from a mysterious caller.

In Hugh Holton's *Time of the Assassins* (2000), an elite trio of assassins is headed by the Baron, a European aristocrat who looks on murder as a fine art. The other male member of the team was born in the impoverished East End of London. Born out of wedlock, he was raised by an aunt. He had asthma, but was a survivor, who "thrived on adversity" (p. 120). By the time he was sixteen, he was the leader of a gang of thugs. He discovered that he was good at killing. Hannah, the female member of the team, is American-born. She grew up in a middle-class family in San Diego, was a cheerleader and an honor student. Then at the age of sixteen, she began to change: "She started viewing her fellow students and some of her teachers oddly. She experienced morbid fantasies in which she envisioned herself torturing and killing each of them" (p. 121). The people she imagined killing began disappearing. When the bodies began turning up, her parents sent her abroad, even though they knew she "was extremely dangerous" (p. 122).

In Holton's *Windy City* (1995), the offenders are a wealthy married couple, Margo and Neil DeWitt. The two are bound by their shared pleasure in killing people. They enjoy reading mysteries and acting out the murders—particularly the more gruesome ones—described in their favorite novels. The husband, Neil, targets young women. Margo enjoys killing children. As a "killer pair,"[101] they are ready and willing to eliminate anyone who they consider a threat. Thinking of an early act of violence, Margo remembers:

> When she was two years old, a doddering aunt had given her a small kitten. The first day, Margo had "broken" the little animal. To this day she could recall her mother's shrieks of horror. The dear woman never again looked at her daughter without fear ... [p. 128].

Margo is not an aberration in her family tree: "Every other generation or so there had been a scandal in the Rapier family" (p. 128). Her violent ancestors include an Army scout, an assassin during the War of 1812, who went too far when he began to kill American soldiers. Another ancestor in the post–Civil War New Orleans was a serial killer who targeted former slaves (p. 128–129). Perhaps because of rumored race mixing in her family line, Margo hates little Black boys and particularly enjoys killing them (p. 128). The duo's victims include a Black male police detective, who disrupts Neil's plan to kill the young White woman with whom the detective lives. Another victim is a White female mystery writer, one of the (fictional) members of the Midwest Chapter of Mystery Writers of America (MWA) providing assistance to the police.

The violent White offenders who appear in works by other African American mystery writers include two wealthy female serial killers, who engage in both rape and murder; a politician and his mother who kill to preserve their family secrets; and a public relations man who kills the woman with whom he mistakenly set up his wealthy client. Other violent White offenders include corrupt police officers, federal agents, and government officials.[102]

Generally African American mystery writers do not depict White offenders as the only White characters in their books. Whites appear not only as offenders, but as victims (sometimes of Black offenders). White are also present as colleagues, friends, and occasionally intimates.

Conclusions

This chapter has focused on violent victimization. In fiction, as in real life, victimization need not be violent to have an impact on victims. Non-violent property offenses can leave the victim feeling insecure and vulnerable. For example, in *Sex, Murder, and a Double Latte* (2005), Kyra Davis's mystery writer protagonist, Sophie Katz, describes coming home after an earlier episode when she believed someone had been in her apartment:

> I went up to my apartment and let my hand rest on the brass doorknob. I stood there for a full two minutes. I wanted to smack myself for being such a wimp. This was my home. Some idiot rearranged my bookshelf and now I was afraid to go inside. Where was the Sophie that had nonchalantly walked through the slums of the city by herself at night while doing research for her novels? ... [p. 117].

In *Dying in the Dark* (2004), Valerie Wilson Wesley's PI Tamara Hayle has a similar reaction when she senses someone has been in her home:

My place had been violated. I was sure of it now, but by whom? And what was he looking for? Had he known I wouldn't be home? Or had he been looking for me? Was he still here? [p. 69].

After determining that the intruder is no longer in the house, Tamara locks her gun back up and collapses on the couch, and is startled again when the phone rings, "It rang four times before I answered it" (p. 70).

In Chassie West's *Killing Kin* (2000), Leigh Ann Warren comes home from a trip to discover a man has not only broken in, but stayed to die in her kitchen. Even though she is a police officer, Leigh Ann feels such a sense of the contamination of her personal space that she is sure that she will never be able to live there again even after the place has been aired out and cleaned.

Yet, in *Killing Kin* (2000), West eventually gives the offender — the dead man — a backstory that explains not only his unfortunate end, but the path that led him to that moment. In their depiction of offenders, African American mystery writers tend to provide enough biographical information for the reader to have some sense of the interplay of personality and environment that determined the offender's life course.

Once the offender has been identified, there is the question of how justice will be achieved. Will he or she be killed at the end by the protagonist, subdued and turned over to the police, or allowed to escape. The next chapter focuses on the matter of "doing justice" in the works of African American mystery writers.

7

*Doing Justice**

In an interview with Samuel Coale (2000), mystery writer Walter Mosley said of his protagonist, Easy Rawlins: "He's trying to impose some sense of justice in a world that has no sense of justice" (p. 203). Historically, African Americans have been distrustful of the criminal justice system. The concept of "blind justice" rendered without bias or prejudice is not one that many African Americans have believed in because of the "dual system" of justice that developed as a structural artifact of the institution of slavery and that remained in place even after the demise of that institution (Kennedy, 1997; Bailey & Green, 1999). Writing in 2006, Bobo and Thompson assert:

> More concretely, we maintain that over the past two to three decades, the United States has enacted a series of policies that have effectively reforged a historically troubled linkage between race and crime, and the functioning of the legal system. Among the effects of these changes are a deep crisis of legitimacy for the legal system in the eyes of black American and a real threat to the promise of equality before the law [p. 445].[103]

Given both past and present, one might expect African American mystery writers to be, if not uniformly critical of the justice system, at least somewhat skeptical of its fairness.

Aside from justice as a concept, there is the matter of "doing justice"—of participating in the criminal justice process and, ideally, helping to achieve a just outcome. However, one might paraphrase critical criminologist William Chambliss, who titled his book *Whose Law, What Order?* (1976), in asking who defines what should be a crime and what the appropriate punishment should be. If one had asked this question of White vigilantes in the South in the late 19th century in pursuit of a Black man that they alleged had assaulted a White

---

*Repeating the caution from the preceding chapters, it may be necessary in sections of this chapter to sometimes reveal a plot twist or an ending in order to illustrate a point. To avoid the "spoilers" that both mystery readers and mystery writers find distressing, author/title will be provided in an endnote rather than in the text. If the reader wishes to avoid this information, the reader should not go to the endnote when a book is being discussed and no author/title is mentioned in the text.

woman, the answer might well have been that a just outcome would be the lynching — preferably with burning — of the accused Black man. No formal trial with judge and jury was thought to be required. Clearly what the Black community deemed just and what the vigilantes deemed just differed markedly.

Even in the modern criminal justice system some observers would argue that those with power and money make the laws that are applied mainly to those who are poor and without power (see e.g., Reiman, 2007). This "conflict" perspective differs from the "consensus" perspective which assumes that most people in our society agree about what the laws should be. Somewhere in the middle are those who would argue that although most people agree about the serious crimes, such as murder and rape, when it comes to "victimless crimes" or "public order offenses" (e.g., prostitution, gambling, and drugs), opinions vary about criminalization and punishment.

There are other issues. A law that is neutral on its face may have differential impact, with greater consequences for one group than another. For example, a vagrancy law that is vigorously enforced has significant impact on the homeless, but none on those who have a place to live. This raises the issue of whether "criminal justice" as a concept should be subsumed under the rubric of "social justice." Should criminologists and criminal justice practitioners— or citizens, in general — be concerned about achieving not only law and order, but also achieving social justice? Should the achievement of a just society be seen as the ultimate solution to the crime problem? If that is the case, should society focus on ensuring an adequate standard of living for all citizens, including adequate education and health care? Going even further, should society be held accountable for the delinquency of children who grow up in impoverished and neglected inner cities? If society is to blame for the social conditions that are correlated with delinquency and later adult criminality, then how should we deal with the concept of "individual responsibility" that is at the heart of our adversarial system of justice?[104]

The Mystery Writer and Justice

One might argue that mystery writers, whatever their racial/ethnic backgrounds, are engaged in discourse about the nature of crime and justice. In mystery novels, the protagonist often carries on an internal monologue and/or narrative in the first-person about the crime and its circumstance. The protagonist talks with others about the investigation and related issues. In modern mystery fiction, these conversations often serve to illustrate the nature of a problem which extends beyond a given offense committed against a given victim (e.g., the investigation of a date rape leads to a discussion of the social problem of binge drinking among college students and what should be done about it).

Commenting on how mystery writers approach the concept of justice in their works, Kelly (1998) observes that writers "associate specific acts with specific consequences." These consequences "constitute a given writer's solution to what is both a technical and a moral problem set by the terms of the story itself" (p. 144). In Norman Kelley's *A Phat Death* (2003), John Matucci, a White police captain that Nina Halligan likes and respects, tells her:

> Justice, Nina.... It's supposed to be about justice. Now, I know you must know outside of your role as an attorney that justice isn't always perfect, but our society is based on the concept of law — and the law as an instrument of human beings is not infallible — but when you ... when you ... [ellipses in original] [p. 54].

The two have this discussion when Matucci comes to the club where Nina's second husband, a musician, is playing. Nina learns that Matucci has just resigned from the police department because of his knowledge of something that he finds morally repugnant. He tells her, "It's all politics. Greed and corruption ... but it's mainly politics." (p. 55). Matucci is killed as he is leaving the club.

In this chapter, we will examine how African American mystery writers depict issues of crime and justice and the functioning of the criminal justice system.

To Protect and Serve

Citizens take seriously the motto "To Protect and Serve" that appears on many police vehicles. They want police officers to both protect them from crime and be there to provide non–law enforcement services when no one else is available. In most departments patrol officers spend a significant amount of time responding to service-related calls rather than engaged in "crime-busting."

In their books, African American mystery writers offer commentary on the traits of both good and bad cops. In Hugh Holton's *Time of the Assassins* (2000), Larry Cole's New York City counterpart is known as "the Spanish Kojak," "Zorro," and "El Detective Magnifico" (p. 105). However, in his own modest assessment of his record as a detective, he has "simply utilized hard work, experience, common sense, and the occasional hunch" (p. 105). These are the same traits that series protagonist Larry Cole displays.

In Eleanor Taylor Bland's *Dead Time* (1992), Marti MacAlister remembers the cop who walked the beat in her neighborhood in Chicago when she was a child. He "wasn't always friendly but he was there ... whether they liked him or not everyone knew him. They all knew his top priority was a crime-free shift" (p. 102). Marti recalls that the officers of her childhood knew the people who lived on their beats (p. 103). In Gammy Singer's *Down and Dirty*, Amos Walker witnesses one cop's commitment to the kids in the community. An Irish cop,

Sergeant McGillihand, who runs the Police Athletic League program in Harlem, comes down hard on one of the kids who is boxing for his lack of effort.

> ... I raised my eyebrows at McGillihand. "Little rough, weren't you?"
> The beet-red of McGillihand's face shifted back to its normal pink color and he said, "Not rough enough. Hanging with the wrong element, he's missed a week of practice. Hammered his butt in front of a crack house and dragged him back here. He's smart — I'm not losing him — here is where he belongs" [p. 60].

Amos approves, observing the sixteen kids working out in the gym, and thinking that if he'd had somebody like McGillihand watching his back, may be he wouldn't have landed in reformatory at sixteen (p. 60).

Research indicates that most citizens are generally satisfied with police services. However, police activities such as "stop and frisk" of suspected drug dealers or gang members are more likely to receive criticism. Special "street units" have been a particular source of tension between the police and residents of urban inner city communities. These units are "proactive" rather than "reactive," often focusing on gangs and drugs. The members of these units often operate in plainclothes. These street units in New York, Los Angeles, and other cities have been involved in high profile cases in which suspects were injured or killed.[105] In a number of works African American mystery writers refer to street units and their activities. For example, in Grace Edwards' series set in Harlem, New York, protagonist, Mali Anderson, has sued the NYPD after leaving the force. Both she and the members of her social network refer with anger to examples of what they perceive as abuse and criminal behavior by the police. In *Do or Die* (2001) when Mali suggests that they rely on her boyfriend, Tad, an NYPD detective to find her father's missing friend, her father tells her that although he respects Tad, he doesn't believe the cops will care. He adds, "The only time they look for a black person is for target practice to pump him with forty-one bullets!" (p. 40).[106] Mali thinks: "What could I say? I thought of Diallo, Glover, Cedeno, Huang, Baez, Rosario, Bumpers. Victims of police brutality and part of a list so long, it sickened me to think about it" (p. 40).

The comments by Mali and her father reflect the low-point that relations between racial/ethnic minority citizens and the NYPD reached in the 1990s. Mayor Rudy Guilliano was perceived as at best indifferent to deteriorating relations, and at worse supportive of aggressive police units that went beyond enforcing the law and engaged in vigilante violence. Those who argued for the effectiveness of Mayor Guilliano's "quality of life" approach to crime control asserted that he and the NYPD had succeed in bringing what had been a spiraling crime rate under control while refusing to cater to special interests (see e.g., Powell, 2007).

However, images of abusive police actions are not limited to works set in New York City. For example, in Gary Hardwick's *Double Dead* (1998) set in Detroit, Ramona, the female protagonist, is the victim of a police officer's use of excessive force:

> ... She was pulled roughly to her feet, and a nightstick was placed over her throat. The cop choked her, cursing and punching her in the side. Ramona struggled to speak but couldn't.
>
> Finally the cop let her go, and she fell to the ground, unable to get up [p. 112].

The use of the "chokehold" by police in real life has sometimes resulted in serious injury or death and charges against police officers (see e.g., Feuer, 2005; Winston, 2007). The recognition of the significance of the technique used by the police officer in subduing Ramona depends on the reader's familiarity with this issue.

In C. M. Miller's *What She Left Behind* (2003), protagonist Audrey Wilson observes the three police officers who walk into the club where she and her brother Bobby are listening to their sister Renita sing. The club owner directs the police officers to their table.

> "Bobby Wilson?" The policeman who stood nearest him said. His blonde hair was trimmed into a neat crew cut, accentuating his angular frame. The wide shoulders most likely offered good support when he needed to apply a strangle hold.
>
> "What's up?" Bobby jerked around to face them, agitated.
>
> "You want to step outside, or you want to do this in here?" The cop was just as belligerent [p. 18].

Bobby is handcuffed and his rights (*Miranda* warning) read. He again demands to know what it's about. He is told that he is wanted for questioning in the death of the mother of his son. After he is lead out, patrons in the club comment on what has just happened. One person observes, "That's how APD is, dawg, always fuckin' wit us!" Other patrons offer their own assessment of the abusive behavior of the Atlanta Police Department (p. 19).

Similarly, in Nichelle Tramble's *The Dying Ground*, protagonist Maceo Redfield, draws an unfavorable comparison between his friends who are involved in criminal activities and the police officers who are assigned to enforce the law in their community:

> ... in the center of the crowd, I spotted two police officers, Phil Blakehorn and Ron Sullevich. The duo were well known and hated within Oakland's Black community, especially in their North Oakland playground. The two of them embodied the worst stereotypes of White cops in Black neighborhoods [p. 148].

Blakenhorn has a baton that he refers to as his "nigger stick for nigger knocking" (p. 148). Maceo notes that at least two of the notches on Blakehorn's baton came from dark-alley encounters with his friend, Holly (p. 148).

Torres (2003) writes: "Contemporary policing has emerged in the U.S. as a key civil rights battleground at lease [sic] for poor, urban communities of color" (p. 71). Critics claim that in field stops and other activities, police officers often engage in "racial profiling" rather than permissible "criminal profiling."[107] Although the courts have said that the police may consider factors relevant to police investigations (e.g., modus operandi), police stops and searches based

solely on the race/ethnicity of the citizen are forbidden. The use of racial profiling on interstate highways has been documented by social scientists and has
resulted in court mandates requiring police data collection on vehicle stops.[108]
Alleged racial profiling in other locations (e.g., customs agents in airports who
detain and search Black women suspected of being drug "mules") has resulted
in class action lawsuits.[109]

In the works of African American mystery writers, references to racial
profiling of Black motorists—"Driving While Black" (DWB)[110]—are frequent.
On occasion, the protagonist has a first-hand encounter with a police officer.
For example, in Eric James Fullilove's *Blowback* (2001), protagonist Richard
Whelan, national security advisor to the president of the United States, is
stopped by two police officers in an unmarked car. They order him to step out
of his vehicle. He thinks:

> *Aw, shit. When they want you to get out of the car they think you're some kind of*
> *drug dealer.* Damn. He carefully got out of the car keeping his hands visible at all
> times, his wallet in his right hand. He pushed the door shut with his hip.
> "Is there a problem, Officer?" he said as politely as he could through gritted
> teeth ... [p. 7].

Protagonists in books by African American mystery writers tend to know
"the drill." They know that keeping their hands in plain sight is well-advised.
They know that even if they are annoyed or irritated, the encounter will go easier if they manage to be polite. However, this does not mean that they always
behave as it might be wise to do. In Pamela Thomas-Graham's *Blue Blood* (1999),
protagonist Nikki Chase, a Harvard economics professor, is visiting Yale University. She is driving in New Haven when she is stopped by a police officer. As
he approaches her car she thinks that even though her collaboration with the
Harvard police on a murder case went well, she still doesn't trust the police.
She remembers the stories that she has heard from her male relatives about
their police encounters. She follows safety measures similar to those used by
Fullilove's Richard Whelan: "After rolling down the window, I carefully placed
my hands on top of the steering wheel. Things were bad enough without some
trigger-happy cop turning me into a statistic" (pp. 24–25).

The police officer points out that Nikki was driving 45 mph in a 25 mph
zone in a neighborhood with children. Although he gives her only a speeding
ticket instead of also writing her a ticket for the expired inspection sticker on
her borrowed car, she is not gracious. She admits to herself that he was right,
but she is still annoyed. The twist in the plot comes when the police officer who
stopped Nikki Chase turns up later as one of the officers assigned to the murder investigation she is involved in. He turns out to be hard-working and con-
scientious. In contrast, the two police officers who stop Fullilove's Richard
Whelan, beat him up, deliberately delaying his arrival at the apartment of his
White girlfriend, who is murdered.

It is this unpredictability of police character and behavior to which African

American protagonists respond. They are wary, distrustful, and uncertain. In Karen Grigsby Bates' *Chosen People* (2006), newspaper columnist Alex Powell relates:

> ... I'd grown to respect some aspects of the LAPD's job since meeting Marron [the white homicide detective from *Plain Brown Wrapper*], but the department has a bad reputation among the city's darker residents, and I'd been cautioned about them almost as soon as I'd moved to L.A....

In an encounter with an unknown police officer, the African American protagonist waits to see how the scene will play out. He or she waits to see what the police officer, who has authority and a gun and the ability to make his/her life unpleasant, will do. In Stephen Carter's *The Emperor of Ocean Park* (2002), Ivy League law professor Talcott Garland is mugged and turns in an alarm. When the police arrive, he is mistaken for the culprit. He is suddenly aware of his jeopardy:

> ... For a moment, I envision a second beating, this time by the campus police. A hot shame rises in my cheeks, as though I have been caught on the brink of a terrible deed. I actually feel *guilty*, of whatever they like ... [p. 326].

He identifies himself as the "tenured professor" who called in the alarm (p. 326).

In real-life, police officers are taught for their own safety and that of citizens to take and to maintain control during encounters. This sometimes leads to conflict with citizens who may perceive a brisk manner as rude, may resist being ordered about, and who, in the case of young men, may feel obliged to prove their masculinity by showing disdain for the police officer and his/her authority.

In Charlotte Carter's Cook County series, set in the 1960s, college student protagonist, Cassandra Lisle, has a profound dislike of the police. In the first book in the series, *Jackson Park* (2003), Cassandra's Uncle Woody calls in a favor owed him by Jack Klaus, a Chicago police detective. Before Cassandra knows that Klaus is a police officer, she is sent to meet him in Marshall Field's department store. She tells the reader that the department store has "always been known as a store for wealthy white people" (p. 57). Even the staff of the store is not integrated. This is also true of Klaus's neighborhood. When Cassandra and Woody drive there to meet with him about what he has found, she comments on the ugliness of the houses and observes:

> ... the quietness of the streets was more menacing than restful.... During the fair-housing marches in neighborhoods like this one, the residents had thrown vegetables at Dr. King and spit on nuns walking arm in arm with him [p. 147].

She is not pacified by the fact Klaus has prepared sandwiches and coffee that he serves to them in the garage that has been turned into a family room. His wife is out, and he tells them that they will not be disturbed (p. 147).

In August 1968, Chicago police clashed with demonstrators as the Democratic Party national convention was taking place in the city. Charlotte Carter's

Trip Wire (2005) is set in December 1968. In this autumn following the "summer of love," Cassandra has moved into a commune in an apartment building. When two members of the group, a charismatic young Black man and his White female lover, the "earth-mother" of the group, are murdered, Cassandra takes charge. When the homicide detective arrives, she observes that he is "[p]oking into our things. Judging us" (p. 29). She demands he show her respect:

> "You never even showed your badge," I said.
> "What?"
> "This isn't the crime scene. This is a private home. You're supposed to show ID when you're in a person's home not to mention a little respect."
> He stared at me for a moment, as if he was thinking about backslapping me.
> "My name is Norris. James Norris. Happy now?"
> I didn't answer [p. 29].

In Blair Walker's *Hidden in Plain View* (1999), journalist Darryl Billups has developed a friendship with Phil Gardner, the detective with whom he worked on an earlier case. When Gardner becomes ill and dies later in the hospital, Billups writes a eulogy for him. However, he finds that Gardner's White partner is distrustful of journalists and needs to be warmed up. Darryl tells the reader, "Cops are naturally clannish and suspicious..." (p. 32). Since they "tend to be cheap too," he hopes to win the partner over by buying him breakfast (p. 32). Later, he has an unpleasant encounter with a Black female police officer. He is attacked and almost killed by a young Black man. The police officer ignores his assertion that he was the one who was attacked until an elderly White man steps forward and tells her that Darryl is telling the truth. Darryl is annoyed that a White man's testimony is necessary before the police officer will believe him (pp. 60–63).

One of the questions of interest to scholars who do research on the police is whether African American officers are perceived differently than their White counterparts by citizens, and conversely whether African American officers behave differently toward citizens— particularly those who are poor, Black, and living in inner city neighborhoods. The findings are somewhat mixed in this regard, but it seems that African American police officers acquire occupational values that are a product of the job socialization that begins in the academy and continues out in the field. As do other officers, they learn, for example, how to evaluate behavior by citizens and what is expected of a good partner. Yet, in some cities, African American police officers are still not fully assimilated into the police subculture. In some departments, tensions between groups of officers remain. Some officers of color have spoken out about racism within their departments.[111]

In books by African American mystery writers, Black protagonists who are police officers sometimes find themselves in ambiguous positions with Black citizens and with other officers. In Grace Edwards' *The Viaduct* (2004), set in 1972, the protagonist, Marin Taylor, a Vietnam vet who is searching for his kidnapped infant, has a conversation with a Black cop (who has a White partner). They are discussing police clearance rates. Marin responds with surprise to what Detective Benjamin has told him:

> "You mean they want to tag me to satisfy their numbers? I don't believe this."
> "How long you been in Harlem, Taylor?"
> "Born here. Raised here. Probably die here."
> "Then you know all about the setups and the throw downs. Mistaken IDs that somehow never get corrected. I don't need to mention how many brothers are doin' hard time for stuff they didn't do..." [p. 88].

In John Ridley's *Those Who Walk in Darkness* (2003), Soledad O'Roark and her White male partner find themselves mediating an argument between a Black man and a Korean American storeowner. As her partner hangs back, Soledad tries to deal with the Black man who thinks she should take his side against the Korean American woman.

In Paula Woods' *Strange Bedfellows* (2006), protagonist Charlotte Justice has a mentor, Burt Rivers, who was her brother's partner and her field training officer. He is now retired from the force. When they meet for coffee, Charlotte recalls how much she learned from him. They discuss his involvement in the program that brought more women onto the force. He tells her that she should feel no embarrassment or shame about having gone for counseling. He himself went after the Rodney King riots, and so did some other officers who won't talk about it (p. 91). In contrast to Burt Rivers, a good cop who is White, Charlotte finds herself working with an African American FBI agent who is ethically challenged. She is forced to confront him when he calls a suspect a "nigger," handcuffs him, and then drives up into the hills to interrogate him. She tells him:

> "If this is the way you get information from people, count me out, okay? And you Feds have the nerve to be on our case [the LAPD] about civil rights violations!"
> "This has nothing to do with the Bureau."
> "What?"
> "I'm just assisting the LAPD in a murder investigation."
> "And trying to sabotage my case..." [p. 137].

She points out that any statement he gets from a suspect who has not been read his *Miranda* rights and who has been coerced into talking will be worthless (p. 137). Later, Charlotte calls a female FBI agent that she knows, an African American woman who is outraged that this agent is sabotaging her own hard work as a recruiting officer.

Some offenses by law enforcement officers in works by African American writers reflect the steady erosion of character of officers who move from minor corruption to major crimes. For example, in one work, an officer whose wife dies moves from minor bribes to heading a gang of police officers who are robbing jewelry stores.[112] In another work, a police officer and his partner move from enforcing drug laws to being on the take to finally committing murder. In the climax, one of them holds a female officer and her child hostage, threatening their lives.[113]

However, police officers who are protagonists note with approval the ethical behavior and professionalism of good cops. In Eleanor Taylor Bland's *Windy City Dying* (2002), Marti MacAlister observes that Slim, the Black vice cop with whom she shares office space, has a reputation for being both aggressive and going by the book:

> Slim worked Vice, not Narcotics, but he had a street rep for coming down hard — legally and relentlessly — on anyone who crossed him.

Marti uses Slim's reputation in an encounter with a petty criminal from whom she and her partner, Vik, are hoping to get information. The man went to school with Slim and knows him well. Marti tells him that she and Slim work together:

> "...I'll make sure he knows that I saw you tonight and that you will be giving me your full cooperation."
> The sweat was rolling down Joe Boy's face now.
> "Detective MacAllister, you got that?"
> "Oh, yes, ma'am. Yes, ma'am" [p. 135].

Marti's respect for Slim as a colleague is noteworthy because of the long-running battle she and Slim have waged about the men's cologne that he douses himself in and their attempts to needle each other (for example, when she finally learns his full name). At various times in the series, Marti and Vik turn to Slim and his partner, Cowboy (who makes excellent coffee) for help with a case or to provide back-up.

In Chassie West's *Killing Kin* (2000), Leigh Ann Warren comments on the integrity of her former partner and ex-boyfriend, Duck. Even though he disappears, taking evidence from a case on which he worked with him. He leaves a note for Leigh Ann assuring her that he has always been a good cop. She finds it hard to believe that he would betray his badge. Other officers in the department share her respect for Duck and help to keep what has happened under wraps until Leigh Ann can find Duck and bring him back.

In *The Legal Limits of the Criminal Sanction* (1968), legal scholar Herbert Packer "describes the criminal justice process as the outcome of competition between two value systems" (Bohm & Haley, 2005, p. 16). The two systems are *crime control* and *due process* (p. 16). In the 1960s, the Supreme Court, led by Chief Justice Earl Warren, rendered a series of decisions that extended the constitutional rights of citizens. Advocates of the crime control model argued that this expansion of rights made it more difficult for the police and prosecutors to do their jobs effectively.

If the police officers are challenged to do their jobs while recognizing the rights of suspects, then prosecutors and defense attorneys also must strike a balance between crime control and due process.

Attorneys and Courts

In Austin Camacho's *Blood and Bone* (2006), Hannibal Jones, former police officer turned trouble-shooter, offers this categorization of lawyers:

> Lawyers, in his experience, came in three brands. Crusaders, like Cindy. Honorable businessmen, like her other boss Dan Balor. And slippery, legalized con men. While he smiled and nodded, he placed Gabe Niesewand into category three [p. 12].

Protagonists who are attorneys are often faced with ethical decisions. For example, in Christopher Darden's *The Trials of Nikki Hill* (1999), assistant district attorney Nikki Hill is basking in the glory and media attention of having won a high profile case when she realizes she has made a mistake. No one checked the pockets of the defendant's jacket. The hot dog that he claimed he was eating is in a pocket. The prosecution has inadvertently withheld evidence from the defense.[114] She and her boss disagree about what should be done. In *Double Dead* (1997), assistant DA Jesse King tells the brother of a Black man that he has prosecuted for rape that he sees neither Black nor White, only "guilty and innocent" (p. 17). Later, when he is assigned to the case of the murdered mayor of Detroit, he is disturbed by the tactics that are being discussed in the prosecution of the mayor's wife. He tells his White colleague, "We'll prosecute this case by the book, Richard, or I'm gone now" (p. 85).

In Gail Ramsey's *Tick Tock* (2004), protagonist Spiegel Cullen is brought into the case by a plea from her ex-boyfriend. His sister, Breanna, a journalist, is accused of the murder of her lover in Bermuda. Their father, a Pennsylvania Congressman, is determined to protect his daughter. However, Breanna's erratic behavior makes the situation worse. To Spiegel's dismay, Breanna turns up at the wake of her lover:

> Breanna stood in the center of the aisle alone, out of place, bewildered. Her makeup was haphazardly applied to her face. She walked up the aisle toward the casket in a full-length fur coat [in May]...
> "Get her out of here!" someone hollered [p. 35].

She is forcibly removed by several men, who escort her to the back of the church and out the door. Spiegel gets her client away "as other mourners were starting to emerge with hate-filled glares" (p. 36). The episode serves to crystallize for Spiegel some awkward aspects of the case. Breanna's lover was a high-school educated parking lot attendant, who had a fiancée. Spiegel has an unstable client who may be guilty.

In real life, the ability of upper class suspects to allegedly "buy justice" with a "dream team" of attorneys has been controversial since at least the 19th century.[115] Only recently has this controversy involved African Americans, who now, as highly paid musicians, athletes, and other professionals, have acquired the resources necessary to hire first-rate representation. The O.J. Simpson case brought this new status of high-profile African American defendants to light. In Pamela Samuels-Young's *Every Reasonable Doubt* (2006), Vernetta Henderson, an employment attorney in a prestigious law firm, is assigned as co-counsel on a murder case. The other attorney, Neddy McClain, specializes in criminal law and is the only other African American woman in the firm. Their client is an African American socialite. When she is offered the case by her boss, Vernetta thinks:

> So that was it. We would no doubt be the first all-black, female defense team to handle such a high-profile case. That would mean coverage in the mainstream media, the legal press, and the black community. O'Reilly was banking on all that publicity bringing more clients through the door ... [p. 21].

Although O'Reilly, her boss, acknowledges that he tries to get as much mileage as possible out of every case, he assures her that he would not assign her and Neddy to the case if he did not think they were the best team to represent the client. Neddy has experience, and Vernetta can learn what she needs to know about criminal cases. He points out this will look good on her resume when she is considered for partnership next year. Vernetta agrees to serve as co-counsel.

In contrast to the "dream team" that these two African American female attorneys provide for their wealthy client, when Barbara Neely's protagonist Blanche White goes to court in *Blanche on the Lam* (1993), she goes alone. Arguably, Blanche's case is much less serious. She is charged with writing checks without sufficient funds to cover them. However, she finds her appearance in court traumatic. Before sentencing her to thirty days and restitution, the White male judge lectures her:

> ... This is the fourth, I repeat, the fourth, time you've been before this court on a bad-check charge. Perhaps some time in a jail cell will convince you to earn your money before you spend it, like the rest of us [p. 1].

Blanche, who is claustrophobic, panics at the thought of being in a jail cell for thirty days (p. 1). She asks to go to the restroom, and as the matron is waiting outside the door, Blanche peeps out and sees reporters surrounding someone. She suspects it is the county commissioner who has been charged with taking bribes. She is sure that, in contrast to her sentence, all he will get is "[a] little bad publicity, and a lot of sympathy from people who might easily be in his position" (p. 5). She is in her position because several of her White employers left town without paying her. Blanche manages to avoid jail by taking it "on the lam" and hiding out.

But it is not unusual for secondary characters in books by African American mystery writers to have served time in prison. In several cases, protagonists also have been incarcerated.

The Prison System

In Walter Mosley's *Black Betty* (1994), protagonist Easy Rawlins goes to meet his friend Mouse who has just gotten out of prison. Mouse arrives at the bus station wearing the same suit and hat that he was wearing on the night that he killed a man. Easy observes that most men who have been in prison would have clothing that is out of style when they are released. "But not Mouse. His tastes were so impeccable that he would have looked good after fifty years in jail" (p. 62). When Easy asks how he is doing, Mouse replies:

> How you think? They got me locked up in a pen like a pig wit' a whole bunch of other pigs. Make me wear that shit. Make me eat shit. An' every motherfuckah there think he could mess wit' me 'cause I'm little [p. 63].

This last statement recalls what African American mystery writer Chester Himes wrote in his autobiography *The Quality of Hurt* (1971) about his prison experience. Himes claimed that although he wasn't a large man, his violent rages caused other prisoners to leave him alone. Similarly Easy observes about Mouse that the men who assumed that he was a target made "a mistake. Mouse was small, "[b]ut he was a killer. If he had any chance to put out your eye or sever a tendon, he did it." (p. 63)

In Walter Mosley's short story collection *Always Outnumbered, Always Outgunned* (1998), Socrates Fortlow has moved to Los Angeles after being released from prison. He has come from Indiana, where he served 27 years in prison for murder. Socrates's struggle to adjust, including the challenges he faces regarding employment, illustrate the re-entry problems faced by ex-prisoners. In "Crimson Shadow," he answers a question about his crime posed by Darryl, a young boy who has killed a neighbor's chicken:

> "What they put you in jail for?" Darryl asked.
> "I killed a man an' raped his woman?"
> "White man?"
> "No."
> "Well ... bye."
> "See ya, li'l brother."
> "I'm sorry ... bout yo' chicken."

Socrates tells him that the chicken, Billy, belonged to the "old lady 'cross the alley" (p. 23). Socrates tells Darryl to come to him if he gets into trouble (p. 23). In a later story in the volume, Darryl does turn to Socrates for help.

In "Midnight Meeting," Socrates and a small group of men try to decide what to do about a man who is committing crimes against people in the neighborhood. One of the men suggests calling the police:

> "I don't believe in goin' t' no cops ovah somethin' like this here," Socrates said.
> "A black man — no matter how hard he is — bein' brutalized by the cops is a hurt to all of us. Goin' to the cops ovah a brother is like askin' for chains" [p. 32].

Later, in "The Wanderer," Socrates tells a man who served in Vietnam about prison: "I either committed a crime or had a crime done to me every day I was in jail. Once you go to prison you belong there" (p. 122). Socrates is commenting here on the brutalizing effect of prison. Although he himself has survived prison, he like other characters challenges the idea — one debated among social scientists as well — that the goal of prison or its outcome is rehabilitation. After twenty-seven years, Socrates, who admits he was a bad man in his youth, has "aged out" of crime. But he is aware of the impact of institutionalization on those who are incarcerated.

Similarly, in Grace Edwards' *Do or Die* (2001), when protagonist Mali Anderson stops to order a meal from Charleston, the owner of a neighborhood eatery, they get into a discussion about JoJo, the young man who makes deliveries. JoJo is doing well, and has been able to afford his own place. Remembering JoJo's plight before he hired him, Charleston complains about the foster care system that warehouses kids until they are eighteen and then cuts them loose: "...next stop naturally is upstate [to prison] and into the system all over again. This time maybe for ten, twenty years" (p. 60). Charleston is referring to the fact that a significant portion of juveniles who are in the social welfare system end up in juvenile correctional facilities and eventually in adult prisons. In New York State, many of those prisoners serving time in prisons located in rural, upstate communities are drawn from downstate, New York City–area communities .

According to critics of the prison system, the location of prisons in upstate New York provides jobs and a boost to the economy of rural, predominantly White communities, but drains economic, social, and political capital from the neighborhoods from which the prisoners come.[116] Hence, Mali's response, "The prison industrial complex is big big [sic] business" (p. 60). Charleston replies that it is really "slavery" all over again. He reminds her that he served time in prison. He intends to make sure that JoJo doesn't end up there (p. 60).

In Gammy Singer's series, Amos Brown also has served time. But as he observes in *Down and Dirty* (2006), "Just because I'm an ex-con don't mean I'm a stupid mother-fucker..." (p. 9). When he goes to see his friend and mentor, Steadwell, who has been arrested, Amos realizes that Steadwell needs a "slick" defense attorney:

> But I figured that Steadwell needed somebody as slick as Prince, because every brother knew that in this city justice meant it was *just us*, niggers that the Man was locking up — and if Steadwell was going to beat this murder rap, Prince was the man for it [p. 29].

Even though Amos himself is an ex-con, former numbers runner, and compulsive gambler, the two buildings he has been left by his father help him to establish himself as a legitimate businessman. Like Charleston, he becomes a source of economic and social capital[117] in his neighborhood. In the social science literature, theoretical questions have to do with the impact of the loss of social and economic capital in the inner city when the middle class and business owners move elsewhere. With the deindustrialization of the inner city and the war on drugs, those who are able to provide jobs and create a social network that provides other resources, such as contacts, become even more important.

In mystery fiction, as Walter Mosley implied about Easy Rawlins, the protagonists are themselves social capital in their communities. They attempt to bring "some sense of justice" to an unjust world.

Doing Justice

The protagonists of these works don't have all the answers. During an investigation, the protagonist may have his/her own assumptions or beliefs called into questions. By the end of the book, the protagonist may have discovered his/her own blind spots and biases. For example, in Norman Kelley's *The Big Mango* (2000), Nina Halligan struggles with her desire to take the law into her own hands. She wants to find and kill the man responsible for the brutal murders of her family. But Anna, her friend and lawyer, warns her about the consequences of vigilante justice, the risk that she will lose her soul in the process.

In the works by African American mystery writers, both protagonist and reader may be required to rethink their expectations about who committed the crime and why and what should be done about it. For example, in one work by an African American mystery writer, the protagonist discovers that the killer is a ten year old child. There is a moment of shock:

> [Protagonist] stared at the little boy, the little monster his mother had created. [Protagonist] feared him, but [protagonist] also felt a pang of sorrow for him.[118]

The protagonist decides that survival is the first imperative in this situation. However, the matter of dealing with the child is taken out of the protagonist's hands by the action of another character.

Although the social science literature indicates that some African Americans may feel ambivalent about mobilizing the police because of concern about how a Black suspect will be treated, the protagonists of African American mystery writers appear generally willing to turn offenders over to the police. When the offender is White and has proven himself (or herself) a bigot, the protagonist may relish the opportunity to see the offender punished. For example, in one work, the protagonist prevents a killer from committing suicide because that would be the easy way out for him.[119] However, the fate of the offender(s) reflects the subgenre in which the author is writing. In hard-boiled fiction, the protagonist is more likely to be involved in a violent confrontation with the offender that results in the offender's death than in classic detective fiction featuring an amateur sleuth.

Conclusions

Shklar (1990), observes, "As long as we have a sense of injustice, we will want not only to understand the forces that cause us pain but also to hold them responsible for it — if we can identify them" (p. 5). In their treatment of the concept of justice in their works, African American mystery writers tend to display a sense of what the injustices are that contribute to the crimes that occur. Moreau (2004) asserts that unequal treatment wrongs individuals when:

   a. It is based upon prejudice or stereotyping;
   b. It perpetuates oppressive power relations;
   c. It leaves some individuals without access to basic goods;
   d. It diminishes individuals' feelings of self-worth.

Unequal treatment also may mean that some victims are not valued and, therefore, some offenders evade justice. In his memoir, *Makes Me Wanna Holler* (1994), Nathan McCall, who served time in prison for robbery before becoming a journalist, eventually for *The Washington Post*, commented on the inequities of the criminal justice system. When he shot and almost killed a Black man, he received 30 days in jail. But when he and his friends robbed a fast-food restaurant in the White part of town, he received a lengthy term in prison. Musing on the worth of Black victims, one fictional protagonist predicts that little will happen in the police search for the Black suspect:

> I didn't think that he'd [the detective] ever locate [the suspect]. If I'd read the man right he was too smart to stay in [city]. He was a black man who was implicated in the murder of other black people. There wouldn't be any national manhunt. They'd wait for him to be arrested on some other charge and then hope that [forensic evidence] would do the job ... [p. 305].[120]

The protagonists in works by African American mystery writers are aware of the factors that affect how justice is rendered. They offer commentary to varying degrees not only on the criminal justice system but social justice. The next section looks at readers' responses to these works and at comments from some African American mystery writers and from scholars of mystery fiction.

PART III

Readers, Writers, and Scholars

Readers and Reading

The protagonists of African American mystery writers tend to be readers. Writing about Walter Mosley's protagonist Easy Rawlins, Panek (2000) notes that "in *A Red Death* and consistently in the later books, Mosley makes his hero an obsessive reader" (p. 188). In *A Little Yellow Dog* (1996), Easy himself says, "I'm a book reader. There's always a book on my nightstand" (p. 102). Gammy Singer's series protagonist, Amos Brown, recounts that he started reading in prison and it became his salvation. The desire to read stopped him from engaging in behavior that would land him in solitary confinement where the only book he was allowed was a bible. Reading in prison provided Amos with the education that he didn't receive on the outside. In *A Landlord's Tale* (2005), he is worried about what will happen the next day and can't sleep, "so I stayed up to read a worn copy of *David Copperfield* and pushed to the happy ending" (p. 45).

It is not uncommon in the works of African American mystery writers to find a protagonist reading a book by an African American mystery writer. In Austin Camacho's *The Troubleshooter* (2004), Hannibal Jones picks up a book while guarding his client's building and makes a comment about the genre:

> ... he got comfortable in his sleeping bag and turned to the first page of one of Walter Mosley's novels about Easy Rawlins. Black detectives, he reflected, were almost as rare in fiction as they were in real life [p. 97].

Actually, in the years since the debut of Easy Rawlins, there has been significant growth in the number of fictional Black detectives created by African American mystery writers. According to a statement Gar Anthony Haywood make in a 1993 interview with the Cleveland *Plain Dealer*, at the time he was "one of only five professional black mystery writers in the United States" (Miller, 1993, p. 8B). More recently, in the introduction to an interview with Eleanor Taylor Bland, mystery scholar Norlisha Crawford (2006b) referred to "the more than forty contemporary African Americans now writing in the genre" (p. 1). The research for this book indicates that there are a number of writers who have published in the genre, but who are known mainly for their works in other fields. As is true of their White peers, most African American writers seem to have "day jobs" (i.e., they are not making a living solely by writing mysteries). However, the number of African Americans writing mysteries has certainly grown since the early 1990s. The question is, are African American mystery writers reaching readers? If they are, how are they received by the people who read their books.

In Alexs D. Pate's satire, *The Multicultiboho Sideshow* (1999), Ichabod "Icky" Word, an unpublished African American writer, holds Bloom, a White Minneapolis detective, hostage. Icky wants to explain how DeWitt McMichael, a White patron of the arts who was supposed to have presented a $500,000 "genius" grant to an artist of color, ended up dead and wrapped in plastic in Icky's living room. As other police officers surround the building, Icky realizes he must get Detective Bloom on his side. He must convince Bloom through his narrative that there is a rational, non-homicidal explanation for what happened that night when the artists of color gathered to await McMichael's decision. Icky must convince Bloom that he is not a rambling madman with a gun. Although the $500,000 grant would have given him the freedom to create, now — as a he holds a police officer hostage — Icky is in a position that might be described as "narrate or die."

This is not the position in which contemporary African American mystery writers find themselves. However, these writers are the literary descendants of those early African American writers who wrote petitions for their own emancipation and of the escaped slaves who wrote slave narratives to further the abolitionist cause. They are the literary descendants of the early Black writers who narrated in order to obtain freedom, write themselves into humanity, and move the race toward both survival and equality. These mystery writers occupy a modern (or post-modern) version of the position James Weldon Johnson identified in the early 20th century. They are still writing for two primary audiences — one Black, one White.

One might argue that whatever their race/ethnicity, mystery readers have in common their attraction to the genre. This does not preclude the possibility that readers from different backgrounds bring different expectations to their reading. We might hypothesize that even though Black readers and White readers[121] share an attraction to mystery fiction, their group experiences in American society shape their engagement with the texts.

Scholarly research on readers and reading is an established field. Among the topics examined: the history of reading, the experience of reading, reading response to specific literary texts, and the conditions under which children become engaged readers (e.g., Miall, 2006; Sullivan, 2007). The research on reader response to popular fiction is limited. The seminal text in this area is Janice Radway's *Reading the Romance* (1984). In his book on the hermeneutics of detection, *The Reader and the Detective Story* (1997), Dove described Radway's book as "[t]he most significant book to date dealing with popular fiction"

(p. 13). In the decade since Dove's book was published, a number of articles have reported research on readers of genre fiction (e.g., Turnbull, 2002). Two of the more recent, Browder (2006) and Sweeney (2003) focus on women reading true crime books. Of significance for this study, Smith (2000) has examined the production and consumption of pulp magazine hard-boiled fiction by working class readers in the 1930s. As will be discussed below, Smith's research raises some issues that are relevant to the readers of works by African American mystery writers.

There is no empirical research dealing with reader engagement with works by African American writers. Commenting on the state of research on popular fiction, Dietzel (2004) observed:

> The field of popular fiction is a relatively unexplored terrain in African American as well as American literary history and criticism. Reasons for this exclusion or oversight are manifold and range from academic practices and aesthetic standards that qualify a text for inclusion in the canon, to the politics of publishing, and the stereotypes or myths that persist about African American readers and their reading habits [p. 156].

This chapter focuses on both the readers and their perceptions. In considering reader interaction with mysteries by African American writers, the concept of "narrative empathy" (Keen, 2006) seems useful.

Narrative Empathy

In Norman Kelley's *A Phat Death* (2003), protagonist Nina Halligan complains during a stressful moment that she is "living out an existence that I wouldn't even want to read about in a fucking detective novel" (p. 129). However, it might well be that readers do want to read about Nina's troubles. After all, the advice often given to mystery writers who want to keep their readers turning pages is to get the protagonist into trouble and then make it worse. But there is also the question of reader identification with a character. Are readers who are not Black or female or who do not share Nina Halligan's political perspective able to feel for and with her. Regarding "narrative empathy," Keen (2006) writes:

> Novelists do not exert complete control over the responses to their fiction. Empathy for a fictional character does not invariably correspond with what the author appears to set up or invite. Situational empathy, which responds primarily to aspects of plot and circumstance, involves less self-extension in imaginative role taking and more recognition of prior (or current) experience.... The generic and formal choices made by authors in crafting fictional worlds play a role in inviting or retarding readers' empathetic responses [p. 215].[122]

This would suggest that the choices made by any writer (e.g., about who the protagonist is, his or her background, and the present situation in which the protagonist finds his/herself) will affect the amount of empathy the reader feels. However, we might also expect that some readers because of their own backgrounds and life-experiences will simply "get" (i.e., understand) some protagonists more readily than others and feel more empathy for their situations. Thus a reader who is a recovering alcoholic might identify and empathize with a protagonist who has a drinking problem. This does not mean that a writer cannot convey what it is like to be addicted to alcohol to the reader who lacks such experience or that a reader may not exercise his or her imagination, summoning other experiences from his or her own background (e.g., an addiction to caffeine).

Because of American social history, the matter of empathizing with a protagonist of another race/ethnicity is complex. This is especially the case when the story takes place in a setting that is unfamiliar to the reader with the focus on issues that in real life provoke tension or conflict between groups. However, in recent years, mystery readers have been seeking out works with protagonists and settings that provide new reading experiences. Mystery readers are more receptive than in the past to works featuring protagonists who are not White males. Yet we might still wonder if there are differences in how White readers and Black readers interact with the same work featuring a Black protagonist. The theory of "tourist reading" describes:

> ... the practice whereby a reader assumes, when presented with a text where the writer and the group represented in the text are ethnically different from herself [or himself] that the text is necessarily an accurate, authentic, and authorized representation of that "other" cultural group [p. 169].

We might suspect that the reader most prone to this type of assumption would be the reader who has had little exposure to real life members of the cultural group about whom he or she is reading. As noted above, in spite of the "illusion of integration" that consumers of the mass media are exposed to in which every social gathering on television commercials or in magazine ads features a cast of laughing people with diverse skin tones and features, most Americans spend much of their private lives in predominantly segregated settings (Diggs-Brown & Steinhorn, 2000). We cannot assume that most readers will have interacted extensively with members of the "other" cultural group about which they are reading.

The dilemma still remains for African American mystery writers that in order to establish themselves in the genre, they need to attract readers from two primary audiences — one Black, one White. These audiences may come to the works of Black mystery writers with differing expectations about what they will or should find. African American readers might want African American mystery writers to provide not only a good mystery but a story that reflects their own experiences and worldviews. White readers, on the other hand, might be put off by works that focus on racial issues. Moreover, each of these audiences is composed of individuals who have varied opinions about social and political issues, whose views may be shaped in various ways by class, gender, age, religion, sexuality, and even region of the country. Thus, we might ask if readers, Black or White, come to works by African American writers with certain expectations or in search of certain gratifications.[123]

Of course, before the reader can respond to the author's book, he or she must first find it. This issue is somewhat complex with regard to books by African American authors. The issue of two audiences comes to the forefront again with a modern twist.

Reaching Readers

In February 1995, an article in *Black Enterprise* (Brown, 1995) reported "a new chapter in book publishing." For the first time, African American writers were finding a sales base in the African American community. Black readers were now making enough money to buy hardcover books, and they were looking for books about Black life and culture. A "new black renaissance" was in the making. Four years later, an article in *Publishers Weekly* (Taylor, 1999) was titled, "A Diverse Market for African-American Books Keeps Growing." Taylor reported that books about the African American experience from poetry and biography to literary and commercial novels were selling well. Now aware of this new group of consumers, publishers, "keenly aware of demographics," were beginning to experiment with specialized marketing and promotion. Major mainstream publishers were developing marketing relationships with African American magazines, such as *Essence* and *Black Enterprise*. They were also launching book clubs aimed specifically at Black readers. This was confirmed by an item in *Book Publishing Report* (2000) titled "Doubleday Direct Has Biggest Launch Ever With Black Book Club." The next year, another article in *Publishers Weekly* (Milliot, 2001) reported, "African-Americans Spent $356 Million on Books in 2000." The statistics came from "The African American Book Buyers Study" conducted by Target Market News. The report found that this figure of $356 million was up from $310 million spent on books in 1999. Clearly, this was a significant and growing market for books. Mainstreams publishers created imprints to serve this expanding market of African American readers. At the same time, independent African American-owned book publishers and bookstores were competing for a share of this market.

The discussion about the boom in Black spending on books became more controversial as a number of issues emerged. One of them had to do with "urban street lit," the literary descendant of the hard-boiled literature of Donald Goines and Robert "Iceberg Slim" Beck. The entrepreneurship and the sales figures of self-published urban street authors led mainstream publishers to create imprints dedicated to serving a market of young readers who were making urban fiction "one of the hottest literary phenomena in recent years" (Wright,

2006; Young, 2006). Critics complained that much of urban street lit was poorly written and glamorized sex and violence in tales of the rise and fall of urban gang members, drug dealers, and the young women who loved thugs. One of the more outspoken critics, novelist Nick Chiles (2006) voiced his objection to not only the books in this genre but the creation of a separate African American literature section in bookstores where these books were shelved side-by-side with other books by African American authors. Chiles op ed piece in the *New York Times* brought the controversy about "book placement" to the forefront in discussions among African American writers.

In an article in *The Wall Street Journal*, Trachtenberg (2006) tackled the question of "Why [the] book industry sees the world split still by race." He described the issue as "a broader debate between assimilation and maintaining a distinct identity. Trachtenberg found that the major chain bookstores varied in their practices with regard to "African American sections." Borders and Waldenbooks (owned by Borders Group Inc.), Wal-Mart Stores, and many airport bookstores had a designated section for books of interest to African American readers. Amazon.com and Barnes & Noble Inc.[124] did not follow this practice. The explanation offered for having an African American section by book retailers was that: (a) it was a convenience for Black readers; and (b) it improved the chances of "new, undiscovered writers" (Trachtenberg, 2006).

In journal articles, in on-line discussion forums, and on blogs, African American writers, particularly writers of genre fiction continue to discuss the issue of book placement. For writers of genre fiction (i.e., romance, mystery/thriller, sci-fi, horror/fantasy), the issue is whether the placement of their books in an African American section in bookstores and in libraries which also maintain such sections means that non–African American readers will be less likely to discover their books. Readers who are looking for genre fiction are unlikely to browse in the "African American literature" section to find a mystery or a romance novel. Therefore, the African American writer of genre fiction — already competing for reader attention because of the many books being published each year — has less visibility and less access to genre readers.

Targeted marketing to African American readers seems to assume that Black readers will be interested in any book with a Black protagonist. When it comes to genre fiction, some African American readers will be interested in romances or mysteries or sci-fi. Others will not. In the case of mysteries, readers may have preferences for certain subgenres (e.g., hard-boiled PI fiction rather than police procedurals). This reduces yet again the segment of African American readers who will buy and read the writer's books. If they also have limited access to other mystery readers, Black writers are at a disadvantage in the marketplace. This is especially the case for those African American mystery writers who are published by independent presses (rather than large corporate publishers) and have limited budgets for marketing and promotion.

As noted above, this placement issue also applies to libraries, where bizarre situations sometime occur. One book in a mystery series by an African American writers will be shelved in the mystery section. A second book in the same series by that author will be shelved in the African American section. Oddly, with this placement scheme, White writers who have mysteries with African American protagonists also are sometimes placed in the African American literature section.

Returning to the original questions, even though more African American mystery writers are being published, are they reaching readers? If so, how are these readers— Black and White — responding to their books? As noted above there is no scholarly research on mystery readers with regard to African American mystery writers. The following section presents the results of a survey of mystery readers.

Mystery Readers Survey

The survey was developed by the author of this book and posted on the Survey Monkey website. Mystery readers were informed of the survey through a posting on DorothyL, a popular on-line discussion group for mystery readers; through e-mails sent to the mystery readers discussion groups listed on MysteryReadersInternational.com; and to the African American book clubs listed on Mosaic.com.[125] In the case of Mosaic.com, the e-mail was sent only to those clubs which indicated in their descriptions that mysteries were among the books that they read.

The response rate was highest for subscribers to DorothyL, where the original posting about the survey was followed with two reminders of the survey. The e-mail communications with the mystery discussion groups and the book clubs were less successful than DorothyL because a significant number of the e-mail addresses listed were not active or "bounced back." When this occurred an attempt was made to resend the bounce-backs individually to ensure that the e-mail address was entered correctly. This was sometimes successful. The e-mail about the survey was sent to the person listed as the contact for the discussion group or book club with the request that the e-mail be shared with members. Several of these contact persons did acknowledge receipt and indicated that the e-mail would be forwarded to members. No follow-up was done with the contact persons for mystery discussion groups and book clubs because the author felt a second e-mail might be more annoying than useful in generating responses. The author suspects the response rate might have been higher if direct contact could have been made with individual members of the discussion groups and book clubs.

In all 163 responses were received to the survey which was available for approximately six weeks. Because of the limited number of responses and the need for further refinement of the questions, what follows should be viewed as a pilot study. Even so, the results provide a solid starting point for future research.

Results of the Survey

Those readers who responded to the announcement about the survey went to the *SurveyMonkey.com*[126] to complete the survey. The respondents first read an introduction to the survey that stated it was a part of research for a book being prepared by the investigator (i.e., the author). Respondents were informed in the introduction that the survey would be anonymous and that they would not be contacted by the investigator. Respondents also were told that comments that they made in response to questions might be used in the book (see Appendix F for the survey).

When asked how they heard about the survey, 73 percent (119) of the 163 respondents reported having heard about it on DorothyL; 16 percent (26) from the Reader/discussion group contact; and 12.3 percent (20) from Other (e.g., "a friend forwarded to me" or "received e-mail"). A number of people who indicated "Other" when asked to specify, listed "Book Club" or "e-mail from my book club." This would suggest the number of respondents who received the information from the discussion group or book club contact may well be higher than indicated by the breakdown. Some respondents may not have understood the category "Reader/discussion group contact" referred to the e-mail that was sent to their contact person. This was a flaw in the survey categories.

Demographic information was collected in order to get some sense of who the respondents were and to aid analysis of responses to the questions. The demographic breakdown of the respondents was by race/ethnicity, sex, and age. Of the 163 persons who responded to the survey, one person skipped Question 2, which requested demographic information. Even so, there were 164 responses to the questions about race/ethnicity and age. This would indicate that 1–2 people who responded to each of these questions selected more than one category.

The majority of the respondents, 79 percent (130) were White/European American. The next largest category was Black/African American, 15 percent (25). Of the remaining respondents, 2 percent (3) were Hispanic/Latina/o; 1 percent (1) was Native American. No respondent identified him/herself as Asian/Asian American. However, 3 percent (5) indicated "Other." This latter category includes at least one person who indicated that he or she is European (as opposed to European American). As this person pointed out in comments, DorothyL has international subscribers. Another person self-identified in his or her final comments as Canadian. It is possible that the people who indicated "Other" all fall into this category of respondents who live outside the United States. The total number of responses to the race/ethnicity question was 164.

With regard to age, most respondents were between 41 and 70. By category, 38 percent (63) were 51–60; 24 percent (40) were 41–50; and 23 percent (38) were 61–70. Among the younger respondents, 9 percent (15) were 31–40; 2 percent (3) were 21–30. At the other end of the age range, 2 percent (4) of respondents were 71–80 and 1 percent (1) respondent was 91–100. No respondent reported his or her age as 81–90. Here again, the total number of responses to this question was 164.

With regard to sex, the majority of the respondents, 85 percent (137) were female. Males were 15 percent (25) of the respondents. The total responses to this question was 162. As noted above, one of the 163 people who responded to the survey did not provide demographic information.

In Question 3, the respondents were asked: "Please describe the type of mystery/detective fiction you most often read." All 163 people completing the survey answered this question. From the subgenres provided, the majority of respondents, 51 percent (83), indicated that they most often read traditional (classic or amateur sleuth). The next largest category was PI (private eye), with 18 percent (29) selecting this category. Of the remaining subgenres, 10 percent (16) selected police procedurals; 9 percent (14) suspense; 4 percent (6) romantic suspense; 3 percent (5) legal thrillers; 1 percent (1) espionage. No respondent selected medical thrillers. However, 6 percent (9) did respond "Other" to this question.

Question 4 asked, "How do you select the mystery/detective fiction that you will read?" All 163 respondents to the survey answered this question. Respondents were able to select more than one category. Table 1 shows the breakdown.

Table 1

How Books Are Selected	*Response Percent (Total)*
Reviews	66.9% (109)
Browsing in bookstore	54.0% (88)
Recommendations from bookstore staff	12.3% (20)
Recommendations from friends	59.5% (97)
Selections made by reading/discussion group	29.4% (48)
Other (please specify)	41.7% (68)

Sixty-seven people who selected "Other" for this category responded to the request to "please specify." The comments included: "I order fiction for public library"; "Read books by favorite authors"; "all of the above"; "browsing in library"; "availability in library, and attractive covers or titles since this is free and I don't lose anything if I don't care for the book"; "Authors I've enjoyed in the past." Other respondents indicated that they read books that had been reviewed or recommended on Dorothy L.

In Question 5, the respondents were provided with a list of 48 African American mystery writers. The majority of the authors were contemporary authors who are presently writing, but the list also included Pauline Hopkins, W. Adolphe Roberts, George S. Schuyler, and Chester Himes. Rudolph Fisher was inadvertently omitted from the list. Two contemporary authors on the list, Hugh Holton and Nora DeLoach, are now deceased. The author of this book, although a mystery writer, did not feel it appropriate to include her own name on the list. The respondents were asked, "Have you read novels or short stories by any of these African American mystery writers?" One hundred and fifty-four (154) of the respondents to the survey answered this question. It was skipped by nine (9) respondents to the survey. Table 2 below provides the breakdown of the writers who had been read by 20 percent or more of the respondents:

Table 2

Author Whose Works You Have Read	Response Percent (Total)
Walter Mosley	82.5% (127)
Gar Anthony Haywood	55.8% (86)
Barbara Neely	51.3% (79)
Eleanor Taylor Bland	46.8% (72)
Valerie Wilson Wesley	46.1% (71)
Paula L. Woods	40.3% (62)
Chassie West	36.4% (56)
Chester Himes	32.5% (50)
Nora DeLoach	32.5% (50)
Gary Phillips	29.2% (45)
Terris McMahan Grimes	26.0% (40)
Grace F. Edwards	25.3% (39)
Hugh Holton	23.4% (36)
Robert O. Greer	20.1% (31)

Other authors who a significant number of respondents had read were: Penny Mickelbury, 19.5 percent (30); Charlotte Carter, 18.2 percent (28); and Pamela Thomas-Graham, 17.5 percent (27). The other authors on the list had all been read by fewer than 10 percent of the respondents. However, 21.4 percent (33) of the respondents to the question also selected "Other," indicating that they had read writers who did not appear on the list.[127]

Questions 6–8 of the survey asked the respondents to think about their responses to books by African American mystery writers. Question 6 stated: "I find it easy to identify with the protagonist in books and short stories by African American mystery writers." The responses to this statement were: Strongly agree, 14 percent (22); Agree, 56 percent (90); Neutral, 26 percent (42); Disagree, 5 percent (7); Strongly Disagree 0 percent (0). Two of the 163 respondents skipped this question.

Question 7 stated: There are certain elements of plot, characterization, and/or setting that I expect to find when I read a book or short story by an African American mystery writer. The responses to this statement were:

Strongly disagree, 7 percent (12); Disagree, 39 percent (63); Neutral, 34 percent (55); Agree, 19 percent (31); Strongly Agree, 1 percent (2). One of the 163 respondents skipped this question.

In Question 8, a list of choices was again provided. The question stated: "If you were asked what elements you might expect to find in books or short stories by African American mystery readers [sic], would you mention any of the following." There was an error in this question. It should have referred to "African American mystery writers." Although a number of respondents pointed this out in their additional comments (Question 9), they indicated that they had read it as intended. By the time the error was noted, many of the respondents had already completed the survey. Therefore, it was not corrected. Table 3 provides the overview of the responses to this question.

Table 3

Elements You Expect to Find in Works	*Response Percent (Total)*
References to African American culture (e.g., music)	64% (103)
References to slavery	5.6% (9)
References to racial profiling by law enforcement	29.8% (48)
Discussion of social issues (e.g., poverty, homelessness)	37.3% (60)
Urban setting	27.3% (44)
Scene set in beauty shop/barber shop	1.9% (3)
Depiction of drug dealing	5.6% (9)
Depiction of gang/gang violence	4.3% (7)
Explicit sex and violence	1.2% (2)
References to religion	15.5% (25)
A protagonist with strong family ties	33.5% (54)
A protagonist with strong ties to the community	22.4% (36)
A protagonist who has served time in prison	2.5% (4)
A protagonist who has been a police officer	7.5% (12)
A protagonist who distrusts the police	18% (29)
Expressions of liberal political views by the protagonist	11.2% (18)
Racial/ethnic slurs directed toward protagonist or others	19.3% (31)
References to homophobia in Black community	4.3% (7)
References to color prejudice in Black community	11.2% (18)
Characters who have been targets of sexual harassment	3.7% (6)
The use of excessive violence by the protagonist	3.1% (5)
The death of the villain at the hands of the protagonist	4.3% (7)
Statements about justice by the protagonist	21.1% (34)
Statements about the American dream by the protagonist	9.9% (16)
No, I have no expectations about what I will find	34.8% (56)

Of the 163 respondents to the survey, 161 responded to this question.

Finally, in Question 9, respondents were given an opportunity for additional comments. The question read: "Is there anything else you would like to add?" Although 104 respondents skipped this question, 59 did have additional comments. The comments were wide-ranging and appear unedited in Appendix B.

Discussion of the Results

In an article in *Ebony*, Christopher Benson (2003) stated that the endorsement that Walter Mosley received from then-presidential candidate Bill Clinton gave a boost to all African American mystery writers. Benson asserted that the attention that followed Clinton's positive review of Mosley's book "created new interest in Black mystery, and a demand for new voices that publishers were eager to meet" (p. 110). Over a decade after this attention, in a *USA Today* review of Mosley's non-genre book, *The Man in My Basement* (2004), Nawotka observed in passing that Mosley "is probably the only living black mystery writer most people can name" (2004, 06d). If "most people" refers to the general public this might well be true.

The people who responded to the Mystery Readers Survey are not representative of the general population because they not only read mystery/detective fiction but also participate in reading forums (whether DorothyL or a book discussion or reading group). These respondents were expected to be better informed than "most people" about the genre and about mystery writers. The respondents were not asked to identify the writers from the list in Question 5 that they had "heard of." This might have yielded a somewhat different answer than the question about writers that they had read. However, the final observations by the respondents in Question 9 suggest there would still have been a significant gap between Walter Mosley, the most read author, and the other African American writers listed. Aside from any initial attention and marketing boost he received because of his celebrity endorsement from Bill Clinton and the subsequent film that was made of his first book, the general consensus of most critics, readers, and other writers is that Mosley is a superb writer. He also has been prolific, with three different genre series (including the Socrates Fortlow short story collections), and a variety of non-genre books, including non-fiction. As Mosley himself observes, he is "representative of a new breed of crime writers and fiction writers" who write "different kinds of books" (Stewart, 2003, p. 1).

When one looks at the other writers who a significant number of White respondents to the survey have read, there seems to be a correlation with: (a) the length of time these writers have been publishing; (b) participation by these writers in mystery organizations and conferences; (c) the nomination of these writers for mystery awards; (d) interviews of these authors in various print and on-line mystery forums; and (e) participation by these authors in on-line discussion groups (e.g., DorothyL). This would suggest that a combination of having more published books, receiving positive critical recognition, and being more visible in the settings that these well-informed White readers frequent increases the likelihood that African American writers will be read. Arguably, this is the same formula that works for other mystery writers.

What remains of interest is the large gap in readership between Mosley and the next African American writer on the list. This is especially intriguing when the list of writers who White respondents have read is examined beside the list of writers read by Black respondents (see Table 4).

Table 4: Comparison of Writers Read by White and Black Respondents

Writers Read	White Respondents N = 122	Black Respondents N = 24
Walter Mosley	103 (84.4%)	17 (70.8%)
Gar Anthony Haywood	74 (60.7%)	7 (29.2%)
Barbara Neely	70 (57.4%	8 (33.3%)
Eleanor Taylor Bland	63 (51.6%)	7 (29.2%)
Valerie Wilson Wesley	55 (45.1%)	12 (50.0%)
Chester Himes	39 (32.0%)	7 (29.2%)
Chassie West	48 (39.3%)	6 (25.0%)
Paula L. Woods	49 (40.2%)	9 (37.5%)
Nora DeLoach	42 (34.4%)	7 (29.2%)
Gary Phillips	34 (27.9%)	7 (29.2%)
Grace F. Edwards	31 (25.4%)	6 (25.0%)
Hugh Holton	31 (25.4%)	4 (16.7%)
Terris McMahan Grimes	31 (25.4%)	6 (25.0%)
Robert O. Greer	25 (20.5%)	6 (25.0%)
Charlotte Carter	25 (20.5%)	2 (8.3%)

Again, these findings should be interpreted with caution because of the relatively small number of respondents. For both Black and White respondents, the demographics were skewed toward women. For Whites, 108 (85.0 percent) of the 128 respondents were female. For Blacks, 22 (88.0 percent) of the total respondents were female. This is not completely unexpected because women are said to "dominate the mystery audience" (Smith, 2000, p. 172).

Comparing the male respondents to the female respondents, one difference that stands out is preferences for type of mystery/detective fiction. Among the females, there was a strong preference for traditional (amateur or classic sleuth) novels, with 73 (56.2 percent) choosing this category. Only 15.4 percent (20) selected PI novels as the type of mystery they most often read. Among males, there was a roughly even split between the two categories, with 33.3 percent (7) reading traditional most often, and 38.1 percent (8) choosing PI. This interest in tough-guy fiction would explain why the men were more likely than the women to have read Chester Himes (61.9 percent of the men compared to 27.5 percent of the women). The percentage of men who had read Walter Mosley was even higher (90.5 percent of the men compared to 80.2 percent of the women). Although some authors were about equally likely to have been read by both men and women (e.g., Gar Anthony Haywood at 52.4 percent and 55.7 percent), the men were more likely to have read male authors and somewhat less likely than the women to have read female authors.

Looking more closely, at the writers read by the Black respondents, what becomes evident is that Black respondents have read more widely across the list of writers. Although not as many Black respondents are reading some of the writers when compared to White respondents, the Black respondents are much more likely to have read writers that White respondents have not. For example, writers not read by 20 percent or more of the White respondents but who are read by at least that percentage of the Black respondents include: Lee Meadows (29.2 percent); Angela Henry (25.0 percent); and Victor R. Alexandria (20.8 percent). Penny Mickelbury who was read by 18.9 percent of White respondents was read by 20.8 percent of Black respondents.

When it came to Question 8, about the elements they might expect to find in books and short stories by African American writers, some differences between males and females emerged (see Table 5).

Table 5

Expect to Find	Male	Female
References to African American culture	70.8% (17)	62.8% (81)
References to racial profiling by law enforcement	37.5% (9)	27.1% (35)
Discussion of social issues	50.0.% (12)	33.3% (35)
Scene set in beauty/barbershop	0.0% (0)	2.3% (3)
Protagonist with strong family tiles	29.2% (7)	34.9% (45)
Protagonist with strong ties to the community	20.8% (5)	24.0% (31)
A protagonist who distrusts the police	33.3% (8)	14.0% (18)
Expressions of homophobia in the black community	16.7% (4)	2.3% (3)
The death of the villain at the hands of the protagonist	4.2% (2)	3.1% (4)
Statements about justice by the protagonist	29.2% (7)	17.8% (23)
I have no expectations about what I will find	29.2% (7)	35.7% (46)

Only three African American males were in the sample, making a racial comparison of the males not particularly useful. But we can compare some of the responses of Black females to Question 8 to those of White females (see Table 6):

Table 6

Expect to Find	Black Females	White Females
References to African American culture	68.2% (15)	61.3% (65)
References to racial profiling	27.3% (6)	27.4% (29)
Discussion of social issues	45.5% (10)	32.1% (34)
Scene set in beauty shop/barbershop	13.6% (3)	0.0% (0)
A protagonist with strong family ties	50.0% (11)	31.1% (33)
A protagonist with strong ties to the community	27.3% (6)	21.7% (23)
A protagonist who distrusts the police	13.6% (3)	15.1% (16)
References to color prejudice in the black community	18.2% (4)	8.5% (9)
Characters who have been targets of sexual harassment	9.1% (3)	2.8% (3)

Expect to Find	Black Females	White Females
Statements about justice by the protagonist	27.3% (6)	16.0% (6)
I have no expectations about what I will find	22.7% (5)	40.6% (43)

These responses to the survey indicate the relevance not only of race but sex of the respondent and the respondent's preferred type of mystery/detective fiction in understanding how these readers perceive works by African American mystery writers. The findings indicate the need for further research to unravel these interactions.

Conclusion

In recent years, some scholars who study reading and readers have become interested in the "sociology of the reader." This is a recognition that although reading is often a solitary activity, it also can be "a communal activity or social process" (Pecoskie, 2005, p. 336). The respondents who took part in this survey, have made their reading of mystery/detective fiction a communal activity. Because their book selections are influenced by others in their reading forums, it is possible that their perceptions, attitudes, and expectations about genre fiction are also shaped in these exchanges. At the same time, as Smith (2000) illustrates in her study of the readers of pulp magazine fiction in the 1930s, readers have "highly personal, 'idiosyncratic' ways" of approaching texts. As Smith observes of her own personal interaction with an organization "dedicated to the reading and advocacy of women's mysteries," the process of reading is a "complex psychic and social process." Those modern readers were involved in "selecting out details of plot, character, or setting with particular resonance for them, and narrating their own concerns through these sites" (p. 5). Undoubtedly, the readers who took part in this survey do much the same when they read mysteries, including those written by African American mystery writers.

In response to Question 9, several readers said they often did not know the racial identity of the author whose book they were reading and really didn't care. One might well ask whether it is even desirable that mystery readers be aware of the race/ethnicity of the author. Isn't it preferable that African American writers (to paraphrase Martin Luther King) be read for the quality of their writing rather than the color of their skin? Would African American writers fare better in the marketplace if their books were simply marketed "color-blind" to genre readers? How could this be done while maintaining the base of African American readers to whom some books are presently targeted? These are intriguing questions that are beyond the scope of this pilot study about how reader respond to the works of African American writers.

Future studies might also consider several other questions. For example, what role do factors such as the historical era in which the book is set play in the response of readers to the works of African American mystery writers. A realistic depiction of White racial violence in a modern setting might engender reactions of both resistance and guilt from a White reader. On the other hand, if an African American writer sets his or her novel in the past, the same White reader might welcome the opportunity for immersion in another time and place. It is possible that the reader also responds to whether the writer seems to be on a "soapbox" (i.e., the champions of a cause that many mystery readers find both distracting and annoying). A question for further research is whether some White readers may indeed expect African American mystery writers to be more likely to deal with social issues in ways that may detract from the mystery.

Returning for a moment to the matter of color-blind reading raised by respondents to the survey. When publishers target African American readers, they are promoting the fact that the works have African American protagonists. Many of the respondents in the survey mentioned that they choose books based on reviews or recommendations from others. Are the reviewers mentioning the race/ethnicity of the protagonists? Is this something that comes up in recommendations in on-line discussions or in book discussion groups? What effect might this have on the respondents' ability to read color-blind?

As noted earlier in this chapter, because of book placement and other marketing strategies, African American writers may be less visible to genre readers than are other mystery/detective writers.[128] It is possible that the African American mystery writers who are read more often by Black respondents than by White respondents may be marketed differently (including placement in bookstores) than those writers who are read more often by White readers. This is a hypothesis that requires further exploration.

In many ways, the issues discussed and the questions that remain unanswered hark back to the discussion in this book of the African American writer's "double audience." The reality is that a double audience does still exist in terms of demographics and perhaps with regard to response to some aspects of an African American writer's work. Arguably, the African American writer needs to reach both audiences and build a base within both to be successful in the market place.

In the next chapter, African American writers offer their thoughts about the mystery genre and their own work. This chapter also includes comments from scholars.

Writers and Scholars Speak

Introduction

Twenty authors representing a cross-section of African American mystery writers at different stages in their careers, ranging from well-established to newcomers, were contacted via e-mail. They were invited to respond to e-mail interview questions. In several cases, no e-mail address was available for the author and a request was sent via website contact or forwarded through another person. No follow-up was done with the writers to encourage them to participate. Seven of the twenty writers responded. These seven author provide the originally sought cross-section of mystery writers. Some felt more comfortable with the format and were more expansive; all offered responses worth pondering. The responses of these seven writers to the e-mail interview questions (repeated for each writer) appear below.

The writer interviews are followed by the responses of scholars to a similar e-mail interview. In the case of these academics, scholars who had expertise related to genre fiction and/or African American mystery writers were sought. Several scholars who were experts in aspects of genre fiction declined because they did not feel informed enough about African American mystery writers to take part. Several others declined because of on-going projects and time constraints. The three scholars who appear below bring a high level of expertise in both genre fiction and African American mystery/detective fiction. Their responses too are thought-provoking.

Interviews with Writers

Grace Edwards

Grace Edwards was born in Harlem. She has an M.A. in Creative Writing from City University New York (CUNY). She is the author of six book and teaches fiction at Marymount Manhattan College and The Frederick Douglass Creative Arts Center.

Q1. Some scholars say that concepts such as "crime" and "justice" have no meaning other than that acquired in the context of human interaction within a given society. Do you agree? If so, what are your thoughts about the concepts of "crime" and "justice" in American society?

"Crime" and "justice" in American society mean different things to different people. In the 1930s justice meant lynching innocent Black men with impunity. On the other hand, when Black people in despair and frustration explode, it's considered a crime.

Q2. In your books and short stories, does your protagonist pretty much reflect your own view of the world and how it operates?

Absolutely! Mali Anderson — the protagonist — is a young Black ex-police officer fired from her job. The white officer involved in the incident gets off scot free. This is a microcosm of the way I see the larger society operating.

Q3. Are there social issues that you feel it important to deal with in your work as a mystery writer?

Indeed. Having grown up in Harlem and experienced the 'benign neglect' of politicians, landlords, and an educational system which guaranteed failure, I understand the root causes of the high rate of black incarceration.

Q4. Who are the writers (genre/non-genre) who have most influenced your own writing?

James Baldwin, Toni Morrison, James Lee Burke, William Faulkner, Charles Dickens, Shakespeare, Zora Neale Hurston, Franz Kafka.

Q5. As an African American writer, do you find it necessary or challenging to strike a balance between "politics" and "art"?

It's challenging. At times, the characters have too much to say regarding politics and it's hard to shut them up.

Q6. Do you think there are certain aspects of American and/or African American life and culture that tend to appear in the works of African American mystery writers?

Yes. And I think it's wonderful. It opens a window into our culture and the way we live and may provide a better understanding of the injury caused by centuries of racial discrimination.

Q7. What do you want readers to find when they come to your books and short stories?

Particularly, I want them to discover and/or appreciate the unique history of Harlem. Generally, I want readers to celebrate the ability of black folks who deal with adversity — whether it's crime, poverty, etc. — we somehow learn how to make a way out of no way — as the old folks used to say. I want the reader to see certain strengths inherent in the characters.

R. Barri Flowers

R. Barri Flowers is a criminologist/crime writer and the author of nearly forty books of fiction and nonfiction, including the legal thrillers *State's Evidence* and *Persuasive Evidence*.

Q1. Some scholars say that concepts such as "crime" and "justice" have no meaning other than that acquired in the context of human interaction within a given society. Do you agree? If so, what are your thoughts about the concepts of "crime" and "justice" in American society?

As a criminologist, I regard the concepts of "crime" and "justice" as having meaning, per se, though still a reflection of interpretation and subjectivity. That is, the terms have meaning because they are defined as such, largely by those in a position of power and authority over the masses.

Radical criminological theorists tend to view crime, especially that involving the working and lower classes, as largely a product of capitalism; with criminal laws or the system of justice serving the interests of the ruling class. The high rate of lower class or street crime is attributed to the economic functioning of the capitalist system, which favors the wealthy; while the more socially harmful crimes such as exploitation and demoralization are largely ignored by the criminal justice system.

While generally subscribing to this school of thought, I also look at "crime" and "justice" from a sociological perspective. That is, I see crime or antisocial behavior in many respects as normal behavior within the context of the social and cultural influences of the deviant; with the notion of justice also highly influenced by the social structure and community principles set forth.

Q2. In your books and short stories, does your protagonist pretty much reflect your own view of the world and how it operates?

Not necessarily. I tend to allow my protagonists to view the world and how it functions in ways that best reflect their characters, idiosyncrasies, and the dynamics of the plot. As a novelist, I like to give my characters the widest range possible in allowing the freedom to be unique unto themselves, while still being people readers can relate to as well as find entertaining.

Q3. Are there social issues that you feel it important to deal with in your work as a mystery writer?

Yes, I would say so. As a criminologist who has written nonfiction books on a number of important social issues, I like to incorporate these into my mystery novels to reflect real life in a fictional context, as well as provide readers more food for thought beyond the crime itself and the process of solving it.

Some of the social issues I have dealt with in my crime and mystery novels include racial and ethnic prejudice, domestic violence, child abuse, sexual assault, sexual exploitation, substance abuse, and Alzheimer's disease.

Q4. Who are the writers (genre/non-genre) who have most influenced your own writing?

There have been many. In nonfiction, I have been influenced by the writings of Cesare Lombroso, Charles Darwin, Sigmund Freud, James Baldwin, and Alex Haley, among others; while in mystery fiction, the writers to whom I have probably been most influenced by have been Dashiell Hammett, M. M. Kaye, Daphne Du Maurier, Erle Stanley Gardner, Raymond Chandler, Truman Capote, Agatha Christie, and Mickey Spillane.

Q5. As an African American writer, do you find it necessary or challenging to strike a balance between "politics" and "art"?

I do not find it necessary to strike such a balance in my fiction, as I am primarily concerned with writing a great story that is less about race and more about human interactions, drama, and the dynamics of an evolving and compelling mystery.

That said, as an African American, I do at times tend to tackle in one form or another the issues of politics, race, ethnicity, and conflicts related to within the context of art.

Q6. Do you think there are certain aspects of American and/or African American life and culture that tend to appear in the works of African American mystery writers?

Yes, there does seem to be among many African American mystery authors a tendency to focus on stark urban settings, and some stereotypical scenarios within—such as impoverishment, violence, use of illegal firearms, substance abuse, domestic violence, gangs, prostitution, unwed mothers, absent fathers, and incarceration.

I prefer to write mystery novels involving characters that give readers a broader picture of African Americans and their role in American society in terms of success, high income, suburbia, middle class, aspirations, travel, and sophistication, within the context of a great mystery drama.

Q7. What do you want readers to find when they come to your books and short stories?

First and foremost, I want readers to find a compelling tale with three-dimensional characters and a strong plot with important subplots in making the story work. Oh, and the conclusion must be satisfying and tie together all the loose ends.

I also want readers to take away from my crime fiction, a prime example of the elements of mystery applied successfully in creating a page-turning suspense novel that will stick with the reader well after finishing the book.

Finally, as an African American mystery writer, I want readers to be able to enjoy a terrific novel that is all about good storytelling and characters that could be any race or ethnicity.

Robert Greer

Robert Greer has written six CJ Floyd mystery novels, two medical thrillers and a short story collection. He lives in Denver where he is a practicing surgical pathologist, research scientist and professor of pathology and medicine at the University of Colorado.

Q1. Some scholars say that concepts such as "crime" and "justice" have no meaning other than that acquired in the context of human interaction within a given society. Do you agree? If so, what are your thoughts about the concepts of "crime" and "justice" in American society?

For me, the term "crime" does have a rather succinct meaning, but I understand that that meaning has to fit in the context of where humanity happens to be at a particular moment in time. A crime that might have been a crime in the third century may no longer be a crime. Whether or not you agree with the issue of what a crime is, has to do, not totally with your point-of-view, unfortunately, but with society's. Although spitting on the sidewalk is no longer a crime, it carries with it, if you happen to be a patient who contracts tuberculosis, because of that act, an ominous, although very rare consequence for us human beings. As a doctor I find the act offensive, and indeed very high risk behavior, although most people would see it as an insignificant part of normal life. So to define crime, is somewhat difficult. Unfortunately in our current society, crime seems too often to be in the eyes of the beholder.

Justice, on the other hand, is easier defined for me. Justice is in fact absolutely an ever moving target — always has been and always will be — and in my mind justice is ephemeral. Some people receive their just deserts, others don't. But that's a whole different story.

Q2. In your books and short stories, does your protagonist pretty much reflect your own view of the world and how it operates?

In my novels and short stories my protagonists tend to reflect my own view of the world. They have a strong sense of right and wrong and I think their sensibilities are very much my own. I tend to stay away from glorifying dark angles and anti-heroes. I'm old school in that respect, I suspect.

Q3. Are there social issues that you feel it important to deal with in your work as a mystery writer?

I certainly deal with social issues in my novels but the compelling reason I write novels is for entertainment, mine and the readers. I have touched on social issues that range from spousal abuse to the Vietnam war, but they represent the background for my stories. I consider myself a story teller foremost, although reviewers and even readers describe my novels as having a much more prominent social context.

Q4. Who are the writers (genre/non-genre) who have most influenced your own writing?

I'm not certain that I've been influenced by many writers but if I had to name a few I would include Mark Twain, Chester Himes, Willa Cather, George Orwell, and Eudora Welty. One thing that all of these writers have in common that I admire is their ability to write succinctly and their masterful ability to write imparting a sense of time and place.

Q5. As an African American writer, do you find it necessary or challenging to strike a balance between "politics" and "art"?

I generally don't consider the issues of either "politics" or "art" when I start to write a novel. Although as it turns out, I am currently writing a suspense novel about the John F. Kennedy assassination. But in that novel I have that character and suspense trump politics. Art, as it were, once again is, is in the eyes of the beholder.

Q6. Do you think there are certain aspects of American and/or African American life and culture that tend to appear in the works of African American mystery writers?

Clearly the larger aspects of the African American life probably appear in any African American mystery writer's work. But that would be true of a person of any ethnicity writing about their particular ethnic group. I'm not sure that there is an absolute difference between a soul food restaurant and an Irish bar, or an Italian bistro in what they truly represent. All in fact represent a fabric of a culture as do the churches and synagogues and holy places and the schools that all ethnic groups inhabit. So African American writers it turns out are simply writing about what they know and what is unique to them, and although such aspects appear in my work as an African American writer, I don't find them in any way unique, they are simply different, yet specific. Unique implies that something stands alone and in the end a restaurant is a restaurant and a man is just a man. Non-African American readers seem to enjoy the voyeurism that goes with viewing black life. I simply describe what I see.

Q7. What do you want readers to find when they come to your books and short stories?

When readers read my books, I want them to be most interested in or to take from my books some sense of the characterizations I render and hopefully also enjoy my attempt at defining place, more particularly the west. I try to define characters and place in a way that is quite different from the typical urban setting that is so often argued to be wholly representative of the black experience.

Gary Phillips

Gary Phillips writes hard-boiled stories with private eyes, thieves, outlaws, bent cops, crooked politicians, and chumps way in over their heads as his characters.

Q1. Some scholars say that concepts such as "crime" and "justice" have no meaning other than that acquired in the context of human interaction within a given society. Do you agree? If so, what are your thoughts about the concepts of "crime" and "justice" in American society?

I think crime and justice and law and order do have a deeper human meaning, though clearly they have a resonance for us due to how any given society or sub-culture responds and interacts with those concepts. In crime, mystery and thriller novels, concepts of street justice invariably play a role or provide a subtext to various stories set in big cities, small cities, rural areas, and so forth. That is, the white collar villain because of their class station and/or political connections may be beyond the law, but justice can be delivered by the protagonist. This doesn't necessarily mean the hero puts a bullet through the bad guy's head — though it could mean this— but sometimes there's clever ways in which the wrong doer is tripped up or gets their just deserts.

So does this mean that justice is always tied to punishment? Probably. And surely the cop on the beat, the one who has to respond to the drunk beating his wife or the knucklehead who's just brained some old man for his social security check feels justified in dealing his or her brand of street justice. Which we might turn a blind eye to until it goes over the line — or we're forced to confront it — as in the recent cell phone taped beating of suspect William Cardenas by two LAPD cops. Well to be accurate, both cops had him on the ground and one of them wailed on Cardenas as a bystander captured this on her cell phone. The video was subsequently posted on Cop Watch, an anti-police abuse website. In fact tracking the advance of technology from that infamous videotaped beating of Rodney King by the cops in 1991 by George Holliday trying out a new video camera to now also impacts perceptions of crime and justice. The fact that a small, easy to carry device can now record these incidents has to give the beat cop pause. You would also think it would make thieves think twice before committing their crimes, but nightly there's some damn headline about some smash and grabber captured on security tape or some such, so I suppose as the cops say, these guys aren't rocket scientists.

Crime and justice have a price tag in America. Enough money you might not be able to beat the rap, but as the TV episodic "Justice" is fond of reminding the viewer, with its focus groups, mock juries, investigators and expert witnesses, an aggressive defense costs plenty. Everyday we know poor and low income black and Latino youths are ground up in the criminal justice system. Not saying they're angels, but if they came from some means, they might be able to get into a diversion program or other possible amelioration of their sentence some of their white counterparts are able to access.

Q2. In your books and short stories, does your protagonist pretty much reflect your own view of the world and how it operates?

In the first novel I wrote, *Violent Spring* set in the aftermath of the '92

civil unrest here in Los Angeles, a look at the racial and social landscape as nav-
igated by the main character, private eye Ivan Monk, that certainly reflected
my world view. I purposely set out in that book to show the city as it existed
then; the tensions, the jockeying for local political power and so on. Now, 14,
15 years down the road, and more novels, short stories and even some crime
and mystery comics I've written, I've portrayed all sorts of protagonists who
are not always the tarnished paladin like Monk in pursuit of the truth and justice. Some of them are venal and selfish and conniving bastards (and women)
out to get over. Still, yeah, something of my world view and how it operates
leaks into all these stories. I'm both hopeful and cynical about the human condition. We know people who do for the sick and shut-in civilians rushing into
a burning building to save a child and that same day hear about some new
atrocity committed in Darfur or Baghdad. It is these contradictions that reside
in all of us that makes for the raw clay from which we as writers use to shape
our characters.

*Q3. Are there social issues that you feel it important to deal with in your work as
a mystery writer?*

The writer's journey I've been on since *Violent Spring* being published in
1993 and now is that while social issues remain important to me, I no longer
feel I have to cram each one or more than one into each story I write. I'll never
forget several years ago a friend of mine, who is a well-respected community
organizer, was disappointed in me for writing *The Jook*, this nourish book of
mine about a grasping pro football player who gets involved in a caper. He'd
read and dug the Monk books with their social and political subtexts, and
expected something along those lines of a mystery novel set against a social and
political backdrop. He found it disturbing that *The Jook* didn't examine issues
of the black athlete, the capitalist owners and all that. He didn't get that for me
the book was a crime story more in the tradition of Donald Goines and Joe Nazel
than applying Marxist or Malcolm X to the crime story motif — though I have
nothing against doing that and may try such in the future.

My point being that while I am affected and look to effect social issues, I
don't want that to get in my way of telling the story. It does mean that unlike
the adage about Western Union and stories not delivering a message, I feel I'm
free to have or not have social issues suffused in my stores.

*Q4. Who are the writers (genre/non-genre) who have most influenced your own
writing?*

In no particular order Stan Lee, Rod Serling, Richard Wright, Ross Mac-
donald and Jack Kirby. Okay, Kirby was primarily a comics artist, but he was
a master storyteller and those dynamic panels and layouts of his still bubble
up in my head today and influence my sense of pacing.

*Q5. As an African American writer, do you find it necessary or challenging to
strike a balance between "politics" and "art"?*

Shades of Shelby Steele and Larry Elder, I don't feel as a black writer I have to "uplift" the race. Maybe this is the function of my age (51), but I'm not burdened with the notion that it's my job to have social and political issues that black folk have to deal with in this country tied up in my work. Having said that, I can't have lived to this age, been brought up like I was, experienced what I have as an African America, and not have that reflected in what I write. So yeah, it's a balancing act of writing fiction with a kind of truth, the ring of authenticity but not being preachy about it. Though for some a mention of racism or inequality in a mystery story is misplaced and being didactic while for others, not enough about such matters is soft-peddling the situation. Ultimately, I have to construct the story the best way I know how in what is best for the particulars of the story.

As a black writer, like any writer, I want to at least have the opportunity to write all types of stories with all types of characters be they be populated with black, Asian, white, gay, straight, men, women, and so on. It's my job to find the humanness and quirkiness that's in all of us and bring that to bear on the page. It also means that if I'm writing about a 19-year-old Cambodian American kid into hip hop growing up in Long Beach, I damn sure had better done my homework because he might talk in rap slang and dress "gangsta," the fact he is who he is means his culture is in the mix even if it's in a subtle way.

Q6. Do you think there are certain aspects of American and/or African American life and culture that tend to appear in the works of African American mystery writers?

Oh of course a lot of the aspects of America and African America life and culture appears in the works of black mystery writers. The barber shop and beauty shop as gathering places, the places where everything from relationships to politics is discussed is one such mainstay. In my novel *Only the Wicked*, old man Marshall Spears, a fixture at the establishment, keels over one day listening to the baseball game in the Abyssinia Barber Shop and Shine Parlor in South Central Los Angeles that Monk frequents, and this sets in motion a plot that involves the private eye's family and sins committed during the Civil Rights Movement. And the blues, that is down home, gut-bucket blues, plays a role in that book as well.

Or take Chester Himes' and for that matter Donald Goines' work as examples of a hyper reality of black life. Himes creates a Harlem of the imagination, a Harlem that he had a passing acquaintance with yet because of his characterization and convoluted stories and situation, drew the reader into a world wholly of his imagination — a world created with him in self-imposed exile.

Same in a lot of ways with Goines' crime-laden novels. Yes, he was a hustler, thief and pimp, and certainly those experiences provided the underpinnings in his work, but he wrote these Blaxploitation-fueled books about this cat Kenyatta a militant gangster out to clean up the ghetto of the criminals, drugs and crooked cops. Ironically written while Goines maintained feeding that monkey, his heroin habit. Outside of the sort of wish fulfillment arena Goines constructs, that sort of brother wouldn't last a week in the real world as cops, the FBI, CIA, whomever, would drop on this dude with both feet. But does it tap something deep and significant in a populace hungry for heroes, yes, it does.

Certainly that explains why some parts of the black community hold up and are respectful of Condoleezza Rice and Colin Powell due to the relative positions of power they've achieved. But are not critical in a class analysis way of what kind of relative power they represent. And if she wasn't Secretary of Sate, wouldn't a woman named Condoleezza be the brunt of jokes by right wing blowhards like Bill O'Reilly and Rush Limbaugh? A name they would stereo-typically use to label welfare queens?

Q7. What do you want readers to find when they come to your books and short stories?

I'd like my readers to be entertained, surprised, amused and maybe even titillated.

Gail Ramsey

Gail Ramsey has written articles on the reciprocal influences of courtroom drama and headline news. She is a trial consultant and author of *Tick Tock*, legal fiction.

Q1. Some scholars say that concepts such as "crime" and "justice" have no meaning other than that acquired in the context of human interaction within a given society. Do you agree? If so, what are your thoughts about the concepts of "crime" and "justice" in American society?

The human experience defines the context of most things. Take the crime of rape, for example, but for the horrid experiences of the victims which gave rape its inherent meanings in our society we may define it differently. A person is raped in our society every two minutes, according to statistics from the Justice Department. The act as well as its post–traumatic stresses albeit often underreported are though clear. There is a place for rape in literature as there is for other crimes and aspects of justice because of what we know about these things. Thus we attach so much importance on the criminal justice process and ultimately the vindication of a guilty or not-guilty verdict.

Q2. In your books and short stories, does your protagonist pretty much reflect your own view of the world and how it operates?

Yes and no. It depends on the story. In *Tick Tock*, because the protagonist orchestrated a high-profile case, sure my own experiences guided her along. So on some creative sensory level, how a protagonist reacts to crime and justice may be bore of my own thoughts. But at other times like the wealthy widow protagonist in my second novel who takes on the world on her own terms, strikingly different from mine, it was I who saw the world through my character's eyes.

Q3. Are there social issues that you feel are important to deal with in your work as a mystery writer?

I try not to use the novel setting as a platform for social issues. Yet, characters are reflective of real people, real places and yes real social issues so in many instances there is no separating the two. A reoccurring theme in my writing is what happens when ordinary people suddenly become headlines news because of crime and justice. To that end, I strive to get across that the lawyers, victims, and even the defendants and the people that love them all have lives beyond the courtroom or the headlines with real personal and private challenges which embodies social issues that we seldom appreciate while watching late-breaking news.

Q4. Who are the writers (genre/non-genre) who have most influenced your own writing?

Lisa Scottoline, Valerie Wilson-Wesley, E Lynn Harris, Walter Mosley, Mary Morrison and Mary Higgins Clark, if only to name my top picks from various genres all abundantly crafty on telling a tale.

Q5. As an African American writer, do you find it necessary or challenging to strike a balance between "politics" and "art"?

On politics or say justice and art, I am challenged by a distrust of politicians and lawyers two of the most prestigious professions of our society. So I try to show both sides of a courtroom in all of its facets—the good and the pathetic. I think that is necessary. Similarly, if a character's political views are germane to a story, those views will resonate, likely though with considerable thought.

Q6. Do you think there are certain aspects of American and/or African American life and culture that tend to appear in the works of African American mystery writers?

What I appreciate most about the African American mystery writing is that we get to see main characters in roles more reflective of our society—African Americans as the lawyers, the detectives, of course, the police officers, and also the trial consultants, legal secretaries, paralegals, etc. As a result of being in these lead roles in culture, it translates to literature where we can more completely and accurately flesh out the many roller-coaster twists of African American life and memorialize it in print and on to the big screen.

Q7. What do you want readers to find when they come to your books and short stories?

Fiction so compelling it could actually be true where readers see themselves in my characters, settings, challenges, defeats, and victories on both sides of the law.

Pamela Samuels-Young

Pamela Samuels-Young is the author of the legal thrillers *In Firm Pursuit* and *Every Reasonable Doubt*. An attorney who specializes in discrimination law, Pamela received her law degree from the University of California at Berkeley.

Q1. Some scholars say that concepts such as "crime" and "justice" have no meaning other than that acquired in the context of human interaction within a given society. Do you agree? If so, what are your thoughts about the concepts of "crime" and "justice" in American society?

In my view, both "crime" and "justice" in American society can be heavily skewed — positively or negatively — by factors such as race, gender, age, economic status, and so forth. As a lawyer, I've witnessed the disparities firsthand. If you can afford the best lawyer, you get the best defense. If you're poor and minority, you'll likely face tougher sentencing even if you have a good attorney. Our nation's disparate sentencing guidelines for those convicted of drug crimes— minorities who use crack are treated far more severely than whites who use cocaine — is a prime example of this.

Q2. In your books and short stories, does your protagonist pretty much reflect your own view of the world and how it operates?

My protagonist definitely incorporates my world view, but I also attempt to show snapshots of how others view the world. I began writing legal fiction because of the absence of women and African American characters in mainstream legal fiction. I wanted to present that viewpoint, which is a perspective that we don't often see in legal fiction.

Q3. Are there social issues that you feel it important to deal with in your work as a mystery writer?

I don't think I consciously set out to attack a particular social issue, but it happened anyway. In *Every Reasonable Doubt*, my two main characters are African American women who work in an all-white law firm. The murder defendant is also an African American woman, while the prosecutor is a Caucasian woman. The novel touches upon racism, affirmative action, the difficult choices working women must face, as well as issues of the adequacy of our legal system.

Q4. Who are the writers (genre/non-genre) who have most influenced your own writing?

My writing has been influenced by many, many writers including James Baldwin, Toni Morrison, Terry McMillan, Walter Mosley, Valerie Wilson Wesley, Joan Didion, Michael Connelly, Tom Wolfe, James Patterson, Bob Woodward and John Grisham.

Q5. As an African American writer, do you find it necessary or challenging to strike a balance between "politics" and "art"?

I view writing novels as a business—a profit-making business. My goal is to write an intriguing legal mystery, one that will entertain readers and sell books. I'm not thinking about politics or art when I sit down to write. My main objective is to entertain. I grew up Compton, California, a community that unfortunately is best known for its crime rate. By virtue of that upbringing and being an African American woman, social and political issues will necessarily seep into my writing.

Q6. Do you think there are certain aspects of American and/or African American life and culture that tend to appear in the works of African American mystery writers?

I think it would be difficult for *any* African American writer *not* to write about their culture. We write what we know. I began writing legal fiction because I wanted to see "my story" in print. But I don't think that's any different for any other race of writers. We all write from our individual perspectives. It's unfortunate, however, that most African American writers are marketed solely to African Americans. There's a perception in the publishing industry that non–African Americans won't read our work and, as a result, we aren't included in the mystery section of book stores. I think that perception is both wrong and discriminatory, but it's not something I expect to see change anytime soon.

Q7. What do you want readers to find when they come to your books and short stories?

Foremost, I want to present readers with engaging legal thrillers. For readers who are not African American, I hope to broaden their perceptions of African Americans, which I think tends to be very limited and primarily negative because of our depiction in the media. When I sat down to write *Every Reasonable Doubt*, I was very excited about telling a story about two savvy, African American female attorneys embroiled in high-profile murder case. I think readers of any race will be able to relate to the ups and downs these women face in the courtroom and in their personal lives.

Gammy Singer

Actress Gammy L. Singer who lives in New York City has turned her talents to writing and her debut novel set in Harlem, *A Landlord's Tale*, told with grit and humor, about ex-con Amos Brown has been optioned for film and television by Laurence Fishburne's Gypsy Cinema Productions. Her second novel in the series, *Down and Dirty*, was released in 2006.

Q1. Some scholars say that concepts such as "crime" and "justice" have no meaning other than that acquired in the context of human interaction within a given society. Do you agree? If so, what are your thoughts about the concepts of "crime" and "justice" in American society?

Social attitudes change, are always in a state of flux. Therefore, concepts such as crime and justice are attitudinal, depending upon the era that is the point of reference. Crime can be defined as what is offensive to the greatest amount of people at a certain time, i.e., it can be a crime in one era to spit on the sidewalk. Or, consider the offense of rape. That crime has had so many variable considerations before coming to be labeled as something punishable — things like ethnicity, status, whether one is married or not, have all factored in. Has it been a crime to rape a black woman in 1800, 1921, 1960, etc.? A little crime, a big crime? Can a wife be raped? Can a woman of lower economic status, or having questionable occupation accuse a powerful man in our justice system and succeed in our courts? Other examples abound — see drugs. However, crime and justice often have nothing to do with "Truth." That is a different discussion. Justice is not always bound up in Truth, at least, not in a manmade legal system.

Q2. In your books and short stories, does your protagonist pretty much reflect your own view of the world and how it operates?

Sometimes, sometimes not. My protagonist is a black male, born in Harlem, who went through the prison system. His attitudes and ways of approaching life would not be mine. However, in writing fiction, I don't think a writer can escape having one's own point of view sift through. I get a kick out of taking the male POV in terms of the male attitude toward woman and all things feminine.

Q3. Are there social issues that you feel it important to deal with in your work as a mystery writer?

Yes, prejudice, injustice in the legal system, corruption in government all are subjects that are part of the world in which my protagonist resides. Whether tackled head on or as a subtle context of the story, these concerns exist, and cannot help but be incorporated into the fiction that I write.

Q4. Who are the writers (genre/non-genre) who have most influenced your own writing?

I'm a weird reader with catholic tastes. I like Amy Tan, Charles Dickens, Jane Austen, Walter Moseley, Ludlum in his prime, James Baldwin. I have other favorites but the list would get too long.

Q5. As an African American writer, do you find it necessary or challenging to strike a balance between "politics" and "art"?

I don't think about it. I just write.

Q6. Do you think there are certain aspects of American and/or African American life and culture that tend to appear in the works of African American mystery writers?

I believe racism is an inescapable subject we can't get away from. Music is another.

Q7. What do you want readers to find when they come to your books and short stories?

I am writing books to entertain people. I want them to like my protagonist, feel for and as him. If they get a message from my writing, that's good, too, but there's no particular polemic I'm pushing.

Chassie West

Chassie West is the author of twenty-five books, including the Leigh Ann Warren series, two of which were Edgar and Anthony nominees.

Q1. Some scholars say that concepts such as "crime" and "justice" have no meaning other than that acquired in the context of human interaction within a given society. Do you agree? If so, what are your thoughts about the concepts of "crime" and "justice" in American society?

I'm not sure how to answer this because I'm not sure what you're asking. I can say that justice in our society can depend on where one falls on the economic ladder. Those on or near the bottom rungs rarely have access to the same quality of protection before or after a crime is committed, or defense in court as those higher up.

Q2. In your books and short stories, does your protagonist pretty much reflect your own view of the world and how it operates?

I think so. Leigh Ann Warren is basically (bless her heart) an optimist. Remembering the policeman who saved her life when she was five, she became a cop because she wanted to be to others what he was to her: someone who had a positive impact on someone else's life, someone who made a difference. She recognizes that the justice system is not always fair but tries to work within it with as even-handed approach as she can.

Q3. Are there social issues that you feel it important to deal with in your work as a mystery writer?

Only in the most broad sense. It was important to me to present a character we rarely see represented in the media, an African American who is law-abiding, employed and probably considered middle class, depending on no one else for his/her survival, content with the concept of life as an unmarried person but open to a relationship in which he/she is an equal partner. This segment of our population is for the most part invisible or non-existent, if we are to believe what we see in headlines or on the small and large screens. Far more often, the public is exposed to opposite ends of the spectrum, those brothers and sisters on the bottom or top rungs. Granted, it's better than it used to be but we rarely see the vast majority of us.

Q4. Who are the writers (genre/non-genre) who have most influenced your own writing?

Too many to name, but off the top of my head Helen McInnes, Alice Walker, Rosa Guy, Sandra Kitt, Nora Roberts, Terris Grimes.

Q5. As an African American writer, do you find it necessary or challenging to strike a balance between "politics" and "art"?

No. I have always admired storytellers and the manner in which they kept me engrossed, engaged, and involved in worlds beyond my own. Storytellers have kept me sane, have been role models. So that has always been my approach, to move a listener or reader beyond their own existence for a while. Whereas politics and art may stumble into a story, they have never been a launching point or platform for me. All I aspire to do is to keep a reader engrossed and caring about a character and what happens to him or her.

Q6. Do you think there are certain aspects of American and/or African American life and culture that tend to appear in the works of African American mystery writers?

One cannot draw an accurate picture of African American life without including the impact that slavery and racism have on each succeeding generation and its psyche. It may or may not be obvious so far as a given character is concerned, but it's there. And we as writers can show not only the damage it's done but the ways in which it has made us stronger as well.

Q7. What do you want readers to find when they come to your books and short stories?

See #5.

Interviews with Scholars

Norlisha F. Crawford

Norlisha Crawford, Assistant Professor, Department of English, and Director, African American Studies Program, University of Wisconsin Oshkosh, writes about the detective fiction of Chester Himes.

Q1. Based on your own research and reading, would you say that there are aspects of plot, setting, and characters that tend to be common in the works of African American mystery writers?

From the first, African American mystery writers have tended to "humanize" their protagonists, especially the heroic figures. These writers, beyond simply offering a compelling read, each understood their creative works would also have to challenge prevailing stereotypes and racialized images that denigrated blacks. The plots in mysteries written by African Americans involve the usual heists, scams, and moneymaking schemes that set the stage for the murders and mayhem that are found in traditional mainstream genre works. And yet, the crimes in African American mysteries inevitably take the central characters to communities, usually African American but sometimes communities that are multiracial and multicultural—for example, Himes' Harlem, Walter Mosley's or Paula Woods' Los Angeles, Barbara Neely's Boston, or Eleanor Taylor Bland's Lincoln Prairie (a stand-in for Waukegan, Illinois). The reader comes to better understand issues of importance in real-world African American communities as she or he follows the story. The detectives, amateur or professional, interact with childhood friends, have spouses or significant others about whom they care, fall in and out of love or romantic relationships, and are introspective regarding their relationships with other citizens of color. They have a more heightened sense of social injustice, relying often on poetic justice balancing the scales for African American clients and citizens in the face of racist restrictions that prevent justice from being color-blind.

Stephen Soitos talks about Chester Himes' Harlem as a "city within a city," in *The Blues Detective*. Reading the novels in Himes' series one finds a complex social structure that is as much a reflection of the setting itself as of the characters who live there. In African American mysteries, characters often speak in vernacular language styles that suggest their racial and ethnic ancestry; reference African American cultural forms and traditions, as they move about the settings of the texts, looking for clues or nursing their wounds when things get tough in their investigations; and discuss, play, or quote lyrics from African American music, including jazz, blues, Motown and R&B. That music often sets the mood or tone for key scenes in African American mysteries. So, as a reader, one must center one's perspectives from an African American point of view, culturally, in order to appreciate the layered nuances of the works. The characters in African American mysteries, unlike most traditional mysteries, especially the hard-boiled, have always been aware of themselves as racialized, and therefore to some degree, politicized. For example, black characters explicitly discuss the wariness among many African American citizens for their local police forces. A long history of discriminatory practices in law enforcement is acknowledged by black characters even if only as an aside or in humor. The conflict of having one foot in an African American community, as a member sharing a cultural identity, while the other foot is in the mainstream world, restoring the societal status quo, is an often-repeated notion that gets interrogated publicly and introspectively by many African American mystery characters.

Q2. How would you describe the roles of race/ethnicity and gender in shaping the worldviews of African American mystery writers about "crime" and "justice"?

In my response to the first question, I suggest this answer as well. The concepts of "crime" and "justice" are tricky for African Americans. Their relationship historically to the national community has been one of making a lie out of the grandly touted ideals of U.S. democracy. Even as the European settlers in the Massachusetts Bay colony were establishing the principles of what would become the democracy we all know today — and as a governmental concept, American-style democracy is a beautiful notion — they were also starting to import forcibly Africans for servitude without human rights or wages. They were setting the stage for introducing chattel slavery. Reading only mainstream genre literature one might imagine that readers did not know of this dichotomy — and least of all, African Americans. But, of course, just the opposite is true: African Americans are always aware of their situation; from Phylis Wheatley to current writers, the case is being made for both interrogating false barriers of racial difference and achieving recognition and rights as fully functioning human beings and citizens. Whether the "Sambo" character or a knife-bearing brute, the "Jezebel" or "mammy," African Americans have challenged in their genre works stereotypes that denied their humanity.

Q3. What observations have you made about the mix or balance of "politics" and "art" in the works of African American mystery writers?

While some African American authors have engaged fully in the debate over whether one can or should create literary art simply for its aesthetic value, those African Americans who have written in the mystery genre seem to have settled on a compelling mix of art and politics in a balance that gives credence to the works.

Q4. Do you have any observations about the responses of various audiences to the works of African American mystery writers?

At popular culture conferences where readers, authors and scholars of the mystery genre meet, I have found those in attendance are self-selected, and therefore are accepting already of African American mystery stories. In the classroom, on the other hand, I have found a more mixed reception. Often in my courses, that have been at universities in rural communities with predominantly white students who have come from predominantly racially segregated environments, students sometimes will reject the racial politics of the protagonists, who are predominantly African American and in urban settings. That rejection occurs most often because those politics are oppositional to mainstream concepts of law and order. Mysteries by African Americans often challenge mainstream notions of police serving simply as protectors for citizens, of justice being made available to any "deserving" citizen, of characters involved in criminal activities as simply deviant from social norms, of poverty as a marker for aberrant values and desires. When ideologies that serve as the backdrops for U.S. politics, economics, history, and just plain racism in practices and traditions, are suggested in the works as the root causes for so-called racial differences, as opposed to genetics, many students are reluctant to change their pre-conceived, or at least their heretofore unquestioned, notions about connections between race and poverty and individual responses to that nexus.

Q5. Is there any thing else you would like to add?

Chester Himes says in *My Life of Absurdity* (1976), the second of his autobiographical works:

> The thought stayed with me all through the time when I was writing [what would become *A Rage in Harlem* (1957)] that this wasn't a detective story I was writing.... It was really what one might call an action story. Maybe it was an unconscious protest against soul brothers always being considered as victims of racism, a protest against racism itself excusing all their sins and major faults [111].

It seems to me that Himes suggests at least two important ideas with this statement. One is an on-going connection with 250 years of African American literary tradition, including with his influential acquaintances, Richard Wright, James Baldwin, and Ralph Ellison. Each of the authors in that tradition have written works that challenge seeing African Americans as anything other than complex human beings. On one hand, Himes was not interested in writing strictly polemical work, simply railing against racism. On the other hand, he was not interested in strictly artistic work, showcasing his creative skills with words used as if beautiful figurative strokes of paint. He wanted to achieve a balance between the two positions. Accordingly, he wrote compelling, fast-paced stories that forced readers to see the world of racial and socio-economic politics upside down. If there were perspectives and actions that could be judged heroic in the novels, they were those of characters that normally would be considered devalued and degraded by mainstream literary characterization norms. This leads to the second idea that Himes' detective series suggests. Yes, his characters may make mistakes in their conduct, and usually the choices they make are predicated on being forced to live within racist constrictions. But lamenting victimization is not the point of Himes showing the social injustices that are associated with black life in urban United States. A frank unsentimental look at the socioeconomic context for the domestic environments that exist for some U.S. citizens, as represented by his Harlem and his characters, so that individual responses to that environment can be assessed by readers as situational, not as deterministic genetically driven markers of race, is what Himes and other African American authors writing in the mystery genre have and do offer.

Maureen T. Reddy

Maureen T. Reddy, chair of English at Rhode Island College, is the author of *Traces, Codes, and Clues: Reading Race in Crime Fiction* and *Sisters in Crime: Feminism and the Crime Novel.*

Q1. Based on your own research and reading, would you say that there are aspects of plot, setting, and characters that tend to be common in the works of African American mystery writers?

Plots often center on the thorny complexities of race matters, as for example in the many "passing" novels published in the 1990s (which I hesitate to name here for fear of giving away plot surprises). In my *Traces, Codes, and Clues: Reading Race in Crime Fiction*, I summarize the recurring features of novels by black women writers featuring black women detectives that together suggest an ideological position opposed to the traditional hard boiled this way: "a black female consciousness in the central position in the text, with that consciousness demonstrably connected to a wider black community and shaped by it; emphasis on the political dimension of friendship between black women; attention to black women's roles as mothers and other-mothers; a focus on the systemic opposition of law and justice; scenes of instruction on the intersections of race and gender; use of a specifically race-based invisibility/hypervisibility theme; and narrative interest in colorism and class issues among people of color, particularly their impact on black women" (76).

Q2. How would you describe the roles of race/ethnicity and gender in shaping the worldviews of African American mystery writers about "crime" and "justice"?

I can't really comment on how writers' world views were shaped, but only about what their fiction demonstrates. There, I think, we see a shared view that racism is absolutely foundational in U.S. society, with all that implies, such as a reasonable distrust of the police as the agents of an unjust social order. Crime fiction traditionally begins in a disruption of order (the crime) and moves toward a restoration of order (the solution, bringing the criminal to "justice"); when the order itself is seen as inherently unjust due to racism, restoring that order is not desirable, a position taken up by much white feminist crime fiction as well as crime fiction by black writers, with the exception of a very few series whose detectives are police officers.

Q3. What observations have you made about the mix or balance of "politics" and "art" in the works of African American mystery writers?

I'm perplexed by this question, as I don't see the two—"politics" and "art"—as separable or even as distinct: art is always political, one way or another. Anyone who would claim otherwise just isn't reading carefully or only recognizes politics when they differ from his/her own.

Q4. Do you have any observations about the responses of various audiences to the works of African American mystery writers?

Because I haven't done a systematic study of audience responses, I'm afraid to generalize. However, my impression is that white readers and readers of color have embraced some black mystery writers for quite different reasons, which is fascinating to me. For instance, browsing through readers' comments on amazon.com — where people sometimes identify themselves by race/ethnicity in the course of their remarks— seldom do white readers seem aware of the deep, serious challenge the Easy Rawlins series poses to the ideological status quo on race, while it is precisely that issue that seems to resonate with readers of color. I was intrigued, and disturbed, when several white reviewers claimed Kris Nelscott's Smokey Dalton series was even better than Walter Mosley's Easy Rawlins books; personally, I find Nelscott's writing clunky and tedious but Mosley's beautiful and powerful. One reviewer said Smokey was a "more compelling" character than Easy. For me, this was all about race: Nelscott is a white woman, Smokey is far more conventional than Easy, the Smokey Dalton books do not seriously undermine the racial status quo. I think white readers may feel more comfortable with Smokey than with Easy, which is not a good thing.

Q5. Is there any thing else you would like to add?

I think gender is central in books by black mystery writers, just as it is in books by white mystery writers. However, in white-authored books, with the significant exception of feminist books, gender is silently reinscribed, taken for granted, whereas even in totally non-feminist black-authored books, gender and sexuality get questioned. I'm thinking of Gar Anthony Haywood's Aaron Gunner series, for instance, where what constitutes black manhood is frequently addressed.

Robert E. Skinner

Robert Skinner has worn the hat of both crime fiction critic and crime fiction writer. Among his books are four dealing with the career of Chester Himes, and six novels in the Wesley Farrell series, including *Skin Deep, Blood Red* and *The Righteous Cut*. He is University Librarian at Xavier University of Louisiana.

Q1. Based on your own research and reading, would you say that there are aspects of plot, setting, and characters that tend to be common in the works of African American mystery writers?

I think that there are some real similarities, particularly among the major figures. The setting tends to be largely an urban one, often set primarily in the African American community. Some black characters may have relationships or live part of their lives in the wider "white world." The hero or heroine, either a professional detective of an unofficial one, may often find that the crime he or she investigates may occur in the black community, but the impetus for the crime often derives from corruption or exploitation from outside by whites. Many African American stories include certain character types: victim, sucker, the black man or woman corrupted or exploited by whites who in turn corrupts or exploits other blacks. White cops, often corrupt or brutal, and corrupt white political figures seem to play a part in many stories.

Q2. How would you describe the roles of race/ethnicity and gender in shaping the worldviews of African American mystery writers about "crime" and "justice"?

The American detective story is, in its most classical form, a story about an outsider, usually a private eye, rogue cop, or everyman who attempts to correct an injustice that law either causes, or at best can't remedy. The worldview of these writers is one that seems to say that the exercise of "law" often subverts or prevents "justice" for the little guy. The detective, often an existential hero with his own code of right and wrong, ignores or breaks the law in order to provide justice for victims who lack the power or money to get it through established legal channels.

I think the African American mystery writer has very similar world view. Racial oppression is very much a political oppression, brought about by the corruption of American institutions. Because he has experienced this political oppression, himself, the African American hero is even more of an outsider than the white private eye. Unlike his white counterpart, he is as much a victim of racial oppression as the African American victim he helps. This gives him a larger stake in the achievement of "justice" for his client. A victory for his client is also, in a smaller way, the hero's victory.

I think the African American hero also recognizes that every victory is a qualified victory. Some justice will be achieved, but a fight against racial/political oppression is more than a fight against corrupt institutions. It is also a fight against the illogic of racism in the human heart. This is beyond the hero's ability to affect.

Q3. What observations have you made about the mix or balance of "politics" and "art" in the works of African American mystery writers?

I haven't noticed a lot of overt political discussion in African American mysteries, but because many stories are about crime in the black community, there is always a socio-political element being subtly played out. When one envisions a "black community" in America, poverty and crime are very much a part of that backdrop. We understand instinctively that American political and economic institutions have played a large part in keeping those communities poor. Poor people have no real political power because they have no economic power. They are trapped in a cycle that only a rare few can escape. Those trapped in the poverty are further oppressed by a black criminal element that preys on its own community.

Q4. Do you have any observations about the responses of various audiences to the works of African American mystery writers?

I think that the fact that there is a significant audience for African American mystery is a very positive comment on a broadening world view among readers. When Chester Himes began publishing his Harlem Domestic Series in America, most of the books were published as paperback originals and consequently got very little attention from reviewers. Although he was the first black crime writer to attract a white audience, there were many of both races who saw his work as dangerous and inflammatory. Now his work is considered part of the canon, is continuously in print, and has even been included in the Library of America. Latter day writers like Walter Mosley and Gar Haywood and others have attracted the attention of both white and black readers and have earned the praise of review establishment. They appear to be immune to the kind of criticism Himes faced.

As a white male writing fiction about African American characters, I have often been interested in the public reception of my own work. When I first began publishing, I was aware of a small, but insistent undercurrent that suggested there was something improper about what I was doing, and that it may be politically incorrect for me to try to imagine the lives of black people. I will note that as time went on, that undercurrent began to fade. I've received a lot of support from both white and black readers, and enjoyed generally positive reviews. I really can't conceive of writing a mystery that doesn't feature black characters.

Q5. Is there any thing else you would like to add?

Having reviewed mysteries on and off for twenty years, I'm aware that there are a lot of mystery novels being published in the United States. It happens that many of them are fairly mediocre and unimaginative. In my opinion, the relative handful of African American writers who work in the mystery field are among the most consistently readable. Black writers have taken material that's been used over and over, put their own indelible stamp on it, and in many regards, infused a tired and overworked genre with new life.

Concluding Thoughts:
Worldviews in Context

The goal of this book was to examine the works of modern African American mystery writers in historical context. In the process, we traveled from the colonial era to the present, examining how African American writers have responded to issues of crime and justice. As the literary heirs of earlier African American writers (who were mindful of the tensions between art and politics in their works), how do modern African American mystery writers deal with the issues of crime and justice? What are the worldviews expressed in the works of modern Black mystery writers?

The answers to these questions are complex. As do other writers, African American mystery writers make pragmatic decisions related to the process and business of writing. For example, in an interview (MysteryOne, 2001), Eleanor Taylor Bland talks about how she made her decision that her protagonist would be a cop. Bland decided to have a police detective as her protagonist because she was a new writer with a busy life (full-time job, infant grandson to raise, attending grad school), and it was easier to have a cop as her sleuth than an amateur or PI who had to "keep falling over bodies." This kind of decision is one that every mystery writer must make. Yet when Bland made this decision, she created the first Black female police detective in a series by an African American mystery writer. Bland's series reflects both her multicultural perspective and her concern with certain social issues (e.g., abused children and the homeless).

African American mystery writers bring their own individual concerns and experiences to their books. However, they are members of a group with a history of legal oppression that is unique in American history. As a group, they share the collective memories of that African American past, which may shape their perspectives on the status of Blacks in contemporary America. Arguably, most American writers bring to their work the cultural influences of the groups with which they identify. What is unique for African Americans is the group experience of slavery and of the dual system of justice that institution spawned.

African Americans have never been completely free of the surveillance, control, and attempts at containment that was the essence of the slavery and racial segregation. Like all Black Americans, they continue to deal with the myths of race in America. This is reflected in the works of modern African American mystery writers. Sometimes as subtext, sometimes as theme, less frequently as an "in your face" indictment of American capitalism and its consequences.

There is often a rather intriguing insider subtext, not essential to the mystery itself, but that undoubtedly enriches the reading experience for those in the know. Sometimes this insider information is shared with the uninformed reader without providing in depth explanation. For example, the matter of a police officer's use of chokehold may be shown as an example of police brutality without discussion of the deaths and lawsuits related to this practice. Or an aspect of the protagonist's personal life may be presented without discussion. For example, in Pamela Samuels-Young's series, her protagonist is a high-powered corporate attorney, married to an electrician (who with a partner owns a small company). The author does not bother to explain that the issue of low marriage rates among Black professional women was deemed provocative enough to merit a cover story in *Newsweek* (Samuels, 2003). According to the story, single Black professional women have much lower rates of marriage than their White female peers because of the limited number of eligible African American males of similar education and economic status. The fact that Samuels-Young's protagonist is portrayed as happily married to a man of lower educational and class status might well be taken as the author's comment about this to the readers who are aware of this issue.

Another aspect the works of these mystery writers is the extent to which the diversity of African American life is portrayed. Modern protagonists have frequent encounters with people from other racial/ethnic and cultural backgrounds. Most of these African American sleuths are middle class and hold positions that take them beyond the boundaries of the communities in which they grew up and sometimes still live. This diversity often extends into the personal lives of the protagonists, who may have friends and lovers from backgrounds distinctly different than their own. This provides writers with opportunities to not only create literary conflict, but to examine difference and its meaning. This diversity also challenges the segregated worlds that has historically characterized genre fiction and only began to sure signs of change in the late twentieth century.

As in real life, African American mystery protagonists who are middle- or even upper-class are often the children of working class parents. They have grandparents who lived or still live in the South. They have elders who told stories of lynching and segregation. African American protagonists who forget where they came from do so at their own risk. Those who remember their roots have resources on which to draw, a context in which to understand the "isms" (e.g., racism, sexism, classism) that they encounter.

Although few African American mystery writers have created gay/lesbian protagonists, they do demonstrate awareness of sexual diversity. Gay/lesbian characters sometimes appear in secondary but continuing roles as the protagonist's colleague or friend. Occasionally, writers deal with discrimination and even hate crimes related to sexuality. In general, the writers seem to view sexuality as another form of diversity that they should incorporate into their works.

Modern mystery writers tend to offer critiques of the social structure that produces crime, poverty, and inequality. Routinely, drugs are presented as the scourge of inner city communities. But even when protagonists express disapproval of addicts and anger toward dealers, they also tend to place the activities of these characters in the larger context of a "war on drugs" that not only failed to reduce the flow of drugs but has worsen police-community relations. But even those protagonists who are generally suspicious of the police acknowledge the existence of an occasional hard-working and fair-minded cop.

To sum up, in books by African American mystery writers:
1 African American culture and the culture of memory play an integral part.
2. Diversity and multiculturalism are expressed in the range of characters and their often intimate involvement in the protagonists' lives.
3. Crime and justice tend to be viewed in the larger context of American history, and the history of conflict with the White-dominated criminal justice system.
4. The political and social views expressed by protagonists and other characters range from liberal to conservative. Conversations between characters often provide an opportunity for discussion/debate of social and political issues.

But, at the same time, African American mystery writers share much in common with other writers. They are hyphenated Americans and products of American popular culture. That comes through in the comments in interviews in which they talk about coming of age in America. These writers attended public schools, watched television, went to movies, read comic books and the "classics" of American literature. They discovered Nancy Drew, rock and roll, and film noir. They hung out, got a job, went to college, and/or got married and had a family. They go to baseball games, attend concerts, vote, volunteer, complain about the life of writers, do all the things that other writers living in America do.

Still, each writer is also unique and his or her personal history influences decisions from whether to write cozy or hardboiled novels to where the protagonist lives, what kind of car he or she drives, and who he or she helps or tries hard to bring down or lock up. Modern African American mystery/detective writers draw on their cultural history, but they are not writing "anti-detective" novels in the manner of Ishmael Reed or Clarence Major. Their works are rooted in the conventions of the genre. African American mystery writers acknowledge that they have been influenced by both the works of writers from the Golden Age of classic detective fiction, hard-boiled fiction, and police procedurals and by their own contemporaries.

On the other hand, there still seems to be that old question about depiction that bedeviled writers of the Harlem Renaissance and still lingers in the minds of some readers. It is understandable that when presented with so many negative images of African American life and culture, readers would like to see protagonists who are smart, courageous, and embody the virtues that they value. As Gary Phillips observes in the preceding chapter, readers sometimes express disappointment about works featuring Black anti-heroes who engage in the behaviors associated with negative stereotypes of Black men and women. By the same token, readers in search of Black role models and depictions of Black culture may express disappointment if an African American character is "not Black enough" and too assimilated into the mainstream. Both of these objections on the part of readers reflect real-life discussions about what is "authentically black" and about class, culture, and stereotyping.

All of these competing forces and colliding interests are reflected in the worldviews of African American mystery writers. There is no one worldview of African American mystery writers, no one perspective. There is a shared sensibility to the legacy of oppression that Blacks and other people of color share. However, African American mystery writers have created protagonists that reject the status of victims. Their protagonists are survivors who bring their own diverse skills to the task of solving crimes and seeking justice.

Appendix A

Biographical Information

The following list is intended to illustrate the diverse backgrounds of African American mystery writers. Not all of the authors who appear elsewhere in this book are listed here. The list includes the authors about whom more (but not always all) information was available in the public domain. This information was gathered from authors' websites, newspaper articles, and biographical listings, and may have changed or have been incorrect in the original source. Birthplace, education, other employment, and other writings are included. Nominations and awards may be incomplete for some authors (see also the list of mystery organization/conference awards in Appendix C).

Alexander, Vincent. Bachelor's degree, psychology, Rockhurst College; M.A., literature, Baker University. Actor; producer; director; composer; musician; founder of Brother 2 Brother Literary Symposium. Poetry and stage plays. Best Murder Mystery 2002 from Sistah Circle Book Club, Dallas, TX.

Bailey, Frankie Y. Danville, VA. Psychology/English, Virginia Tech; M.A. and Ph.D., criminal justice, State University of New York at Albany. Associate professor, School of Criminal Justice, SUNY Albany. Nonfiction on crime and mass media/popular culture; crime history. Edgar nomination (nonfiction); Anthony and Macavity nominations (nonfiction).

Bates, Karen Grigsby. Connecticut. B.A., Wellesley College in sociology and Black studies; studied at Ghana University; completed executive management program at Yale University. Journalist/contributor to numerous magazines, Los Angeles–based correspondent for NPR's *Day to Day*; alternate host, *Tavis Smiley Show*. Nonfiction, including book on etiquette.

Bland, Eleanor Taylor. Boston, MA. Bachelor's degree, accounting and education. Former accountant at Abbott Laboratories.

Carter, Stephen L. Washington, D.C. B.A., Stanford; J.D., Yale Law School. Professor, Yale Law. Nonfiction about culture, law and religion. Louisville-Grawemeyer award in religion.

Chambers, Christopher. Former U.S. Department of Justice lawyer; professor, Georgetown University; faculty, University of Maryland/UMUC. Anthologies, short fiction, comic books, graphic anthology (edited with Gary Phillips).

Cose, Ellis. Chicago. M.A., science, technology, and public policy, George Washington University. Columnist and contributing editor, *Newsweek*; former chair, editorial board, *New York Daily News*; editorial board, *Chicago Sun-Times, Time, Detroit Free Press*. Nonfiction about race, affirmative action, politics, and other topics. Vision

Award, Maynard Institute for Journalism Education; Unity Award, Society of Professional Journalists.

Darden, Christopher. Richmond, CA. B.A., San Jose State University; J.D., University of California, Hastings College of the Law. Former prosecutor, Los Angeles County District Attorney's Office; faculty, California State University and Southwestern University School of Law; founded Darden & Associates, Inc.

DeLoach, Nora (1940–2001). Orlando, FL. Social worker. Nominated, Georgia Author of the Year in 2000 and 2001.

Due, Tananarive. Florida. B.S., journalism, Northwestern; M.A., English, University of Leeds. Former journalist/columnist, *Miami Herald*. Historical, horror, and other fiction. American Book Award; nominated for Bram Stoker Award; nominated for NAACP Image Award.

Edwards, Grace. Harlem, NY. M.A., creative writing, CUNY. Writing instructor at Writer's Voice (NYC).

Flowers, R. Barri. Detroit. B.A., M.S., Criminal justice, Michigan State University. Literary criminologist. Crime nonfiction, true crime and romance. Michigan State University Wall of Fame.

Greer, Robert. Columbus, OH. Chemistry and journalism, Miami University (Ohio); dentistry degree, Howard University; medical degree, Boston University. Professor of pathology, medicine, surgery, and dentistry, University of Colorado. Founder of literary magazine, *The High Plains Literary Review*; rancher.

Grimes, Terris McMahan. Tucker, AR. Degree in English, California State University. Feature writer for *Sacramento Observer*. Double Anthony Award; Agatha nomination.

Hayes, Teddy. Cleveland, OH. Writer/producer for American Television Network; writing teacher; former producer, music videos; stage producer (lives in London).

Holton, Hugh (1947–2001). Chicago. B.A. and M.A., Roosevelt University. Chicago police officer, 1969–2001. Readers' Choice Award.

Haywood, Gar Anthony. Baldwin Hills, CA. Computer service technician. Television writer, episodes for *New York Undercover* and *The District*; newspaper articles. St. Martin's/Private Eye Writers Best First Novel.

Henry, Angela. Springfield, OH. B.A., English lit, Ohio University. Reference specialist, community college library; columnist; founder of website, MystNoir. MystNoir named USA Today.com "Hot Site"; Golden Web Award.

Lamar, Jake. Bronx, NY. Harvard University. Former *Time* magazine editor; now full-time novelist (lives in Paris).

Lovell, Glenville. Parish Land, Christ Church (Barbados). Dancer; playwright (lives in New York). Plays, short stories, non-genre novels. 2002 Frank Collymore Literary Award for play.

McEachin, James. Rennert, NC. Military; policeman; fireman; record producer; actor, network television, including star of police drama series *Tenafly*; short film maker. The Benjamin Franklin Award; 2007 GI Film Festival Award for Best Short Film.

Meadows, Lee E. Detroit. Ph.D., Michigan State University in higher education and management. Former MSU administrator; assistant professor; consultant, organizational change; host in 1990s of weekly radio program (*The Book Beat*).

Mickelbury, Penny. Atlanta. B.A., Sociology, University of Georgia. Former newspaper, radio and TV reporter. Playwright. Lambda Literary Award for *Night Songs* and *Where to Choose*; runner-up *Booklist*'s Best Crime Novels, 1988–89.

Miller, Cora (C.M.). Cincinnati. University of Cincinnati grad. Financial planner.

Mosley, Walter. Los Angeles. Political science degree. Computer programmer; board of directors of National Book Awards; board of trustees, Goddard College. Other fiction including blues, science fiction, and erotica; nonfiction. Numerous awards, including Edgar, Shamus, Grammy Award for liner notes; Anisfield Award; O. Henry Award; Sundance Institute "Risktaker Award" finalist; NAACP Award in Fiction.

Neely, Barbara. Lebanon, PA. M.A., urban and regional planning, University of Pittsburgh. Host of radio program *Commonwealth Journal* (WUMB-FM); founder of community-based program for female offenders; documentary maker. Short story writer. Winner of Agatha, Macavity, and Anthony; winner of Go on Girl! Book Club Award for Debut Novel.

Phillips, Gary. Los Angeles. Degree in graphic design. Community organizer; graphic designer; printer. Anthologies, graphic novels; columnist, *Mystery Scene* magazine; supernatural stories; chapter on coalition building.

Ramsey, Gail. Administration of justice degree, Temple University; M.A., communication, litigation, public relations, American University. Work with law firms, assisting lawyers in trial presentations. Essay on Pier 34 case (Philadelphia); articles on law and media. Winner of Art Sanctuary's annual award for Pier 34 essay.

Ridley, John. Milwaukee. TV and film writer/producer. Morning show panelist, commentator. Excellence Award, National Association of Black Journalists.

Samuels-Young, Pamela. Compton, CA. B.A., journalism, University of Southern California; M.A., broadcasting, Northwestern; J.D., University of California, Berkeley. TV news writer; corporate attorney; legal consultant, *Soul Food* (Showtime). Winner, Black Expression Book Club Annual Fiction Writing Award.

Singer, Gammy L. Cincinnati. University of Hawaii drama major; M.A. degree program, writing popular fiction, Seton Hall. Former school teacher; actor. Four Dramalogue Awards; NAACP Theater Award.

Thomas-Graham, Pamela. Detroit. Harvard Law and Business Schools. Former president and CEO of CSNBC; current president of Liz Claiborne. *Crain's New York Business*, "40 Under 40."

Underwood, Blair. Tacoma, WA. Carnegie Mellon School of Drama. Actor, including *L.A. Law, City of Angels,* and *Sex and the City*; co-founder, Artists for New South Africa, 1989. Four NAACP Image Awards; *People*, "50 Most Beautiful People" (2000).

Wesley, Valerie Wilson. Connecticut. M.A., Howard University, education; Columbia Graduate School of Journalism. Former executive editor and contributing editor, *Essence* magazine. "Willimena" children's series; women's fiction. Grist Award from New York chapter, National Association of Black Journalists.

West, Chassie. New York. Drama degree, Howard University. Former administrative assistant, Baltimore College; acted in community theater. Young adult (including *Nancy Drew*); romantic suspense.

Woods, Paula. Los Angeles. B.A., English and Black studies; M.A. degree from University of California, Los Angeles. Moseley Fellow in Creative Writing at Pomona College (taught writing course); speaker/lecturer. Editor of anthology; author/editor of nonfiction books; book reviewer, *Los Angeles Times* and *Washington Post*. Mystery anthology nominated, Anthony and Macavity; received Black Caucus of American Library Association award (ALA); Macavity, Edgar, and Anthony nominations, Best First mystery; Best First award from Black Caucus of ALA.

Books of Post-1987 Authors in the Sample

The first year listed is the copyright date of the book. If another edition of the book was used in the sample, the publication date for that edition follows in brackets.

Bailey, Frankie Y. *Death's Favorite Child* (2000)
_____. *A Dead Man's Honor* (2001)
_____. *Old Murders* (2003)
_____. *You Should Have Died on Monday* (2007)
Baker, Nikki. *The Lavender House Murder* (1992)
Bates, Karen Grigsby. *Plain Brown Wrapper* (2001 [2005])
_____. *Chosen People* (2006)
Bland, Eleanor Taylor. *Dead Time* (1992)
_____. *Slow Burn* (1993)
_____. *Done Wrong* (1995 [1996])
_____. *Scream in Silence* (2000 [2001])
_____. *Whispers in the Dark* (2001)
_____. *Windy City Dying* (2002)
_____. *Fatal Remains* (2003)
_____. *A Cold and Silent Dying* (2004)
_____. *A Dark and Deadly Deception* (2005)
Brown, Elaine Meryl. *Lemon City* (2004)
Camacho, Austin S. *The Troubleshooter* (2004)
_____. *Blood and Bone* (2006)
Carter, Charlotte. *Coq au Vin* (1999)
_____. *Drumsticks* (2000)
_____. *Jackson Park* (2003)
_____. *Trip Wire* (2005)
Carter, Stephen L. *The Emperor of Ocean Park* (2002)
Chambers, Christopher. *Sympathy for the Devil* (2001)

_____. *A Prayer for Deliverance* (2003)
Coleman, Evelyn. *What a Woman's Gotta Do* (1998)
Darden, Christopher, and Lochte, Dick. *The Trials of Nikki Hill* (1999)
_____ and _____. *L.A. Justice* (2001)
Davis, Kyra. *Sex, Murder, and a Double Latte* (2005)
_____. *Passion, Betrayal and Killer Highlights* (2006)
DeLoach, Nora. *Mama Stalks the Past* (1997 [1998])
_____. *Mama Rocks the Empty Cradle* (1998 [1999])
_____. *Mama Cracks a Mask of Innocence* (2001)
Edwards, Grace F. *A Toast Before Dying* (1998 [1999])
_____. *No Time to Die* (1999)
_____. *Do or Die* (2000 [2001])
_____. *The Viaduct* (2003)
Flowers, R. Barri. *Justice Served* (2005)
_____. *State's Evidence* (2006)
Fullilove, Eric James. *Blowback* (2001)
Greer, Robert. *The Devil's Hatband* (1996)
_____. *The Devil's Backbone* (1998 [1999])
_____. *Limited Time* (2000)
_____. *Heat Shock* (2003)
_____. *Resurrecting Langston Blue* (2005)
_____. *The Fourth Perspective* (2006)
Grimes, Terris McMahan. *Somebody Else's Child* (1996)

_____. *Blood Will Tell* (1997)
Hardwick, Gary. *Double Dead* (1997 [1998])
_____. *The Executioner's Game* (2005)
Hayes, Teddy. *Blood Red Blues* (1998)
_____. *Dead By Popular Demand* (2000)
Haywood, Gar Anthony (see also Shannon, Ray). *Fear of the Dark* (1988)
_____. *Going Nowhere Fast* (1994 [1995])
_____. *Bad News Travels Fast* (1995)
_____. *It's Not a Pretty Sight* (1996)
_____. *When Last Seen Alive* (1997)
_____. *All the Lucky Ones Are Dead* (1999 [2000])
Henry, Angela. *Tangled Roots* (2006)
_____. *Diva's Last Curtain Call* (2007)
Holton, Hugh. *Presumed Dead* (1994 [1995)]
_____. *Windy City* (1995 [1996])
_____. *Red Lightning* (1998)
_____. *Violent Crimes* (1997 [1998])
_____. *Time of the Assassins* (2000)
_____. *The Devil's Shadow* (2001)
Joe, Yolanda (as Garland, Ardella). *Hit Time* (2002 [2003])
_____. (as _____). *Video Cowboys* (2005 [2006])
Johnson, Keith Lee. *Sugar & Spice* (2003)
Kelley, Norman. *The Big Mango* (2000)
_____ (2002 [2003]). *A Phat Death (Or, The Last Days of Noir Soul)*
Lamar, Jake. *If 6 Were 9* (2001)
_____. *Rendezvous Eighteenth* (2003)
Lovell, Glenville. *Too Beautiful to Die* (2003)
_____. *Love and Death in Brooklyn* (2004)
Meadows, Lee. *Silent Suspicion* (2000)
Mickelbury, Penny. *Keeping Secrets* (1994)
_____. *Night Songs* (1995)
_____. *Where to Choose* (1999 [2001])
_____. *The Step Between* (2000)
Miller, C.M. *Taxes, Death, & Trouble* (2001)
_____. *What She Left Behind* (2003)
Mosley, Walter. *Devil in a Blue Dress* (1990)
_____. *A Red Death* (1991 [1992])
_____. *White Butterfly* (1992 [1993])
_____. *Black Betty* (1994)
_____. *A Little Yellow Dog* (1996 [1997])
_____. *Gone Fishin'* (1997 [1998])
_____. *Always Outnumbers, Always Outgunned* (1998)
_____. *Walkin' the Dog* (1999)
_____. *Fearless Jones* (2001 [2002])
_____. *Fear Itself* (2003 [2004])
_____. *Six Easy Pieces* (2003)
_____. *Little Scarlet* (2004 [2005])

_____. *Fear of the Dark* (2006)
Neely, Barbara. *Blanche on the Lam* (1992 [1993])
_____. *Blanche Among the Talented Tenth* (1994 [1995])
_____. *Blanche Cleans Up* (1998 [1999])
_____. *Blanche Passes Go* (2000 [2001])
Olden, Marc. *Kisaeng* (1991)
_____. *The Ghost* (1999)
Phillips, Gary. *Violent Spring* (1994)
_____. *Perdition, U.S.A.* (1996)
_____. *The Jook* (1999)
_____. *High Hand* (2000 [2001])
_____. *Shooter's Point* (2001 [2002])
_____. *Monkology* (2004)
Ramsey, Gail. *Tick Tock* (2004)
Ridley, John. *Those Who Walk in Darkness* (2003)
Samuels-Young, Pamela. *Every Reasonable Doubt* (2006)
_____. *In Firm Pursuit* (2007)
Shannon, Ray. *Man Eater* (2003)
_____. *Firecracker* (2004)
Singer, Gammy. *A Landlord's Tale* (2005)
_____. *Down and Dirty* (2006)
Smith, Ian. *The Blackbird Papers* (2004)
Smith-Levin, Judith. *Green Money* (2000)
_____. *Reckless Eyeballin'* (2001)
Thomas-Graham, Pamela. *A Darker Shade of Crimson* (1998)
_____. *Blue Blood* (1999)
_____. *Orange Crushed* (2004)
Tramble, Nichelle D. *The Dying Ground* (2001 [2006])
Underwood, Blair; Due Tananarive, and Barnes, Steven. *Casanegra* (2007)
Walker, Blair. *Up Jumped the Devil* (1997)
_____. *Hidden in Plain View* (1999)
_____. *Don't Believe Your Lying Eyes* (2002)
Walker, Persia. *Harlem Redux* (2002)
Wesley, Valerie Wilson. *Dying in the Dark* (2004)
_____. *Easier to Kill* (1998 [1999])
_____. *When Death Comes Stealing* (1994)
_____. *Where Evil Sleeps* (1996 [1997])
West, Chassie. *Killer Chameleon* (2004)
_____. *Killing Kin* (2000)
_____. *Killer Riches* (2001 [2004])
_____. *Sunrise* (1994)
Woods, Paula L. *Inner City Blues* (1999 [2000])
_____. *Stormy Weather* (2001 [2003])
_____. *Strange Bedfellows* (2006)

Appendix C

Nominations and Awards

A. Agatha Award (Malice Domestic)

1996 — Best First Novel Nominee   Terris McMahan Grimes (*Somebody Else's Child*)

1992 — Best First Novel Winner   Barbara Neely (*Blanche on the Lam*)

B. Anthony Award (Bouchercon)

1993 — Best First Novel Winner   Barbara Neely (*Blanche on the Lam*)

1996 — Best Short Story Winner   Gar Anthony Haywood ("And Pray Nobody Sees You")

1997 — Best First Novel Winner   Terris McMahan Grimes (*Somebody Else's Child*)

1997 — Best Paperback Winner   Terris McMahan Grimes (*Somebody Else's Child*)

2000 — Best First Novel Nominee   Paula L. Woods (*Inner City Blues*)

2001 — Best Novel Nominee   Chassie West (*Killing Kin*)

2005 — Best Non-Fiction Nominee   Frankie Y. Bailey and Steven Chermak (*Famous American Crimes and Trials*, 5-vol. set)

2005 — Best Cover Art Nominee   Michael Kellner; Gary Phillips (*Monkology*)

C. Chester Himes Award (Friends of Chester Himes)

1996 — Gar Anthony Haywood
1997 — Terris Grimes [McMahan]
1998 — Walter Mosley
1999 — Robert Greer
2000 — Eleanor Taylor Bland

2001 — Alice Holman
2002 — Renay Jackson
2003 — Gary Phillips
2004 — No award given

D. Edgar Award (Mystery Writers of America)

1969 — Best Juvenile Novel Winner   Virginia Hamilton (*The House of Dies Drear*)

1970 — Best Novel Nominee   Chester Himes (*Blind Man with a Pistol*)

1978 — Best Paperback Original Novel Nominee   Marc Olden (*They've Killed Anna*)

1991 — Best First Novel Nominee   Walter Mosley (*Devil in a Blue Dress*)

1992 — Best Critical/Biographical Work Nominee Frankie Y. Bailey (*Out of the Woodpile: Black Characters in Crime and Detective Fiction*)

1993 — Best Novel Nominee Walter Mosley (*White Butterfly*)

1995 — Best Paperback Original Nominee Chassie West (*Sunrise*)

1996 — Best Motion Picture Nominee Carl Franklin, director (*Devil in a Blue Dress*)

1997 — Best Critical/Biographical Work Nominee Stephen F. Soitos (*The Blues Detective: A Study of African American Detective Fiction*)

2000 — Best First Novel Nominee Paula L. Woods (*Inner City Blues*)

2000 — Best Play Nominee Thulani Davis (*Everybody's Ruby*)

2001 — Best Paperback Original Nominee Chassie West (*Killing Kin*)

2006 — Best Play Winner Gary Earl Ross (*Matter of Intent*)

2008 — Best Juvenile Novel Nominee Evelyn Colman (*Shadows on Society Hill*)

E. Macavity Award (Mystery Readers International)

1993 — Best First Novel Winner Barbara Neely (*Blanche on the Lam*)

2000 — Best First Mystery Novel Winner Paula L. Woods (*Inner City Blues*)

2005 — Best Nonfiction Nominee Frankie Y. Bailey and Steven Chermak (*Famous American Crimes and Trials*, Vol. 1)

F. Shamus Award (Private Eye Writers)

1987 — St. Martin's Press/PWA Best First Private Eye Contest Winner Gar Anthony Haywood (*Fear of the Dark*)

1989 — Best First P.I. Novel Winner Gar Anthony Haywood (*Fear of the Dark*)

1991 — Best First P.I. Novel Winner Walter Mosley (*Devil in a Blue Dress*)

1994 — Best P.I. Short Story Nominee Walter Mosley ("The Watt's Lion")

1995 — Best First P.I. Novel Nominee Valerie Wilson Wesley (*When Death Comes Stealing*)

1996 — Best P.I. Short Story Nominee Gar Anthony Haywood ("And Pray Nobody Sees You")

2001 — Best P.I. Short Story Nominee Gary Phillips ("The Sleeping Detective")

2006 — Best P.I. Novel Nominee Walter Mosley (*Cinnamon Kiss*)

Checklist of Mystery/Detective Fiction, Film and Television

Novels

Alexandria, Vincent. *If Walls Could Talk,* We Must X-L Publishing, re-issue, 2004.
_____. *Black Rain,* We Must X-L Publishing, 2004.
_____. *Postal Blues,* We Must X-L Publishing, re-issue, 2004.
Anderson, Maggie. *Murder by Prophecy,* ReGeJe Press, 1998.
Anthony, Mark. *The Take Down,* St. Martin's Press, 2006.
Anthony, Sterling. *Cookie Cutter,* Ballantine, 1999.
Arnold, N. Xavier *The Genocide File,* Tana Lake, 1997.
_____. *Day of the Moon,* Chicago Spectrum, 2004.
Bailey, Frankie Y. *Death's Favorite Child,* Overmountain Press, 2000.
_____. *A Dead Man's Honor,* Overmountain Press, 2001.
_____. *Old Murders,* Overmountain Press, 2003.
_____. *You Should Have Died on Monday,* Overmountain Press, 2007.
Baker, Nikki. *Lavender House Murder,* Naiad Press, 1992.
_____. *Long Goodbyes,* Naiad Press, 1993.
_____. *The Ultimate Exit Strategy,* Naiad Press, 1993.
_____. *In the Game.* Naiad Press, 1994/
Banks, Jacqueline Turner. *Maid in the Shade,* ReGeJe Press, 1998.
Banks, Leslie Esdaile. *Blind Trust,* Kensington, 2005.
_____. *Betrayal of The Trust,* Kensington, 2005.
_____. *Shattered Trust,* Dafina, 2006.
_____. *No Trust,* Dafina, 2007.
Bates, Karen Grigsby. *Chosen People,* Avon Books, 2006.
_____. *Plain Brown Wrapper,* Avon Books, 2001.
Beamon, M. C. *Dark Recesses,* Writers Club Press, 2000.
_____. *Eyewitness,* Aventine Press, 2002.
Benson, Christopher. *Special Interest,* Third World, 2001.
Benson, Erick G. *The Weight Pile Murders,* iUniverse.com, 2001.
Bland, Eleanor Taylor. *Dead Time,* St. Martin's Press, 1992.
_____. *Slow Burn,* St. Martin's Press, 1993.
_____. *Gone Quiet,* St. Martin's Press, 1994.
_____. *Done Wrong,* St. Martin's Press, 1995.
_____. *Keep Still,* St. Martin's Press, 1996
_____. *See No Evil,* St. Martin's Press, 1998.

_____. *Tell No Tales,* St. Martin's Press, 1999.

_____. *Scream in Silence,* St. Martin's Press, 2000.

_____. *Whispers in the Dark,* St. Martin's Press, 2001.

_____. *Windy City Dying,* St. Martin's Press, 2002.

_____. *Fatal Remains,* St. Martin's Press, 2003.

_____. *A Cold and Silent Dying,* St. Martin's Press, 2004.

_____. *A Dark and Deadly Deception,* St. Martin's Press, 2005.

Boyd, Randy. *Uprising,* West Beach Books, 2001.

_____. *The Devil Inside,* West Beach Books, 2002.

Briscoe, Edward et al. *Distant Revenge,* iUniverse.com, 2000.

Brookshire, LaJoyce. *Web of Deception,* Retnuh Relations, 1998.

Brown, Elaine Meryl. *Lemon City,* One World/Ballantine, 2004.

_____. *Playing by the Rules,* One World/Ballantine, 2006.

Bruce, John Edward. *The Black Sleuth,* Northeastern University Press, 2002.

Bullard, Linda McKeever. *Shades of Justice,* Dutton, 1998.

Burney, Claudia Mair. *Murder, Mayhem, and a Fine Man,* Navpress Publishing, 2006.

_____. *Death, Deceit & Some Smooth Jazz,* Howard Books/Simon & Schuster, 2008 [2006].

Camacho, Austin. *The Troubleshooter,* Intrigue Publishing, 2004.

_____. *The Payback Assignment,* Intrigue Publishing, 2005.

_____. *Blood and Bone,* Echelon Press, 2006.

Carter, Charlotte. *Rhode Island Red,* Consortium, 1997.

_____. *Coq au Vin,* Mysterious Press, 1999.

_____. *Drumsticks,* Mysterious Press, 2000.

_____. *Walking Bones,* Serpent's Tail, 2002.

_____. *Jackson Park,* One World, 2003.

_____. *Trip Wire,* One World, 2005.

Carter, Stephen L. *The Emperor of Ocean Park,* Vintage, 2002.

_____. *New England White,* Knopf, 2007.

Chambers, Christopher. *Sympathy for the Devil,* Crown, 2001.

_____. *A Prayer for Deliverance,* Crown, 2003.

Cleage, Pearl. *Babylon Sisters,* One World/Ballantine, 2005.

Coleman, Evelyn.*What a Woman's Gotta Do,* Simon & Schuster, 1998.

_____. *Mystery of the Dark Tower,* Pleasant, 2000.

Coram, Robert. *Running Dead,* Signet, 1993.

_____. *Kill the Angels,* Signet, 1996.

_____. *Atlanta Heat,* Signet, 1997.

_____. *Dead South,* Signet, 1999.

Cose, Ellis. *The Best Defense,* HarperCollins, 1998.

Cuthbert, Margaret. *Silent Cradle,* Pocket Books, 1998.

Darden, Christopher, and Dick Lochte. *The Trials of Nikki Hill,* Warner, 1999.

_____. *L.A. Justice,* Warner, 2000.

_____. *The Last Defense,* New American Library, 2002.

_____. *Lawless,* Onyx, 2005.

Davis, Kyra. *Sex, Murder, and a Double Latte,* Red Dress Ink, 2005.

_____. *Passion, Betrayal and Killer Highlights,* Red Dress Ink, 2006.

_____. *Obsession, Deceit and Really Dark Chocolate,* Red Dress Ink, 2007.

Davis, Thulani. *Maker of Saints,* Penguin, 1997.

DeLoach, Nora. *Mama Solves a Murder,* Holloway House, 1994.

_____. *Mama Traps a Killer,* Holloway House, 1995.

_____. *Mama Stands Accused,* Holloway House, 1997.

_____. *Mama Stalks the Past*, Bantam, 1997.

_____. *Mama Pursues Murderous Shadows*, Holloway House, 1997.

_____. *Mama Rocks the Empty Cradle*, Bantam, 1998.

_____. *Mama Saves a Victim*, Bantam, 2000.

_____. *Mama Cracks a Mask of Innocence*, Bantam, 2001.

Edwards, Grace. *If I Should Die*, Doubleday, 1997.

_____. *No Time to Kill*, Doubleday, 1998.

_____. *A Toast Before Dying*, Doubleday, 1999.

_____. *Do or Die*, Doubleday, 2000.

_____. *The Viaduct*, Doubleday, 2003.

Edwards, Louis. *N: A Romantic Thriller*, Dutton, 1997.

Fisher, Rudolph. *The Conjure–Man Dies: A Mystery of Dark Harlem*, University Michigan Press, 1998.

Fleming, Barbara. *Hot Stones, Cold Death*, Silver Maple Press, 2001.

Flowers, R. Barri. *Deadly Secrets in the Motor City*, iUniverse.com, 2000.

_____. *Damning Evidence*, iUniverse.com, 2000.

_____. *Murder in the Rose City*, iUniverse.com, 2000.

_____. *When Night Falls*, Xlibris, 2000.

_____. *Positive ID*, iUniverse.com, 2000.

_____. *Scheme of Things*, Sadorian, 2002.

_____. *Persuasive Evidence*, Leisure Books, 2004.

_____. *Justice Served*, Leisure Books, 2005.

_____. *State's Evidence*, Leisure Books, 2006.

Ford, Clyde W. *Red Herring*, Mystic Voyager Books, 2005.

_____. *The Long Mile*, Midnight Ink, 2005.

_____. *Deuces Wild*, Midnight Ink, 2006.

Fullilove, Eric James. *Blowback*, Amistad Press, 2001.

Garland, Ardella (see Joe, Yolanda).

Gause-Jackson, Arlene. *Howling Against the Wind*, Winston-Derek, 1999.

George, Nelson. *Nightwork*, Touchstone, 2003.

_____. *The Accidental Hunter*, Tandem Library, 2005.

Gibson, John. *Dummy*, Greenfield Publishers, 1997.

Greer, Robert O. *The Devil's Hatband*, Mysterious Press, 1996.

_____. *The Devil's Red Nickel*, Mysterious Press, 1997.

_____. *The Devil's Backbone*, Mysterious Press, 1998.

_____. *Limited Time*, Mysterious Press, 2000.

_____. *Heat Shock*, Mysterious Press, 2003.

_____. *Resurrecting Langston Blue*, Frog Books, 2005.

_____. *The Fourth Perspective*, Frog Books, 2006.

_____. *The Mongoose Deception*, Frog Books, 2007.

Grimes, Terris McMahan. *Somebody Else's Child*, Signet/Onyx, 1996.

_____. *Blood Will Tell*, Signet/Onyx, 1997.

_____. *Other Duties as Required*, Signet, 2000.

Hardwick, Gary. *Cold Medina*, Dutton, 1996.

_____. *Double Dead*, Dutton, 1997.

_____. *Supreme Court*, William Morrow, 1999.

_____. *Color of Justice*, William Morrow, 2002.

_____. *The Executioner's Game*, William Morrow, 2005.

Hayes, Teddy. *Blood Red Blues*, Justin, Charles & Co, 1998.

_____. *Dead By Popular Demand*, Justin, Charles & Co, 2000.

_____. *As Wrong as Two Left Shoes*, The X Press 2003.

Haywood, Gar Anthony (see Shannon, Ray). *Fear of the Dark,* St. Martin's, 1988.
_____. *Not Long for This World,* G. P. Putnam, 1990.
_____. *You Can Die Trying,* St. Martin's Press, 1993.
_____. *Going Nowhere Fast,* Putnam, 1994.
_____. *Bad New Travels Fast,* G. P. Putnam, 1995.
_____. *It's Not a Pretty Sight,* St. Martin's Press, 1996.
_____. *When Last Seen Alive,* Putnam, 1998.
_____. *All the Lucky Ones Are Dead,* Putnam, 1999.
Henry, Angela. *The Pleasure of His Company,* Pagefee Publishing, 2002.
_____. *The Company You Keep,* Kimani Press, 2006.
_____. *Tangled Roots,* Kimani Press, 2006.
_____. *Diva's Last Curtain Call,* Kimani Press, 2007.
Himes, Chester. *A Rage in Harlem* (1957), Vintage 1989.
_____. *Real Cool Killers* (1959), Vintage, 1988.
_____. *The Crazy Kill* (1959), Vintage, 1989.
_____. *All Shot Up* (1960), Thunder's Mouth, 1996.
_____. *Big Gold Dream* (1960), Thunder's Mouth Press, 1996.
_____. *Cotton Comes to Harlem* (1965), Vintage, 1988.
_____. *The Heat's On* (1966), Vintage, 1988.
_____. *Run Man Run* (1966), Carroll & Graf, 1995.
_____. *Blind Man with a Pistol* (1969), Schocken Books, 1987.
_____. *Plan B* (1993), University Press of Mississippi, 1994.
Holman, Alice. *The Last Days Murder List,* Highbridge Press, 2000.
Holton, Hugh. *Presumed Dead,* Forge, 1995.
_____. *Windy City,* Forge, 1995.
_____. *Chicago Blues,* Forge, 1996.
_____. *Violent Crimes,* Forge, 1997.
_____. *Red Lightning,* Forge, 1998.
_____. *The Left Hand of God,* Forge, 1999.
_____. *Time of the Assassins,* Forge, 2000.
_____. *The Devil's Shadow,* Forge, 2001.
_____. *Critical Element,* Forge, 2002.
Hopkins, Pauline. *Hagar's Daughter,* The X Press, 2003.
Jackson, Renay. *Oaktown Devil,* Frog, 2004.
_____. *Shakey's Loose,* Frog, 2004.
_____. *Turf War,* Frog, 2004.
_____. *Crack City,* Frog, 2006.
_____. *Peanut's Revenge,* Frog, 2006.
Jefferson, Roland. *The School on 103rd Street,* W.W. Norton, 1997 [1976].
_____. *Damaged Goods,* Milligan Books, 2003.
Joe, Yolanda. *Falling Leaves of Ivy,* Longmeadow, 1992.
_____. *Details at 10,* Simon & Schuster, 2002.
_____. *Video Cowboys,* Simon & Schuster, 2005.
Johnson, Keith Lee. *Sugar & Spice,* 2003.
Johnson, Lisa Jones. *A Dead Man Speaks,* Genesis Press, 2006.
Johnson, Mat. *Hunting in Harlem,* Bloombury, USA, 2003.
Johnson, Rique. *Love and Justice,* Strebor Books, 2003.
_____. *A Dangerous Return,* Strebor Books, 2007.
_____. *Whispers from a Troubled Heart,* Strebor Books, 2007.
Jones, Solomon. *Pipe Dream,* Random House, 2001.
_____. *The Bridge,* St. Martin's Press, 2003.

_____. *Ride or Die,* St. Martin's Press, 2004.

Kay, Terri. *A Promise of Revenge (The Death of Javier),* Xlibris, 2003.

_____. *The Secret at St. Sans,* Xlibris, 2004.

Kelley, Norman. *Black Heat,* Amistad Press, 2001 [1997].

_____. *The Big Mango,* Akashic Books, 2000.

_____. *A Phat Death (Or, The Last Days of Noir Soul),* Amistad Press, 2002.

_____. *The Bridge,* St. Martin's Minotaur, 2003.

Lamar, Jake. *If 6 Were 9,* Crown, 2001.

_____. *Rendezvous Eighteenth,* St. Martin's Minotaur, 2003.

_____. *The Ghosts of Saint-Michel,* St. Martin's Minotaur, 2006.

Lawrence, Christopher. *All About Mary,* MF Unlimited, 2001.

_____. *Dog 'Em,* MF Unlimited, 2002.

_____. *Mary's Little Lamb,* MF Unlimited, 2003.

Lewis, Shelby. *Simply Wonderful,* Kimani Press, 2000.

Lindsay, Tony. *One Dead Preacher,* Black Words, 2000.

_____. *Prayer of Prey,* Black Words, 2002.

_____. *Street Possessions,* United Brothers, 2005.

_____. *One Dead Lawyer,* Urban Books, 2007.

Lovell, Glenville. *Too Beautiful to Die,* Putnam, 2003.

_____. *Love and Death in Brooklyn,* Putnam, 2004.

Major, Clarence. *Reflex & Bone Structure,* Mercury House, 1996.

Mallette, Gloria. *When We Practice to Deceive,* Holloway House, 1995.

_____. *Shades of Jade,* Villard, 2001.

_____. *Promises to Keep,* Villard, 2002.

Mason, Clifford. *The Case of Ashanti Gold,* St. Martin's, 1985.

_____. *Jamaica Run,* St. Martin's, 1987.

McEachin, James. *Heroin Factor,* Rharl Publishing, 1999.

_____. *Say Goodnight to the Boys in Blue,* Rharl Publishing, 2000.

Meadows, Lee E. *Silent Conspiracy,* Proctor, 1996.

_____. *Silent Suspicion,* Proctor, 2000.

Mickelbury, Penny. *Keeping Secrets,* Naiad Press, 1994.

_____. *Night Songs,* Naiad Press, 1995.

_____. *One Must Wait,* Simon & Schuster, 1998.

_____. *Where to Choose,* Simon & Schuster, 1999.

_____. *The Step Between,* Simon & Schuster, 2000.

_____. *Paradise Interrupted,* Simon & Schuster, 2001.

_____. *Love Notes,* Migibooks, 2002.

_____. *Darkness Descending,* Kings Crossing, 2005.

_____. *Two Graves Dug,* Five Star, 2005.

Miller, C.M. *Taxes, Death, and Trouble,* Writers Club Press, 2000.

_____. *Accural Way to Die,* Writers Club Press, 2001.

_____. *What She Left Behind,* iUniverse, Inc., 2003.

_____. *Dead Broke,* iUniverse, Inc., 2005.

Mosley, Walter. *Devil in a Blue Dress,* W.W. Norton, 1990.

_____. *A Red Death,* W. W. Norton, 1991.

_____. *White Butterfly,* W. W. Norton, 1992.

_____. *Black Betty,* W.W. Norton, 1994.

_____. *A Little Yellow Dog,* W.W. Norton, 1995.

_____. *Gone Fishin',* Black Classic Press, 1997.

_____. *Always Outnumbered, Always Outgunned,* W.W. Norton, 1997.

_____. *Walkin' the Dog,* Little, Brown, 1999.

_____. *Fearless Jones,* Little, Brown, 2001.
_____. *Bad Boy Brawly Brown,* Little, Brown, 2002.
_____. *Fear Itself,* Little, Brown, 2003.
_____. *Six Easy Pieces: Easy Rawlins Stories,* Atria Books, 2003.
_____. *Little Scarlet,* Little, Brown, 2004.
_____. *Fear of the Dark,* Little, Brown, 2006.
_____. *Blonde Faith,* Little, Brown, 2007.
Neeley, Barbara. *Blanche on the Lam,* St. Martin's Press, 1992.
_____. *Blanche Among the Talented Tenth,* St. Martin's Press, 1994.
_____. *Blanche Cleans Up,* Penguin, 1998.
_____. *Blanche Passes Go,* Viking, 2000.
Olden, Marc. *Kisaeng,* Zebra, 1992.
_____. *Fear's Justice,* Villard, 1996.
_____. *The Ghost,* Simon & Schuster, 1999.
Parker, Percy Spurlark. *Good Girls Don't Get Murdered,* Scribner's Sons, 1974.
Perry, Charles. *Portrait of a Young Man Drowning,* W.W. Norton, 1996.
Phaire, Dorothy. *Almost Out of Love,* Writers Club Press, 1999.
_____. *Murder and the Masquerade,* iUniverse, 2007.
Pharr, Robert Deane. *Giveadamn Brown,* W. W. Norton, 1997.
Phillips, Gary. *Violent Spring* (1994), Point Blank Books, 2004.
_____. *Perdition, U.S.A,* John Brown Books, 1996.
_____. *Bad Night Is Falling,* Prime Crime, 1998.
_____. *Jook,* Really Great Books, 1999.
_____. *High Hand,* Kensington Books, 2000.
_____. *Only the Wicked,* Write Way, 2000.
_____. *Shooter's Point,* Kensington Books, 2001.
_____. *The Perpetrators,* Uglytown Productions, 2002.
_____. *Bangers,* Kensington/Dafina, 2003.
_____. *Monkology,* Dennis McMillan, 2004.
Ramsey, Gail. *Tick Tock,* Sug Books, 2004.
Reed, Ishmael. *Mumbo Jumbo,* Doubleday, 1972.
_____. *The Last Days of Louisiana Red,* Random House, 1974.
Rhodes, Evie. *Criss Coss,* Kensington, 2006.
Rhodes, Jewell Parker. *Voodoo Season,* Atria Books, 2005.
Ridley, John. *Stray Dogs,* Ballantine, 1997.
_____. *Love Is a Racket,* Knopf, 1998.
_____. *Everybody Smokes in Hell,* Knopf, 1999.
_____. *Those Who Walk in Darkness,* Aspect, 2003.
_____. *The Drift,* One World, 2003.
Riley, Cole (pseudo. Fleming, Robert). *Dark Blood Moon,* Holloway House, 1995.
Roberts, W. Adolphe. *The Haunting Hand,* Macauley, 1926.
_____. *The Top-Floor Killer,* Nicholson and Watson, 1935.
_____. *The Mind Reader,* Macauley, 1929.
Samuels-Young, Pamela. *Every Reasonable Doubt,* Kimani Press, 2006.
_____. *In Firm Pursuit,* Kimani Press, 2007.
Saxton, Lisa. *Caught in a Rundown,* Scribner, 1997.
Schuyler, George. *Black Empire,* Northeastern University Press, 1985.
_____. *Ethiopian Stories,* Northeastern University Press, 1991.
Shannon, Ray (see Haywood, Gar Anthony). *Maneater,* G. P. Putnam, 2003.
_____. *Firecracker,* G. P. Putnam, 2005.
Singer, Gammy *A Landlord's Tale,* Kensington, 2005.

_____. *Down and Dirty,* Kensington, 2006.

Smith-Levin, Judith. *Do Not Go Gently,* HarperCollins, 1996.

_____. *The Hoodoo Man,* Ballantine, 1998.

_____. *Green Money,* Ballantine, 2000.

_____. *Reckless Eyeballin',* Fawcett, 2001.

Tervalon, Jervey. *Dead Above Ground,* Atria, 2000.

_____. *Lita,* Atria, 2003.

Thomas-Graham, Pamela. *A Darker Shade of Crimson,* Simon & Schuster, 1998.

_____. *Blue Blood,* Simon & Schuster, 1999.

_____. *Orange Crushed,* Simon & Schuster, 2004.

Tillis, Tracey. *Deadly Masquerade,* Dell, 1994.

_____. *Flashpoint,* Signet/Onyx, 1997.

_____. *Final Act,* Signet/Onyx, 1998.

_____. *Final Hour,* Onyx, 1999.

Toples, Portia. *Bad Medicine,* Hilliard & Harris, 2004.

Tramble, Nichelle. *The Dying Ground,* Strivers Row, 2001.

_____. *The Last King,* Strivers Row, 2004.

Underwood, Blair; Due, Tananarive; and Barnes, Steve. *Casanegra,* Atria, 2007.

Van Dyke, Henry. *Dead Piano,* W.W. Norton, 1997.

Walker, Blair S. *Up Jumped the Devil,* Avon, 1997.

_____. *Hidden in Plain View,* Avon, 1999.

_____. *Don't Believe Your Lying Eyes,* Ballantine, 2002.

Walker, Persia. *Harlem Redux,* Simon & Schuster, 2002.

Wesley, Valerie Wilson. *When Death Comes Stealing,* Putnam, 1994.

_____. *Devil's Gonna Get Him,* Putnam, 1995.

_____. *Where Evil Sleeps,* Putnam, 1996.

_____. *No Hiding Place,* Putnam, 1997.

_____. *Easier to Kill,* Putnam, 1998.

_____. *The Devil Riding,* Putnam, 2000.

_____. *Dying in the Dark,* One World/Ballantine, 2004.

_____. *Of Blood and Sorrow,* One World/Ballantine, 2008.

West, Chassie. *Sunrise,* HarperTorch, 1994.

_____. *Loss of Innocence,* HarperTorch, 1997.

_____. *Killing Kin,* HarperTorch, 2000.

_____. *Killer Riches,* HarperTorch, 2001.

_____. *Killer Chameleon,* HarperTorch, 2004.

Whitehead, Colson. *The Intuitionist,* Anchor, 2000.

Woods, Paula L. *Inner City Blues,* W.W. Norton, 1999.

_____. *Stormy Weather,* W.W. Norton, 2001.

_____. *Dirty Laundry,* One World/Ballantine, 2003.

_____. *Strange Bedfellows,* One World/Ballantine, 2006.

Novels for Children/Young Adults

Canterbury, Patricia *The Secret of St. Gabriel's Tower,* ReGeJe, 1998.

_____. *Carlotta's Secret,* RBC. 2001.

Coleman, Evelyn. *Mystery of the Dark Tower: A Bessie Mystery,* American Girl, 2000.

_____. *Circle of Fire,* American Girl, 2001.

_____. *Shadows on Society Hill: An Addy Mystery,* American Girl, 2007.

Hamilton, Virginia *The House of Dies Drear,* Macmillan, 1969.

_____. *The Mystery of Drear House,* Greenwillow, 1987.

Plays

Davis, Thulani. *Everybody's Ruby.*
Fuller, Charles. *A Soldier's Story.*
Graham, Shirley. *It's Morning* (1940).
Johnson, Douglas Georgia. *Safe* (© 1929).
Jones, Leroi (Baraka, Amiri). *The Dutchman.*
Ross, Gary Earl. *Picture Perfect.*
Thurman, Wallace (with Rapp, William Journan). *Harlem: A Melodrama of Negro Life in Harlem* (1929).

Short Stories in Anthologies

Anthology: Bland, Eleanor, ed. (2004). *Shades of Black: Crime and Mystery Stories by African American Writers.* New York: Berkley Prime Crime.

Bailey, Frankie Y. *Since You Way Away.*
Banks, Jacqueline Turner. *The Cookout.*
Benson, Chris. *Double Dealing.*
Bland, Eleanor Taylor and Bland, Anthony. *Murder on the Southwest Chief.*
Canterbury, Patricia E. *The Secret of the 369th Infantry Nurse.*
Chambers, Christopher. *Doggy Style.*
Clark, Tracy P. *For Services Rendered.*
Coleman, Evelyn. *The Pride of a Woman.*
Edwards, Grace F. *The Blind Alley.*
Greer, Robert. *A Matter of Policy.*
Grimes, Terris McMahan. *Small Colored World.*
Haywood, Gar Anthony. *Better Dead Than Wed.*
Holton, Hugh. *The Werewolf File.*
Hunter, Geri Spencer. *Déjà Vu.*
Jackson, Dicey Scroggins. *Survival.*
Lovell, Glenville. *When Blood Runs to Water.*
Meadows, Lee E. *A Small Matter.*
Mickelbury, Penny. *More Than One Way.*
Mosley, Walter. *Bombardier.*
Parker, Percy Spurlark. *A Favorable Murder.*
Phillips, Gary. *Beginner's Luck.*
Shipps, Charles. *God of the Pond.*

Anthology: Woods, Paula L., ed. (1995). *Spooks, Spies, and Private Eyes: Black Mystery, Crime, and Suspense Fiction.* New York: Doubleday.

Allison, Hughes. *Corollary.*
Bland, Eleanor Taylor. *The Man Who Said I'm Not.*
Dunbar-Nelson, Alice. *Summer Session.*
Greenlee, Sam. Excerpt from *The Spook Who Sat by the Door.*
Haywood, Gar Anthony. *And Pray Nobody Sees You.*
Himes, Chester. *His Last Day.*
Holton, Hugh. *The Thirteenth Amendment.*
Hopkins, Pauline E. *Talma Gordon.*
León , Aya De. *Tell Me Moore.*
Mickelbury, Penny. Excerpt from *Night Songs.*

Mosley, Walter. *Fearless.*
Neely, Barbara. *Spilled Salt.*
Parker, Percy Spurlark. *Death and the Point Spread.*
Petry, Ann. *On Saturday the Siren Sounds at Noon.*
Phillips, Gary. *Dead Man's Shadow.*
Phillips, Mike. *Personal Woman.*
Schuyler, George S. writing as William Stockton. *The Shoemaker Murder.*
Sherman, Charlotte Watson. *Killing Color.*
Simon, Njami. Excerpt from *Coffin & Co.*
Williams, John A. Excerpt from *The Man Who Cried I Am.*
Wright, Richard. *The Man Who Killed a Shadow.*

Films/Television Shows Based on Books

Himes, Chester. *A Rage in Harlem*; *Cotton Comes to Harlem*; *Come Back, Charleston Blue.*
Mosley, Walter. *Devil in a Blue Dress*; *Always Outnumbered, Always Outgunned* (HBO).
Ridley, John. *U Turn* (based on *Stray Dogs*); *Those Who Walk in Darkness.*

Index to Topics in the Books in the Sample

See below for an overview of some of the topics that appear in the books in the sample (see Appendix B). For fuller discussions of the most important topics the reader should see the text. When no page numbers are listed for the books below, the reference is to the book as a whole.

Academics/Academic Settings
Bailey, Frankie Y. *A Dead Man's Honor; Old Murders.* Carter, Stephen L. *The Emperor of Ocean Park; New England White.* Thomas-Graham, Pamela. *Blue Blood; A Darker Shade of Crimson; Orange Crushed.*

Affirmative Action
As Motive for Murder: Cose, Ellis. *The Best Defense.*
Assumption About Black Female Cop: Walker, Blair. *Don't Believe Your Lying Eyes.*

AIDS (HIV-Positive)
AIDS, Character Infected: Singer, Gammy. *A Landlord's Tale; Down & Dirty.*
Reaction to Celebrities HIV-Positive: Woods, Paula L. *Stormy Weather* (p. 219).
Status Relevant to Crime: Bailey, Frankie Y. *Old Murders.*

Alcohol
Protagonist Has Drunken Episode: Carter, Charlotte. *Drumsticks* (pp. 1–2).

American Dream
Carter, Charlotte. *Drumsticks.* Coleman, Evelyn. *What a Woman's Gotta Do* (p. 11).

Associations/Organizations
Black Fraternity (Loyalty): Grimes, Terris McMahan. *Blood Will Tell* (p. 197).
Black Nationalists: Mosley, Walter. *Bad Boy Brawly Brown.*
Jack & Jill (Children in): Grimes, Terris. McMahan *Blood Will Tell* (p. 24).

Athletes/Sports
Basketball, Professional: Miller, C. M. *What She Left Behind.*
Former Baseball Star: Tramble, Nichelle. *The Dying Ground.*
Former Professional Football Player: Phillips, Gary. *The Jook.*
Prizefighting: Phillips, Gary. *Shooter's Point.*
Rodeo Riding: Greer, Robert O. *The Devil's Backbone.*

Attorneys

AFFORDING A GOOD LAWYER: "O.J.'s dream team was not available for what Bert was able to scrape together" (Edwards, Grace. *A Toast Before Dying*, p. 24).

GUILT ABOUT CLIENT WHO COMMITS ANOTHER CRIME: Mickelbury, Penny. *Where to Choose* (pp. 8–9).

PUBLIC DEFENDER (HARD WORKING): Wesley, Valerie Wilson. *Death Comes Stealing* (pp. 63–64).

TRIALS/COURTROOM: Darden, Christopher, and Dick Lochte. *The Trials of Nikki Hill*; *L.A. Justice*. Davis, Kyra. *Passion, Betrayal and Killer Highlights*. Flowers, R. Barrie. *Justice Served*; *State's Evidence*. Ramsey, Gail. *Tick Tock*. Samuels-Young, Pamela. *Every Reasonable Doubt*; *Firm Pursuits*.

Barbershop (*and see* the text)

BARBER AS ARTIST: Edwards, Grace. *No Time to Die* (p. 73).

OPENING SCENE SET IN: Tramble, Nichelle. *The Dying Ground*.

Barroom Encounters (*and see* the text)

Camacho, Austin S. *Blood and Bone* (pp. 1–3).

Beauty Shop (*and see* the text)

PRESENCE OF WHITE COSMETOLOGIST IN BLACK SHOP: Wesley, Valerie Wilson. *Easier to Kill* (pp. 72–73).

Body Image (*see also* Sexuality)

POSITIVE SELF-IMAGE OF SIZE 16 PROTAGONIST: Neely, Barbara. *Blanche Among the Talented Tenth* (pp. 1–3).

Cars/Driving

CLASSIC CAR: Greer, Robert O. *The Devil's Hatband*.

DRIVING AS PLEASURE: Mickelbury, Penny. *Where to Choose* (p. 32).

Central Intelligence Agency (CIA)

Holton, Hugh. *Time of the Assassins*.

Children/Parenting

ABUSIVE MOTHER—SLEUTH'S MEMORIES: Wesley, Valerie Wilson. *Devil's Gonna Get Him* (p. 43).

ABUSIVE/NON-ABUSIVE FATHERS: Mosley, Walter. *A Little Yellow Dog*.

COMMITTING CRIME TO PROVIDE MEDICAL CARE FOR SICK CHILD: Mosley, Walter. *Cinnamon Kiss*.

CONFLICT BETWEEN KIDS/ELDERLY WOMAN: Neely, Barbara. *Blanche Cleans Up* (pp. 154–155).

CRIMINAL CHILD: "Mrs. Carson has four other hard-working and law-abiding children, but sticky-fingered Stevie is the apple of her eye, and she won't hear a word against him" (Henry, Angela. *Tangled Roots*, p. 173).

DECEPTION OF PARENTS ABOUT LIFESTYLE: Carter, Charlotte. *Drumsticks*; *Coq au vin*.

EMPTY NEST LOOMING: Wesley, Valerie Wilson. *Dying in the Dark* (p. 126).

FATHER FIGURE/MOTHER FIGURE: Wesley, Valerie Wilson. *Dying in the Dark* (pp. 65, 67).

FATHER ON SON'S RESPONSE TO RACIAL SLUR: Grimes, Terris McMahan. *Blood Will Tell* (pp. 138–139).

IMPACT ABSENCE/LOSS OF PARENTS: Bailey, Frankie Y. *Lizzie Stuart* series. West, Chassie. *Leigh Ann Warren* series.

INCEST: Hayes, Teddy. *Dead by Popular Demand*.

Church (*and see* the text)

Cities/Countries (*and see* the text)

Class

Domestic Violence (*see* the text)

Domestic Workers (*and see* the text)

CLEANING WOMAN WHO IS ALSO SUBSTITUTE TEACHER: West, Chassie. *Killer Chameleon.*

Drugs (*and see* the text)

ADDICT IN FAMILY: Bland, Eleanor Taylor. *A Cold and Silent Dying; Done Wrong* (p. 27). Lovell, Glenville. *Love and Death in Brooklyn.* Hardwick, Gary. *Double Deal.*

ROLE IN THE PLOT: Camacho, Austin. *The Troubleshooter.* DeLoach, Nora. *Mama Cracks a Mask of Innocence.* Grimes, Terris McMahan. *Somebody Else's Child.* Hardwick, Gary. *The Executioner's Song.* Holton, Hugh. *The Time of the Assassins.* Joe, Yolanda. *Video Cowboy.* Mosley, Walter. *A Little Yellow Dog.* Singer, Gammy. *A Landlord's Tale.* Woods, Paula L. *Inner City Blues.*

Education

DELINQUENT BOYS FROM PRIVATE SCHOOL: Smith-Levin, Judith. *Green Money.*

GHETTO DRUG DEALER EXCELLING IN COLLEGE CHEMISTRY COURSES: Tramble, Nichelle. *The Dying Ground.*

HAPPY CHILDREN IN ILLEGAL NURSERY SCHOOL: Mosley, Walter. *Black Betty* (pp. 32–33).

HIGH SCHOOL CRIME: DeLoach, Nora. *Mama Cracks a Mask of Innocence.*

PRIVATE SCHOOLS, CONCERN ABOUT INFLUENCE: Neely, Barbara. *Blanche Among the Talented Tenth.*

SEMI-LITERATE ATHLETE: Phillips, Gary. *The Jook.*

Environment/Environmental Crime

ENVIRONMENTAL CRIME/POLLUTION: Bland, Eleanor Taylor. *A Cold and Silent Dying.* Greer, Robert. *Heat Shock.* Kelley, Norman. *The Big Mango.* Smith, Ian. *The Blackbird Papers.*

ENVIRONMENTAL JUSTICE ACTIVISM: Neely, Barbara. *Blanche.*

Entrepreneurs (*and see* the text)

BLACK BUSINESSWOMAN IN NEW SOUTH: Neely, Barbara. *Blanche Passes Go.*

Ethics/Values

ABOUT ACCEPTING "BLOOD MONEY": Wesley, Valerie Wilson. *Where Evil Sleeps* (p. 260).

ABOUT DRAWING FRIEND INTO TROUBLE: Phillips, Gary. *High Hand* (p. 55).

ETHICS OF BREAKING THE LAW: Kelley, Norman. *The Big Mango.*

ETHICS OF SURVEILLANCE: Mickelbury, Penny. *The Step Between* (p. 19).

JOURNALISM AND PROTAGONIST'S ETHICS: "I hate sneaking.... But in television news you do what you have to do" (Joe, Yolanda. *Hit Time*, p. 195).

MEDICAL ETHICS: Greer, Robert. *Limited Time.*

OBLIGATION TO DEAD CLIENT: Wesley, Valerie Wilson. *Dying in the Dark* (p. 18).

OF INVESTIGATING OWN EX-LOVER: Wesley, Valerie Wilson. *Devil's Gonna Get Him.*

PROSECUTORS' DECISIONS: Darden, Christopher, and Dick Lochte. *The Trials of Nikki Hill.* Hardwick, Gary. *Double Dead.*

REACTION TO SHOOTING/KILLING: Phillips, Gary. *High Hand.* West, Chassie. *Sunrise.*

REFUSAL TO COVER UP FOR SUPERIOR: Camacho, Austin. *The Troubleshooter* (p. 83).

REFUSING CHAMPAGNE ON DUTY: Smith-Levin, Judith. *Reckless Eyeballin'* (p. 147).

RESEARCH ETHICS: Bailey, Frankie Y. *Old Murders.*

THROWAWAY ETHIC OF LIFE: Baker, Nikki. *The Lavender House Murder.*

TORTURE: Kelley, Norman. *The Big Mango* (p. 67).

WHAT SLEUTH VALUES: "There are three things in this life I cherish: my independence, my son Jamal, and my peace of mind" (Wesley, Valerie Wilson. *When Death Comes Stealing*, p. 17).

Excitement of Confrontation

"There was respect in his eyes as he looked at me over the hand he held to his wound, 'Look, Zelmont.' 'Shut the hell up.' I was enjoying this. The tingling I got in my gut was like sex with Davida. 'Don't say a goddamn thing unless it's how soon you gonna have my cash'" (Phillips, Gary. *The Jook*, p. 15).

Federal Bureau of Investigation (FBI)

AFRICAN AMERICAN AGENT: Chambers, Christopher. Angela Bivens series. Johnson, Keith Lee. *Sugar & Spice*. Smith, Ian. *The Blackbird Papers*. Woods, Paula L. *Strange Bedfellows*.
DEAD AGENT: Lovell, Glenville. *Too Beautiful to Die*.
COINTELPRO: Bailey, Frankie Y. *You Should Have Died on Monday*.
WHITE AGENT AS SCHOOL CLASSMATE OF PROTAGONIST'S FRIEND: West, Chassie. *Killer Riches*.
WITNESS PROTECTION PROGRAM: Haywood, Gar Anthony. *Going Nowhere Fast*.

Foster Care (*see* the text)

Funeral/Death Rituals

FOOD/COOKING: Bland, Eleanor Taylor. *Done Wrong* (p. 6).
FUNERALS/ WAKES: Bailey, Frankie. *A Dead Man's Honor*. Ramsey, Gail. *Tick Tock*. Wesley, Valerie Wilson. *When Death Comes Stealing*.

Gangs (*and see* the text)

INITIATION AND VIOLENCE: Miller, C. M. *Taxes, Death, & Trouble*.

Gay/Lesbian Character (*see* Sexuality *and see* the text)

Gossip/Rumor (*and see* the text)

ROLE OF RUMOR IN RIOT: Wesley, Valerie Wilson. *When Death Comes Stealing* (p. 23).
RUMOR MAN SEEKING REVENGE AGAINST PROTAGONIST: Edwards, Grace. *No Time to Die* (p. 84).

Guns (*and see* the text)

ELDERLY WOMEN WITH GUNS: Grimes, Terris McMahan. *Somebody Else's Child*. Henry, Angela. *Tangled Roots* (p. 171).
PROTAGONIST'S FEELINGS ABOUT GUNS: Bailey, Frankie Y. *You Should Have Died on Monday*.

Hair (*and see* the text)

"She had the kind of wavy and shoulder length, kink-free hair many little black girls would kill their Barbie dolls for even today" (Neely, Barbara. *Blanche Among the Talented Tenth*, p. 19).
DISAGREEMENT WITH ELDER ABOUT STYLE: Neely, Barbara. *Blanche on the Lam*.
GROOMING RITUAL: Grimes, Terris McMahan. *Blood Will Tell* (p. 84).
INSULT DIRECTED AT BLACK WOMAN (DREADS): Miller, C. M. *Taxes, Death, & Trouble* (p. 189).
LACK OF GROOMING CAUSE FOR CONCERN: Edwards, Grace. *No Time to Die* (p. 115).

Hate Crimes (*and see* the text)

AGAINST GAYS/LESBIANS: Mickelbury, Penny. *Keeping Secrets*.
BY WHITE SUPREMACISTS: Walker, Blair. *Up Jumped the Devil*.

Homeless Persons (*see also* Victims *and see* the text)

HUMANITY/VALUE: Camacho, Austin. *The Troubleshooter* (p. 37).
IMPORTANT ROLE IN PLOT: Bailey, Frankie Y. *A Dead Man's Honor*. Mosley, Walter. *Little Scarlet*.

Immigrants
Greer, Robert L. *The Fourth Perspective*. Greer, Robert L. *Heat Shock*. Mickelbury, Penny. *Where to Choose*.

Indians (*see* Native Americans)

Informants (*and see* the text)
"TOWN HISTORIANS": DeLoach, Nora. *Mama Rocks the Empty Cradle* (p. 12).

Intelligence
CHARACTER WITH MOSAICISM, DIFFERENT INTELLIGENCE: Neely, Barbara. *Blanche on the Lam*.

Internal Revenue Service (IRS)
Mosley, Walter. *White Butterfly*.

Jews
BLACK COMMUNITY: Mosley, Walter. *A Red Death*.
JEWISH BOSS: Bates, Karen Grigsby. *Plain Brown Wrapper* (pp. 73–74).
JEWISH P.I. AND FRIEND: Mosley, Walter. *Cinnamon Kiss*.

Juke Joint
Brown, Elaine. *Lemon City* (p. 147).

Justice (*and see* the text)
LACK OF FOR NEGROES: Mosley, Walter. *Devil in a Blue Dress* (p. 121).

Korean American (*and see* the text)
Phillips, Gary. *Violent Spring*. Woods, Paula. *Dirty Laundry*.

Latinos and Hispanics
AS CHARACTER: Bailey, Frankie. *Death's Favorite Child*; *You Should Have Died on Monday*. Greer, Robert. *Heat Shock*. Mickelbury, Penny. *Two Graves Dug*. Olden, Marc. *The Ghost*. Woods, Paula L. *Dirty Laundry*.

Library/Librarians
Bailey, Frankie. *You Should Have Died on Monday*. Mosley, Walter. *White Butterfly* (pp. 54–55).

Lynching
Bailey, Frankie. *A Dead Man's Honor*.

Masculinity
COOL POSE/STYLE: Camacho, Austin S. *Blood and Bone*.
MANLINESS: Mosley, Walter. *Fear Itself*.
MEN CRYING: Mosley, Walter. *White Butterfly* (p. 181).

Media (*see also* Sleuths *and see* the text)
AFRICAN AMERICAN MEDIA, CRIME INVOLVING: Bates, Karen Grigsby. *Plain Brown Wrapper*.
COVERAGE OF BLACK LIFE: Mosley, Walter. *Devil in a Blue Dress* (pp. 160–161). Mosley, Walter. *White Butterfly* (p. 16).
COVERAGE OF BLACK VICTIMS: "They carried the body away on a stretcher when the photographers were through — police photographer, not newsmen. A black woman getting killed wasn't photographic material for the newspapers in 1956" (Mosley, Walter. *White Butterfly*).

COVERAGE OF PROTAGONIST'S ACTIVITIES: Darden, Christopher, and Dick Lochte. *The Trials of Nikki Hill*. Greer, Robert. *The Devil's Hatband* (p. 12). Samuels-Young, Pamela. *Every Reasonable Doubt* (p. 14).

Migrants
POST–WORLD WAR II LOS ANGELES: Mosley, Walter. *Devil in a Blue Dress*.

Military
CONTINUING CHARACTERS WHO ARE FORMER MILITARY: Bailey, Frankie. Lizzie Stuart series. Camacho, Austin. Hannibal Jones series. Greer, Robert. CJ Floyd series.
MILITARY BRATS: Tramble, Nichelle. *The Dying Ground* (p. 85).

Million Man March
Haywood, Gar Anthony. *When Last Seen Alive*.

Misogyny
Bland, Eleanor Taylor. *A Cold and Silent Dying*. Mickelbury, Penny. *Night Songs*. Phillips, Gary. *Shooter's Point*.

Murder for Hire
Joe, Yolanda. *Hit Time*. Smith-Levin, Judith. *Reckless Eyeballin'*.

Murder Methods (*and see* the text)
POISONING: DeLoach, Nora. *Mama Stalks the Past*.
THROAT CUT: Bates, Karen Grigsby. *Chosen People*.
THROWN HUNTING KNIVES: Mickelbury, Penny. *Night Songs*.

Music
BLUES: Phillips, Gary. *Only the Wicked*.
MOTOWN: Joe, Yolanda. *Hit Time*.
MUSIC TO GROUND/SET MOOD: Comacho, Austin. *Blood and Bones* (p. 160). Neely, Blanche. *Blanche on the Lame* (p. 77). Singer, Gammy. *A Landlord's Tale* (p. 25).
RAP: Davis, Kyra. *Sex, Murder and a Double Latte*. Hayes, Teddy. *Dead by Popular Demand*.

Mystery Fiction (*and see* the text)
LOCKED ROOM: "Chainey had never read an Agatha Christie novel, but from what she understood, this kind of locked-room puzzle was at the heart of some of her stories" (Phillips, Gary. *Shooter's Point*, p. 56).
MYSTERY WRITER AS SLEUTH: "I don't care what anyone said, writing the Alicia Bright mysteries did qualify me to be an amateur sleuth" (Davis, Kyra. *Passion, Betrayal, and Killer Highlights*, p. 59).

Native Americans
CULTURE AND HISTORY: Bland, Eleanor Taylor. *Fatal Remains*.
VICTIMS AND OFFENDERS: Greer, Robert. *The Fourth Perspective*. Holton, Hugh. *Red Lightning*.

Neighborhoods (*and see* the text)
HYDE PARK (CHICAGO): Carter, Charlotte. *Jackson Park*; *Trip Wire*.
LINCOLN PARK (CHICAGO): Joe, Yolanda. *Hit Time* (p. 39).
SOUTHEAST L.A., 1963: Mosley, Walter. *A Little Yellow Dog* (pp. 24–25).
TIMES SQUARE (NEW YORK): Carter, Charlotte. *Drumstick* (p. 13).
WOODLAWN (CHICAGO): Joe, Yolanda. *Video Cowboys* (p. 176?).

Neo-Nazis/Skinheads/White Supremacists
Phillips, Gary. *Perdition, U.S.A.* Walker, Blair. *Up Jumped the Devil.*

Non-Lethal Crimes (*see also* other felonies by name)
BAD CHECKS: Neely, Barbara. *Blanche on the Lam.*
CON GAME: Bland, Eleanor Taylor. *Scream in Silence.* Grimes, Terris McMahan. *Blood Will Tell.*
FENCING STOLEN PROPERTY: Singer, Gammy. *Down & Dirty.* Tramble, Nichelle. *The Dying Ground* (pp. 247–248).
HOSTAGE-TAKING: Bland, Eleanor Taylor *Slow Burn.* Joe, Yolanda. *Video Cowboy.*
IDENTITY THEFT: West, Chassie. *Killer Chameleon.*
KIDNAPPING: West, Chassie. *Killer Riches.*

Organized Crime
CONTROL OF TERRITORY: Camacho, Austin. *The Troubleshooter.*
CRIME LORD: Singer, Gammy. *A Landlord's Tale.*
GANGSTERS IN HARLEM (HISTORY): Mickelbury, Penny. *Two Graves Dug.*
IN CHICAGO, 1960S: Bailey, Frankie Y. *You Should Have Died on Monday.*

Patriotism/Espionage/National Security
Fullilove, Eric James. *Blowback.* Hardwick, Gary. *The Executioner's Game.* Horton, Hugh. *Time of the Assassins.*

Pets in Household (*and see* the text)
CATS: Davis, Kyra. Sophie Katz series.
DOGS: Bailey, Frankie Y. Lizzie Stuart series. Bland, Eleanor Taylor. Marti McAllister series. Edward, Grace. Mali Anderson series. "He was the love of my little girl's life, so I accepted his hatred" (Mosley, Walter. *Big Boy Brawly Brown*, p. 5).

Pimps/Prostitutes
AS CHARACTERS: Edwards, Grace. *Do or Die.* Mickelbury, Penny. *Night Songs.* Smith-Levin, Judith. *Green Money.* Wesley, Valerie Wilson. *Easier to Kill.*
BROTHEL: Carter, Charlotte. *Jackson Park.*
HELPING CLIENT LEAVE PROSTITUTE: Comacho, Austin. *Blood and Bone.*
SEX WORK AND FAMILY VALUES: Neely, Barbara. *Blanche Cleans Up* (p. 72).
WHITE PIMP: Holton, Hugh. *Windy City* (p. 235).

Police
"I've never been comfortable talking to the police even when I was one of them...." (Wesley, Valerie Wilson. *Easier to Kill*, p. 128).
AFRICAN AMERICAN DETECTIVE AS OUTSIDER: Mosley, Walter. *White Butterfly.*
CHICANO DETECTIVE: Mosley, Walter. *A Little Yellow Dog.*
COP SUICIDE: Bland, Eleanor Taylor. *Done Wrong.*
CORRUPTION/CRIME: Holton, Hugh. *Time of the Assassins.* Kelley, Norman. *A Phat Death.* Smith-Levin, Judith. *Reckless Eyeballin'.* Woods, Paula L. *Inner City Blues.*
ENCOUNTER BETWEEN PROTAGONIST AND RUDE COP: Mickelbury, Penny. *Where to Choose* (p. 89).
IMPACT OF MOD SQUAD ON BLACK COP: Brown, Elaine. *Lemon City* (p. 187).
INABILITY TO DISTINGUISH GOOD KIDS FROM BAD: Thomas-Graham, Pamela. *Blue Blood* (p. 190).
LESBIAN/DYKE JOKES ABOUT FEMALE COPS: Woods, Paula. *Dirty Laundry.*
REACTION OF BLACK DETECTIVE TO RACIST WHITE CITIZEN/VICTIM: Smith-Levin Judith. *Green Money.*
STREET JUSTICE BY WHITE COP: Mosley, Walter. *White Butterfly* (p. 48).

Politics
FAMILY VALUES AND CANDIDATE: Neely, Barbara. *Blanche Cleans Up.*
POLITICAL COMMENTARY: Kelley, Norman. *A Big Mango; A Phat Death.*
URBAN POLITICS: Woods, Paula. *Dirty Laundry.*

Popular Culture
"I wouldn't cast this guy as a bank robber no more than I'd cast Britney Spears in a remake of *The Flying Nun*" (Joe, Yolanda. *Video Cowboys*, p. 12).
BLACK CULTURE/WHITE CONSUMPTION: Kelley, Norman. *The Big Mango* (p. 48).
BLACK HOLLYWOOD/FILMMAKERS: Woods, Paula. *Dirty Laundry.*
FILM GANGSTERS/TV COPS AS ROLE MODELS: Tramble, Nichelle. *The Dying Ground.*
FILM SERIAL KILLER AS POINT OF REFERENCE: Phillips, Gary. *Shooter's Point.*
FORMER BLACK STAR/VICTIM: Henry, Angela. *Diva's Last Curtain Call.*
IMPORTANT CLUE TO SOLUTION OF CRIMES: "Curious, I opened it. A review of *Macbeth*, onstage in Chicago. Why would anyone send this to me?" (West, Chassie. *Killer Chameleon*, p. 24).
JIM BROWN FILMS: Haywood, Gar Anthony. *All the Lucky Ones Are Dead* (pp. 256–257).
PORNOGRAPHY/PEDOPHILE: Neely, Barbara. *Blanche Cleans Up.*

Poverty (*see* the text)

Prisons (*and see* the text)
ANGOLA PRISON FARM AND BLUES: Tramble, Nichelle. *The Dying Ground* (pp. 166–167).
CORRUPT GUARD: Singer, Gammy. *A Landlord's Tale* (p. 61).
EXECUTION BLACK WOMAN: Bailey, Frankie Y. *Old Murders.*
PAROLE OFFICER: Joe, Yolanda. *Video Cowboys* (pp. 139–140).
RE-ENTRY OF PRISONER: Mosley, Walter. Socrates Fortlaw series.

Racism/Race Relations (*and see* the text)
BLACK MALE VICTIMS/ALLEGED "RAP WAR": Carter, Charlotte. *Drumsticks.*
"DARKIES' DISEASE": Neely, Barbara. *Blanche on the Lam.*
EXTRA SEAT ON BUS (WHITES AVOID SITTING BESIDE): Neely, Barbara. *Blanche Among the Talented Tenth* (p. 11).
GENERIC BLACK MALE ASSAILANT: Carter, Charlotte. *Drumsticks* (p. 29). Thomas-Graham, Pamela. *Blue Blood.*
IN EUROPE: Mosley, Walter. *Bad Boy Brawly Brown* (p. 250).
IN LANGUAGE: Neely, Barbara. *Blanche on the Lam* (p. 122).
IN PROFESSIONAL SKATEBOARDING COMMUNITY: Tramble, Nichelle. *The Dying Ground* (p. 51).
MOCKING DIALECT RESPONSE TO INSULT: Smith-Levin, Judith. *Reckless Eyeballin'* (pp. 154–155).
RACIAL HOAX: Thomas-Graham, Pamela. *Blue Blood.*
RACIAL IDENTITY AS PLOT ELEMENT: Bates, Kathy Grisby. *Plain Brown Wrapper.* Edwards, Grace. *A Toast Before Dying.* Henry, Angela. *Diva's Last Curtain Call.* Mosley, Walter. *Devil in a Blue Dress.* Thomas-Graham, Pamela. *A Darker Shade of Crimson.* Walker, Persia. *Harlem Redux.* Woods, Paula L. *Strange Bedfellows.*
RACISM TOWARD BLACK/CHINESE MALE WHEN HE WAS CHILD/TEENAGER: Mickelbury, Penny. *Where to Choose* (p. 53).
REACTION OF WHITE WOMAN TO GALLANT OFFER OF HELP: Singer, Gammy. *Down and Dirty* (p. 33).
WEARING "MASK" WITH EMPLOYER: Neely, Barbara. *Blanche on the Lam* (p. 16).

Rape
BY STEP-FATHER: Wesley, Valerie Wilson. *Easier to Kill.*
FLASHBACK TO RAPE AT SIGHT OF OFFENDER: Neely, Barbara. *Blanche Passes Go.*
IN PRISON: Johnson, Keith Lee. *Sugar & Spice.*
RESPONSE OF RAPE SURVIVORS TO CRIME: Bland, Eleanor Taylor. *Scream in Silence.* Holton, Hugh. *Violent Crimes.*
SERIAL RAPIST OF CHILDREN: Mickelbury, Penny. *Two Graves Dug.*
WIFE ACCUSES PROTAGONIST OF RAPING HER: Mosley, Walter. *White Butterfly* (p. 39).

Reading (*see* the text)

Religion/Spirituality (*see also* Church *and see* the text)
PROTAGONIST'S PRAYER: Wesley, Valerie Wilson. *When Death Comes Stealing* (p.42).
PROTAGONIST'S SPIRITUAL RITUALS: Neely, Barbara. *Blanche Among the Talented Tenth.*

Reputation/Public Image
"That's what I call P-Funk — when the public won't let you be a regular person and gets oh so cruel about it. My undercover corns would just have to suffer undercover"(Joe, Yolanda. *Hit Time*, p. 14).
PROTAGONIST ON MAINTAINING STREET REP: Camacho, Austin. *Blood and Bones* (p. 132). Joe, Yolanda. *Video Cowboys* (p. 225). Phillips, Gary. *The Jook* (pp. 16–17).

Revenge (*and see* the text)
Bland, Eleanor Taylor. *Scream in Silence.* Johnson, Keith Lee. *Sugar & Spice.* Kelley, Norman. *The Big Mango.* Ridley, John. *Those Who Walk in Darkness.*

Riots (*and see* the text)
IN CHICAGO: Carter, Charlotte. *Jackson Park.*
IN LOS ANGELES: Mosley, Walter. *Little Scarlet.* Phillips, Gary. *Violent Spring.* Woods, Paula. *Inner City Blues.*
IN NEWARK: Wesley, Valerie Wilson. *When Death Comes Stealing.*

Segregation (*and see* the text)
SELF-SEGREGATION: Brown, Elaine. *Lemon City.*

Serial Killers (*and see* the text)
Bland, Eleanor Taylor. *A Cold and Silent Dying.* Edwards, Grace. *No Time to Die.* Flowers, F. Barrie. *Justice Served.* Holton, Hugh. *Violent Crimes; Windy City.* Johnson, Keith. *Sugar & Spice.* Mickelbury, Penny. *Keeping Secrets; Night Songs.* Mosley, Walter. *Little Scarlet.* Phillips, Gary. *Perdition, U.S.A.* Woods, Paula L. *Stormy Weather* (p. 86).

Sexual Harassment (*see* Work/Workplace)

Sexuality (*see also* Victims)
FEMALE ALLURE/SENSUALITY: Mosley, Walter. *Black Betty; Cinnamon Kiss; Devil in a Blue Dress; Gone Fishin'.* Neely, Barbara. *Blanche Passes Go* (pp. 2, 5). Thomas-Graham, Pamela. *Blue Blood.* Wesley, Valerie Wilson. *Where Evil Sleeps.*
HOMOSEXUALITY/BISEXUALITY/HOMOPHOBIA: Bailey, Frankie Y. *Death's Favorite Child.* Baker, Nikki. *The Lavender House Murder.* Haywood, Gar Anthony. *All the Lucky Ones Are Dead.* Kelley, Norman. *Nina Halligan series.* Mickelbury, Penny. *Keeping Secrets; Night Songs.*
TEMPTATION SEXUAL EXPERIMENTATION/EXPLORATION: Phillips, Gary. *High Hand* (166–167).

Sickle Cell Anemia
OTHER CHARACTER WITH: Wesley, Valerie Wilson. *Devil's Gonna Get Him.*
PROTAGONIST WITH: Hayes, Teddy. Devil Barnett series.

Skin Color (*see also* Racial Identity)
BLACKBALLING BY LIGHT-SKINNED WOMAN: Wesley, Valerie Wilson. *Devil's Gonna Get Him* (p. 37).
COLONIALISM/COLORISM ON CARIBBEAN ISLAND: Kelley, Norman. *The Big Mango* (p. 55).
CONSEQUENCES APPEARING WHITE FOR OFFENDER: Kelley, Norman. *A Phat Death.*
DARK-SKINNED PROTAGONIST (ASSUMPTIONS ABOUT/RESPONSES TO): Neely, Barbara. Blanche White series.
LIGHT-SKINNED PROTAGONIST (ASSUMPTIONS ABOUT/RESPONSES TO): Bates, Karen Grigsby. Alex Powell series. Woods, Paula L. Charlotte Justice series.

Slavery (*and see* the text)
MAINE AND RUNAWAY SLAVES: Neely, Barbara. *Blanche Among the Talented Tenth* (p. 5).

Storytelling (*and see* the text)
BLACK HUMOR/COMEDIAN: Phillips, Gary. *Shooter's Point* (p. 175).
FAMILY LEGEND ABOUT GRANDFATHER AND KKK: Joe, Yolanda. *Hit Time* (pp. 111–113).
FRIEND (MOUSE) AS LEGEND: "... the most perfect human being a black man could imagine. He was a lover and a killer and one of the best storytellers you ever heard" (Mosley, Walter. *Bad Boy Brawly Brown*, p. 237).

Suburbs
AS PRISON: Comacho, Austin. *Blood and Bones* (p. 244).
INFORMAL CONTROL/NORMS: Grimes, Terris McMahan. *Blood Will Tell* (p. 101).

Urban Inner City (*see* the text)

Victims (*see* the text)

Vigilante/Vigilante Group
Carter, Charlotte. *Drumsticks*; *Trip Wire*. Flowers, R. Barrie. *Justice Served*. Hayes, Teddy. *Dead by Popular Demand*. Neely, Barbara. *Blanche Cleans Up.*

War and Aftermath (*and see* the text)
IMPACT ON MEN WHO SERVED: Bland, Eleanor Taylor. *Windy City.* Carter, Charlotte. *Jackson Park.* Greer, Robert L. *The Resurrection of Langston Blue.* Mosley, Walter. *Devil in a Blue Dress.*
SAVING RACIST DURING WAR: Mosley, Walter. *Fear Itself* (p. 204).
WAR CRIMES: Carter, Charlotte. *Trip Wire.* Greer, Robert O. *The Resurrection of Langston Blue.* Holton, Hugh. *Time of the Assassins* (p. 120).

Work/Workplace
BLACK MALE LABORERS/WORKERS: Miller, C.M. *Taxes, Death, & Trouble.*
PROTESTANT WORK ETHIC: Mosley, Walter. *Black Betty* (pp. 44–63).
SEXUAL HARASSMENT: Neely, Barbara. *Blanches Passes Go* (pp. 21–22). Grimes, Terris McMahan. *Blood Will Tell.* Samuels-Young, Pamela. *Firm Pursuit.*
STYLE OF WORKING MAN: Neely, Barbara. *Blanche Passes Go* (p. 1).
WORKPLACE VIOLENCE: Grimes, Terris McMahan. *Blood Will Tell* (pp. 16–17).

APPENDIX F

Readers Survey

Description of Survey (Excerpted)

This survey is a part of a project conducted by Professor Frankie Y. Bailey of the State University of New York at Albany's School of Criminal Justice. The data collected will be included in a book by Professor Bailey titled *African American Mystery Writers*.

Although comments from your survey may be quoted in the book, you will not be identified by name or location (that information will not be collected in this survey). Your e-mail address may be temporarily stored in the archives of SurveyMonkey.com while the survey is in progress.

You will not be contacted concerning this survey. However, you may see the results in the published book.

Professor Bailey may be reached at: [mailing address, telephone number, and e-mail address provided].

Survey Questions

1. **How did you hear about this survey?**
   DorothyL
   Reader/discussion group contact
   Other (please specify)

2. **Please provide the following demographic information.**
   About you: Race/Ethnicity   Sex   Age

3. **Please describe the type of mystery detective fiction you most often read.**
   Reading habits: Subgenres [listed]

4. **How do you select the mystery/detective fiction that you will read?**
   Reviews
   Browsing in bookstore
   Recommendations from bookstore staff
   Recommendations from friends
   Selections made by reading/discussion group
   Other (please specify)

5. Have you read novels or short stories by any of these African American mystery writers?

> [authors listed]

6. I find it easy to identify with the protagonists in books and short stories by African American mystery writers.

	Strongly				Strongly
	Agree	Agree	Neutral	Disagree	Disagree

> Your response to this statement:

7. There are certain element of plot, characterization, and/or setting that I expect to find when I read a book or short story by an African American mystery writer.

	Strongly				Strongly
	Agree	Agree	Neutral	Disagree	Disagree

> Your response to this statement:

8. If you were asked what elements you might expect to find in books or short stories by African American mystery readers [sic], would you mention any of the following?

> References to African American culture (e.g., music)
> References to slavery
> References to racial profiling by law enforcement
> Discussion of social issues (e.g., poverty, homelessness)
> Urban setting
> Scene set in beauty shop/barber shop
> Depiction of gangs/gang violence
> Explicit sex and violence
> References to religion
> A protagonist with strong family ties
> A protagonist with strong ties to the community
> A protagonist who has served time in prison
> A protagonist who has been a police officer
> A protagonist who distrusts the police
> Expressions of liberal political views by protagonist
> Racial/ethnic slurs directed toward protagonist or others
> References to homophobia in black community
> Characters who have been targets of sexual harassment
> The use of excessive violence by the protagonist
> The death of the villain at the hands of the protagonist
> Statements about justice by the protagonist
> Statements about the American dream by the protagonist
> No, I have no expectations about what I will find

9. Is there anything else you would like to add?

> [End of survey — respondents were thanked for participating]

Responses to Question 9

These comments have not been edited for grammar, spelling, or content. The responses are in precise chronological order; hour and minute notations are eliminated.

and Date of Response

1. 10/17/2006 • I ended up skipping this list. Yes, there are a lot on there I'd expect to find — even HOPE to find — because that's why I read, say, Faye Kellerman. To learn a little bit more about Jewish culture and tradition. AT THE SAME TIME, I hope I'm open to so much more. And I hope I haven't fallen into a horrible, confining slot where people must fall into predictable patterns. Blick!

2. 10/17/2006 • I don't "expect" to find things/characteristics in an author's work not previously known to me. This is different than being less than surprised when core historical themes crop up.

3. 10/17/2006 • I read mostly British mysteries, so the black characters are generally Caribbean-British or African-British. I am happy to find black characters from all walks of life as both heroes and villains.

4. 10/17/2006 • I don't usually pay any attention to ethnicity in choosing authors or protagonists. I just like a good mystery.

5. 10/17/2006 • With the exceptions of Mosley and Darden, I didn't know some of the writers I've read are African American and don't much care as long as I find a good story, well told.

6. 10/17/2006 • Since I've never read a mystery by a AAMW, I would expect some of the same elements I'd find in a thriller / romantic suspense written by a white author.

7. 10/17/2006 • I don't read a particular author because of skin color ... but rather to get a glimpse into a different cultural world or perspective.

8. 10/17/2006 • I'm disappointed that I don't find more "middle America" themes in black mysteries. Mysteries set in Iowa, small town America where there are black folks. That's why my novels take place in northern California in small towns.

9. 10/17/2006 • I look for interesting books and stories, not paying that much attention to who the author is. However, cultural references fascinatge me. I've enjoyed books about Tibet, historical mysteries (like Walter Moseley's that draw you in to post-war California).

10. 10/17/2006 • I expect to find this things no more or less than I do in books by other authors. I do look for culture references (though that need not be racial, it may be geographical) because I like that in mysteries. Some of these are distinctive in certain books (Mosley and working toward the American dream, but not necessarily unique to African-American writers.

11. 10/17/2006 • Most of the time I am not sure I would know that the writer was black. I wonder if there is a large black community of mystery readers ... and of mystery buyers. That may sound racist, but although about 10 pct of our Atlanta suburb is black middle and upper class, I never see blacks in the bookstore. In the library they are always with children.

12. 10/18/2006 • PLEASE NOTE: I answered the above because the question asked "might expect." I wouldn't necessarily expect any of the above, but I have found most of the above at one time or another.

13. 10/18/2006 • I'm sure that somewhere along the way I've read a book written by an African American, but off-hand I can't give you a name. As far as queston 8 goes, I think that would depend on the the story line.

14. 10/18/2006 • I like to be suprised by the story line without being hand-helded to each point. I do not like to have the same requiste characters all of the time ie. the whore, drug dealer, abusive male partner, con artist without any intelligence, etc.

15. 10/18/2006 • I am only interested in gay detectives. Though I know of few African American novelists or script writers by their cultural identity, I am intrigued by the number of African American police officers and sleuths on television and in movies, fewer in novels. Unless I am mistaken in Mr. Boyd's cultural identity, you really should look at his impressive work.

16. 10/19/2006 • I always hope to find some insight culturally that I have not been aware of before reading the book.

17. 10/19/2006 • Seems an incomplete survey.

18. 10/19/2006 • I didn't know that there were so many African-American mystery writers. The list has motivated me to read more of these writers!

19. 10/19/2006 • I know I have read mysteries by African American authors, but it's not been recent enough to remember the names, and I didn't recognize any of the ones in the list. I know I enjoyed them at the time and didn't find it hard to relate at all.

20. 10/20/2006 • I expect to find all the same characteristics in novels by caucasian or other authors too. I don't choose a book because of the skin color of the author.

21. 10/25/2006 • I like reading about people different than myself including stories set in foreign countries. I would like to read more stories with African American protagonists but it seems as though they aren't promoted as well as they might be.

22. 10/26/2006 • Many of the books have a sense of humor. I especially like the viewpoint of someone not in the main stream (also found in other sub-cultures such as Indian, Gay, Inuit, etc) and books from other countries (most often Canadian, British (including Ireland/Scotland/Wales) but I'm open to others).

23. 10/26/2006 • I am not usually aware of the color of an author unless there is a picture of them on the book. Just as I often don't know the sex of an author. I am more aware of the sub-genre area such as legal or police procedural.

24. 10/26/2006 • Good idea to do this survey.

25. 11/4/2006 • As someone who pays little or no attention to the author of mysteries, I really have no expectations or ideas about what the author might introduce into the book. I just want a good novel to read and the authors I checked have given me that.

26. 11/4/2006 • I look for an interesting story, characters and place and a protagonist I care about. I like to be given a glimpse into a culture that's different from my own experience. Grace F. Edwards' books are favorites. And then there's the writing. No one in any genre of literature is better than Walter Mosley. He does it all.

27. 11/5/2006 • to question 8, I usually see some reference to tension between the races. I'm pretty surprised when I don't. I also tend to pick AA authors who focus on strong women characters (of any race) because that's what I like.

28. 11/5/2006 • I read such a wide variety of mysteries that I've come to the point of view that I should read each mystery without too many preconceptions ... which isn't always easy, but makes for some interesting reading sometimes.

29. 11/5/2006 • Issues that arise for the protagonist in the workplace and/or society due to or perceived to be due to race/someone's response unconscious or deliberate.

30. 11/6/2006 • My expectations from a black author are no different from any other author. There have been authors that I have read that I was unaware of their ethnic background.

31. 11/8/2006 • I actually hope that the writing is really well done and researched and I will see that it was an African American author after I finish without any preconceived notions or expectations.

32. 11/9/2006 • I don't pick a book because of the ethnicity of the author. I could care less what the author looks like, only if he/she can write.

33. 11/26/2006 • I am Canadian, and am frequently surprised to discover that a book I have just enjoyed was written by an African-American. It never enters my mind.

34. 11/27/2006 • It's more of what I've found in books by African Americans than what I expect. All I want is a good book and a chance to see our society from a different perspective.

35. 11/27/2006 • Until I've read an author I don't have an expectation about anything so specific as the things listed above. I may have an expectation about the amount of humor or of violence in the book based on the flap copy, but that's about as far as I can go with an expectation until I've read something by an author. Once I've read something, I guess I kind of expect more of the same in future books.

36. 11/27/2006 • Just that I'm kind of embarrassed at how few of the books by the writers listed that I've read.

37. 11/28/2006 • I just read books based on the descriptions on the back or jacket blurb and whether I'd like the climate/setting/characters.

38. 12/2/2006 • A lot of my expectations of African-American authors are the same as those of other authors. Yet somehow I don't identify with the protagonists or with the culture very much. Thus I tend not to read African-American authors. To put this is perspective, I have only a few favorite white American authors. I will read a Brisish/European author way before most American writers, maybe because more Americans tend to write legal thrillers and I don't care for them as much as I like traditional police procedurals.

39. 12/8/2006 • Just that I'd like to see more books by Gar and Barbara Neely.

40. 11/29/2006 • I'd like to try and clarify my answers to 6–8. I don't have trouble caring about the characters, and recognizing the ways the characters are like me, but I'm not sure "identify" is the right word to describe it. I also very much appreciate a chance to see the world from a different viewpoint than my own when I am reading. I am not surprised if any of the things in the list in #8 appear, but I don't expect that all mysteries by African-American authors will have these elements, and I also expect to see some of these elements in mysteries by non–African-American authors. If I have expectations, it is that I will find characters, settings, plots, that will catch my attention, fit enough with the world as I know it to have a "ring of truth," and show me a little bit different way to look at the world or think about life and all it encompasses.

41. 11/27/2006 • Regarding expectations: I did not check the last item on the list because I do have expectations. I expect the books to be well written and entertaining. The books I've read by those whose names I checked off on the list of authors all wrote wonderful, entertaining and thoughtful books and I enjoyed them all.

42. 11/27/2006 • I have many of the above authors in my "to be read" piles, but I haven't technically read them yet (Eleanor Taylor Bland, Nora DeLoach, Robert O. Greer, Terris McMahan Grimes, Barbara Neely, Gary Phillips, Pamela Thomas-Graham, Chassie West, Paula L. Woods). Good luck with your study!

43. 11/27/2006 • Conflicts with other ethnic groups and other cultures. Unmarried mothers— many children Grandparent presence.

44. 11/27/2006 • Some African-American characters in books by non–African-American writers have been well-developed, such as those in works by Elmore Leonard.

45. 11/27/2006 • I expect some differences from a story with a caucasian protagonist, but what I expect specifically has more to do with what kind of mystery it is in general, and what is the setting — Grace Edwards world is not Pamela Thomas-Graham's, (just as Lawrence Block's is not Margaret Marons).

46. 10/21/2006 • All that matters is that the story is good. Who cares about the race of the author?

47. 10/20/2006 • N/A

48. 10/19/2006 • There are so many differences among the African-American authors whose books I read that my expectations vary from author to author — just as they do for all other authors. I mean, Gar Anthony Haywood and Eleanor Taylor Bland are marvelous writers, but their milieus are very, very different.

49. 10/17/2006 • I might expect to find references to color *consciousness*, rather than prejudice, within the community.

50. 10/17/2006 • My reading really depends on how much I identify with the protagonist — I like to read about women like me even if the cultural background is different.

51. 10/17/2006 • I assume question #8 was supposed to read "mystery writers" rather than "mystery readers."

52. 10/17/2006 • It is all about the story.

53. 10/18/2006 • I subscribe to Alfred Hitchcock and Ellery Queesn Mystery magazines, so I'm sure I've read short stories from these writers if they've appeared in these magazines. The thing is, I can never remember the authors of the stories. Now if you had a list of the series main characters, those I remember. I remember Mosley and Neely because I've purchsed their novels.

54. 11/27/2006 • I was a critique partner for an African American writer of chicklit. Critiqued 5 of her books until she sold. Reading her work was an in-depth study of another culture. Many of the things you listed here were included in her books. But, I've found the same elements in many of the mysteries I read.

55. 11/5/2006 • If I'm reading it, I expect to identify with the protagonist somewhat. Sure, I'm not African-American, but I am interested in righting wrongs and finding out how other people live and what their culture is all about. I expect to like the character so if there is too much foul language or violence, I'm ducking out.

56. 11/1/2006 • I'm not sure what the point of these questions is — why would I expect to find any of that list of things in a novel by an African-American SPECIFICALLY? I put "tradional" for my type of mystery, but I don't like cozies, I like P.D. James, and I expected to find a lot of the things on that list up there (statements about justice, for instance, and references to religion, and others) in ANY mystery I'd be interested in reading, no matter who wrote it. None of the list (except possibly slavery) seems specific to the African-American experience exclusive of all other American experiences.

57. 10/26/2006 • Interesting and important survey! My answers to both #6 & #7 are based on the fact that I've read very little so I don't feel I can generalize at this point. I am turned off when protagonists are unapologetically homophobic or misogynic and I seem to remember that the only Mosley mystery I read fell into the latter category, or perhaps I judged the author to be a misogynist. Either way, I never picked up another of his. Would love to read some mysteries where the protagonist is a black lesbian.

58. 10/23/2006 • No.

59. 11/6/2006 • I read virtually all of the subgenres you listed and just chose one to have something to put down.

Notes

1. Chinn (2000) states: "Currently, racial identity is explicitly defined and quantified through parentage on the one hand and self-identification on the other (what Werner Sollors has called the tension between descent and consent identities)" (p. 3).

2. I capitalize both "Black" and "White" throughout the text, but observe the capitalization used by other authors in quotations. I use African American and Black interchangeably throughout the book. This study focuses on writers who are African Americans. When the author is an immigrant, but has been listed in various sources as an African American author and now lives in the United States, that author has been included. When an African American author living abroad has written mysteries that are published and available in the United States, I have included that author. I have not included foreign-born authors of African descent who live in other countries. I have included the several authors who are bi-racial, but who are identified or self-identify as African American.

3. See also Patterson (1982) for his discussion of slavery as "social death."

4. In the formula coined in 1783, slaves counted as "three fifth of a man" for purposes of representation in Congress. This opened the door for the continuing struggle between the "free" states and the "slave" states to maintain the balance of power between them as new states entered the Union.

5. See, for example, White & White (2000) on the perceptions of antebellum European American listeners who described the discordant and inappropriate sounds made by Black preachers and their Black congregations.

6. In justifying the enslavement of Blacks, slaveholders and their allies (including members of the clergy) referred to the alleged curse visited upon Ham, the son of Noah who had seen his father, naked, that Ham's descendants should be the slaves of men.

7. Greenwich's master, Captain Obadiah Johnson, a church deacon, did not free him. When Johnson died, Greenwich and his wife Peg were willed to Johnson's son. They were later sold to another family member. Finally, on July 4, 1776, they were sold to Benjamin Bacon, who allowed the couple to buy their freedom (Seeman, p. 402).

8. Cima (2000), analyzing the invisibility/visibility of both Black and White authors and critics during this era, states: "The 'blackening' of both black and unlicensed white women in public has traditionally meant that 'licensed' white women critics have tried to protect their virtue by writing through various pseudonymous veils, veils which sometimes threatened to marginalize them or transform them into representatives of white womanhood" (p. 472). Required to be visible, Wheatley challenged perceptions about Black intelligence. Cima states, "Domesticating her talent, those who called her 'genius' avoided having to acknowledge the shifting class basis of racial formulations" (p. 482).

9. After receiving her freedom, Wheatley died in poverty while trying to provide for herself and her daughter. Her last published poem was dedicated to George Washington.

10. Pamphlets were an important means of disseminating information in the early republic. Harrell (2006) finds that "African American pamphlets called for social, political, economic, and religious reform" (p. 173).

11. Bruce (2001) points to the *Confessions* of Virginia slave rebel Nat Turner, recorded by White lawyer, Thomas Gray, as another radical Black voice. The *Confessions* were published after Turner's execution, about a year after the final edition of Walker's *Appeal*.

12. Forbes writes: "A major self-help effort was the Negro convention movement, which began in 1817 as a response to the American Colonization Society's effort to rid the nation of free Blacks. The conventions provided a

forum for Africans to protest and coalesce as they recognized and fought against their precarious position in a nation that sanctioned the enslavement of Africans" (p. 157).

13. For discussion of the rhetoric of Garnet's speech, including the influence of Lord Byron, see Forbes (2003).

14. Of this tension in the movement, Coates (1999) observes: "Garrison had provided Douglass with the platform, both literally and figuratively, from which he could passionately plead for the end of slavery. Ironically, by 1845, many of the more conservative elements within the antislavery movement, Garrison included, began to view Douglass as a threat" (p. 88).

15. See McDorman (2006) on the Dred Scott case (*Scott v. Sanford*, 1857). In this case, Dred Scott, who had been taken into a free state by his master, sued for his freedom. Chief Justice Roger Taney declared in the Court's decision that Blacks were not citizens and had no rights that White citizens need respect.

16. However, Foster (2005) argues convincingly that the history of African American print culture begins before the publication of the *Freedom's Journal* in 1827. She describes the African American mutual aid and benevolent societies and the African American church as "progenitors of an African American press" (p. 721). Foster states, "Eighteen seventeen is the date when the first known African American publishing company, the African Methodist Episcopal (AME) Book Concern, was established." By 1841, the Book Concern had established "what is considered by some as the first African-American literary journal, the *AME Magazine*, and a few years later, in 1852, the Book Concern established the *Christian Recorder*, the longest continuously printed African American newspaper" (p. 722). Richard Allen, who had helped to establish the Book Concern, "joined with several other black leaders" from several states to found the *Freedom's Journal* in 1827 (p. 722).

17. Ridicule of the Black middle class and their alleged pretensions was common during this period by critics who claimed they were unfit "for true American respectability" (Bruce, 2001, p. 217; see also White and White, 1998).

18. Based on content analysis of black antislavery newspapers in New York State, Shortell (2004) asserts: "Black abolitionists sustained a more radical critique of American society than their white colleagues. The same forces that generated a conservative outlook, with regard to reform, among northern whites produced militancy among blacks" (p. 80).

19. However, Coates (1999) argues: "Ignored, dismissed, or misquoted in the other major papers, Douglass came to believe that he

had no other choice but to start his own newspaper. This newspaper would provide him a vehicle to express his own sentiments in his own way to those interested in abolition" (p. 88).

20. Jacobs (2000) finds that Douglass "was one of the most ardent supporters of the idea of a national black press." Douglass argued that building successful public institutions would allow African Americans to reach "both whites and blacks who were 'outside' of the African American communicative spaces organized by the convention movement." According to Jacobs, Douglass saw the Black press as both protecting cultural autonomy and allowing for "interpublic engagement" (Jacobs, p. 37).

21. The eighteenth century narrative by Olaudah Equiano (*The Interesting Narrative of the Life of Olaudah Equiano*) is now considered a classic of the genre. However, as Mulvey argues, the narrative published after Equiano's escape to England presents a voice that is "aristocratic, genteel, Augustan, and deferential, more English than American." It is not the voice of the classic American slave narrative, which is "democratic, businesslike, plainspoken, and self-assertive" (Mulvey, 2004, p. 18).

22. See Bell (2001) on the literary marketplace in the 1840s and 1850s. He finds: "Book publishing, by the 1840s, had consolidated into dominant forms in major cities ... and increased capitalization and efficiencies of the production and distribution had made an increasingly national market available to native writers" (p. 137). In spite of setbacks following the financial panic of 1857, literary magazines also flourished (p. 138–140). During this era, American women novelists were particularly successful (p. 142).

23. Regarding female oppression, see e.g., Coates (1999) on the cooperation and tensions between male abolitionists and early feminists both Black and White.

24. Nat Turner was a slave who led a rebellion in Virginia in 1831. He became symbolic of the rebellious, violent slave who was the nightmare of White slaveowners. Turner was captured and executed. In 1967, White novelist, William Styron, published Nat Turner's *Confessions*, a first-person narrative that prompted an angry response from some African American scholars (see Bailey and Green, 1999, p.)

25. Cutter (1996) argues that in her writing, Jacobs obtained a "critical literacy" that Douglass did not. That is Jacobs was able to acquire the master's language and then use it in a subversive way that challenged its assumptions. Douglass, on the other hand, wrote within the assumptions of the language.

26. Rohrbach (2001) suggests that fiction

was not a favored form among the editors of the early abolitionist newspapers and escaped slaves who associated fiction with lying (as opposed to veracity). Rohrbach quotes an 1838 article in the *Colored America* that observed "most novels and romances have no value because they are immoral" (pp. 729–730).

27. In his introduction to *My Bondage and My Freedom*, Edwards (2005) argues that this second book reflects Douglass's growing independence of thought, his now extensive experience as a writer of editorials, articles, and reviews, and his immersion into the genre of autobiographical writing by reading books by white authors and reviewing "a good number of the twenty-one slave narratives published between 1846 and 1855" (p. xix). Edwards writes: In other words, *My Bondages and My Freedom* became necessary in part as a result of this extensive experience and exposure to a wide segment of the American literary scene" (p. xix).

28. Blake was first serialized in Thomas Hamilton's *Anglo-African Magazine* from January to July 1859, and then later in the now retitled *Weekly Anglo-African* (Okker, p. 101). Okker asserts that even though the 1859 text was incomplete, it signified a "remarkable point in the history of American and African American literature; namely the first time African American fiction had ever been published in the United States in either book or periodical" (p. 102).

29. As activists, Harper and other educated women in the postbellum era and into the early 20th century found themselves confronting the images of Black women that were being perpetuated in the mythology of the Old South. In 1923, even as the struggle to enact an anti-lynching bill was underway, African American clubwomen mobilized to protest the efforts by the United Daughters of the Confederacy to erect a statue to "Mammy." At the same time, the clubwomen took on the task of restoring and maintaining the home of Frederick Douglass (Johnson, 2005).

30. Reviewing studies on lynching, Perloff (2000) notes the tendency of the White mainstream press in the South to support the actions of the White vigilantes. Outside the region, the *Chicago Tribune* and the *New York Times* were pioneers in the anti-lynching movement. However, Perloff notes the "blind spots" of the *Times*, "the harshest critic of lynching" (p. 323) in assuming Blacks were guilty of the crimes they were accused of committing and more prone to rape than Whites. Change in the attitudes of Southern White newspapers came in the early 20th century and reflected the boosterism of the "commercial

civic elite" and in the North, the impact of the Progressive movement (p. 355).

31. "In his first publication exclusively devoted to crime," W.E.B. Du Bois, the Ivy League-educated sociologist and historian who would later become a civil rights activist identified four causes of crime in the African American community: the convict lease system; the attitude of the courts, lawlessness of the mob, and segregation (Gabbidon, 2001, p. 587)

32. However, see Gussow 2002a and 2002b on the coded depiction of racial violence in blues music.

33. For example, both James Weldon Johnson and W.E.B. Du Bois, officials in the NAACP, had first-hand knowledge of the violence of the South. Johnson reported barely escaping a potentially lethal situation when he was mistakenly thought to be walking with a White woman (actually a light-skinned Black woman). Du Bois was on faculty at Atlanta University in 1906 when the Atlanta riot occurred (see Bailey & Green, 1999).

34. See Gillman (2003) for discussion of Chesnutt's book in contrast to White novelist Thomas Dixon's fictionalized account of the riot in *The Leopard's Spots* (1902).

35. For more on Hopkins's tenure at *Colored American Magazine* see Doreski (1996).

36. More germane to her crime fiction, Knadler (2002) notes: "Initially appointed as editor of the women's section, Hopkins soon became a main contributor, often writing under pseudonyms like Alan Pinkerton, the founder of the famous detective agency, to disguise the extent of her authorship..." (pp. 63–64).

37. However, book collector Wyatt Houston Day (1999) reports the discovery of a serialized novelette in *Frank Leslie's Boys' and Girls' Weekly*, an illustrated 19th century magazine. Day has located 10 of the 12 issues, published in 1880–1881. The novelette features Nicodemus, the Detective from Africa. Day suspects the author, Capt. Elmer Hardinge, was a ghost writer or a "house name" used by staff members. Day observes that although it was a "revolutionary concept" to have an African American as the heroic protagonist, the novelette contains the stereotypes "in speech and phraseology" that Leslie would have believed his readers expected.

38. At the same time, an audience of African American readers had appeared. Commenting on rates of African American literacy in a 1938 article, Detweiler reports: "According to to the 1920 census, among African Americans over the age of nine, 6,211,064 were literate. By 1930, that number had increased to 7,778,664."

Based on "the best available information; three African American newspapers— the *Pittsburgh Courier*, the *Baltimore Afro-American*, and the *Chicago Defender*— each had a circulation of 50,000 or more" (Detweiler, p. 395).

39. Coates (1999) asserts that Du Bois had decided to start *The Crisis* because he, like Frederick Douglass, was "well aware of how the press and other media were used for propaganda purposes.... As an academician, Du Bois's principal weapons were his research and publications, which painstakingly attempted to understand the problem of race" (p. 95).

40. As Bernard (2005) notes that the symposium did not ask the writers how White characters should be portrayed in fiction by African American writers. However, the presence of White characters in Black-authored works allowed the authors to deal with "the white presence in Harlem" as "interlopers." Bernard states: "...literary landscapes were as much a means to punish and control white ways in Harlem, as they were opportunities to construct ideal white intimates, equals across the color line, useful in the New Negro enterprise to re-construct the black self..." (p. 409).

41. Richardson (2005) notes: "To discourage behavior detrimental to racial uplift — such as wearing house slippers in public, using profanity, and talking loud — the Urban League distributed pamphlets in the 1920s to African American Southern migrants newly arrived in Detroit" (p. 7). This was in fact the role of the Urban League in urban areas— to provide aid, information and assistance to black migrants and to offer education programs and employment workshops (see Bailey and Green, 1999; see also Williams, 2001).

42. Restrictive covenants were legal obligations placed on deeds limiting the use or sale of property. In this case, the intent was to ensure that the property would not be sold to African Americans or others who were considered unacceptable as neighbors.

43. Critiquing Du Bois's study, Scruggs (1993) observes: "What Du Bois did not see in his brilliant study is that street life, alley life, and juke joints made the city bearable for those at the bottom. What he did perceptively see was that blacks' high death rate (especially infant mortality) and high crime rate, and other social ills, were caused by the intolerable conditions of a city that was riddled with race prejudice..." (p. 23).

44. In a 1927 essay titled "The Caucasian Storms Harlem," Fisher had expressed his feeling on returning to Harlem after living in Washington, D.C. Finding that many of the Harlem nightclubs and cabarets were now catering to White patrons and excluding

Blacks, Fisher felt not only uncomfortable but out of place (Bernard, 2005, p. 412).

45. Cain's novels, *The Postman Always Rings Twice* (1934) and *Double Indemnity* (1935), were inspired by the real-life 1927 Ruth Snyder-Judd Gray murder case, involving a New York housewife and her corset salesman lover who killed her husband. Snyder was portrayed as a stylish, blonde femme fatale by the prosecution and in the media coverage of the case.

46. Another reference to the convention of the "least likely suspect" occurs when Bubber pauses in his investigation to see a movie "in which the villainous murderer turned out to be a sweet young girl of eighteen." This does nothing to spark Bubber's mental processes. He goes to have pigtails and hoppin'-john at a café and think some more about the case (p. 231).

47. In Christie's novel the doctor/narrator turns out to be the killer.

48. I will generally try to avoid revealing the endings to the contemporary mystery novels discussed in Section II. However, with early genre fiction, much discussed by scholars, the solutions are often revealed in the context of discussion. In the case of early genre fiction, knowing "whodunit" is more likely to add to the reader's enjoyment and appreciation of the structure of the work than subtract from it.

49. See Knadler (2004) for discussion of domestic violence in Harlem Renaissance era tabloids.

50. "Double-consciousness" is a reference to Du Bois's oft-quoted assertion that African Americans are ever conscious of themselves as they are seen by Whites. In *The Souls of Black Folk* (1903) Du Bois wrote: "[T]he Negro is a sort of seventh son, born with a veil, and gifted with second-sight in this American world, — a world which yields him no true self-consciousness, but only lets him see himself through the revelation of the other world. It is a peculiar sensation, this sense of always looking at one's self through the eyes of others.... One ever feels his twoness, — an American, a Negro; two souls, two thoughts, two unreconciled strivings; two warring ideals in one dark body, whose dogged strength alone keeps if from being torn asunder" (p. 215).

51. In 1931, Schuyler published a novel, *Slaves Today: A Story of Liberia*, that "provides a literary window into the politics of black identity in the early years of the Great Depression" (Putnam, 2006, p. 235). This work deals with the plight of Liberian labor in the African diaspora. The publication of Schuyler's book occurred in the same year that the Scottsboro Boys, nine African American youths, were accused of the gang rapes of two young White

women on a slow-moving train in rural Alabama. The series of trials that followed galvanized both African Americans and the Communist Party. (For information about the Scottsboro case see Carter, 1979. For discussion of the media coverage of the case see also Acker, 2007; Ross, 1999).

52. One of the African American patrons of the Harlem Renaissance, A'Lelia Walker was the daughter of Madam C. J. Walker, the famed entrepreneur. Madame Walker had been born the child of freed slaves and created a hair-care empire that made her incredibly wealthy. A'Leila Walker maintained a salon for Harlem artists, writers, and musicians until her death in 1931.

53. See Ellis (2006) on Black masculinity in contained space in the novel.

54. See also Hakutani (1996) who draws parallels between *Native Son* and Mark Twain's *Pudd'nhead Wilson* in that "both [authors] narrate in the full conviction that the crimes they dramatize are the inevitable products of American society" (p. 72).

55. A racial hoax is perpetrated when a false accusation is made that depends for believability on the stereotypes about the members of a racial/ethnic group (see Russell, 1998).

56. The story was published in 1946 in France and in 1949 in the United States.

57. In a Washington, D.C. murder case, Julius Fisher, a Black janitor at the National Cathedral, was sentenced to death for killing a White female librarian. See *Fisher v. United States*, 328 U.S. 463.

58. The essay was a review of Wright's autobiographical *Black Boy* (1945).

59. However, Jarrett argues that Ellison rejected both the "tight, well-made Jamesian novel" and the "hardboiled novel with its dedication to physical violence" as a vehicle for capturing the diversity and fluidity of Negro life" (p. 87).

60. See also Jimoh, 2000, pp. 116–130 on blues themes in Petry's novel.

61. See Roberts (2004) for his discussion of the influence of lynching and police violence on Ellison's work. Roberts discusses Ellison's short story about a lynching, "A Party Down at the Square," told from the perspective of a White boy (p. 105).

62. In 1980, White novelist Norman Mailer had a strikingly similar experience with White prisoner, Jack Abbott. After helping Abbott to publish *In the Belly of the Beast*, the book Abbott had written in prison, Mailer advocated for his parole. Six weeks after his release from prison, Abbott stabbed a young man to death.

63. See Wheeler, 2000, pp. 105–106 on the "containment policy" that perpetuated segregation in post–World War II American in spite of the push toward social justice.

64. Bryant (2003) reminds us that in a letter to his agent Himes refers to his novels as "domestic" rather than "detective" novels. Himes described "the crime and vice" of the novels as simply "an integral factor in the domestic life of any 'ghetto'" (p. 99).

65. Criminologist Packer (1968) argues that there are two competing models of how the criminal justice system should function: due process (emphasizing the rights of the suspect) or crime control (focusing on stopping crime).

66. Himes was arrested but received "a two year suspended sentence and five-year bench parole" [prison if he committed another crime within five years] (Himes, 1971, p. 46).

67. Harold and DeLuca (2005) make a similar observation. They assert that by the time of the murder of 14 year old Emmett Till in Money, Mississippi in 1955 by two White men for an alleged wolf whistle at a White woman, "lynching was no longer an acceptable public spectacle, though it was still an acceptable community practice.... Racial violence had gone 'underground'" (p. 269).

68. "CBS Reports: In the Killing Fields of America" (January 1995) was the title of a controversial TV documentary.

69. See Weisenburger (1998) on the true-life case of Margaret Garner and the 19th century use of classical allusions to Medea in depicting Garner as a murdering mother.

70. Cawelti (1971) asserts: "All cultural products contain a mixture of two elements: conventions and inventions" (p. 37). In the case of mystery novels, the conventions would be the conventions of the genre "known to both the creator and his audience." The inventions "are elements which are uniquely imagined by the creator such as new kinds of characters, ideas or linguistic forms" (p. 37)

71. See e.g. Gabbidon and Greene (2005) on perceptions.

72. It is my understanding that Christopher Darden's writing partner, Dick Lochte, is not an African American mystery writer. He is included here as Mr. Darden's co-author.

73. Barbara Neely's name appears as "BarbaraNeely" on her website. I am using the traditional separation of first and last name.

74. The earliest gay Black sleuths were created by White writers such as Joseph Brandsetter and George Baxt.

75. Film scholars have identified the enduring stereotype of "the magic Negro" in films such as *Ghost* (1990), *The Green Mile* (1999), and *The Legend of Bagger Vance* (2000). The "magic Negro" is there to provide aid and comfort to the White characters in the film.

76. When she was a reporter for the *Washington Post*, Cooke wrote a Pulitzer-winning story about a Black child junkie. The story turned out to be fraudulent.

77. Christie Love (played by Theresa Graves) was a Black undercover cop on the television show *Get Christie Love!* (1974–1975). Her catch phrase was, "You're under arrest, sugar!"

78. Brackets appear in the original.

79. Appointed by President Lyndon Johnson and chaired by former Illinois governor, Otto Kerner, this commission was known as The National Advisory Commission on Civil Disorders. Its charge was to investigate the underlying causes of the series of riots occurring in American cities in the 1960s.

80. Reginald Denny, a White truck driver passing through the area was pulled from his truck and beaten by several Black men. In the absence of a police presence, he was rescued and taken to safety by other Black citizens. Denny's attackers were charged with attempted murder. The case became another flashpoint in the Black community.

81. Shortly before the 1992 riot, the media played repeatedly a videotape of an altercation between a Korean American storeowner named Mrs. Du and Black teenager, LaTasha Hollings. After an argument over a bottle of orange juice, Mrs. Du shot LaTasha Hollings. Mrs. Du was sentenced to a fine, probation, and community service. During the 1992 riot, the media carried images of armed Korean Americans merchants guarding their businesses.

82. During World War II, the LAPD attracted national and international attention by its handling of the "Zoot Suit" riots that occurred between off-duty servicemen and zoot-suit clad Chicano youth. However, the department also was known for its professionalism. In the 1950s and 1960s, it was the police department immortalized in the *Dragnet* radio, later television, series featuring Sergeant Joe Friday (see Alford, 2004; Cosgrove, 2005).

83. Yancy (2005) writes: "To have one's dark body invaded by the white gaze and then to have that body returned as distorted is a powerful experience of violation. The experience presupposes an anti–Black lived context, a context within which whiteness gets reproduced and the white body as norm is reinscribed" (p. 217).

84. For discussion of food/cooking, see Henderson, 2007. For discussion on racism and grief in the Black community. See Rosenblatt & Wallace, 2005. See Banks-Wallace and Parks (2001). See Majors and Billson (1992) on impression management by Black males. See also Appendix E in this book.

85. See Bohm & Haley (2005) for their critique of the war on drugs. They conclude that among the other negative outcomes has been the "hugely expensive" diversion of resources from more important projects with little lasting effect (pp. 212–213).

86. Black flight to the suburbs could only occur after restrictive covenants were struck down.

87. Carole Ann discovers what is happening is related to the smuggling of illegal Mexican immigrants and involves a woman that both she and her mother know and trust.

88. This was illustrated in coverage of the mass murders by a student at Virginia Tech, in the college town of Blacksburg.

89. See Courtwright (1996) and Nisbett & Cohen (1996) for their theories about the connection between honor and masculinity and its link to White male honor violence. These theories are debated among historians and social scientists, but it does seem that the young, poor, inner city Black male's response to insult is rooted in masculine perceptions of insult and appropriate response. The issue is whether this can be traced as a historical progression from White gentleman who fought duels to the American West and finally to the urban inner city.

90. In New York City, where the penny press (affordable newspapers for the working class) was born, two sensational crimes, the murder of brothel prostitute Helen Jewett and the unsolved death of Mary Rogers, became prototypes for sensational media coverage.

91. This assumes that the case goes to trial rather than being plea-bargained.

92. The "battered woman syndrome" is not a defense for homicide. It is introduced as an explanation of the woman's state of mind. Although there is now more recognition of the cycle of violence in such relationships, the battered woman syndrome is still controversial among those who argue it is a "get out of jail free" card for women who kill. Some feminists also object to the use of the syndrome because they say it presents women as "victims" rather than "survivors" of abuse. It is important to note that most battered women do not kill their partners. In fact, the rate of battered women who kill has gone down. The rate of men who kill their partners has not (see e.g., Edwards, 2007).

93. Research suggests some African American and other women of color hesitate to call the police or fail to press charges after the police are called because of concern that the offender (whom they may love) will be abused by the police. Many localities have mandatory arrest policies that allow the police to arrest the

abusive spouse even if the woman chooses not to press charges.

94. Bystanders who witness an assault or other crime often hesitate to intervene directly because they may be unsure of what is going on and/or may fear that they themselves will be harmed. The scene in the bar is a textbook example of "diffusion of responsibility"; everyone — except Ronnie — waits for someone else to do something (see Latané & Darley, 1970).

95. The debate about both term and films remains lively. The term comes from the assertion that the films—featuring strong, assertive Black protagonists who take on evil and corrupt white police officers, mobsters, and supervillains— declined in quality over time. Critics of the genre also objected to films in which the protagonist was a criminal or characters were stereotypes. Fans of the genre point out that this was the first time that Black actors— men and women — were allowed to play action heroes. They argue that the genre reflected the larger trends in American popular culture (e.g., the James Bond films). For discussion, see Bogle, 1991.

96. Walker (1998) asserts: "Without any question, the primary victims of the nation's drug crisis were young black men. The only question was which of them did more harm, drugs or the war on drugs. In 1995 the Sentencing Project found that, on any given day, 30 percent of African American men between the ages of twenty and twenty-nine were in the hands of the criminal justice system: in prison or jail or on probation or parole" (p. 230).

97. The reference is to Charles Whitman, the University of Texas at Austin student who in 1966 launched a sniper attack from an administrative building observation deck. He killed 14 people, wounded 31.

98. See Gabbidon & Greene, 2005 for discussion of the death penalty issues.

99. The author (title) in order: Chassie West (*Sunrise*); Robert Greer (*Limited Time*); Gar Anthony Haywood (*Going Nowhere Fast*); Walter Mosley (*White Butterfly*); Yolanda Joe (*Hit Time*); Judith Smith-Levin (*Reckless Eyeballin'*); Nikki Baker (*The Lavender House Murder*); Frankie Y. Bailey (*Death's Favorite Child*).

100. This privilege is complicated for white female offenders by gender stereotypes concerning femininity and of the "good wife" and "good mother" (see e.g., Bailey & Hale, 2004).

101. Two people who kill together and who reinforce each other's homicidal tendencies are often referred to in true crime literature as a "killer pair." One of the pair is often the dominant member.

102. The titles in order: Keith Lee Johnson (*Sugar & Spice*); Terris McMahan Grimes (*Somebody Else's Child*); Frankie Y. Bailey (*Old Murders*).

103. See also Taxman, Byrne, & Patlavina (2005); Hurwitz & Peffley (2005).

104. Although the concept of justice incorporates various forms of justice, the definition of justice used here is fundamental fairness.

105. The NYPD street crime unit has been the subject of a significant amount of controversy. See e.g., Rashbaum & Baker (2002); Newman (2001). For a more thorough examination of policing in New York, see McArdle & Erzen (2001).

106. This is a reference to the 1999 shooting of Amadou Diallo, a Guinea immigrant, who was shot by members of the Street Crimes Unit, as he stood in the foyer of his apartment building. The four officers, who fired 41 shots, were acquitted after a jury trial.

107. Heumann & Cassack (2003) write: "Before there was racial profiling, there was criminal profiling, or just plain profiling. Criminal profiling has been described as the 'process of inferring distinctive personality characteristics of individuals responsible for committing criminal acts' (p. 11). In contrast, the term 'racial profiling' came into common usage in the mid–1990s 'to describe specific types of police practices, although those practices actually began more than a decade before that...'" (p. 2).

108. For discussion of issues related to racial profiling see Gabbidon & Greene, 2005.

109. For discussion of the racial profiling of African American women and customs activities at airports see Newsome (2003).

110. See Russell (2004) on driving while Black and "corollary phenomena" such as "Walking While Black," "Idling While Black," "Standing While Black" and "Shopping While Black" (99–101). Russell discusses the "various ways that Blackness has been criminalized and associated with deviance" (104).

111. For an overview of police recruitment of officers of color see Raganella & White (2004). For example of recent law suit regarding racial discrimination in an urban police department see Murray (2007).

112. Hugh Holton, *Time of the Assassins* (2000).

113. Paula L. Woods, *Inner City Blues* (1999).

114. Prosecutors have a constitutional duty to share all evidence in a case with the defense. Failure to do so is prosecutorial misconduct.

115. In cases such as Congressman Sickles and Lizzie Borden.

116. For discussion of the empirical research on prison siting in rural communities see King, Mauer, and Huling (2004).

117. Rosenfeld, Messner, & Baumer (2001) write: "Social capital refers in general terms to cooperative social relationships that facilitate the realization of collective goals. ... it manifests itself in mutually reinforcing relationships between interpersonal trust and civic engagement " (p. 1).

118. Christopher Darden and Dick Lochte (2000) *L. A. Justice*, p. 421. The protagonist is Nikki Hill.

119. Pamela Graham–Thomas, *Blue Blood* (1999).

120. Walter Mosley, *A Little Yellow Dog* (1996).

121. Ignoring for the moment other readers of color, and speaking of White readers as if they too do not belong to various ethnic groups.

122. Keen (2006) goes on to speculate that some readers may respond to "the author's use of formulaic conventions of a thriller or a romance novel." She notes that "for other readers (perhaps better educated and attuned to literary effects) unusual or striking representations promote foregrounding and open the way to empathetic reading" (p. 215).

123. The use of the word gratifications is not intended to invoke a debate about "uses and gratifications" theory in media research. It is used more generally here and not intended to suggest that this is the best or only approach to studying reader responses to this fiction.

124. Barnes and Noble reported that the corporation does maintain stand alone sections in its Atlanta and Oakland stores, cities with large Black populations.

125. Based on the website descriptions of each group: DorothyL is a "discussion and idea list for the lovers of the mystery genre." The listserve was founded in 1991 by a group of librarians. Mystery Readers International is "the largest mystery fan/reader organization in the world. It is "open to readers, fans, critics, editors, publishers, and writers." MosaicBooks.com is "the quintessential place for booklovers." The website provides a meeting place for bookclubs and provides promotional opportunities to authors.

126. Survey Monkey is one of a number of websites where scholars and others may construct a survey and make it available to respondents.

127. Among the authors mentioned were Judith Smith-Levine (inadvertently not included on the list) and Austin Camacho (whom the author met for the first time after the survey was prepared). Also mentioned was Patricia Canterbury, an author of young adult mysteries. Although young adult mysteries are included in the directory, the author did not think the majority of the respondents would have read works by the authors. A numbers of writers that the author had identified as writing in other genres (e.g., romance, mainstream fiction, horror/suspense) were mentioned. Some of these authors do appear in the directory. All mystery writers mentioned by respondents who did not appear in the author's directory were added to the list.

128. This also may be true of other groups of writers who are identified in some fashion that places them outside the mainstream. For example, mystery writers who are gay and lesbian may have similar concerns/issues about marketing, including book placement.

Bibliography

Abbott, L. (1992). *"Play That Barber Shop Chord": A Case for the African American Origin of Barbershop Harmony*. Champaign: University of Illinois Press.

Acker, J. (2007). *Scottsboro and Its Legacy: The Cases That Challenged American Legal and Social Justice*. Westport, CT: Praeger Publishers.

Agozino, B. (1995). "Radical Criminology in African Literature." *International Sociology*, 10 (3).

Alford, H. (2004). "The Zoot Suit: Its History and Influence." *Fashion Theory*, 8 (2), 225–236.

Allen, C. (2005). *Peculiar Passages: Black Women Playwrights, 1875 to 2000*. New York: Peter Lang.

Allison, H. (1948). "Corollary." *Ellery Queen Mystery Magazine*. Reprinted in Woods, P.L. (Ed.). (1995). *Spooks, Spies, & Private Eyes*, pp. 70–88. New York: Doubleday.

Amber, J. (2007). "The Streets Are Watching." *Essence*, 37 (9).

Anderson, E. (2000). *Code of the Street: Decency, Violence, and the Moral Life of the Inner City*. New York: W.W. Norton.

Bailey, F. Y. (1999). "Blanche on the Lam, or the Invisible Woman Speaks." In Klein, K. G. (Ed.), *Diversity and Detective Fiction* (pp. 186–204). Bowling Green, OH: Bowling Green State University Popular Press.

_____. (1991). *Out of the Woodpile: Black Characters in Crime and Detective Fiction*. Westport, CT: Greenwood Press.

_____, and A. P. Green (1999). *"Law Never Here": A Social History of African American Responses to Issues of Crime and Justice*. Westport, CT: Greenwood Press.

_____, and D. H. Hale (2004). *Blood on Her Hands: The Social Construction of Women, Sexuality, and Murder*. Belmont, CA: Wadsworth Publishing.

Bailyn, B. (Ed.). (1993) *The Debate on the Constitution: Federalist and Antifederalist Speeches,*

Articles and Letters During the Struggle Over Ratification, 2 vols. New York.

Baker, H. A. (1985). *Blues, Ideology, and Afro-American Literature: A Vernacular Theory*. Chicago: University of Chicago Press.

Balshaw, M. (2000). *Looking for Harlem: Urban Aesthetics in African-American Literature*. London & Sterling, VA: Pluto Press.

Banks, W. M. (1996). *Black Intellectuals: Race and Responsibility in American Life*. New York: W. W. Norton.

Banks-Wallace, J., and L. Parks (2001). "'So That Our Souls Don't Get Damaged': The Impact of Racism on Maternal Thinking and Practice Related to the Protection of Daughters." *Issues in Mental Health Nursing*, 22 (1), 77–89.

Barlow, M. H. (1998). "Race and the Problem of Crime in *Time* and *Newsweek* Cover Stories, 1946 to 1995." *Social Justice*, 25 (2), 149–183.

Barnes, A. S. (1993). "White Mistresses and African-American Domestic Workers: Ideals for Change." *Anthropological Quarterly*, 66 (1).

Barnes, S. L. (2005). "Black Church Culture and Community Action." *Social Forces*, 84 (2), 967–994.

Basu, B. (1996). "Public and Private Discourses and the Black Female Subject: Gayl Jones' *Eva's Man*." *Callaloo*, 19 (1), 193–208.

Batker, C. (1998). "'Love Me Like I Like to Be': The Sexual Politics of Hurston's *Their Eyes Were Watching God*, the Classic Blues, and the Black Women's Club Movement." *African American Review*, 32 (2), 199–213.

Baum, R. M. (1994). "Early-American Literature: Reassessing the Black Contribution." *Eighteenth-Century Studies*, 27 (4), 533–549.

Baumer, E. P. (2002). "Neighborhood Disadvantage and Police Notification by Victims of Violence." *Criminology*, 40 (3), 579–616.

Bell, M. D. (2001). *Cultural, Genre, and Liter-*

ary Vocation: Selected Essays on American Literature. Chicago & London: The University of Chicago Press.

Bellah, R. N., R. Madsen, W. M. Sullivan, A. Swidler, and S. M. Tipton (1986 [1985]). *Habits of the Heart: Individualism and Commitment in American Life.* New York: Perennial Library.

Berger, A. A. (1997). *Narratives in Popular Culture, Media, and Everyday Life.* Thousands Oaks, CA: Sage Publications.

Berger, P., and T. Lackman (1966). *The Social Construction of Reality: A Treatise of the Sociology of Knowledge.* Garden City, NY: Doubleday.

Berger, R. A. (1997). "'The Black Dick': Race, Sexuality, and Discourse in the L.A. Novels of Walter Mosley." *African American Review,* 31 (2).

Bergman, J. (2004). "'Everything We Hoped She'd Be': Contending Forces in Hopkins Scholarship." *African American Review.*

Berlant, L. (1993) "The Queen of America Goes to Washington City: Harriet Jacobs, Frances Harper, Anita Hill." *American Literature,* 65 (3), 574.

Bernard, E. (2005). "Unlike Many Others: Exceptional White Characters in Harlem Renaissance Fiction." *Modernism/Modernity,* 12 (3), 407–423.

Birnbaum, M. (1999). "Racial Hysteria: Female Pathology and Race Politics in Frances Harper's Iola Leroy and W. D. Howells's *An Imperative Duty.*" *African American Review,* 33 (1), 7–23.

Bland, E. T. (2004). *Shades of Black: Crime and Mystery Stories by African American Authors.* New York: Berkley Publishing Group.

Boan, D. (2002). *The Black "I": Author and Audience in African American Literature.* New York: Peter Lang.

Bobo, J. (1995). *Black Women as Cultural Readers.* New York: Columbia University Press.

Bobo, L. D., and V. Thompson (2006). "Unfair by Design: The War on Drugs, Race, and the Legitimacy of the Criminal Justice System." *Social Research,* 73 (2), 445–472.

Bogle, D. (1991). *Toms, Coons, Mulattoes, Mammies, and Bucks: An Interpretive History of Blacks in American Films.* New York: Continuum.

Bohm, R. M., and K. N. Haley (2005). *Introduction to Criminal Justice: Updated 4th Edition.* New York: McGraw-Hill.

Book Publishing Report. (2000, 02/21). "Doubleday Direct Has Biggest Launch Ever with Black Book Club," 25 (8).

Boyd, H. (2002). "The Man and the Plan: Conspiracy Theories and Paranoia in Our Culture." *Black Issues Book Review,* 4 (2), 38–40.

Boyd, R. L. (2000). "Race, Labor Market Disadvantage, and Survivalist Entrepreneurship: Black Women in the Urban North During the Great Depression." *Sociological Forum,* 15 (4), 647–670.

Braham, P. (1997). "Violence and Patriotism: La Novela Negra from Chester Himes to Paco Ignacio Taibo II." *Journal of American Culture,* 20 (2).

Breen, J. (05/28/2001). "Black Mystery: The Life and Work of Chester Himes." *The Weekly Standard,* Books & Arts, p. 35.

Bremer, S. H. (1990). "Home in Harlem, New York: Lessons from the Harlem Renaissance Writers." *PMLA,* 105 (1), Special Topic: African and African American Literature, 47–56.

Breu, C. (2005). *Hard-Boiled Masculinities.* Minneapolis & London: University of Minnesota Press.

Brook, V. (Ed.) (2006). *You Should See Yourself: Jewish Identity in Postmodern American Culture.* New Brunswick, NJ: Rutgers University Press.

Brooks, K. (1996). "Mammies, Bucks, and Wenches: Minstrelsy, Racial Pornography, and Racial Politics in Pauline Hopkins's *Hagar's Daughter.*" In Gruesser, J. C. (Ed.). *The Unruly Voice: Rediscovering Pauline Elizabeth Hopkins,* pp. 119–157. Urbana & Chicago: University of Illinois Press.

Brown, C. (1995). "Writing a New Chapter in Book Publishing." *Black Enterprise,* 25 (7).

Brown, E. (2000). "Mothering and Parenting Styles." In Burgers, N. J. and Brown, E., (Eds.), *African American Women: An Ecological Perspective,* pp. 53–82. New York and London: Falmer Press.

Brown, E. B., and G. D. Kimball (1995). "Mapping the Terrain of Black Richmond." *Journal of Urban History,* 21 (3), 296–346.

Browning, S. L., and L. Cao (1992). "The Impact of Race on Criminal Justice Ideology." *Justice Quarterly,* 9 (4), 685–701.

Bruce, D. D., Jr. (2001). *The Origins of African American Literature, 1680–1865.* Charlottesville & London: University Press of Virginia.

Bruce, J. E. (2002 [ ]). *The Black Sleuth.* Edited with Introduction by Gruesser, J. C. Boston: Northeastern University Press.

Brundage, F. (1991). "'To Howl Loudly': John Mitchell Jr. and His Campaign Against Lynching in Virginia." *Canadian Review of American Studies,* 22 (3).

Bryant, C. G. (2005). "'*The Soul Has Bandaged Moments*'! Reading the African American Gothic in Wright's 'Big boy Leaves Home,'" Morrison's *Beloved,* and Gomez's *Gilda.* *African American Review,* 39 (4), 541–553.

Bryant, J. H. (2003). *"Born in a Mighty Bad Land": The Violent Man in African American Folklore and Fiction.* Bloomington, IN: Indiana University Press.

_____. (1997). *Racial Violence in the African American Novel: Victims and Heroes.* Amherst: University of Massachusetts Press.

Bunyan, S. (2003). "No Order from Chaos: The Absence of Chandler's Extra-Legal Space in the Detective Fiction of Chester Himes and Walter Mosley." *Studies in the Novel,* 35 (3), 339–365.

Burman, S., and P. Allen-Meares (1994). "Neglected Victims of Murder: Children's Witness to Parental Homicide." *National Association of Social Workers,* 39 (1), 28–34.

Butler, R. (2005). "The Loeb and Leopold Case: A Neglected Source for Richard Wright's *Native Son.*" *African American Review,* 39 (4), 555–567.

Byrd, A. D. and Tharps, L. L. (2001). *Hair story: Untangling the Roots of Black Hair in America.* New York: St. Martin's Press.

Carter, D. T. (2007). *Scottsboro: A Tragedy of the American South,* rev. ed. Baton Rouge: Louisiana State University Press.

Cavaan, A. M. (10/9/2000). "Fiction on the Edge; Publisher Uses Hip-Hop Blend of Violence to Attract Young Black Male Readers; Publisher Targets Underserved Urban Audience." *The Boston Herald,* Arts & Life, p. 39.

Cawelti, J. G. (1976). *Adventure, Mystery, Romance: Formula Stories as Art and Popular Culture.* Chicago: University of Chicago Press.

Chambliss, W. (1976). "Whose Law? What Order?" New York: John Wiley & Sons.

Chandler, R. (1944). "The Simple Art of Murder." *The Atlantic Monthly.* Reprinted in Chandler, R. (1950). *The Simple Art of Murder.* Boston: Houghton Mifflin.

Charlton, M., C. Pette, and C. Burbaum (2004). "Reading Strategies in Everyday Life: Different Ways of Reading a Novel Which Make a Distinction." *Poetics Today,* 25 (2), 241–263.

Chesnutt, C. W. (1972 [1899]). *The Wife of His Youth and Other Stories.* Ann Arbor: The University of Michigan Press.

Chiles, N. (1/4/2006). "Their Eyes Were Reading Smut." *The New York Times,* Section A; Column 1, Editorial Desk, p. 15.

Chinn, S. E. (2000). *Technology and the Logic of American Racism: A Cultural History of the Body of Evidence.* London & New York: Continuum.

Christian, B. T. (1999). "Politically Incorrect Struggles/Syndromes." In Nunez, E. and Greene, B. M. (Eds.), *Defining Ourselves:*

Black Writers in the 90s (pp. 137–145). New York: Peter Lang.

Cima, G. G. (2000). "Black and Unmarked: Phillis Wheatley, Mercy Otis Warren, and the Limits of Strategic Anonymity." *Theatre Journal,* 52 (4), 465–495.

Clabough, C. (2006). "'Toward An All-Inclusive Structure': The Early Fiction of Gayl Jones." *Callaloo,* 29 (2), 634–657.

Clark, K. (1999). "Re-(W)righting Black Male Subjectivity: The Communal Poetics of Ernest Gaines's *A Gathering of Old Men.*" *Callaloo* 22 1), 195–207.

Coale, S. (2000). *The Mystery of Mysteries: Cultural Differences and Designs.* Bowling Green, OH: Bowling Green State University Popular Press.

Coates, R. D. (1999). "Social Action, Radical Dialectics, and Popular Protests: Treatment of African American Leaders and Intellectuals by the Press." *Journal of Black Studies,* 30 (1), 85–102.

Cochran, D. (1996). "So Much Nonsense Must Make Sense: The Black Vision of Chester Himes." *Midwest Quarterly,* 38 (1).

Cohen, M. (2000) *Murder Most Fair: The Appeal of Mystery Fiction.* Madison: Fairleigh Dickinson University Press.

Coleman, L. (1997). "Carl Van Vechten Presents the New Negro." In Kramer, V. A. and Russ, R. A. (Eds), *Harlem Renaissance Re-Examined: A Revised and Expanded Edition* (pp. 133–150). Troy, NY: The Whitston Publishing Company.

Collins, P. H. (2000 [1990]). *Black Feminist Thought: Knowledge, Consciousness, and the Politics of Empowerment* (Rev. 10th Ann. 2nd ed.). New York and London: Routledge.

_____. (1998). *Fighting Words: Black Women and the Search for Justice.* Minneapolis: University of Minnesota.

Cook, W. W. (1999) "What Is Reborn in a Renaissance?" In Nunez, E. and Greene, B.M. (Eds.), *Defining Ourselves: Black Writers in the 90s* (pp. 187–191). New York: Peter Lang.

Copes, H., K. R. Kerley, and A. Carroll (2002). "Killed in the Act: A Descriptive Analysis of Crime-Precipitated Homicide." *Homicide Studies,* 6 (3), 240–257.

Corbould, C. (2007). "Streets, Sounds and Identity in Interwar Harlem." *Journal of Social History,* 40 (4), 859–894.

Cordell, S. A. (2006). "'The Case Was Very Black Against Her': Pauline Hopkins and the Politics of Racial Ambiguity at the *Colored American Magazine.*" *American Periodicals: A Journal of History, Criticism, and Bibliography,* 16 (1), 52–73.

Cornelius, J. D. (1991). *When I Can Read My Title Clear: Literacy, Slavery, and Religion in the Antebellum South.* Columbia: University of South Carolina Press.

Corrigan, M. (2005). *Leave Me Alone, I'm Reading: Finding and Losing Myself in Books.* New York: Vintage Books.

Cose, E. (1993). *The Rage of a Privileged Class.* New York: HarperCollins.

Cosgrove, S. (2005). "The Zoot-Suit and Style Warfare." In Cameron, A. (Ed.), *Looking for America: The Visual Production of Nation and People* (pp. 264–280). Malden, MA & Oxford, UK: Blackwell Publishing.

Courtwright, D. T. (1996). *Violent Land: Single Men and Social Disorder from the Frontier to the Inner City.* Cambridge: Harvard University Press.

Crane, G. D. (1997). "The Path of Law and Literature." *American Literary History,* 9 (4), 758–775.

Crawford, N. (2006a). "Good, Bad, and Beautiful: Chester Himes's Femmes in Harlem." *NWSA Journal,* 18 (2), 193–217.

_____. (2006b). "An Interview with Eleanor Taylor Bland." *Heldref Publications.* Online at http://www.heldref.org/storfull.php.

Crooks, R. (1995). "From the Far Side of the Urban Frontier: The Detective Fiction of Chester Himes and Walter Mosley." *College Literature,* 22 (3).

Cutter, M. J. (1996). "Dismantling 'The Master's House': Critical Literacy in Harriet Jacobs' *Incidents in the Life of a Slave Girl.*" *Callaloo,* 19 (1), 209–225.

Davidson, M., and R. A. Friedman (1998). "When Excuses Don't Work: The Persistent Injustice Effect Among Black Managers." *Administrative Science Quarterly,* 43 (1), 154–183.

Davis, A. (1975). "Joan Little: The Dialectics of Rape." *Ms. Magazine* (on line).

Davis, A. J. (2005). "Shatterings: Violent Disruptions of Homeplace." In *Jubilee* and *The Street. MELUS,* 30 (4). 25–51.

_____. (2005). "To Build a Nation: Black Women Writers, Black Nationalism, and the Violent Reduction of Wholeness." *Frontiers: A Journal of Women's Studies,* 26 (3), 24–53.

Dawahare, A. (1999). "From No Man's Land to Mother-Land: Emasculation and Nationalism in Richard Wright's Depression Era Urban Novels." *African American Review,* 33 (3), 451–466.

Dawkins, L. (2004). "From Madonna to Medea: Maternal Infanticide in African American Women's Literature of the Harlem Renaissance." *Literature Interpretation Theory,* 15, 223–240.

Day, W. H. (1999, Feb/Mar). "Book Collector Stalks Detective from Africa." *American Visions,* 4 (1). (on line).

Dayan, J. (2001). "Legal Slaves and Civil Bodies." *Nepantla: Views from South,* 2 (1), 3–39.

DeCoste, D. M. (1998). "To Blot it All Out: The Politics of Realism in Richard Wright's Native Son." *Style,* 32 (1), 127–

Décuré, N. (1999). "In Search of Our Sisters' Mean Streets: The Politics of Sex, Race, and Class in Black Women's Crime Fiction." In Klein, K. G. (Ed.), *Diversity and Detective Fiction* (pp. 158–185). Bowling Green, OH: Bowling Green State University Popular Press.

DeLamotte, E. (2004?). "'Collusions of the Mystery': Ideology and the Gothic in *Hagar's Daughter.*" *Gothic Studies,* 6 (1), 69–79.

DeLombard, J. (2001). "'Eye-Witness to the Cruelty': Southern Violence and Northern Testimony in Frederick Douglass's 1845 Narrative." *American Literature,* 73 (2), 245–275.

Desai, G., F. Smith, and S. Nair (2003). "Introduction: Law, Literature, and Ethnic Subjects." MELUS, 28 (1), 3–16.

Detweiler, F. G. (1938). "The Negro Press Today." *The American Journal of Sociology,* Vol. 44, No. 3, 391–400.

Deutsch, L. J. (1979). "'The Streets of Harlem': The Short Stories of Rudolph Fisher." *Phylon,* 40 (2), 159–171.

Diawara, M. (1993). "Noir by Noirs: Towards a New Realism in Black Cinema." *African American Review,* 27 (4), 525–537.

Dietzel, S. B. (2004). "The African American Novel and Popular Culture." In Graham, M. (Ed.), *Cambridge Companion to the African American Novel* (pp. 156–170). Cambridge, UK: Cambridge University Press.

Diggs-Brown, B., and L. Steinhorn (2000). *By the Color of Our Skin: The Illusion of Integration and the Reality of Race.* New York: Plume/Penguin.

Dines, G., and J. M. Humez (Eds). (1995). *Gender, Race and Class in Media: A Text- Reader.* Thousand Oaks, CA: Sage Publications.

Doreski, C. K. (1996). "Inherited Rhetoric and Authentic History: Pauline Hopkins at the *Colored American Magazine.*" In Gruesser, J. C. (Ed.). *The Unruly Voice: Rediscovering Pauline Elizabeth Hopkins,* pp. 71–97. Urbana & Chicago: University of Illinois Press.

Douglass, F. (2003 [1845]). *Narrative of the Life of Frederick Douglass, An American Slave.* Introduction and Notes by O'Meally, R. New York: Barnes & Noble Classics.

_____. (1852). "What to the Slave Is the 4th of July?" In Foner, P.S. (Ed.). (1950). *The Life and Writings of Frederick Douglass,* Vol. 11, Pre-Civil War Decade, 1850–1860. New York: International Publishers.

Dove, G. N. (1997). *The Reader and the Detec-*

tive Story. Bowling Green, OH: Bowling Green State University Popular Press.

Du Bois, W. E. B. (1973 [1899]). *The Philadelphia Negro: A Social Study.* Millwood, NY: Kraus-Thomson Organization.

_____. (1965 [1903)]. *The Souls of Black Folk: Essays and Sketches.* Reprinted in *Three Negro Classics.* New York Avon Books.

Dunn, J. L. (2005). "'Victims' and 'Survivors': Emerging Vocabularies of Motive for 'Battered Women Who Stay.'" *Sociological Inquiry,* 75 (1), 1–30.

Durant, T. J., Jr., and J. S. Louden (1986). "The Black Middle Class in America: Historical and Contemporary Perspectives." *Phylon,* 47 (4), 253–263.

Durham, J. R. (1990). "The City in Recent American Fiction: Listening to Black Urban Voices." *College English,* 52 (7), 764–775.

Edwards, B. H. (2005). "Introduction." In Douglass, F. (2005). *My Bondage and My Freedom.* Barnes & Noble Classics.

Edwards, S. (2007). "Descent into Murder: Provocation's Stricture — the Prognosis of Women Who Kill Men Who Abuse Them." *Journal of Criminal Law,* 71 (4), 342–361.

Elias, R. (1986). *The Politics of Victimization: Victims, Victimology and Human Rights.* New York: Oxford University Press.

Ellis, A. J. (2006). "'Boys in the Hood': Black Male Community in Richard Wright's *Native Son.*" Callaloo, 29 (1), 182–201.

_____. (2002). "Where Is Bigger's Humanity? Black Male Community in Richard Wright's *Native Son.*" *ANQ,* 15 (3).

Ellison, R. (1964). "Richard Wright's Blues." In *Shadow and Act,* pp. 77–94. New York: Random House.

English, D. K. (2006). "The Modern in the Postmodern: Walter Mosley, Barbara Neely, and the Politics of Contemporary African-American Detective Fiction." *American Literary History,* 18 (4), 772–796.

Entman, R. M., and A. Rojecki (2000). *The Black Image in the White Mind: Media and Race in America.* Chicago & London: The University of Chicago Press.

Equiano, O. (1789). *The Interesting Narrative of the Life of Olaudah Equiano, or Gustavus Vassa, the African, Written by Himself,* London, Vol. I. Available on line at Project Gutenberg.

Ernest, J. (1992). "From Mysteries to Histories: Cultural Pedagogy in Frances E. W. Harper's *Iola Leroy.*" *American Literature,* 64 (3), 497–518.

_____. (2002). "Liberation Historiography: African-American Historians Before the Civil War." *American Literary History,* 14 (3), 413–443.

Fabi, M. G. (2004). "Reconstructing the Race: The Novel After Slavery." In Graham, M. (Ed), *Cambridge Companion to the African American Novel* (pp. 49). Cambridge, UK: Cambridge University Press.

Fabre, M. (1973). *The Unfinished Quest of Richard Wright.* New York: William Morrow.

Fanuzzi, R. (2001). "Frederick Douglass's 'Colored Newspapers': Identity Politics in Black and White." In Vogel, T. (Ed.), *The Black Press: New Literary and Historical Essays* (pp. 55–70). New Brunswick, NJ: Rutgers University Press.

Felson, M. (2002). *Crime and Everyday Life,* 3rd. ed. Thousand Oaks, CA: Sage Publications.

Feuer, A. (2005, 4/15). "Ex-Officer Convicted in Choking Death Is to Leave Prison." *New York Times,* Section B; Column 2; Metropolitan Desk; p. 3.

Finch, E., and V. E. Munro (2007). "The Demon Drink and the Demonized Woman: Socio-Sexual Stereotypes and Responsibility Attribution in Rape Trials Involving Intoxicants." *Social & Legal Studies,* 16 (4), 592–614.

Fine, D. (2000). *Imaging Los Angeles: A City in Fiction.* Albuquerque: University of New Mexico Press.

Fisher, R. (1992 [1932]). *The Conjure–Man Dies: A Mystery of Dark Harlem.* Ann Arbor: University of Michigan Press.

_____. (1994 [1928)]. *The Walls of Jericho.* Ann Arbor: The University of Michigan Press.

_____, and Perry, M.(ed). (1987). *The Short Fiction of Rudolph Fisher.* Westport, CT: Greenwood Press.

Fishkin, S. F., and C. L. Peterson (2001). "'We Hold These Truths to Be Self-Evident': The Rhetoric of Frederick Douglass's Journals." In Vogel, T. (Ed.), *The Black Press: New Literary and Historical Essays* (pp. 71–89). New Brunswick, NJ: Rutgers University Press.

Fister, B. (2005). "'Reading as a Contact Sport': Online Book Groups and the Social Dimensions of Reading." *Reference & User Services Quarterly,* 44 (4), 303–309.

Fleet, C. V. (2004). *African-American Mysteries. Collection Management,* 29?, (3/4). 83–99.

Fluck, W. (2003). "Fiction and Justice." *New Literary History,* 34 (1), 19–42.

Forbes, E. (2003). "Every Man Fights for His Freedom: The Rhetoric of African American Resistance in the Mid-Nineteenth Century." In Jackson, R. L., II and Richardson, E. B. (Eds.), *Understanding African American Rhetoric: Classical Origins to Contemporary Innovations* (pp. 155–170). New York: Routledge.

Ford, J.M., and A. A. Beveridge (2004). "'Bad' Neighborhoods, Fast Food, 'Sleaky' Businesses, and Drug Dealers: Relations Between the Location of Licit and Illict Businesses in the Urban Environment." *Journal of Drug Issues*, 34, (1), 51–76.

Foreman, P. G. (1997). "'Reading Aright': White Slavery, Black Referents, and the Strategy of Histotextuality in *Iola Leroy*." *The Yale Journal of Criticism*, 10 (2), 327–354.

Foster, F. S. (2005). "A Narrative of the Interesting Origins and (Somewhat) Surprising Developments of African-American Print Culture." *American Literary History*, 17 (4), 714–740.

Fouché, R. (2006) "Say it Loud, I'm Black and I'm Proud: African Americans, American Artifactual Culture, and Black Vernacular Technological Creativity." *American Quarterly*, 58 (3), 639–661.

Fox, R. L., R. W. Van Sickel, and T. L. Steiger (2007). *Tabloid Justice: Criminal Justice in An Age of Media Frenzy*, 2nd ed. Boulder, CO: Lynn Rienner Publishers.

Frank, R. (2003). "When Bad Things Happen in Good Places: Pastoralism in Big-City Newspaper Coverage of Small-Town Violence." *Rural Sociology*, 68 (2), 207–230.

Free, M. P., Jr. (2004). "Race and Criminal Justice in the United States: Some Introductory Remarks." In Free, M.P., Jr., (Ed.), *Racial Issues in Criminal Justice: The Case of African Americans* (pp. 1–5). Monsey, NY: Criminal Justice Press.

Freistheler, B., Lascala, E. A., Gruenewald, P., and Treno, A. J. (2005). "An Examination of Drug Activity: Effects on Neighborhood Social Organization on the Development of Drug Distribution Systems." *Substance Use & Misuse*, 40, 671–686.

Fullilove, M. T., V. Héon, W. Jimenez, C. Parsons, L. L. Green, and R. E. Fullilove (1998). "Injury and Anomie: Effects of Violence on An Inner-City Community." *American Journal of Public Health*, 88 (6), 924–927.

Gabbidon, S. L. (2001). W. E. B. Du Bois: "Pioneering American Criminologist." *Journal of Black Studies*, 31 (5), 581–599.

_____, and Greene, H. T. (2005). *Race and Crime*. Thousand Oaks, CA: Sage Publications.

Garnet, H. H. (1994 [1848]. "An Address to the Slaves of the United States of America (Rejected by the National Convention, 1843)." In *Walker's Appeal and Garnet's Address to the Slaves of the United States of America* (pp. 89–96). Nashville, TN: James C. Winston Publishing.

Gates, H. L., Jr. (2000 [1979]). "Preface to Blackness: Text and Pretext." In Napier, W. (Ed.), *African American Literary Theory: A Reader* (pp. 147–164). New York & London: New York University Press.

_____. (1998). *The Signifying Monkey: A Theory of Afro-American Literary Criticism*. New York: Oxford University Press.

Ghachem, M. W. (2007). "The Slave's Two Bodies: The Life of An American Legal Fiction." *The William and Mary Quarterly*, 60 (4).

Gibson, J.W. (1993). *Warrior Dreams: Paramilitary Culture in Post-Vietnam America*. New York: Farrar, Straus & Giroux.

Giles, P. (2001) "Narrative Reversals and Power Exchanges: Frederick Douglass and British Culture." *American Literature*, 73 (4), 779–810.

Gillman, S. (2003). *Blood Talk: American Race Melodrama and the Culture of the Occult*. Chicago & London: The University of Chicago Press.

Goetz, E. G. (1996). "The U.S. War on Drugs as Urban Policy." *International Journal of Urban & Regional Research*, 20 (3), 539–549.

Gosselin, A. J. (Ed.). (1999). *Multicultural Detective Fiction: Murder from the "Other" Side*. New York & London: Garland.

_____. (1999). "The Psychology of Uncertainty: (Re)Inscribing Indeterminacy in Rudolph Fisher's *The Conjure–Man Dies*." *Other Voices*, 1 (3).

_____. (1998). "The World Would Do Better to Ask Why Is Frimbo Sherlock Holmes?: Investigating Liminality in Rudolph Fisher's *The Conjure–Man Dies*." *African American Review*, 32 (4), 607–619.

Gounard, J. F. (1978). "Richard Wright's 'The Man Who Lived Underground': A Literary Analysis." *Journal of Black Studies*, 8 (3), 381–386.

Grantdt, J. E. (2004). *Kinds of Blue: The Jazz Aesthetic in African American Narrative*. Columbus: The Ohio State University Press.

Gray, R. (2004). *A History of American Literature*. Malden, MA and Oxford: Blackwell.

Green, C., and I. I. Smart (1997). "Ebonics as Cultural Resistance." *Peace Review*, 9 (4).

Green, R. K. (2005). *Voices in Black Political Thought*. New York: Peter Lang.

Greene, H. T. (2004). "Do African American Police Make a Difference?" In Free, M. D., Jr. (Ed.), *Racial Issues in Criminal Justice: The Case of African Americans* (pp. 207–220). Monsey, NY: Criminal Justice Press.

Greene, S. E. (1974). *Books for Pleasure: Popular Fiction 1914–1945*. Bowling Green, OH: Bowling Green University Popular Press.

Greenlee, S. (1969). *The Spook Who Sat by the Door*. New York: Richard W. Baron.

Greeson, J. R. (2001). "The 'Mysteries and Miseries' of North Carolina: New York City, Urban Gothic Fiction, and *Incidents in the Life of a Slave Girl.*" *American Literature*, 73 (2), 277–309.

Grenander, M. E. (1977). "Criminal Responsibility in *Native Son* and *Knock on Any Door.*" *American Literature*, 49 (2), 221–233.

Griffin, F. J. (1995) "'*Who Set You Flowin'?*': The African-American Migration Narrative." New York: Oxford University Press.

Griggs, S. E. (2003 [1899]). *Imperium in Imperio: A Study of the Negro Race Problem.* New York: Modern Library.

Gruesser, J. C. (2002). "Introduction: The Mysteries of the Black Sleuth." In Bruce, J. E.. *The Black Sleuth* (pp. ix–xxxiii). Boston: Northeastern University Press.

Gunning, S. (1996). *Race, Rape, and Lynching: The Red Record of American Literature, 1890–1912.* New York: Oxford University Press.

Gussow, A. (2003). "'Fingering the Jagged Grain': Ellison's Wright and the Southern Blues Violence." *Boundary* 2 30 (2), 137–155.

_____. (2002a). *Seems Like Murder Here: Southern Violence and the Blues Tradition.* Chicago: The University of Chicago Press.

_____. (2002b). "'Shoot Myself a Cop': Mamie Smith's 'Crazy Blues' as Social Text." *Callaloo*, 25 (1), 8–44.

Gutjahr, P. C. (2002). "No Longer Left Behind: Amazon.com, Reader-Response, and the Changing Fortunes of the Christian Novel in America." *Book History*, 5, 209–236.

Guttman, S. (2001). "What Bigger Killed For: Rereading Violence Against Women in *Native Son.*" *Texas Studies in Literature and Language*, 43 (2), 169–193.

Hagan, J., and F. Kay (2007). "Even Lawyers Get the Blues: Gender, Depression, and Job Satisfaction in Legal Practice." *Law & Society Review*, 41 (1), 51–78.

Hakutani, Y. (1996). *Richard Wright and Racial Discourse.* Columbia & London: University of Missouri Press.

Halttunen, K. (1998). *Murder Most Foul: The Killer and the American Gothic Imagination.* Cambridge: Harvard University Press.

Hansen, H. (2006). "The Ethnonarrative Approach." *Human Relations*, 58 (8), 1049–1075.

Harding, V., R. D. G. Kelley, and E. Lewis (2005). "We Changed the World: 1945–1970." In Kelley, R. D. G. and Lewis, E. (Eds.), *To Make Our World Anew* (vol. II): A History of African Americans from 1880 (pp. 167–264). Oxford & New York: Oxford University Press.

Harold, C., and K. M. DeLuca (2005). "Behold the Corpse: Violent Images and the Case of Emmett Till." *Rhetoric & Public Affairs*, 8 (2), 263–286.

Harrell, W. J., Jr. (2006). "A Call to Consciousness and Action: Mapping the African-American Jeremiad." *Canadian Review of American Studies*, 36 (2), 149–180.

Harris, K. J., and K. M. Kacmar (2005). "Easing the Strain: The Buffer Role of Supervisors in the Perceptions of Politics-Strain Relationship." *Journal of Occupational and Organizational Psychology*, 78, 337–354.

Harris, T. (1998). "The Blues in African American Literature." *Arkansas Review: A Journal of Delta Studies*, 29 (2).

_____. (1995). "This Disease Called Strength: Some Observations on the Compensating Construction of Black Female Character." *Literature and Medicine*, 14 (1), 109–126.

Hart, R. C. (1973). "Black-White Literary Relations in the Harlem Renaissance." *American Literature*, 44 (4), 612–628.

Haslam, J. (2005?). "'The Strange Ideas of Right and Justice': Prison, Slavery, and Other Horrors in *The Bondswoman's Narrative.*" *Gothic Studies*, 7 (1), 29–40.

Hathaway, R. V. (2005). "The Signifyin(g) Detective: Barbara Neely's *Blanche White, Undercover in Plain Sight.*" *Critique*, 46 (4), 320–332.

Henderson, L. (2007). "Ebony Jr! and 'Soul Food': The Construction of Middle-Class African American Identity Through the Use of Traditional Southern Foodways." *MELUS*, 32 (4), 81–97.

Henri, F. (1976) *Black Migration: Movement North, 1900–1920.* New York: Anchor Books.

Henry, M. (2004). "He Is a 'Bad Mother *$%@!#*' [sic]: *Shaft* and Contemporary Black Masculinity." *African American Review*, 38 (1), pp. 119–126.

Herman, M. A. (2005). *Fighting in the Streets: Ethnic Succession and Urban Unrest in Twentieth Century America.* New York: Peter Lang Publishing.

Hester, M. (1994). "An Examination of the Relationship Between Race and Gender in An Early Twentieth Century Drama: A Study of Angelina Weld Grimké's Play *Rachel.*" Proceedings of the 78th Annual Meeting. *The Journal of Negro History*, 79 (2), 248–256.

Heumann, M., and L. Cassack (2003). *Good Cop, Bad Cop: Racial Profiling and Competing Views of Justice.* New York: Peter Lang.

Hicks, H. (2003). "'This Strange Communion': Surveillance and Spectatorship in Ann Petry's *The Street.*" *African American Review*, 37 (1).

Hill, R. A. (Ed.). (1994). "Introduction." In Schuyler, G. S. *Ethiopian Stories* (pp. 1–50). Boston: Northeastern University Press.

Himes, C. (1976). *My Life of Absurdity: The Autobiography of Chester Himes, Volume II*. Garden City, NY: Doubleday.

_____. (1971). *The Quality of Hurt: The Early Years. The Autobiography of Chester Himes*. New York: Paragon House.

Hirschinger, N. B., J. A. Grisso, D. B. Wallace, K. F. McCollum, D. Schwarz, M. D. Sammel, C. Bresinger, and E. Anderson (2003). "A Case-Control Study of Female-to-Female Nonintimate Violence in an Urban Area." *American Journal of Public Health*, 93 (7).

Hoffert, B. (1998). "Book Report: What Public Libraries Buy and How Much They Spend." *Library Journal*, 123 (3).

Hogue, E. L. (2002). "Postmodern, Traditional Cultural Forms, and the African American Narrative: Major's Reflex, Morrison's Jazz, and Reed's *Mumbo Jumbo*." *Novel*, 169–192.

Hood, T. C. (1995). "The Practical Consequences of Sociology's Pursuit of 'Justice for All.'" *Social Forces*, 74 (1), 1–14.

hooks, b. (1992). *Black Looks: Race and Representation*. Boston: South End Press.

Hopkins, P. (2000 [1901–1902]). *Hagar's Daughter*. London, UK: Black Classics.

Horsley, L. (2005). *Twentieth Century Crime Fiction*. New York: Oxford University Press.

_____. (2001). *The Noir Thriller*. New York: Palgrave.

Howell, P. (1998). "Crime and the City Solution: Crime Fiction, Urban Knowledge, and Radical Geography." *Antipode*, 30 (4), 357.

Hughes, P. C., and A. N. Heuman (2006). "The Communication of Solidarity in Friendships Among African American Women." *Qualitative Research Reports in Communication*, 7 (1), 33–41.

Hurwitz, J., and M. Peffley (2005). "Explaining the Great Racial Divide: Perceptions of Fairness in the U.S. Criminal Justice System." *The Journal of Politics*, 67 (3), 762–783.

Hutchinson, G. (2004). "The Novel of the Negro Renaissance." In Graham, M. (Ed.), *The Cambridge Companion to the African American Novel* (pp. 50–69). Cambridge, UK: Cambridge University Press.

Itagaki, L. M. (2003). "Transgressing Race and Community in Chester Himes's *If He Hollers Let Him Go*." *African American Review*, 37 (1).

Jablon, M. (1997). *Black Metafiction: Self-Consciousness in African American Literature*. Iowa City: University of Iowa Press.

Jackson, L. P. (1999). "Ralph Ellison, Sharpies, Rinehart, and Politics in *Invisible Man*." *Massachusetts Review*, 40 (1).

Jacobs, R. N. (2000). *Race, Media, and the Crisis of Civil Society: From Watts to Rodney King*. Cambridge, UK & New York: Cambridge University Press.

_____. (1996). "Civil Society and Crisis: Culture, Discourse, and the Rodney King Beating." *American Journal of Sociology*, 101 (5), 1238–72.

Jargowsky, P. A., and R. Yang (2006). "The 'Underclass' Revisited: A Social Problem in Decline." *Journal of Urban Affairs*, 28 (1), 55–70.

Jarrett, T. D. (1954). "Recent Fiction by Negroes." *College English*, 2 (16), 85–91.

Jefferson, T. (1955 [1785]). *Notes on the State of Virginia*. (W. Peden, Ed. and Introd.). Chapel Hill: University of North Carolina Press.

_____. (1964 [1861]). *Notes on the State of Virginia*. New York: Harper and Row.

Jimoh, A. Y. (2002). *Spiritual Blues and Jazz People in African American Fiction: Living in Paradox*. Knoxville: The University of Tennessee Press.

Johnson, J. M. (2005). "'Ye Gave Them a Stone': African American Women's Clubs, the Frederick Douglass Home, and the Black Mammy Monument." *Journal of Women's History*, 17 (1), 62–86.

Joiner, L. L. (2005, July/Aug.). "Looking Back: 40 Years After the 1965 Watts Riot." *The Crisis*, p. 9.

Jones, E. (1976). *Eva's Man*. Boston: Beacon Press.

Jones, G. (2003). "Poverty and the Limits of Literary Criticism." *American Literary History*, 15 (4), 765–792.

Jones, L. (1963). *Blues People: The Negro Experience in White America and the Music that Developed from it*. New York: Morris Quill Paperbacks.

Jordan, W. D. (1974 [1968]). *The White Man's Burden: Historical Origins of Racism in the United States*. London, Oxford & New York: Oxford University Press.

Joseph, P. (2002). "The Verdict from the Porch: Zora Neale Hurston and Reparative Justice." *American Literature*, 74 (3), 455–483.

Kadonaga, L. (1998). "Strange Countries and Secret Worlds in Ruth Rendell's Crime Novels[a]." *Geographical Review*, 88 (3).

Keen, S. (2006). "A Theory of Narrative Empathy." *Narrative*, 14 (3), 207–236.

Kellner, B. (1997). "'Refined Racism': White Patronage in the Harlem Renaissance." In Kramer, V. A. and Russ, R. A. (Eds), *Harlem Renaissance Re-Examined: A Revised and Expanded Edition* (pp. 121–132). Troy, NY: The Whitston Publishing Company.

Kelly, J. (2000). "I Thought I Was Writing Realism." *American Legacy: Celebrating African-American History & Culture*, 6 (3).

Kelly, R. G. (1998). *Mystery Fiction and Modern Life*. Jackson: University Press of Mississippi.

Kennedy, L. (1999). "Black Noir: Race and Urban Space in Walter Mosley's Detective Fiction." In Klein, K. G. (Ed.), *Diversity and Detective Fiction* (pp. 224–239). Bowling Green, OH: Bowling Green State University Popular Press.

Kennedy, R. (1997). *Race, Crime, and the Law*. New York: Pantheon Books.

Kerr, A. E. (2005). "The Paper Bag Principle: Of the Myth and the Notion of Colorism." *Journal of American Folklore*, 118, 271–289.

King, R. S., M. Mauer, and T. Huling (2004). "An Analysis of the Economics of Prison Siting in Rural Communites." *Criminology and Public Policy*, 3 (3), 453–480.

Kinnamon, K. (1969). "*Native Son*: The Personal, Social, and Political Background." *Phylon*, 30 (1), 66–72.

Klein, K. G. (Ed.). (1999). *Diversity and Detective Fiction*. Bowling Green, OH: Bowling Green State University Popular Press.

_____. (1988). *The Woman Detective: Gender & Genre*. Urbana and Chicago: University of Illinois Press.

Knadler, S. (2004). "Domestic Violence in the Harlem Renaissance: Remaking the Record in Nella Larsen's *Passing* and Toni Morrison's *Jazz*." *African American Review*, 38 (1), 99–118.

Knadler, S. P. (2002). "The Fugitive Race: Minority Writers Resisting Whiteness." Jackson: University Press of Mississippi.

Koskela, H., and S. Tani (2005). "'Sold out!': Women's Practices of Resistance Against Prostitution Related Sexual Harassment." *Women's Studies International Forum*, 28 (5), 418–429.

Lacy, K. R. (2004). "Black Spaces, Black Places: Strategic Assimilation and Identity Construction in Middle-Class Suburbia." *Ethnic and Racial Studies*, 27 (6), 908–930.

Latané, B., and J. Darley (1970). *The Unresponsive Bystander: Why Doesn't He Help?* New York: Appleton-Century-Crofts.

Lauritsen, J. L., and R. J. Schaum (2004). "The Social Ecology of Violence Against Women." *Criminology*, 42 (2), 323–357.

Lee, A. R. (1976). "Violence Real and Imagined: The World of Chester Himes' Novels." *Negro American Literature Forum*, 10 (1), 13–22.

Lee, B. A. and Schreck, C. J. (2005). "Danger on the Streets: Marginality and Victimization Among Homeless People." *American Behavioral Scientist*, 48 (8), 1055–1081.

Lenz, B. (2004). "Postcolonial Fiction and the Outsider Within: Toward a Literary Practice of Feminist Standpoint Theory." *NWSA Journal*, 16 (2), 98–120.

Lenz, G. H. (1988). "Symbolic Space, Communal Rituals, and the Surreality of the Urban Ghetto: Harlem in Black Literature from the 1920s to the 1960s." *Callaloo*, 35, 309–345.

Levine, R. S. (2001). "Circulating the Nation: David Walker, the Missouri Compromise, and the Rise of the Black Press." In Vogel, T. (Ed.), *The Black Press: New Literary and Historical Essays* (pp. 17–36). New Brunswick, NJ & London: Rutgers University Press.

Lewis, D. L. (1997). *When Harlem Was in Vogue*. New York: Penguin Books.

Lewis, E. (1995). "Connecting Memory, Self, and the Power of Place in African American Urban History." *Journal of Urban History*, 21 (3), 347–371.

Libretti, T. (1999). "Lucha Corpi and the Politics of Detective Fiction." In Gosselin, A. J. (Ed.), *Multicultural Detective Fiction: Murder from the "Other" Side* (pp. 61–81). New York & London: Garland.

Light, I., and C. Rosenstein (1995). *Race, Ethnicity, and Entrepreneurship in Urban America*. New York: Aldine de Gruyter.

Lindsay, T. (09/2001). "A Brief History of African-American Mysteries." *Black Issues Book Review*.

Lipschultz, J. H., and M. L. Hilt (2002). *Crime and Local Television News: Dramatic, Breaking, and Live from the Scene*. Mahwah, NJ: Lawrence Erlbaum.

Lock, H. (1994). *A Case of Mis-taken Identity: Detective Undercurrents in Recent African American Fiction*. New York: Peter Lang.

Ludwig, S. (1998). "Ishmael Reed's Inductive Narratology of Detection: A Narratology of Free Voices." *African American Review*, 32 (3).

Lutes, J. M. (2007). "Lynching Coverage and the American Reporter-Novelist." *American Literary History*, 19 (2), 456–481.

Madriz, E. (1997). *Nothing Bad Happens to Good Girls*. Berkeley & L.A.: University of California Press.

Major, C. (1975). *Reflex and Bone Structure*. New York: Fiction Collective.

Majors, R., and J. M. Billson (1992). *Cool Pose: The Dilemmas of Black Manhood in America*. New York: Lexington Press.

Majors, Y. J. (2003). "Shoptalk: Teaching and Learning in an African American Hair Salon." *Mind, Culture, and Activity*, 10 (4), 289–310.

Malmgren, C. D. (2001). *Anatomy of Murder: Mystery, Detective and Crime Fiction*. Bowling Green, OH: Bowling Green State University Popular Press.

Marberry, C. (2005). *Cuttin' Up: Wit and Wisdom from Black Barber Shops*. New York: Doubleday.

Martin, R. (1988). *Ishmael Reed and the New*

Black Aesthetic Critics. Houndsmill, UK: The Macmillan Press.

Martin, S. E. (1994). "'Outsider Within' the Station House: The Impact of Race and Gender on Black Women Police." *Social Problems*, 41, 383–400.

May, R. A. B. (2001). *Talking at Trena's: Everyday Conversations at an African American Tavern.* New York and London: New York University Press.

_____. (2000). "Race Talk and Local Collective Memory Among African American Men in a Neighborhood Tavern." *Qualitative Sociology*, 23 (2), 201–214.

McArdle, A. (2005). "The Confluence of Law and Antebellum Black Literature: Lawyerly Discourse as Rhetoric of Empowerment." *Cardozo Studies in Law and Literature*, 17 (183).

_____, and Erzen, T. (2001). *Zero Tolerance: Quality of Life and the New Police Brutality in New York City.* New York and London: New York University Press.

McCabe, M. P., and M. Wauchope (2005). "Behavioural Characteristics of Rapists." *Journal of Sexual Aggression*, 11 (3), 235–247.

McCaffrey, L., and S. Gregory (1979). "*Major's Reflex and Bone Structure* and the Anti-Detective Tradition." *Black American Literature Forum*, 13 (2), 39–45.

McCall, N. (1994). *Makes Me Wanna Holler.* New York: Random House.

McCann, S. (2002). "Chester Himes, Black Hard-Boiled Master." *The Common Review: The Magazine of the Great Books Foundation*, 1 (1).

McCluskey, J., Jr. (1987). *The City of Refuge: The Collected Stories of Rudolph Fisher.* Columbia: University of Missouri Press.

_____. (1983). "Two Steppin': Richard Wright's Encounter with Blue-Jazz." *American Literature*, 55 (3), 332.

McCoy, B. (2005). "Paratext, Citation, and Academic Desire in Ishmael Reed's *Mumbo Jumbo*." *Contemporary Literature*, 46 (4), 604–635.

McDorman, T. F. (2006). "History, Collective Memory, and the Supreme Court: Debating 'the People' Through the *Dred Scott* Controversy." *Southern Communication Journal*, 71 (3), 213–234.

McGee, C. (11/11/2006). "For Readers, a New Forum for Black Literature." *The New York Times*, Section B, Column 3; The Arts/Cultural Desk, p. 7.

McKenzie, M. M. (2004). "Spaces for Readers: The Novels of Toni Morrison." In Graham, M. (Ed.), *Cambridge Companion to the African American Novel* (pp. 221–232). Cambridge, UK: Cambridge University Press.

Meier, A. (1995 [1966]). *Negro Thought in America 1880–1915: Racial Ideologies in the Age of Booker T. Washington.* Ann Arbor: The University of Michigan Press.

Meiners, E. R. (1999). "Writing (on) Fragments." *International Journal of Qualitative Studies in Education*, 12 (4).

Meriwether, L. (1970). *Daddy Was a Number Runner.* New York: Prentice Hall.

Miall, D. S. (2006). "Empirical Approaches to Studying Literary Readers: The State of the Discipline." *Book History*, 9, 291–311.

Mikko, J. T. (1999). "'A [B]igger's Place': Lynching and Specularity in Richard Wright's 'Fire and Cloud' and *Native Son*." *African American Review*, 33 (1), .

Mikula, G., B. Petri, and N. Tanzer (1990). "What People Regard as Unjust: Types and Structures of Everyday Experiences of Injustice." *European Journal of Psychology*, 20, 133–149.

Miller, J., T. Z. Like, and P. Levin (1998). "The Caucasian Evasion: Victims, Exceptions, and Defenders of the Faith." In Mann, C. R. and Zatz, M. (Eds.). *Images of Color/Images of Crime* (pp. 217–233). Los Angeles: Roxbury.

Miller, W. F. (1993, 08/28). "Shortage of Black Peers Is a Mystery to Writer." *Plain Dealer* (Cleveland, OH), Metro, p. 8B.

Milliot, J. (2001). "African-Americans Spent $356 Million on Books in 2000." *Publishers Weekly*, 248 (33).

Mitchell, K. S. (1996). "Ever After: Reading the Women Who Read (and Re-Write) Romances." *Theatre Topics*, 6 (1), 51–69.

Molesworth, J. M. (2006). "Equiano's Loud Voice: Witnessing the Performance of *The Interesting Narrative*." *Texas Studies in Literature & Language*, 48 (2), 123–144.

Mor Barak, M. E., and A. Levin (2002). "Outside of the Corporate Mainstream and Excluded from the Work Community: A Study of Diversity, Job Satisfaction and Well Being." *Community, Work & Family*, 5 (2), 133–157.

Morgan, S. I. (2004). "Rethinking Social Realism: African American Art and Literature, 1930–1953." Athens and London: The University of Georgia Press.

Monto, M. A. (2004). "Female Prostitution, Customers, and Violence." *Violence Against Women*, 10 (2), 160–188.

Morrison, T. (1998 [1987]). *Beloved.* New York: Plume/Penguin.

_____. (1992). *Playing in the Dark: Whiteness and the Literary Imagination.* New York: Vintage Books.

Mullen, B. (1996). "Popular Fronts: Negro Story Magazine and the African American Literary Response to World War II." *African American Review*, 30 (1), 5–15.

Mullen, B. V. (2001). *Popular Fronts: Chicago and African American Cultural Politics, 1935–1946*. Urbana and Chicago: University of Illinois Press.

Mulvey, C. (2004). "Freeing the Voice, Creating the Self: The Novel and Slavery." In Graham, M. (Ed.), *The Cambridge Companion to the African American Novel* (pp. 17–33). Cambridge, UK: Cambridge University Press.

Murray, L. A. (2007, 4/26). "Detectives Sue NYPD." *New York Amsterdam News*, 98 (18).

Musser, J. (1998). "African American Women's Short Stories in the Harlem Renaissance: Bridging a Tradition." *MELUS*, 23 (2), Varieties of Ethnic Criticism, 27–47.

Musser, J. A. (2002). "'The Blood Will Flow Back to You': The Reactionary Proletarian Fiction of Marita Bonner." *Canadian Review of American Studies*, 32 (1).

Mystery One Bookstore. (2001, Nov.). "Eleanor Taylor Bland Interview." Available online at http://www.mysteryone.com/EleanorTaylorBlandInterview.htm.

Nelson, A. M. (2005). *Swing Papa* and *Barry Jordan*: Comic Strips and Black Newspapers in Postwar Toledo. *Proceedings of the Ohio Academy of History*, 61–74.

Nerad, J. C. (2003). "Slippery Language and False Dilemmas: The Passing Novels of Child, Howells, and Harper." *American Literature*, 75 (4), 813–841.

Nettler, G. (1982). *Killing One Another*. Cincinnati: Anderson Publishing.

Newman, A. (2001, 1/26). "Ruling in Street Crime Case Could Expand List of Plaintiffs." *New York Times*.

Newsome, Y. D. (2003). "Border Patrol: The U.S. Customs Services and the Racial Profiling of African American Women." *Journal of African American Studies*, 7 (3), 31–57.

Nickerson, C. (1997). "Murder as Social Criticism." *American Literary History*, 9 (4), 744–757.

Nickerson, C. R. (1998). *The Web of Iniquity: Early Detective Fiction by American Women*. Durham & London: Duke University Press.

Nisbett, R. E., and D. Cohen (1996). *Culture of Honor: The Psychology of Violence in the South*. Boulder, CO: Westview Press.

Norton-Hawk, M. (2004). "A Comparison of Pimp- and Non–Pimp-Controlled Women." *Violence Against Women*, 10 (2). 189–194.

Nussbaum, M. C. (1995). *Poetic Justice: The Literary Imagination and Public Life*. Boston: Beacon Press.

Okker, P. (2003). *Social Stories: The Magazine Novel in Nineteenth-Century America*. Charlottesville & London: University of Virginia Press.

Oldenburg, R. (1989). *The Great Good Place: Cafes, Coffee Shops, Community Centers, Beauty Parlors, General Stores, Bars, Hangouts, and How They Get You Through the Day*. New York: Paragon House.

Oliver, W. (1994). *Violent Social World of Black Men*. San Francisco, CA: Jossey-Bass Publications.

Ortega, A., S. O. Brenner, and P. Leather (2007). "Occupational Stress, Coping and Personality in the Police: An SEM Study." *International Journal of Police Science & Management*, 9 (1), 36–50.

Osborne, G. (2001). "Old School Masters of Blaxploitation Lit: The Lives and Works of Iceberg Slim and Donald Goines." *Black Issues Book Review*, 3 (5).

Ostrowski, C. (2006). "Slavery, Labor Reform, and Intertextuality in Antebellum Print Culture: The Slave Narrative and the City-Mysteries Novel." *African American Review*, 40 (3), 493–506.

Packer, H. (1968). *The Legal Limits of the Criminal Sanction*. Stanford: Stanford University Press.

Page, P. (1999). *Reclaiming Community in Contemporary African American Fiction*. Jackson: University Press of Mississippi.

Pain, R. and Francis, P. (2004). "Living with Crime: Spaces of Risk for Homeless Young People." *Children's Geographies*, 2 (1), 95–110.

Panek, L. L. (2003). *The American Police Novel: A History*. Jefferson, NC and London: McFarland.

_____. (2000). *New Hard-Boiled Writers 1970s-1990s*. Bowling Green, OH: Bowling Green State University Popular Press.

Pate, A. D. (1999). *The Multicultiboho Sideshow*. New York: Bard/Avon Books.

Patterson, O. (1982). *Slavery and Social Death: A Comparative Study*. Cambridge: Harvard University Press.

Patton, T. O. (2006). "Hey Girl, Am I More Than My Hair?: African American Women and Their Struggles with Beauty, Body Image, and Hair." *NSWA Journal*, 18 (2), 24–51.

Patton, V. K. (2000). *Women in Chains: The Legacy of Slavery in Black Women's Fiction*. Albany, NY: State University of New York Press.

Payne, B. K., B. L. Berg, and I. Y. Sun (2005). "Policing in Small Town America: Dogs, Drunks, Disorder, and Dysfunction." *Journal of Criminal Justice*, 33, 31–41.

Pecoskie, J. L. (2005). "The Intersection of 'Community' Within the Reading Experience: Lesbian Women's Reflections on the Book as Text and Object." *The Canadian*

Journal of Information and Library Science, 29 (3), 335–349.

Penzler, O. (4/18/2005). "Anatomy of a Mystery." *Publishers Weekly,* 252 (16).

Perloff, R. M. (2000). "The Press and Lynchings of African Americans." *Journal of Black Studies,* 30 (3), 315–330.

Petry, A. (1946). *The Street.* Boston: Houghton Mifflin.

Phillips, E. N. (2001). "Doing More Than Heads: African American Women Healing, Resisting, and Uplifting Others in St. Petersburg, Florida." *Frontiers: A Journal of Women's Studies,* 22 (2), 25–42.

Phillips, G. (1998). "The Cool, the Square and the Tough: The Archetypes of Black Male Characters in Mystery and Crime Novels." *Black Scholar,* 28 (1), 27–32.

Pierce, J. L., M. P. O'Driscoll, and A. M. Coghlan (2004). "Work Environment Structure and Psychological Ownership: The Mediating Effects of Control." *The Journal of Social Psychology,* 144 (5), 504–534.

Porter, D. (1981). *The Pursuit of Crime: Art and Ideology in Detective Fiction.* London: Yale University Press.

Powell, M. (2007, 7/22). "In a Volatile City, a Stern Line on Race and Politics." *New York Times,* Section A, Column 0, Metropolitan Desk; The Long Run; p. 1.

Pratofiorito, E. (2001). "'To Demand Your Sympathy and Aid': Our Nig and the Problem of No Audience." *Journal of American & Comparative Cultures,* 24 (1/2).

Prince, V. S. (2004*). Burnin' Down the House: Home in African American Literature.* New York: Columbia University Press.

Putnam, A. (2006). "'Modern Slaves': The Liberian Labor Crisis and the Politics of Race and Class." *Rhetoric & Public Affairs,* 9 (2), 235–256.

Quillian, L., and D. Pager (2001). "Black Neighbors, Higher Crime? The Role of Racial Stereotypes in Evaluations of Neighborhood Crime." *American Journal of Sociology,* 107 (3), 717–767.

Quinn, E. (2001). "'Pimpin' Ain't Easy': Work, Play, and 'Lifestylization' of the Black Pimp Figure in Early 1970s America." In Ward, B. (Ed.), *Media, Culture, and the Modern African American Freedom Struggle* (pp. 211–232). Gainesville: University Press of Florida.

Radway, J. (1984). *Reading the Romance.* Chapel Hill: University of North Carolina Press.

Radway, J. A. (1995). "Women Read the Romance: The Interaction of Text and Context." In Dines, G. and Humez, J. M. (Eds.), *Gender, Race and Class in Media: A Text-*

Reader (pp. 202–214). Thousand Oaks & London: Sage Publications.

Raganella, A. J., and M. D. White (2004). "Race, Gender, and Motivation for Becoming a Police Officer: Implications for Building a Representative Police Department." *Journal of Criminal Justice,* 32 (6), 501–513.

Rampersad, A. (1986). *The Life of Langston Hughes, Vol. I: 1902–1941. I, Too, Sing America.* New York and Oxford: Oxford University Press.

Ramaprasad, J. (1996). "How Four Newspapers Covered the 1992 Los Angeles 'Riots.'" In Berry, V. T. and Manning-Miller, C. L. (Eds.), *Mediated Messages and African-American Culture: Contemporary Issues* (pp. 76–95). Thousand Oaks, CA and London: Sage Publications.

Raphael, J., and D. L. Shapiro (2004). "Violence in Indoor and Outdoor Prostitution Venues." *Violence Against Women,* 10 (2), 126–139.

Rashbaum, W. K., and A. Baker (2002, 4/10). "Police Commissioner Closing Controversial Street Crime Unit." *New York Times,* 151 (52084), pB1.

Reddy, M. T. (2003). *Traces, Codes, and Clues: Reading Race in Crime Fiction.* New Brunswick, NJ: Rutgers University Press.

Reed, I. (1988). *Writin' Is Fightin': Thirty-Seven Years of Boxing on Paper.* New York: Atheneum.

_____. (1974). *The Last Days of Louisiana Red.* New York: Random House.

_____. (1972). *Mumbo Jumbo.* Garden City, NY: Doubleday.

Reilly, J. M. (1972). "Richard Wright's Apprenticeship." *Journal of Black Studies,* 2 (4), 439–460.

Reiman, J. (2006). *The Rich Get Richer and the Poor Get Prison: Ideology, Class, and Criminal Justice,* 8th ed. Boston: Allyn & Bacon.

Rice, T. J. (2003). "Mapping Complexity in the Fiction of Umberto Eco." *Critique,* 44 (4).

Richardson, R. (2005). "Charles Fuller's Southern Specter and the Geography of Black Masculinity." *American Literature,* 77 (1), 7–32.

Riedel, M., and J. Best (1998). "Patterns in Intimate Partner Homicide: California, 1987–1996." *Homicide Studies,* 2 (3), 305–320.

Riley, L. (2005). "Neonaticide: A Grounded Theory Study." *Journal of Human Behavior in Social Environment,* 12 (4), 1–42.

Roberts, B. (2004). "Reading Ralph Ellison Synthesizing the CP and NAACP: Sympathetic Narrative Strategy, Sympathetic Bodies." *Journal of Narrative Theory,* 34 (1), 88–110.

Robertson, S. (2005). "What's Law Got to Do with It?: Legal Records and Sexual Histories." *Journal of the History of Sexuality*, 14 (1/2), 161–185.

Robinson, C. J. (1997). *Black Movements in America*. New York & London: Routledge.

Rodgers, L. R. (1997). *Cannan Bound: The African-American Great Migration Novel*. Urbana & Chicago: University of Illinois Press.

Rodriguez, R. E. (2005). *Brown Gumshoes: Detective Fiction and the Search for Chicano/a Identity*. Austin: University of Texas Press.

Rohrbach, A. (2001). "'Truth Stronger and Stranger Than Fiction': "Reexamining William Lloyd Garrison's Liberator." *American Literature*, 73 (4), 727–755.

_____. (1999). "To Be Continued: Double Identity, Multiplicity and Antigenealogy as Narrative Strategies in Pauline Hopkins' Magazine Fiction." *Callaloo*, 22 (2), 483–498.

Rooks, N. M. (2004). *Ladies' Pages: African American Women's Magazines and the Culture That Made Them*. New Brunswick, NJ & London: Rutgers University Press.

Rosen, S. J. (1995). "African American Anti-Semitism and Himes's Lonely Crusade." *MELUS*, 20 (2), 47–68.

Rosenblatt, P. C., and B. R. Wallace (2005). "Narratives of Grieving African-Americans About Racism in the Lives of Deceased Family Members." *Death Studies*, 29, 217–235.

Rosenfeld, R., S. Messner, E. P. Baumer (2001). "Social Capital and Homicide." *Social Forces*, 80 (1).

Ross, F. G. J. (1999). "Mobilizing the Masses: The Cleveland Call and Post and the Scottsboro Incident." *The Journal of Negro History*, 84 (1), 48–60.

Ross, M. B. (2004). *Manning the Race: Reforming Black Men in the Jim Crow Era*. New York and London: New York University Press.

Roth, L. (2004). *Inspecting Jews: American Jewish Detective Stories*. New Brunswick, NJ & London: Rutgers University Press.

Rubinstein, D. (1988). "The Concept of Justice in Sociology." *Theory and Society*, Vol. 17, No. 4, 527–550.

Ruble, N. M., and W. L. Turner (2000). "A Systemic Analysis of the Dynamics and Organization of Urban Street Gangs." *The American Journal of Family Therapy*, 28, 117–132.

Rushdy, A.H.A. (2001). *Remembering Generations: Race and Family in Contemporary African American Fiction*. Chapel Hill and London: The University of North Carolina Press.

Russell, K. (1998). *The Color of Crime: Racial Hoaxes, White Fear, Black Protectionism, Police Harassment, and Other Macroaggressions*. New York: New York University Press.

Russell, K. K. (2004). "'Driving While Black': Corollary Phenomena and Collateral Consequences." In Free, M. D., Jr. (Ed.), *Racial Issues in Criminal Justice: The Case of African Americans* (pp. 97–111). Monsey, NY: Criminal Justice Press.

Samuels, A. (2003, 03/03). "Time to Tell It Like It Is." *Newsweek*, Cover Story, p. 52.

Sanchez, D., and R. T. Carter (2005). "Exploring the Relationship Between Racial Identity and Religious Orientation Among African American College Students." *Journal of College Student Development*, 46 (3), 280–295.

Sante, L. (1992). *Low Life: Lures and Snares of Old New York*. New York: Vintage.

Santino, J. (1991). *Miles of Smiles, Years of Struggle: Stories of Black Pullman Porters*. Urbana and Chicago: University of Illinois Press.

Sarkisian, N. (2007). "Street Men, Family Men: Race and Men's Extended Family Integration." *Social Forces*, 86 (2), 763–794.

Sasson, T. (1995). *Crime Talk: How Citizens Construct a Social Problem*. New York: Aldine De Gruyter.

Schuyler, G. S. (writing as Brooks, S. I.). (1991). *Black Empire*. Boston: Northeastern University Press.

_____. (1999 [1931]). *Black No More*. New York: The Modern Library.

_____. (1994). "The Ethiopian Murder Mystery: A Story of Love and International Intrigue." In Schuyler, G. S. *Ethiopian Stories* (pp. 51–122). Boston: Northeastern University Press.

_____. (1931). *Slaves Today: A Story of Liberia*. New York: Brewer, Warren, and Putnam.

Schwartz, R. B. (2002). *Nice and Noir: Contemporary American Crime Fiction*. Columbia & London: University of Missouri Press.

Scruggs, C. (1977). "'All Dressed Up but No Place to Go': The Black Writer and His Audience During the Harlem Renaissance." *American Literature*, 48 (4), 543–563.

_____. (1993). *Sweet Home: Invisible Cities in the Afro-American Novel*. Baltimore and London. The John Hopkins University Press.

Sennett, R. (1990). *The Conscience of the Eye: The Design and Social Life of Cities*. New York: W. W. Norton.

Seraile, W. (2003). *Bruce Grit: The Black Nationalist Writings of John Edward Bruce*. Knoxville: The University of Tennessee Press.

Sharpe, P., F. E. Mascia-Lees, and C. B. Cohen (1990). "White Women and Black Men: Differential Responses to Reading Black Women's Texts." *College English*, 52 (2), 142–153.

Sheehan, R. C., and V. B. Van Hasselt (2003).

"Identifying Law Enforcement Stress Reactions Early." *FBI Law Enforcement Bulletin*, 72 (9), pp. 12–17.

Shihadeh, E. S., and N. Flynn (1996). "Segregation and Crime: The Effect of Black Social Isolation on the Rates of Black Urban Violence." *Social Forces*, 74 (4), 1325–1352.

Shklar, J. N. (1990). *The Faces of Injustice*. New Haven & London: Yale University Press.

Shortell, T. (2004). "The Rhetoric of Black Abolitionism: An Exploratory Analysis of Antislavery Newspapers in New York State." *Social Science History*, 28 (1), 75–109.

Shulman, D. (2000). "Professionals' Accounts for Work-Related Deceptions." *Symbolic Interaction*, 23 (3), 259–281.

Sisney, M. F. (1990). "The View from the Outside: Black Novels of Manners." In Bowers, B. K. and Brothers, B. (Eds.), *Reading and Writing Woman's Lives: A Study of the Novel of Manners* (pp. 171–185). Ann Arbor: University of Michigan Press.

Skinner, R. (1998). "Chester Himes and the Birth of the 'Ethnic' Detective Story." *Mystery Readers International*, 14 (3).

_____. (1989). *2 Guns from Harlem: The Detective Fiction of Chester Himes*. Bowling Green, OH: Bowling Green State University Popular Press.

Slotkin, R. (1973). *Regeneration Through Violence: The Mythology of the American Frontier*. Middletown, CT: Weslyan University Press.

Smith, E. A. (2000). *Hard-Boiled: Working-Class Readers and Pulp Magazines*. Philadelphia: Temple University.

Smith, J. C. (Ed.). (1988). *Images of Blacks in American Culture: A Reference Guide to Information Sources*. Westport, CT: Greenwood Press.

Smith, M. M. (2006). *How Race Is Made: Slavery, Segregation, and the Senses*. Chapel Hill: The University of North Carolina Press.

Smith, S. M. (2000). "'Looking At One's Self Through the Eyes of Others': W. E. B. Du Bois's Photography for the 1900 Paris Exposition." *African American Review*, 34 (4), 581–599.

Smitherman, G. (1985). *Talkin and Testifyin: The Language of Black America*. Detroit: Wayne State University Press.

Smith-Shomade, B. E. (2003). "'Rock-a-Bye, Baby!': Black Women Disrupting Gangs and Constructing Hip-Hop Gangsta Films." *Cinema Journal*, 42 (2), 25–40.

Soitos, S. F. (1999). "Queering the 'I': Black Lesbian Detective Fiction." In Gosselin, A. (Ed.), *Multicultural Detective Fiction: Murder from the "Other" Side* (pp. 105–121). New York & London: Garland.

_____. (1996). *The Blues Detective: A Study of African American Detective Fiction*. Amherst: The University of Massachusetts Press.

Sparrow, K. H. (2000). "Dating and Mating Patterns." In Burgers, N.J. and Brown, E. (Eds.), *African American Women: An Ecological Perspective* (pp. 41–52). New York and London: Falmer.

Spellers, R. E. (2003). "The Kink Factor: A Womanist Discourse Analysis of African American Mother/Daughter Perspectives on Negotiating Black Hair/Body Politics." In Jackson, R. L., II and Richardson, E. B. (Eds.), *Understanding African American Rhetoric: Classical Origins of Contemporary Innovations* (pp. 223–243). New York: Routledge.

Spilka, M. (1997). "Lesson 6. Ann Petry's Determinist Dilemma: Unchosen Violence in 'Like a Winding Sheet.'" In *Eight Lessons in Love: A Domestic Violence Reader* (pp. 262–288). Columbia & London: University of Missouri Press.

Squires, G. D., and C. E. Kubrin (2005). "Privileged Places: Race, Uneven Development and the Geography of Opportunity in Urban America." *Urban Studies*, 42 (1), 47–68.

Stabile, C. A. (2006). *White Victims, Black Villains: Gender, Race, and Crime News in US Culture*. New York and London: Routledge.

Stewart, P. (2007). "Who Is Kin? Family Definition and African American Families." *Journal of Human Behavior in the Social Environment*, 15 (2/3), pp. 163–181.

Strange, C. (1999). "Murder and Meanings in U.S. Historiography." *Feminist Studies*, 25 (3), 679–697.

Strohm, S. M. (1999). "The Black Press and the Black Community: *The Los Angeles Sentinel's* Coverage of the Watts Riots." In Mander, M. S. (Ed.), *Framing Friction: Media and Social Conflict* (pp. 58–88). Urbana and Chicago: University of Chicago Press.

Sundstrom, R. R. (2003). "Race and Place: Social Space in the Production of Human Kinds." *Philosophy & Geography*, 6 (1), 83–95.

Surrette, R. (2007). *Media, Crime, and Criminal Justice: Images, Realities, and Policies*. Belmont, CA: Wadsworth.

Swan, N. (1995). "Thirty-One of New York Murder Victims Had Cocaine in Their Bodies." *NIDA Notes*, 10 (2).

Sweeney, M. (2006). "'Something Rogue': Commensurability, Commodification, Crime, and Justice in Toni Morrison's Later Fiction." *MFS Modern Fiction Studies*, 52 (2), 440–469.

_____. (2004). "Racial House, Big House, Home: Contemporary Abolitionism in Toni

Morrison's *Paradise.*" *Meridians: Feminism, Race, Transnationalism,* 4 (2), 40–67.

_____. (2003). "Living to Read True Crime: Theorizations from Prison." *Discourse,* 25 (1/2), 55–80.

Swope, R. (2002). "Crossing Western Space, or the Hoodoo Detective on the Boundary in Ishmael Reed's *Mumbo Jumbo.*" *African American Review,* 36 (4), 611–628.

Taylor, C. (1999, 12/13). "A Diverse Market for African-American Books Keeps Growing." *Publishers Weekly,* 246 (50).

Taxman, F., J. M. Byrne, and A. Pattavina (2005). "Racial Disparity and the Legitimacy of the Criminal Justice System: Exploring Consequences for Deterrence." *Journal of Health Care for the Poor and Undeserved,* 16 (4), 57–77.

Thomas, H. N. (1988). *From Folklore to Fiction: A Study of Folk Heroes and Rituals in the Black American Novel.* New York & Westport, CT: Greenwood.

"To Our Patrons." (1827). *Freedom's Journal,* 1 (1), 1. Available in digital form at Wisconsin History Society, Library-Archives, on line.

Toch, H. (2001). *Stress in Policing.* Washington, D.C.: American Psychological Association.

Tolnay, S. E., and E. M. Beck (1995). *A Festival of Violence: An Analysis of Southern Lynchings, 1882–1930.* Urbana and Chicago: University of Illinois Press.

Torres, S. (2003). *Black, White, and in Color: Television and Black Civil Rights.* Princeton & Oxford: Princeton University Press.

Trachtenberg, J. A. (01/03/2007). "Where Does It Belong?: Friction Over Black Authors' Fiction." *Wall Street Journal,* Features, p. 35.

_____. (12/06/2006). "Dividing Lines: Why Book Industry Sees the World Split Still by Race." *The Wall Street Journal Online,* Page One.

Travis, M. A. (1998). *Reading Cultures: The Construction of Readers in the Twentieth Century.* Carbondale and Edwardsville, IL: Southern Illinois University Press.

Tulloch, M. I. (2004). "Parental Fear of Crime." *Journal of Sociology,* 40 (4), 362–377.

Turnbull, S. (2002). "'Nice Dress, Take It Off': Crime, Romance and the Pleasure of the Text." *International Journal of Cultural Studies,* 5 (1), 67–82.

Turner, J. R. (1998). "Coffin Ed Johnson and Grave Digger Jones: Violence and Humor in the Mystery Novels of Chester Himes." *Black Scholar,* 28 (1).

Turner, P. A. (1998). "From Talma Gordon to Theresa Galloway: Images of African American Women in Mysteries." *Black Scholar,* 28 (1).

_____. (1993). *I Heard It Through the Grapevine: Rumor in African-American Culture.* Berkeley: University of California Press.

USA Today (Dec. 20, 2005). "Murder Rate in Small Cities Jumps 13%." Section: News, p. 03a.

Van Deburg, W. L. (1997). *Black Camelot: African-American Cultural Heroes in Their Times, 1960–1980.* Chicago & London: The University of Chicago Press.

van Dijk, T. A. (1993) "Stories and Racism." In Mumby, D.K. (Ed.), *Narratives and Social Control: Critical Perspectives* (pp. 121–142). Newbury, CA: Sage Publications.

Van Fleet, C. (2004). "African-American Mysteries." In Overmier, J. and Taylor, R. H. (Eds.), *Managing the Mystery Collection: From Creation to Consumption* (pp. 83–99). The Haworth Information Press.

Van Vechten, C. (1926). *Nigger Heaven.* New York: Knopf.

Vedantum, S. (1/23/2005). "See No Bias; Many Americans Believe They Are Not Prejudiced." *The Washington Post,* Magazine; (w12).

Vermeule, B. (2006). *Gossip and Literary Narrative. Philosophy and Literature,* 30 (1), 102–117.

Vogel, T. (2001). "The New Face of Black Labor." In Vogel, T. (Ed.), *The Black Press: New Literary and Historical Essays* (pp. 37–54). New Brunswick, NJ & London: Rutgers University Press.

Voss, K. (1998). "Replacing L.A.: *Mi Familia, Devil in a Blue Dress,* and Screening the Other Los Angeles." *Wide Angle,* 20 (3), 157–181.

Walker, A. (1992). *The Color Purple.* New York: Harcourt Brace.

Walker, D. (1994 [1829/1830]. "Appeal, in Four Articles, Together with a Preamble, to the Colored Citizens of the World." In *Walker's Appeal and Garnet's Address to the Slaves of the United States of America* (pp. 9–88). Nashville, TN: James C. Winston Publishing.

Walker, L. E. (1980). *Battered Women.* New York: Harper Paperbacks.

Walker, S. (1998). *Popular Justice: A History of American Criminal Justice,* 2nd ed. New York: Oxford University Press.

Wallace, H. (2007). *Victimology: Legal, Psychological, and Social Perspectives,* 2nd ed. Fresno: California State University.

Wallace, M. (1979). *Black Macho and the Myth of the Superwoman.* New York: Doubleday.

Walls, D. W. (1985). "The Clue Undetected in Richard Wright's *Native Son.*" *American Literature,* 57 (1), 125–128.

Walters, W. W. (1994). "Limited Options:

Strategic Maneuverings in Himes's Harlem." *African American Review*, 28 (4), 615–631.

Ward, E. G. (2005). "Homophobia, Hypermasculinity and the US Black Church." *Culture, Health & Sexuality*, 7 (5), 493–504.

Ward, J. W., Jr. (2004). "Everybody's Protest Novel: The Era of Richard Wright." In Graham, M. (Ed.), *The Cambridge Companion to the African American Novel* (pp. 173–188). Cambridge, UK: Cambridge University Press.

Warr, M., and C. G. Ellison (2000). "Rethinking Social Reactions to Crime: Personal and Altruistic Fear in Family Households." *The American Journal of Sociology*, 106 (3), 551–578.

Weisenburger, S. (1998). *Modern Medea: A Family Story of Slavery and Child-Murder from the Old South*. New York: Hill and Wang.

Weixlmann, J. (1991–1992). "African American Deconstruction of the Novel in the Work of Ishmael Reed and Clarence Major." *MELUS*, 17 (4), 57–79.

Wesley, M. C. (2003). *Violent Adventure: Contemporary Fiction by American Men*. Charlottesville & London: University of Virginia Press.

West, S. (1998). "Tip-Toeing on the Tightrope: A Personal Essay on Black Writer Ambivalence." *African American Review*, 32 (2)

Whalan, M. (2005). "'The Only Real White Democracy' and the Language of Liberation: The Great War, France, and African American Culture in the 1920s." *MFS Modern Fiction Studies*, 51 (4), 775–800.

Wheeler, E. A. (2001). *Uncontained: Urban Fiction in Postwar America*. New Brunswick, NJ & London: Rutgers University Press.

White, S., and G. White (2000). "'At Intervals I Was Nearly Stunned by the Noise He Made': Listening to African American Religious Sound in the Era of Slavery." *American Nineteenth Century History*, 1 (1), 34–61.

_____, and _____. (1998). *Stylin': African American Expressive Culture from Its Beginnings to the Zoot Suit*. Ithaca & London: Cornell University Press.

Whitehead, M. (2003). "From Moral Space to the Morality of Scale: The Case of the Sustainable Region." *Ethics, Place, & Environment*, 6 (3), 235–257.

Willett, C. (2001). *The Soul of Justice: Social Bonds and Racial Hubris*. Ithaca and London: Cornell University Press.

William, J. A. (1967). "The Man Who Cried I Am." New York: Little Brown & Co.

Williams, C. (2001). "The *Guide for Colored Travelers*: A Reflection of the Urban

League." *Journal of American and Comparative Cultures*, 24 (3/4), 71–79.

Wilson, A. (1996). "Death and the Mainstream: Lesbian Detective Fiction and the Killing of the Coming-Out Story." *Feminist Studies*, 22 (2), 251.

Wilson, W. J. (1987). *The Truly Disadvantaged: The Inner City, the Underclass, and Public Policy*. Chicago: University of Chicago Press.

Winton, R. (2007, 9/29). "LAPD Officer Agrees to Quit in Wake of Charges." *Los Angeles Times*, California; Metro Desk, Part B, p. 3.

Wintz, C. D. (1988). *Black Culture and the Harlem Renaissance*. Houston, TX: Rice University Press.

Wolfgang, M. E. (1958). *Patterns in Criminal Homicide*. Philadelphia: University of Pennsylvania.

Wood, J. K. (2005). "In Whose Name? Crime Victim Policy and the Punishing Power of Protection." *NWSA Journal*, 17 (3), 1–17.

Woods, P. L. (Ed.). (1995). *Spooks, Spies, and Private Eyes: Black Mystery, Crime, and Suspense Fiction of the 20th Century*. New York: Doubleday.

Worth, R. F. (1995). "*Nigger Heaven* and the Harlem Renaissance." *African American Review*, 29 (3).

Wright, D. (2006, 7/1). "Streetwise Urban Fiction." *Library Journal*, 131 (12).

Wright, R. (1987 [1940]). "The Man Who Killed a Shadow." In *Eight Men: Stories by Richard Wright* (pp. 193–209). New York: Thunder Mouth Press.

_____. (1992 [1940]). *Native Son*. New York: HarperPerennial.

Yancy, G. (2005). "Whiteness and the Return of the Black Body." *The Journal of Speculative Philosophy*, 19 (4), 215–241.

Yarborough, R. (1988). "Introduction." In Hopkins, P. E., *Contending Forces* (pp. xxvii–xlvii). New York & Oxford: Oxford University Press.

_____. (1981). "The Quest for the American Dream in Three Afro-American Novels: *If the Hollers Let Him Go, The Street*, and *Invisible Man*." MELUS 8 (Winter): 33–59.

Yoder, J. D. and Berendsen, L. L. (2001). "'Outsider Within' the Firehouse: African American and White Women Firefighters." *Psychology of Women Quarterly*, 25 (1), 27–36.

Young, E. (2006). "Urban Lit Goes Legit." *Black Issues Book Review*, 8 (5), 20–23.

Young, H. B. (2005). "Inheriting the Criminalized Black Body: Race, Gender, and Slavery in *Eva's Man*." *African American Review*, 39 (3), 377–393.

Young, M. (1998). "Walter Mosley, Detective

Fiction and Black Culture." *Journal of Popular Culture*, 32 (1), 141–150.

Zangrando, R. L. (1980). *The NAACP Crusade Against Lynching, 1909–1950*. Philadelphia: Temple University Press.

Zirin, A. (2000). "Richard Wright: 'Using Words as a Weapon.'" *International Socialist Review*, 14.

Index